PRISCILLIAN OF AVILA

PRISCILLIAN
OF AVILA

THE OCCULT
AND THE CHARISMATIC
IN THE
EARLY CHURCH

HENRY CHADWICK

OXFORD
AT THE CLARENDON PRESS
1976

Oxford University Press, Ely House, London W. 1

GLASGOW NEW YORK TORONTO MELBOURNE WELLINGTON
CAPE TOWN IBADAN NAIROBI DAR ES SALAAM LUSAKA ADDIS ABABA
DELHI BOMBAY CALCUTTA MADRAS KARACHI DACCA
KUALA LUMPUR SINGAPORE HONG KONG TOKYO

ISBN 0 19 826643 X

© *Oxford University Press 1976*

*Printed in Great Britain
at the University Press, Oxford
by Vivian Ridler
Printer to the University*

PRISCILLAE

FILIAE DILECTISSIMAE

PREFACE

PRISCILLIAN, bishop of Avila 381–5, led an evangelical ascetic movement in the Spanish churches, which encouraged charismatic prophecy among both men and women, with the study of heretical apocrypha. His frankly avowed interest in the occult left him open to accusations of sorcery and Manicheism. In 385 he was tortured and executed by imperial order at Trier, the first, and in antiquity almost the only, heretic to suffer formal capital punishment from the secular arm. The present study seeks to push beyond the prevailing agnosticism of recent scholarship about the character of his personal beliefs and to examine the social and political pressures which produced the tragedy of his execution.

The twentieth century, sceptical of the very existence of an immaterial order of things, is increasingly absorbed, even morbidly fascinated, by the phenomena of the spirit world, the charismatic gifts of spiritual power, and the hidden forces of evil and witchcraft. The central figure of this book shared this double fascination. While this is a technical historical study that seeks to understand Priscillian in the context of the later Roman empire at the time of its disintegration under the impact of barbarian invasion and inflation, the story is not, I believe, of merely antiquarian interest.

The second chapter, on the thought of Priscillian and his followers, is the core of the attempt to penetrate the mind of this distant and strange man. But it will be a section to be read more quickly by those who want the narrative of the man and his tragedy and of the tenacious community in Galicia which, for over 200 years, treasured the memory of his martyrdom at a shrine which is a possible explanation of the mysterious origins of Compostela.

To make the narrative easier I have often used modern place-names. English readers are more familiar with Saragossa than with Caesaraugusta (or even Zaragoza). But I have not tried to be consistent.

I have to thank Mr. J. K. Cordy, Mrs. J. M. Argyle, the editorial staff of the Clarendon Press, Dr. M. Winterbottom, and Dr. A. M. Crabbe whose vigilance has put me much in their debt.

Oxford, August 1975

CONTENTS

Abbreviations   xi

Bibliographical Note on the Primary Sources   xiii

I. The Sorcerer's Apprentice   1

II. The Teaching of Priscillian   57

III. Priscillian's End and its Consequences   111

IV. The Honour of the Martyr of Trier   170

APPENDIX. The Priscillianist Professions and the Judgement of the Council of Toledo, 400   234

Index   241

ABBREVIATIONS

ACO	*Acta Conciliorum Oecumenicorum*, ed. E. Schwartz.
Anal. Boll.	*Analecta Bollandiana.*
Byz. Z.	*Byzantinische Zeitschrift.*
CLA	*Codices Latini Antiquiores*, by E. A. Lowe.
Clavis	*Clavis Patrum Latinorum*, editio altera, by E. Dekkers.
CSEL	*Corpus Scriptorum Ecclesiasticorum Latinorum.*
DACL	*Dictionnaire d'archéologie chrétienne et de liturgie.*
HTR	*Harvard Theological Review.*
JRS	*Journal of Roman Studies.*
JTS	*Journal of Theological Studies.*
MGH	*Monumenta Germaniae Historica.*
PGM	*Papyri Graecae Magicae*, ed. K. Preisendanz.
PLRE	*The Prosopography of the Later Roman Empire*, I, ed. A. H. M. Jones, J. R. Martindale, J. Morris.
PL	J. P. Migne, *Patrologia Latina.*
PL Suppl.	A. Hamman, *Patrologiae Latinae Supplementum*, 5 volumes.
PG	J. P. Migne, *Patrologia Graeco-Latina.*
PO	*Pastrologia Orientalis*
PW	*Realenzyklopädie der classischen Altertumswissenschaft*, ed. Pauly-Wissowa.
RAC	*Reallexikon für Antike und Christentum.*
ThLL	*Thesaurus Linguae Latinae.*
TU	*Texte und Untersuchungen zur Geschichte der altchristlichen Literatur.*
ZDMG	*Zeitschrift der deutschen morgenländischen Gesellschaft.*
ZNW	*Zeitschrift für die neutestamentliche Wissenschaft.*
Z. wiss. Theol.	*Zeitschrift für wissenschaftliche Theologie.*

BIBLIOGRAPHICAL NOTE ON THE
PRIMARY SOURCES

1. Priscillian's canons on the Pauline epistles as revised by Peregrinus are edited by G. Schepss in *CSEL* 18 (1889), and in the second volume of the Oxford Vulgate, *Novum Testamentum Domini Nostri Iesu Christi Latine secundum editionem sancti Hieronymi*, ed. Wordsworth and White, ii (1913–41), 17–32 (cf. also pp. 44–61 on Priscillian's sections). Schepss's edition is reprinted by A. Hamman in *PL Suppl.* ii. 1391–1413.

2. Orosius, *Ad Aurelium Augustinum commonitorium de errore Priscillianistarum et Origenistarum*, is critically edited by Schepss in *CSEL* 18.

3. The anonymous Priscillianist tractates contained in the Würzburg codex, found by Schepss in the autumn of 1885, are edited in *CSEL* 18. They are reprinted in *PL Suppl.* ii. 1413–83.

4. The anonymous tractate in the Laon codex, *De Trinitate catholicae fidei*, is edited by G. Morin, *Études, textes, découvertes* (Paris, 1913), and reprinted in *PL Suppl.* ii. 1487–1507.

5. The Monarchian gospel prologues: see p. 102, n. 1, for editions.

6. The *Chronicle* (or Sacred History) of Sulpicius Severus is edited from the solitary manuscript by C. Halm in *CSEL* 1 (1866), who also edits the Life of St. Martin and the Dialogues. The Life of St. Martin is now best read in the richly annotated edition of J. Fontaine, *Sources chrétiennes* 133–5 (Paris, 1967–9).

7. Spanish conciliar documents, e.g. the councils of Elvira, Saragossa, and Toledo (400), are printed conveniently by J. Vives, *Concilios visigóticos e hispano-romanos* (Madrid, 1963), but may also be found in *PL* 84 or in standard collections such as Mansi, or Labbe, or Labbe–Coleti.

8. Jerome is quoted either from Migne or by Vallarsi's pages, given both in Migne and in *Corpus Christianorum*.

The principal secondary works are given at p. 8, n. 1.

I

THE SORCERER'S APPRENTICE

Early Christianity in Spain

THE apostle Paul's declared ambition was to found churches in Spain and, if we may believe Clement of Rome, he succeeded. The existence of churches in Spain is attested by Irenaeus and Tertullian. The location of some of these communities first becomes clear with Cyprian's 67th letter, strictly the letter of his African council of the year 254, supporting the puritan party at Mérida and at León and Astorga, where the bishops had lapsed in the Decian persecution and the laity assumed the right and the duty of electing successors. The African letter attests a church at Saragossa. That at this time there was also a community in Tarragona is shown by the Acts of the martyrdom of St. Fructuosus.[1] It seems clear that evangelization spread along the Ebro valley. We do not hear of gnosticism or Montanism troubling Spanish churches. Late in the fourth century bishop Pacianus of Barcelona (below, p. 4) wrote against an advocate of severe penitential discipline named Sympronianus who was a Novatianist. But heresy is not prominent among the problems facing the Spanish bishops who met in council early in the fourth century, probably soon after the Great Persecution, at Iliberri or Elvira (modern Atarfe, 7 km. north-west of Granada). The bishops were gathered from thirty-three sees mainly in the southeast of the peninsula. Ossius of Cordoba was prominent.

The eighty-one canons of the council of Elvira[2] show how

---

[1] The *Acta S. Fructuosi* are in H. A. Musurillo, *The Acts of the Christian Martyrs* (Oxford, 1972), with good translation and notes. Bishop Martialis (whether of Emerita or of Asturica is not clear—see G. W. Clarke in *Latomus* 30 (1971), 1141–4) offended further by belonging to a convivial pagan club owning a necropolis where the bishop had his family tomb instead of in the Christian cemetery.

[2] On the council of Elvira there is an old monograph by A. W. W. Dale (1882), and a hostile essay by S. Laeuchli, *Power and Sexuality* (Philadelphia, 1972). The bishops' names and the canons are preserved in the Hispana canonical collection. F. A. Gonzalez's edition (1808) is reprinted in *PL* 84. 301–10, or H. T. Bruns, *Canones apostolorum et conciliorum* ii (1839), 1–12. The text of the Escorial codex d. 1. 2

successful the mission in Spain has been. The large number of
adherents to the faith has led to compromise with idolatry. Some
believers, including bishops and other clergy, have conspicuously
failed to keep the rules in regard to sexual purity. Among the
clergy some are mainly engaged in commerce. Laymen are
accepting pagan priesthoods. The council prescribes penalties.
But it is remarkable how mild the canons can be in certain cases.
If a Christian lady wilfully beats her slave girl to death, she must
do a mere seven years' penance before restoration to communion,
five years if she did not actually intend so drastic a consequence
(canon 5). Pagans of reasonably good life who desire baptism
on their sick bed may be granted their wish, without instruction,
to secure their destiny hereafter (39). Some catechumens are
content not to appear in church for years on end (45, 'per in-
finita tempora'). Church members include some considerable
landowners (40), who have so many slaves on their estates that
they fear sharp collective reaction if they try to suppress polytheistic images, a fear which the council, while deploring the
fact, treats with respect (41). Evidently landowners do not wish
to be pressed by their bishops into action that will endanger
good labour relations. A similar anxiety for tranquil toleration
appears in canon 80, forbidding the ordaining of freedmen whose
patron is a heathen. On the other hand, Christians should not
eat with Jews (50), a community numerous in Spain by 300, and
must not ask the rabbi to bless their fields which would nullify
the blessing pronounced by the bishop (49).[1]

One remarkable canon (6) excommunicates those who compass
death by sorcery, 'since this entails idolatrous practices'. This
penetration of black magic within the Church long survived.
In 667 a council of Toledo, held when Julian was consecrated
bishop of the Visigothic capital, deplored the saying of masses
'for the deaths of enemies' from motives of ill will or revenge;
and the censure was repeated at Toledo in 694. Such prayer for
revenge is not peculiar to old Spain. Giraldus Cambrensis early

(anno 976) is printed by J. Vives, *Concilios visigóticos e hispano-romanos* (Madrid, 1963).
A critical text is given by A. C. Vega in *España sagrada* 56 (1957), 199–222.

[1] Ancient Spanish formulas for blessing crops are printed in M. Férotin's edition
of the Mozarabic *Liber ordinum* (1904, repr. 1969), 167–70. In southern Spain where
rainfall is low, prayers to avert drought remain important today. (See below, p. 53.)
Evidence for the Jews in Spain is collected by W. P. Bowers in *JTS*, n.s. 26 (1975),
395–402.

in the thirteenth century tells of Welsh clergy repeating a requiem mass ten times over a waxen image to bring about the chosen enemy's death within ten days. Augustine tells of a wronged widow at Caesarea in Cappadocia who at a baptistery pronounced a curse on her ten children which struck them all with sickness and drove them round the world seeking healing, found by the eldest at the shrine of St. Laurence 'recently constructed at Ravenna' and by the sixth son and his sister from relics of St. Stephen at Ancona and in Africa.[1] The bishops in council at Elvira thought it self-evident that sorcery could cause death; but so did all ancient men (below, p. 141).

A five-year excommunication is imposed on parents who marry their daughters to Jews or to heretics unwilling to become catholics (16). Marriage to a pagan husband is discouraged but carries no penalty unless he is a priest; it is frankly conceded that Christian girls outnumber the supply of Christian husbands (15), a social situation that long held good. Ambrose once comments that pagan suitors, to win a girl refused by her Christian parents, pretend to be believers, but in the end their pretence is always shown up. Marriage was the point at which religion and class came into obvious conflict.[2]

Spain evidently has its proportion of resident heretics. The canons of Elvira prescribe procedure for accepting converts from sects (22), forbidding their ordination (51). Unhappily there is no hint of the nature of the heresies. All bishops and especially he who occupies the first see ('prima cathedra') have special responsibility for ascertaining the orthodoxy of immigrant travellers bringing letters of communion (58), a canon that may suggest heresy to be largely an imported commodity. The bishop of the 'first see' in Spain was probably, as in North Africa, the senior bishop by consecration; and at Elvira the presidency of the

---

[1] See Férotin, *Liber ordinum* 332; Conc. Tolet. XVII, can. 5; Giraldus, *Gemma ecclesiastica* 1. 49, ed. Brewer, ii. 137; Augustine, *Sermo* 322; *De civ. Dei* 22. 8. On Ancona, below, p. 178. For death by sorcery see (e.g.) Lucan vi. 529–30; Byzantine instances in Moschus, *Pratum* 145 (*PG* 87. 3008–9), Evagrius, *HE* 5. 3. Prayer for revenge is discouraged by Basil, *Ep.* 199. 29; cf. Moschus 175 on a mother praying the Virgin to avenge her daughter when the emperor Zeno got her with child.

[2] Ambrose, *Expl. Ps.* 118. 20. 48 (*CSEL* 62. 468). See a touching story in Moschus 201 (*PG* 87. 3089D), how parents providentially found for their daughter a believing husband of the right class by leaving her praying in a church with the faith that the first man to speak to her would be her intended (a variant of *sortes biblicae*).

council fell to the bishop of near-by Acci (Guadix), the name of Ossius of Cordoba appearing second. A reference in canon 58 either to Rome or to an incipient metropolitan structure is unlikely.[1]

Canon 43 discloses that not all Christians in Spain have been regarding Pentecost as a feast of obligation and expresses fear that this may lead to a 'new heresy'. A variant reading here suggests that the deviation consisted in celebrating Pentecost on the fortieth rather than on the fiftieth day after Easter. The distinction between Ascension Day and Pentecost was not yet clear. In the 380s Filastrius of Brescia (below, pp. 9–10) specifies four festivals in the year: Nativity, Epiphany, the Passion 'in pascha', and 'the day on which he ascended to heaven about Pentecost'.[2]

The canons of Elvira reflect a social situation where Christianity is penetrating the higher classes, a process of which there is other supporting evidence. In the time of Constantine the Great a Christian poet in Spain, of senatorial standing, C. Vettius Aquilinus Juvencus,[3] became a presbyter in the church and wrote an epic on the Gospels in Vergilian hexameters. He was confident that if Vergil and Homer enjoyed immortality with their pagan lies, his poem on divine truth would last at least as long, indeed beyond the end of time, so that his poem would be counted to him for righteousness at the Last Judgement. In the middle years of the fourth century another noble Spaniard, Acilius Severus, composed an autobiography of mixed prose and poetry, which he called *Catastrophe or Trial* (the title being in Greek).[4] Another aristocrat Pacianus (above, p. 1) became bishop of Barcelona soon after this time, and lived on to die at an advanced age after

---

[1] The fourth council of Toledo (633), canon 4, notes that episcopal seniority depends on the date of consecration (*PL* 84. 366c). Harnack, *Mission und Ausbreitung*[4], p. 923, n. 3, mistakenly thought seniority hung on the foundation of the see, i.e. that Guadix was the earliest bishopric in Spain. That canon 58 refers to Rome was argued by P. Batiffol in *JTS* 23 (1922), 263–70 = *Cathedra Petri* (1938), pp. 105 ff., with supplementary reply to Jülicher's criticism. His view has found little favour; cf. D. Mansilla, 'Orígenes de la organisación metropolitana en la iglesia española', *Hispania sacra* 12 (1959), 255.

[2] Filastrius 140 (*CSEL* 38. 111). See A. Cabié, *La Pentecôte* (1965), pp. 181–3.

[3] Edited by J. Huemer, *CSEL* 24 (1891). See Jerome, *Vir. inl.* 84 (*TU* 14. 1); *Ep.* 70. 5 (*ad Magnum*). His work influenced Prudentius and later Christian poets. See P. G. van der Nat, 'Die Praefatio der Evangelienparaphrase des Iuvencus', in *Romanitas et Christianitas, Studia J. H. Waszink oblata* (1973), 249–57.

[4] Jerome, *Vir. inl.* 111. The title is a striking anticipation of Peter Abelard; but Jerome does not tell us the nature of Acilius' misfortunes.

378.[1] His son Nummius Aemilianus Dexter was a zealous Christian who enjoyed a distinguished public career (proconsul of Asia, 379–87; *comes rei privatae* in the East, 387; praetorian prefect of Italy, 395). Jerome dedicated to him his *Lives of Illustrious Men* in which special attention is paid to Spanish and Aquitanian figures.[2]

It is evident that the ordination of several members of the landowning class to the episcopate would raise problems. The 15th canon of the council of Serdica in 342 shows Ossius of Cordoba anxious about a situation where some bishops own estates distant from the city where their see is; because of their need to care for their land and trading interests they are absent for lengthy periods. Ossius proposes for the council's assent a ruling that such landowning bishops may not be absent for more than three weeks in the year, and while on leave are not to celebrate mass privately and neglect attendance at the local church. At the beginning of the fifth century the Aquitanian Sulpicius Severus (biographer of Martin of Tours and historian of Priscillianism) bitterly attacked the western bishops of his time whose principal care was either to maximize the return from their estates, or, if they were not landowners, to go about begging, so that in either case, whether rich or poor, their single obsession was money (below, ch. III, p. 121, n. 4).

The divisive impact of heresy and schism deeply affected the Spanish churches in the decade after 357, the year in which the aged Ossius of Cordoba was brought by Potamius of Olisipo (Lisbon)[3] and by the western Arians, Valens of Mursa (Osijek), and Ursacius of Singidunum (Belgrade), to sign his name to the Arian creed denounced by Hilary of Poitiers as 'the blasphemy of Sirmium'. Ossius returned to Spain armed with a letter from

---

[1] Jerome, *Vir. inl.* 106.

[2] See A. Feder, *Studien zum Schriftstellerkatalog des hl. Hieronymus* (Freiburg, 1927) esp. pp. 142 ff.; H. Crouzel, 'S. Jérôme et ses amis toulousains', *Bulletin litt. eccl.* = *Mélanges É. Griffe* (1972), 125–46. Other Christian nobles of Spain include Prudentius the poet and probably Egeria the pilgrim (below, p. 166). For brief discussion see K. F. Stroheker, 'Spanische Senatoren der spätrömischen und westgotischen Zeit', *Madrider Mitteilungen* 4 (1963), 107–32 at p. 118.

[3] For recent discussion see A. M. Moreira, *Potamius de Lisbonne et la controverse arienne* (Louvain, 1969); V. de Clercq, *Ossius of Cordova*, pp. 474–530; M. Simonetti, 'La crisi ariana e l'inizio della riflessione teologica in Spagna', in *Hispania romana*, colloquium of the Accademia dei Lincei: Problemi attuali di scienza e di cultura (Rome, 1974), pp. 127–47.

Constantius threatening dire penalties for any who refused communion with him. The old man soon died, but his name was erased from the list of those commemorated at the eucharist in Spanish churches of orthodox confession.

After the disastrous surrender to Arianism by the western bishops of the council of Ariminum (Rimini) in 359, Lucifer of Calaris (Cagliari) in Sardinia refused communion with all those in any way involved in the pollution, and turned Sardinia into an autocephalous island in which the true church could be preserved.[1] From Spain, however, the Luciferian group received moral support from Gregory, bishop of Iliberri, a weighty figure among the Spanish bishops, from whose pen there have been preserved exegetical tractates and an anti-Arian work *De fide*.[2] Gregory vehemently defends the 'equality' of Father, Son, and Holy Spirit.[3]

Jerome says that there were three bishops who never compromised with Arianism: Lucifer, Gregory, and Philo of Libya.[4] The petition to the emperors, submitted in the winter of 383/4 to Theodosius at Constantinople by the Luciferian presbyters Marcellinus and Faustinus, preserved in the Avellana collection, treats Gregory of Elvira as being in every sense a full member of the Luciferian group, and mentions a visit paid by Gregory to Lucifer in Sardinia in the middle sixties.[5] The petition also mentions the sufferings endured by a Spanish presbyter, Vincentius, who held communion with Gregory of Elvira and in consequence was subjected to threats of physical violence organized by two bishops, Luciosus (whose see is unknown) and Hyginus—evidently the bishop of Cordoba who plays an ambivalent role in the Priscillianist affair.[6]

Theodosius issued an order that Gregory of Elvira, and those

[1] Ambrose, *De excessu Satyri fratris* i. 47 (*CSEL* 73. 235). Since in antiquity to refuse communion meant refusal to accept rather than refusal to give, the 'schism' of the Luciferians on Sardinia was more a theoretical matter which raised practical problems for Sardinians only when travelling on the mainland. The Luciferians established their own independent congregation in Rome (*Avellana* 11. 77 ff.).

[2] See V. Bulhart's edition in *Corpus Christianorum* 69 (1967).

[3] *Tract. de libris ss. scripturarum* xiv (p. 110 Bulhart = *PL Suppl.* i. 443a 15) 'aequalis potestas et indifferens virtus'.

[4] *Chron.* ad ann. 370. On Philo see Synesius, *Ep.* 67 (*PG* 66. 1416–17).

[5] *Avell.* 11. 33 ff.; 90. The document is re-edited by M. Simonetti in *Corpus Christianorum* 69 (1967); differences from Günther's text in *CSEL* 35 are slight.

[6] *Avell.* 11. 73–6. A bishop Lucius played a part in the anti-Priscillianist synod of Saragossa in October 380 (below, p. 13).

in communion with him, must be unmolested.[1] It is clear, accordingly, that Gregory remained in possession of his see at Elvira, whatever problems this may have raised for other bishops in Spain, of whose integrity in orthodoxy he had dark suspicions. When Jerome wrote his *Lives of Illustrious Men* in 392 or 393, he included a paragraph on Gregory's works and noted that the old man was still living.[2] The later Mozarabic church did not look back on him as a dangerous schismatic, but commemorated him on 24 April.[3] It is therefore likely that the Spanish church felt compelled by Theodosius' decree of toleration to allow Gregory to stay in possession of his church until his death, no man forbidding him. This would explain the fact that throughout the Priscillianist crisis, 380–5, we have no evidence of any intervention in the debate on the part of Gregory. The only possible allusion to any action touching the church at Elvira at this time is concerned with Gregory's rigorism towards the signatories of the creed of Ariminum (below, p. 30).

[1] *Avell.* IIA (*CSEL* 35. 45–6). Theodosius required of the presbyter Faustinus a written confession of faith rebutting charges of Sabellianism brought against him: see Faustinus' confession in *Corpus Christianorum* 69. 357 (ed. Simonetti) = *PL* 13. 79–80. The charge may have arisen from Faustinus' anti-Arian tract on the Trinity dedicated to the empress Flaccilla: ed. Simonetti, pp. 295–353 (= *PL* 13. 37–80); though this text is also careful to disown Sabellianism (§ 12), its emphasis is on the unity of God. The penultimate sentence declares Faustinus' intention: to justify his refusal to accept communion from Arians as no mere 'vain superstition'.

[2] *Vir. inl.* 105 'Gregorius Baeticus Eliberi episcopus usque ad extremam senectutem diversos mediocri sermone tractatus composuit et de Fide elegantem librum; hodieque superesse dicitur.' If Gregory continued at Elvira without joining his episcopal colleagues for synods, his position would be paralleled by that of Martin of Tours after 385 in Gaul (Sulp. Sev. *Dial.* iii. 13. 6). For 393 as the date of Jerome's work see P. Nautin in *Rev. d'hist. eccl.* 56 (1961), 33. 392 is defended by T. D. Barnes, *Tertullian* (Oxford, 1971), pp. 235–6, and by J. N. D. Kelly, *Jerome* (London, 1975), p. 174.

[3] Isidore of Seville copies from *Avellana* II the Luciferian anecdote of the clash between Gregory of Elvira and Ossius when Ossius returned to Spain after compromising with radical Arianism at Sirmium in 357; Gregory's fortitude for the faith so struck Ossius' conscience that he fell dead (*Vir. inl.* 14). His feastday is attested in the Cordoba calendar, compiled in 961 by Recemundus, Bishop of Elvira (for whom Liutprand of Cremona wrote his *Antapodosis*), and dedicated to the caliph of Cordoba: see Férotin, *Liber ordinum*, 463. A century earlier Usuard inserted Gregory's name in the Martyrology on the same day—see J. Dubois's edition (1965), p. 218, and B. de Gaiffier in *Anal. Boll.* 55 (1937), 279. Usuard had travelled in Spain in search of relics and visited Cordoba in 858. See also José Aldazábal, 'Influencia de Gregorio de Elvira y de Justo de Urgel en el Liber Psalmographus hispanico', *Fons vivus, miscellanea liturgica in memoria di don Eusebio Maria Vismara* (Zürich, 1971), pp. 125–42.

The emergence of Priscillianism

In the seventies of the fourth century the Spanish churches were stirred by a new voice. A devout cultivated layman of high, probably senatorial, standing, named Priscillianus,[1] began to ask his fellow Christians to take their baptismal renunciation more seriously and to give more time to special spiritual study. The instruction that they were receiving from their bishops in the cities was no doubt good. But the ordinariness and the humdrum character of this limited experience were failing to answer the longing for deeper feeling, for greater inwardness, for alerter sensitivity to the hidden forces of evil, and for a wider comprehension of the divine mystery. Something of the atmosphere of Priscillian's evangelical message can be seen in eleven Priscillianist tractates preserved in a codex at Würzburg University Library of the fifth or sixth century, the salient character of which is examined in the next chapter. Typical is the absoluteness of their demand: 'None can be Christ's disciple if he loves anyone more than God', and the acceptance of baptism entails 'a total abandonment of the foul darkness of secular activities' (*Tract.* ii, pp. 34 f. Schepss). Priscillian's followers are called to strenuous Bible study: 'To us learning is... scripture and to know the power of the living word' (i, p. 28, 26). They study the scriptures to understand the depth of Satan (i, p. 13, 24). So they may learn to transcend the gravitational pull of the body and rise to the things of the spirit. Therefore Priscillian's call is strongly ascetic; marriage and procreation become venial failures, but the spiritual man is celibate, dedicated to voluntary poverty, practising vegetarianism to make himself more readily open to the charismatic gift of prophecy.

The call was not addressed merely to isolated individuals, but

[1] A full survey of research to 1964 is given by B. Vollmann, *Studien zum Priszillianismus* (1965), to be supplemented, and in places modified, by his article 'Priscillianus' in *PW* Suppl. xiv (1974), 485–559, now the best survey available. Both have a good bibliography. Otherwise the main works on Priscillian remain E. C. Babut, *Priscillien et le priscillianisme* (1909); A Puech, 'Les origines du Priscillianisme et l'orthodoxie de Priscillien', in *Bulletin d'ancienne litt. et d'archéol. chrétiennes* 2 (1912), 81–95, 161–213; J. A. Davids, *De Orosio et S. Augustino Priscillianistarum adversariis commentatio historica et philologica*, Diss., The Hague (1930); A. d'Alès, *Priscillien et l'Espagne chrétienne* (1936). The best contribution by recent Spanish scholarship is by J. M. Ramos y Loscertales, *Prisciliano: gesta rerum* (Salamanca, 1952), in part highly speculative; but there are magistral pages on the subject in Florez's *España sagrada*.

to all the faithful willing to give an unreserved dedication to Christ their God. Nevertheless, the hearing of the call was not easy without withdrawal. Accordingly, Priscillian invited Christians to come aside, to leave the busy city, and to withdraw to special retreats at country villas or up in the hills. Before a great festival like the Epiphany on 6 January, they should prepare themselves by ascetic retirement into the mountains for three weeks. Similarly before Easter the days of Lent called for a deepening of the spiritual life by leaving the distractions of the town and going off (like the Lord in the wilderness) to cells and houses in the hill-country, which might be outside their own diocese, beyond the controlling hand of the local bishop. There they could receive advanced instruction in biblical exegesis with Priscillian or some other layman as their teacher.

What forces lay behind this ascetic movement it is hard to say. The ideals of Egyptian hermits were beginning to exert an influence in the western provinces, as the Life of St. Martin of Tours bears witness or Ponticianus' record in Augustine's *Confessions* viii of the catalytic effect on two *agentes in rebus* at Trier (undated but before 381) of a Latin version of Athanasius' Life of Antony.[1] Moreover, the late sixties of the fourth century were a time of high expectation that the end of the world was near. One line of traditional exegesis said that Antichrist was no super-human or demonic figure but a man within history,[2] a view making it easy to identify him with Julian the Apostate. Antichrist was expected to rebuild the Temple at Jerusalem, as Julian had vainly attempted to do. His failure did not quench the expectation. Martin (whose life is that of a wandering charismatic) told his disciple Postumianus how Antichrist had already been born and would shortly come to power in the East to make his capital at a rebuilt Jerusalem.[3] Filastrius, writing at Brescia in the 380s

[1] See the edition of the Life of St. Martin by J. Fontaine in *Sources chrétiennes* 133–5 (1967–9), and the excellent Freiburg-im-Breisgau thesis by W. Schatz, 'Studien zur Geschichte und Vorstellungswelt des frühen abendländischen Mönchtum' (1957), unhappily unprinted; I have used a microfilm in the Bodleian Library. Schatz interprets Priscillian in the light of the beliefs reflected in the *Apophthegmata patrum*.
[2] Irenaeus, *Adv. haereses* 5. 25. 1 (ii. 390 f. Harvey); Jerome, *In Danielem* vii. 8 (*PL* 25. 555); John Chrysostom, *In II Thess. hom.* 3. 2 (*PG* 62. 482).
[3] Sulpicius Severus, *Dial.* ii. 14. Excited interest in the date of the coming of Antichrist is shown in the anonymous *Consultationes Zacchaei et Apollonii* 3. 7–8 (*PL* 20. 1159–63), a work of about A.D. 400 (below, p. 146): if Antichrist comes Christ's second advent will follow quickly (1161C). All the signs are here (1162).

where he became bishop after ascetic wanderings about the
Empire in search of heretical enormity and exegetical eccen-
tricity, reports a strong belief that the end had been calculated to
occur 365 years after Christ's coming.[1] In his Life of St.
Martin, Sulpicius Severus tells of a young man in Spain who claimed to be
Elijah, the precursor of the second Advent; on acquiring a large
following he raised a greater claim that in him Christ himself
had come again, and among those now convinced by him was
a bishop named Rufus.[2] A markedly illuminist element was
present among the western ascetics, as in the Nitrian desert. In
Gaul a hermit named Anatolius, who joined the circle of cells
round Martin, held converse with angels, and was miraculously
granted a scarlet robe after a midnight visitation when the ground
thudded with dancing feet and his cell was aglow with light.[3]
The ascetic movement in the West was accompanied by apocalyptic excitement with the expectation of visions and prophecies.
These were days in which the mystery of iniquity was surely at
work, and vigilant disciples would be alert to uncover the hidden
plots of the powers of darkness. For Priscillian, though visions
of light do not seem to have been the experience of his followers,
the hope of the end was certainly a potent factor. The very
contentions aroused by the ascetic movement which he led in
Spain were seen as a sign of 'the power of the last time'.[4] His
followers were convinced that 'all the world lies in the evil one'
(1 John 5 : 19, cited in *Tract.* v, p. 57, 16).

Accordingly withdrawal was the call of the hour. Yet Priscillian
made no attempt to create an organized monastic movement with
communities living permanently under rule and wearing a special
habit. His followers seem to have been members of coherent
fraternities and sororities or mixed groups, but are not asked to
go permanently apart into separate houses. They are to come
away for limited periods of retreat, determined in relation to the
great festivals of the Church calendar. Moreover, he does not
turn his followers away from the normal sacramental life of the
Church or discourage them from seeking holy orders as an
ambition for power incompatible with monastic humility. He
wants reform within the Church, not apart from it, and hopes to
put a dedicated ascetic into every see in Spain.

[1] Filastrius 106 (*CSEL* 38. 65).   [2] *Vita Martini* 24.
[3] *Vita Martini* 23.   [4] Priscillian, *Tract.* ii, p. 35, 6–7.

When the detailed content of the Würzburg tractates comes to be considered, it will be seen that Priscillianist exegesis of holy scripture has idiosyncratic qualities. Hilary of Poitiers is influential, and several of the tractates are liberally sprinkled with quotations and allusions. But Priscillian (if he is the main author of the tractates) has evidently come late to the study of theology, and writes rather in the manner of an autodidact to whom has been granted a discernment of special meanings in the sacred text. Nothing is more certain than that he is not the product of a school. Fourth-century Spain did not provide a rich soil for serious theology. Its bishops no doubt included good men but, as at all times, they could not but reflect the style of their laity. The reports suggest that the Spanish clergy were not only recruited from merchants, landowners, and government administrators, but also continued to pursue these secular avocations in plurality with their priestly duties. They had little time to produce a strong coherent theology to underpin their preaching and teaching.

When early in the fifth century a Spanish theologian named Consentius, living on some islands which were probably the Balearic islands, became concerned about fundamental dogmas such as the Trinity, the Person of Christ, and the resurrection, he sent his own peculiar private efforts to Augustine of Hippo to beg for criticism and help—which indeed he received in Augustine's 120th letter and at greater length than Augustine thought him likely to expect. Consentius confessed to a sense of isolation and of 'working on his own', which must have been a general experience among any aspiring Iberian divines of that time. Augustine thought that he needed a considerable degree of help.

Where Priscillian's family estate was and where his activities began is not known. His ascetic movement first created controversy when it affected the churches in Baetica and Lusitania in southern Spain. The message spread westwards and northwards into the hills of Galicia. Soon it was across the Pyrenees penetrating Aquitaine.[1] Links between the churches on both sides of

---

[1] 'Aquitania' at this period is the regular term for southern Gaul, as opposed to 'Galliae', the Gauls, which means the northern provinces. The prefect resided at Trier till about 401 when he moved to Arles. The imperial vicar, as Vienne became vulnerable to attack, moved to Bordeaux. The divisions and subdivisions of the southern provinces varied from time to time; the documents sometimes call

the Pyrenees were close at this time; there was no frontier or language barrier. So Vigilantius could come from Calagurris on the north side of the mountains to become a presbyter in Barcelona, and the great Aquitanian noble Paulinus of Nola, baptized by bishop Delphinus of Bordeaux, was ordained at Barcelona.[1] Priscillian's movement had something of that contagion characteristic of a revival Awakening and, like such movements in later times, its effect came to be passionately divisive. Alarm began to be felt by the neighbours. Hyginus of Cordoba was disturbed and consulted his Lusitanian colleague Hydatius of Mérida, who was more than disturbed.[2] On 4 October 380 twelve anxious bishops assembled in council at Caesaraugusta (Saragossa) in the province Tarraconensis. The Hispana canon collection has preserved the list of those attending and something of their decisions.[3] The Aquitanians sent important delegates.

The council of Saragossa

The Acts of the council record the names of the twelve bishops and the text of their eight canons or *sententiae*. The bishops' sees are not recorded, but the first two names are familiar in ecclesiastical documents of the time: Phoebadius, bishop of Agen (Aginnum), and Delphinus, bishop of Bordeaux (Burdigala).[4] There may have been other Aquitanians present, but they cannot be identified as such. Auxentius (or Augentius) is probably of Toledo. Ildefonsus mentions Audentius as bishop of Toledo about this time;[5] and perhaps he is the Audentius of Gennadius

Aquitaine 'the five provinces', sometimes 'the seven provinces'. From 381 there were seven provinces, but the old name of five was often used. For a clear statement see A. Chastagnol, 'Le Diocèse civile d'Aquitaine au bas-empire', *Bulletin de la société nat. des antiquaires de France*, 1970, pp. 272–90.

[1] Gennadius, *Vir. inl.* 36; Paulin. Nol. *Ep.* 1. 10; 3. 4.
[2] Sulpicius Severus, *Chron.* ii. 46. 8.
[3] The record of the council of Saragossa, preserved in the Hispana canon-collection, is printed in Bruns, ii. 13; Lauchert, p. 175; Vives, p. 16; Gonzalez's edition in *PL* 84. 315–18.
[4] On Phoebadius and Delphinus see L. Duchesne, *Fastes épiscopaux de l'ancienne Gaule* ii[2] (1910), 60, 63. Phoebadius is spelt 'Fitadius' in the *Acta* of Saragossa, 'Foegadius' in Sulpicius Severus and the *Acta* of Valence, 'Segatius' in Ambrose, *Ep.* 87 (to Phoebadius and Delphinus commending Polybius, ex-proconsul of Africa, travelling from Milan into Aquitaine; the joint address is probably to be explained from the fact that Phoebadius was the senior and so 'presiding' bishop, whereas Delphinus was bishop of the metropolis of the province).
[5] Ildefonsus, *Vir. inl.* 2 (*PL* 96. 199).

of Massilia (Marseille) (*Vir. inl.* 14), a Spanish bishop who wrote against Manichees, Sabellians, Arians, and Photinians (below, p. 172 n. 1). Symposius is of Asturica. The extent of his presence will appear (below, p. 28). Valerius is almost certainly the local bishop of Saragossa, since Prudentius mentions with pride a family of Valerii which has produced several bishops of Saragossa.[1] Carterius may be the Spanish digamist defended by Jerome, *Ep.* 69, and conceivably also the Galician divine recalled by Braulio of Saragossa in his letter to Fructuosus (below, p. 230). The bishop Lucius who read out the agreed canons cannot be bishop of Tarraco, as Babut conjectured,[2] because only five years later Himerius of Tarraco enjoyed great seniority as a bishop (below, p. 30). But he may be identical with the Luciosus who had assisted Hyginus of Cordoba in harassing Luciferian supporters of Gregory of Elvira (above, p. 6).[3] 'Idacius' is the bishop of Emerita, Itacius probably of Ossonuba (below, p. 20). Names otherwise unknown are Eutychius, Ampelius, Splendonius. The absence of the name of Hyginus of Cordoba is striking. It is clear from the second tractate (p. 40, 8–10) that Hyginus did not attend (below, p. 25).

The presence and prominence of the two Aquitanians need not mean that the initiative in summoning the synod has lain north of the Pyrenees. But it appears that concern about Priscillian has been just as strong in Aquitaine as in Spain. Phoebadius' name no doubt stands first because of his seniority in years of consecration. He had become a bishop in the fifties and had played the role of a moderate in 359 at the unhappy general council of Ariminum where, according to the proud Aquitanian tradition, he had been 'most constant' for orthodoxy against Arianism.[4] (The decisions of Ariminum rapidly came to appear so disastrous that almost no bishop present could later be found to have supported them.) In 374 he had presided, probably again on grounds of seniority rather than because of rights attaching to the see of Agen, at a Gallic council in Valence (Valentia), at which the Gallic bishops set out to 'review matters that because of the holiness of the Church cannot be accepted,

[1] *Peristephanon* iv. 79–80. A Valerius of Saragossa was at Elvira.

[2] *Priscillien*, p. 99, n. 2, with whom concurs J. Matthews, *Western Aristocracies and Imperial Court* (Oxford, 1975), p. 16, n. 4.

[3] *Avell.* ii. 75 (*CSEL* 35. 27. 20).

[4] Sulpicius Severus, *Chron.* ii. 44. 1.

yet because of the usurpation of custom cannot be condemned'.[1] Among the problems facing the bishops at Valence are the acceptability of married clergy and the reluctance of some to accept the call to ordination, which they seek to avoid on the ground that they are unworthy; i.e. an ascetic renunciation which rejects the pastoral office of the priesthood as 'secular'.[2] That the tension imposed on the local church by the ascetic ideal is an element in the Priscillianist crisis is evident from the record of the synod at Saragossa in October, probably of the year 380.

The canons of Saragossa deplore many things in the situation: (*a*) women attending Bible-readings ('lectio') in the houses of men to whom they are unrelated ('alieni'); (*b*) fasting on Sundays and withdrawal from the worship of the church during Lent and in the period from 17 December to 6 January; (*c*) receiving the eucharistic elements in the church without immediately consuming them; (*d*) recession into cells and mountain retreats ('latibula cubiculorum ac montium'); (*e*) walking with unshod feet; (*f*) clergy abandoning the duties of their office to become monks; (*g*) virgins taking the veil before the age of forty and without doing so formally in the presence of the bishop; (*h*) the title of 'teacher' being granted to unauthorized persons (presumably laymen).

Among these complaints particular interest attached to the censure of those who withdraw during Lent and in the period from 17 December to 6 January, and who evidently kept up their fasting on Sundays falling in these periods. This canon of Saragossa is therefore a very early testimony to the observance of Advent, the fast being begun on the day of the pagan Saturnalia and no doubt understood as a protest against that riotous festival. Since the three-week period runs till 6 January, it is probable

[1] The *Acta* of this council are critically edited by C. H. Turner, *Eccles. occid. monumenta iuris antiqu.* i. 417–24, and by C. Munier, *Concilia Galliae a. 314–a. 506 (Corpus Christianorum* 148, 1963), pp. 35–42.

[2] In at least one case, at Fréjus, a reluctant ordinand had embarrassed the church by confessing, falsely, to grave crimes. The synod agreed that such lies should not be regarded as white. When in 452 Peter the Iberian reluctantly came to be consecrated bishop, he confessed himself both a sinner and a heretic, but was required to withdraw his confession of heresy before ordination (Zacharias Schol. *HE* iii. 4). The correct formula came to be 'I am sinful but orthodox'; cf. Theodore of Studios, *Ep.* I. 25 (*PG* 99. 989A); or the Mozarabic prayer for the departed: 'licet enim peccavit, Patrem et Filium et Spiritum non negavit sed credidit . . .' (Férotin, *Liber ordinum* 123).

that the festival of Christ's Nativity on 25 December has not yet spread generally to Spain. Attestation of an Advent lasting three weeks appears also in a fragment ascribed to Hilary of Poitiers preserved by quotation in an eleventh- or twelfth-century tract where it is quoted as from his 'Liber officiorum'.[1] The notion that Hilary wrote about liturgical ceremonies (as that title would imply) is probably a deduction from the fragment itself, which therefore enjoyed some independent circulation; the medieval author did not have a full text of Hilary before him. Probably the fragment comes from Hilary's *Tractatus mysteriorum*, a work of biblical exegesis extant in a very fragmentary condition, surviving partly through remnants of an eleventh-century codex at Arezzo bound up with parts of another eleventh-century codex containing Egeria's pilgrimage, partly through excerpts in a Cassino manuscript (cod. 257) written by Peter the Deacon in 1137. Apart from the precariousness of its transmission the only substantial argument against accepting the fragment as Hilary's is the assumption that Advent was not observed in the fourth century; and this assumption is destroyed by the canon of Saragossa.[2]

The Great Advent Antiphons to the Magnificat at Latin Vespers, *O Sapientia*, etc., are first attested in the ninth century by Amalarius of Metz, but as familiar texts long in general use.[3] The placing of *O Sapientia* on 17 December as the beginning of the series may be a remnant of an Advent that began on this date. The Great Antiphons, however, are very unlikely to be of Spanish origin; they are not in the León Antiphonary.[4] Another

---

[1] *PL* 142. 1066 and 1086–7.

[2] The fragment is rejected by G. Mercati in *JTS* 8 (1907), 429 = E. Bishop, *Liturgica historica* (1918, repr. 1962), pp. 209–10; B. Botte, *Les Origines de la Noël et de l'Épiphanie* (1932), pp. 47–8; J. P. Brisson in his edition of the *Tractatus mysteriorum* in *Sources chrétiennes* 19 *bis* (1967). It is accepted by W. C. Bishop in *JTS* 10 (1909), 127; A. Wilmart in *Rev. Bénéd.* 27 (1910), 500–13; A. Feder, *CSEL* 65, praefatio, p. xi; text, pp. 16–17. I would not confidently affirm authenticity, but observe only the frailty of the negative arguments used by Mercati and especially by Brisson.

[3] Amalarius, *De ordine antiphonarii* 12–13 (ed. J. M. Hanssens, *Studi e testi* 140, pp. 43–4). The text of the O Antiphons may be conveniently found in the Latin Breviary. The English Advent hymn, 'O come O come Emmanuel', is a version of them. For the view that a possible echo of *O Sapientia* may be found in Boethius, *Consol.* iii. 12 (64), see J. A. Cabaniss in *Speculum* 22 (1947), 440–2.

[4] The León Antiphonary is edited by L. Brou and J. Vives (Barcelona, 1959). On Spanish Advent antiphons see J. M. Martín Patino in *Miscelanea Camillas* 45 (1966), 191–243.

possible remnant of the original beginning of Advent in fourth-
century Spain may be discerned perhaps in the fact that in the
Visigothic period the Spanish churches are found observing
the Annunciation not in March but on 18 December.[1]

One of the complaints against the Priscillianists which Turibius
of Astorga reported to pope Leo the Great (below, p. 212) was
that 'they fast on Christ's Nativity and on Sunday'.[2] It is unclear
whether the Priscillianists thought the humiliation of God in
submitting to the indignities of human birth should be a matter
for fasting and penitence, or whether during the first half of the
fifth century the festival on 25 December had come to be generally
observed in the Spanish churches except in Priscillianist Galicia
which may have kept to the older Spanish observance of the
Nativity on 6 January.[3] Turibius' suggestion that they fasted
on 25 December because they held a docetic Christology can
certainly be ignored.

A three-week fast before Epiphany is also attested in a letter,
ascribed in the manuscript (St. Gall 190, of the ninth century) to
Jerome, which Dom Morin thought possibly the work of the
Galician Bachiarius of the first quarter of the fifth century (below,
p. 168). The letter presupposes the observance of 25 December as
well as 6 January, and regards 25 December as a time for prayer
in solitude on the ground that Joseph, being a man of proper
feeling, would certainly have left the Virgin Mary alone in labour
at the time of the birth of Jesus.[4]

An attempt to argue that the Spanish churches were observing
25 December as early as the fourth century, at least by 384, has
been based on Siricius' letter of February 385 to Himerius, bishop

[1] See the Mozarabic calendars printed by Férotin, *Liber ordinum* 490–1, 518; the
mass text in his *Liber sacramentorum* 50–1; and the Mozarabic prayer book of cod.
Veron. LXXXIX (84) written probably at Tarragona before the Arab invasion,
edited by J. Vives, *Oracional visigótico* (Barcelona, 1946), pp. 67–80.

[2] Leo, *Ep.* 15. 4 (*PL* 54. 632A); Vollmann, *Studien*, p. 157. Turibius' statement
reappears in the fourth anathema of the first council of Bracara of 561: C. W.
Barlow, *Martini Bracarensis opera* (1950), p. 107; *PL* 84. 563D.

[3] On the latter hypothesis there could be an analogy with the Donatists if it were
more certain than it is that the Donatists did not come to observe 25 December.

[4] The letter, *Quamlibet sciam*, edited by G. Morin in *Rev. Bénéd.* 40 (1928), 293, is
reprinted by Hamman in *PL Suppl.* i. 1038–44. There may be polemic against the
requirement of penitential quietness at Christmas in Ambrosiaster's commentary on
Phil. 2:8, where he attacks exegetes who say that Christ took the form of a servant
when born as man rather than when he was humiliated on the cross as a sinner
(*CSEL* 81. 3, 140).

of Tarraco (Tarragona).[1] This document partly echoes Himerius' own words (addressed to Siricius' predecessor, Damasus, who died in November 384), in which Himerius had mentioned the general Spanish custom of baptizing on 'Christ's nativity or (*seu*) Epiphany', for which Siricius uses the characteristic Spanish term *apparitio*, and even on saints' days. Siricius, knowing only the Italian tradition which reserved baptism to Easter and Pentecost, expresses dismay at this liturgical freedom which diminishes the solemnity of the act. The word *apparitio* for Epiphany makes it virtually certain that Siricius is in part citing Himerius; but it does not follow that the church at Tarragona in 384 has both the Nativity on 25 December and Epiphany on 6 January. In late Latin the word *seu* or *sive*, like *vel* and *aut*, can mean either 'or' or 'and'. The January festival, at all stages of its history tending to be overloaded with significations, is for fourth-century Spain, as in the Greek East, the feast of both Nativity and Baptism, and nothing in Siricius' letter precludes this. Probably, therefore, the feast on 25 December made its way into the Spanish calendar more slowly—just as the Mozarabs long celebrated the Holy Innocents on 8 January (*Allisio Infantum*) and came to accept a date in December only from the tenth century.[2]

A second practice deplored by the synod at Saragossa (canon 4) is that of going with bare feet: 'nudis pedibus incedere'. At first sight the modern reader naturally takes this to be an ascetic mortification. It is likely to have been more than that, and two possible interpretations may be founded on the ancient evidence. On the one hand, Filastrius describes a 'heresy' according to which it is a duty for Christians to walk barefoot because Moses was told to take off his shoes at the burning bush and because Isaiah walked barefoot for three years.[3] Filastrius is no doubt misleading in suggesting that this was the mark of one particular discalced sect. John Cassian (*Inst.* i. 9) records that Egyptian monks removed their shoes for eucharistic communion. But there is further evidence that at this time in north Italy such practices

[1] B. Botte, *Les Origines de la Noël et de l'Épiphanie*, pp. 49–50.
[2] See Férotin's note, *Liber ordinum* 451, no. 8. The Cordoba calendar of the year 961 puts the commemoration on 8 January and also on the Greek date of 29 December. For *apparitio* = Epiphany see Isidore of Seville, *Eccl. offic.* i. 27. 2 (PL 83. 762C). The letter *Quamlibet sciam*, however, uses *Epiphania*, which introduces hesitation about its Spanish origin.
[3] Filastrius 81 (*CSEL* 38. 43), copied by Augustine, *Haer.* 68.

were causing controversy. Christ had sent out the apostles with
the command to wear no shoes (Matt. 10: 10).¹ The fifth sermon
of Gaudentius, Filastrius' successor as bishop of Brescia, trium-
phantly proves from John the Baptist's protestation of his un-
worthiness that Jesus himself must have worn shoes which John
felt too humble to untie.² Gaudentius' sermon shows that the
practice was a live issue. Ambrosiaster's commentary on 1 Cor.
12: 23 praises the moral lives of barefoot Christians in humble
clothing.

On the other hand, going with bare feet may have had a magical
or ritual association, and the majority of ancient texts would
suggest that this would be the understood meaning. That sacrifices must be offered unshod was a Pythagorean principle, and
appears in the precepts of a number of ancient sanctuaries,
opinion among ancient antiquarians being divided whether the
cultic taboo was based on objection to the hide of animals or to
the knots which tied the shoe.³ Bare feet were a special requirement for the efficacy of prayers offered in time of drought.⁴ The
rites of country magic used by peasants to make their crops grow
demanded processions round the fields without shoes, in some
places without further clothing. The elder Pliny preserves a
report from Metrodorus of Scepsis that caterpillars, worms,
beetles, and other pests drop dead when menstruous women
walk naked about the cornfields, a discovery made in Cappadocia

---

¹ Ambrose, *Expl. Ps.* 118. 17. 18.
² Gaudentius, *Serm.* 5 (*CSEL* 68. 43–8; *PL* 20. 871–7).
³ On Pythagorean principles see Aristotle as cited by Iamblichus, *Vita Pythagorae*
85 and 105. Of ancient shrines, evidence exists for Ialysus, Rhodes (Dittenberger,
Sylloge ii. 560), Lycosura in Arcadia (ibid. 939), the temple of Isis at Coptos in Egypt
(despite scorpion infestation, Aelian, *Hist. anim.* 10. 23), the temple of Artemis in
Crete (Solinus, xi. 8, p. 73 Mommsen). Animal hide: Ovid, *Fasti* i. 629. Knots:
Servius, *Ad Aen.* iv. 518. On superstitions about knots see Joh. Chrys. *Hom. in
I Cor.* xii. 7 (13), *PG* 61. 105. Hippolytus (*Apost. trad.* 21) directs that at baptism
women must untie their hair; cf. Clem. Alex. *Paed.* ii. 62. W. C. van Unnik adduces
rabbinic parallels, *Vigiliae Christianae* i (1947), 77–100. Pliny (*NH* 22. 61) preserves
a remedy for fever, tying knots that are loosed only after the fever has gone, and
mentions (*NH* 26. 93) how an abscess can be healed with a poultice applied by a
fasting and naked virgin, a story illustrating the magical potency of fasting, nudity,
and virginity. For cultic nudity in antiquity see J. Heckenbach, *De nuditate sacra
sacrisque vinculis* (1911); P. Oppenheim, *RAC* i. 1186–93 s.v. 'Barfüssigkeit' (1950);
W. Speyer, 'Die Segenskraft des göttlichen Fusses', *Romanitas et Christianitas, Studia
J. H. Waszink oblata* (1973), 293–309.
⁴ So the Roman procession to the Capitol called Nudipedalia: Petronius 44;
Suetonius, *Aug.* 100. 4; Tertullian, *Apol.* 40. 14; *Ieiun.* 16. 5.

where the peasant women ceremonially walk through the fields with their clothes hitched up above their waist, while in other places they proceed barefoot with hair dishevelled and without a knot in their girdles.[1] That magical power increases if the feet are naked is axiomatic in antiquity.[2]

Such notions did not die out with the coming of Christianity. In his 55th letter, to Januarius, Augustine remarks that it is easier to persuade a confirmed drinker to forsake his bottle than to dissuade a man from walking barefoot for eight days, so great is the force of cultic custom ('praesumptio').[3] Early medieval processions at Rogationtide sometimes required unshod feet.[4] The nakedness required of candidates for baptism was sometimes less than total, and then took the form of leaving off shoes, especially for the exorcism, unction, and water rite.[5] The ancient evidence, in short, for regarding bare feet as necessary for cultic acts, like Moses at the bush, or any entrant to a mosque, is so widespread that the council of Saragossa may well have been objecting either to the survival of a pagan superstition or to a magical ceremony.

---

[1] Pliny, *NH* 28. 78. For Metrodorus see F. Jacoby, *Die Fragmente der griechischen Historiker* 184.

[2] Pliny, *NH* 29. 131; Horace, *Sat.* i. 8. 23 ff.; Tibullus i. 5. 55; Ovid, *Metam.* vii. 180–6; Juvenal vi. 446; Philostratus, *V. Apoll. Tyan.* vi. 10. On the apotropaic effect of displaying sexual parts see Plutarch, *Mulierum virtutes* 248B, and much evidence gathered by C. Bonner, 'The Trial of S. Eugenia', *American Journal of Philology* 41 (1920), 253–64. Cf. also below, p. 52, n. 3.

[3] Augustine, *Ep.* 55. 35.

[4] See a variant reading in canon 33 of the council of Mainz of 813 in *MGH Leges* II. ii. 1 (1904), 269.

[5] Exorcism: Dionysius Areopagita, *Eccl. hier.* ii. 2. 6; 3. 5; thereon F. J. Dölger, *Der Exorzismus im altchristlichen Taufritual* (1909, repr. 1967), pp. 107–14. Unction: Joh. Chrys. *Ad illuminandos catech.* i. 2 (*PG* 49. 225); Joh. Diac. (perhaps the later pope John I, 523–6), *Ep. ad. Senarium* 6 (ed. Wilmart in *Studi e testi* 59, p. 172; *PL* 59. 403A). The Syrian custom of baptizands at Apamea being exorcised with bare feet is mentioned in the Acts of the council of Constantinople 536 (Mansi VIII. 1111 = *ACO* iii. 99. 31). On baptismal nakedness see Cyril of Jerusalem, *Cat. myst.* ii. 2, implying removal of more than shoes; Zeno of Verona, i. 23 (ii. 35), p. 70 Löfstedt, 'nudi demergitis'; Palladius, *Dial. de vita Joh. Chrys.* 2, p. 13, 3–6 Coleman-Norton. Moschus, *Pratum* 3 (*PG* 87. 2855), tells how the monastic presbyter Conon, called to baptize a beautiful Persian girl, was granted the gift of indifference by a vision of John the Baptist; a story showing that, though the ancients were accustomed to mixed bathing without clothing in public baths, at least in a monastic context the baptismal ceremony could fail to realize that recovery of Adam and Eve's innocence before the Fall which the total removal of clothing was intended to symbolize. Ambrose, *Expl. Ps.* 61. 32 (*CSEL* 64. 396) says that sexual shame is caused only by sin: 'nulla enim esset verecundia genitalium si culpa non esset.' So, also *De Ioseph* 5. 25 (*CSEL* 32. 2; 90. 12) 'he alone is naked whom guilt has made naked'; and *De Isaac* 5. 43; 6. 55. Baptismal loincloths are Arian: *PO* 23. 281.

Accordingly, there may be more than meets the eye behind the canon of the council censuring the apparently harmless practice of walking without shoes. Certainly the records of Saragossa offer no hint whether the Priscillianists felt bound to take literally Christ's mission charge, or whether they were motivated by ritual considerations. The attraction of the second possibility is made more plausible by the fact, as will emerge, that Priscillian was suspected of having taken part in peasant ceremonies designed to ensure the right climate for the crops, and was an unashamed possessor of an amulet inscribed with God's name (below, p. 54).

The Manichee question at Saragossa

According to Sulpicius Severus, whose Aquitanian background and relation to Martin of Tours gave him an impassioned interest in Priscillianism, which he describes in language modelled on Sallust's account of Catiline's conspiracy,[1] Priscillian's movement began when he fell under the influence of an aristocratic lady named Agape and an orator Elpidius, both of whom had been friendly with a gnostic teacher Mark of Memphis, who came to Spain from Egypt. Priscillian, he continues, soon attracted a group round him, especially of women. His circle came to include at least two bishops, Instantius and Salvianus, who even bound themselves to Priscillian by an oath, at which point Hyginus of Cordoba became apprehensive and turned to Hydatius of Mérida. The location of the sees of Instantius and Salvianus is not given; probably they were in Lusitania, and the metropolitan of Mérida would be concerned.

On being put on the alert by Hyginus, Hydatius of Mérida turned for support to an episcopal colleague Ithacius, the name of whose see is unfortunately miswritten in the solitary manuscript of the chronicle of Sulpicius Severus which is the only authority at this point. The scribe wrote 'Ithacio Sossubensi episcopo'. Since C. Sigonius's edition of the chronicle (1581), it has been generally accepted that the most plausible correction of 'Sossubensi', which corresponds to the name of no known city in Roman Spain, is 'Ossonubensi', thus making Ithacius bishop of

[1] *Chron.* ii. 46. 1 ff. On Sallust's influence on Severus' portrait of Priscillian see J. Fontaine in *Classica et Iberica, in honour of J. M. F. Marique* (1975), 355–92.

Ossonuba, modern Estoi near Faro in the Algarve, a place then enjoying good communications with Emerita. The only alternative worth considering might be Sisapo or Saesapo in Baetica (modern Almadén) in the hills some 70 miles east of Emerita,[1] but its claims are less than those of Ossonuba. Ithacius of Ossonuba was to play a cardinal role in the story, always with Hydatius the spearhead of the opposition to Priscillian, the principal accuser at his trial, and thereafter a divisive figure among the bishops of both Spain and Gaul. Isidore of Seville includes him in his catalogue of illustrious men and, while failing to mention his see, adds to our information by giving his *cognomen*, Ithacius Clarus, and by saying that he 'wrote a book in the form of an apologia, in which he shows Priscillian's hateful doctrines and arts of sorcery and disgraceful lechery, observing that the teacher of Priscillian was a certain Mark of Memphis, a disciple of Mani, and a most learned expert in the magic art.'[2]

The comparison of Isidore's summary of Ithacius' apologia with Sulpicius Severus' account of the origins of Priscillian's movement makes it as good as certain that Sulpicius Severus was drawing upon Ithacius' book as a main source.[3] It follows that the assertion of Priscillian's dependence on Mark of Memphis is not a neutral report, but comes from a bitterly hostile writer desperately anxious to defend the unpleasant part that he had taken in the prosecution of an episcopal colleague. Memphis was famous throughout antiquity as a principal centre of the magic art, and a text of Jerome attests that it retained its vitality in his time. At its underground shrines adepts could learn how to ride on crocodiles or how to force broomsticks to serve man.[4] Therefore

---

[1] A. Tovar, *Iberische Landeskunde* i, *Baetica* (Baden-Baden, 1974), pp. 96–7.
[2] Isid. Hispal., *Vir. inl.* 15 (*PL* 83. 1092): 'Ithacius Hispaniarum episcopus, cognomento et eloquio Clarus, scripsit quemdam librum sub apologetici specie, in quo detestanda Priscilliani dogmata et maleficiorum eius artes libidinumque eius probra demonstrat, ostendens Marcum quemdam Memphiticum magicae artis scientissimum discipulum fuisse Manis et Priscilliani magistrum . . .'.
[3] Babut, *Priscillien*, pp. 36–8; d'Alès, *Priscillien*, pp. 11–12, concurs.
[4] On Memphitic magic see (e.g.) Ezek. 30: 13; Lucan iv. 449; Lucian, *Philopseudes* 34, etc.; Jerome, *Vita Hilarionis* 21; *In Esaiam* v, on 19: 11–13 (*PL* 24. 188), 'Memphim quoque magicis artibus deditam pristini usque ad praesens tempus vestigia erroris ostendunt.' A ninth-century text (Ps.-Anastasius Sinaita, *Disput. adv. Iud.* 2, *PG* 89. 1233A) says that divination at Memphis has been abolished; presumably this occurred in the fifth century, before the Arab invasion. Ability to ride on a crocodile is a charism of Egyptian holy men; see the anonymous apophthegm, Nau 46 (*Revue de l'Orient chrétien* 12, 1907, 176).

the statement that Mark came from Memphis is almost certainly
an invention of Ithacius to add verisimilitude to his portrait of
Priscillian the sorcerer's apprentice.

If Sulpicius Severus were the sole text at this point, it might be
natural to accept that there really was a fourth-century migrant
named Mark who came from Egypt to Spain, though whether
he was an Origenist ascetic or a Manichee (Egypt being well
supplied with either type) is a question dependent on the critical
estimate which of these positions most closely approximates to
that attested by Priscillianist writings. Trade between Alexandria
and Spain at this period was so normal and everyday that Palladius
attests a Greek epithet *Spanodromos* for Egyptian merchants
regularly 'on the Spanish run'.[1] However, Jerome and texts of the
early fifth century which give clear signs of having been similarly
dependent upon Ithacius' book for their information about
Priscillian, identify Mark with the second-century gnostic teacher
to whom Irenaeus devotes several chapters in the first book of
his *Adversus haereses* (below, p. 152). A second-century gnostic
cannot have been a disciple of the third-century Mani, but so
nice a point of chronology would seem unimportant to a hot
controversialist such as Ithacius. In all probability Ithacius'
apologia identified Mark the source of Priscillianism with the
Mark of Irenaeus. Accordingly, while there is not the least
improbability about the hypothesis that Priscillian may have been
given the impetus to start his ascetic reform by the arrival of an
immigrant to Spain from the East, 'Mark of Memphis' can be
eliminated from the prosopography of the fourth century.[2]

This critical evaluation of the sources is prerequisite if the
question can be properly put, whether Ithacius or Hydatius
raised the alarm about para-Manichee ideas and practices as
early as the council of Saragossa. If Mark of Memphis is an
invention of Ithacius' apologia, at what date did Ithacius begin
to accuse Priscillian of Manicheism, sorcery, and lechery?

At first sight it may appear most unlikely that this charge

---

[1] *Historia Lausiaca* 14.

[2] V. C. de Clercq, 'Ossius of Cordova and the origins of Priscillianism', *Studia Patristica* i (*TU* 63, 1957), 601–6, suggests identifying Mark of Memphis with a Mark whom Ossius is accused of having injured by the eastern council of Serdica in 342 (*CSEL* 65. 66). If this presupposes that the eastern synod risked prejudicing its case by implicitly supporting the cause of a Manichee, it is too improbable to merit consideration.

had been brought as early as October 380 since, if the bogy of
Manicheism really had been prominently brought before the
bishops at that council, which Ithacius attended, then their
counter-reaction is amazing in its moderation. Had the bishops
been unanimously agreed that they faced an insidious and hated
heresy, by general consent held in abhorrence by authority and
all sensible men, the synod might have been expected to react
sharply. Yet the canons of Saragossa keep a strange silence. They
conspicuously fail to mention dogmatic deviation as the ground
for alarm. Only one of the *sententiae* at Saragossa brings us within
sight of real Manicheism, namely, the insistence that those who
receive the eucharistic elements at mass must consume them.
This might mean that the Priscillianists, while accepting and
consuming the bread, were abstaining from the chalice, a practice
common among crypto-Manichees, for the Manichees regarded
wine as 'the poison of the princes of darkness'.[1] In Rome during
the time of Leo the Great a secret group of Manichees was
detected by observers watching whether or not they drank from
the chalice.[2] But of course it is at least as natural to interpret the
Saragossan canon to mean that some Priscillianists, and perhaps
others, were accepting the host at the eucharist and taking it
away for private reservation, perhaps to be consumed on those
Sundays in Advent or Lent when they had retired to their mountain retreats and their lay-directed Bible-readings.

Nevertheless, it is not difficult to show that it would be wholly
misleading to treat the particular practices censured in the
sententiae as exhausting the agenda of the council of Saragossa.
The second of the Würzburg tractates, the petition of the Priscillianist bishops to pope Damasus (below, p. 38), mentions
two quite different matters as having been part of the debate at
Saragossa. At the council Hydatius of Emerita had laid before
the synod a memorandum on discipline of life ('commonitorium
quod velut agendae vitae poneret disciplinam'), a text that may
have been a draft for the canons. More important, the second
tractate reports that during the course of the debate in the council
Hydatius had cried out: 'Let what should be condemned be
condemned; let what is superfluous not be read.' ('Damnanda

---

[1] Augustine, *De moribus Manich.* xvi. 46.
[2] Leo, *Sermo* 42. 5 (PL 54. 280A; *Corpus Christianorum* 138A, p. 247, ed.
Chavasse).

damnentur, superflua non legantur.')[1] This utterance is quoted in the context of a defence of reading apocryphal texts. At Saragossa, therefore, Hydatius urged the council not only to condemn heretical apocrypha but to prohibit the study of orthodox apocrypha, 'superfluous' because, in so far as their orthodoxy is assessed by the criterion of the canon of scripture, they can add nothing to the doctrine contained in the canon. The canons of the council are wholly silent on this point, and may show that Hydatius failed to win sufficient support. Yet the Manichees were well known to hold apocryphal Acts of the apostles in deep reverence, and it was association with heresy that made apocrypha dangerous. It follows that more was said about heresy at Saragossa than can be discerned from the text of the *sententiae*.

The Priscillianist position is set out at length especially in the acephalous third tractate (below, p. 81), an emotionally charged and eloquent reply to Hydatius' attack. The essential core of the argument is that the biblical writers themselves cite non-canonical texts (Jude cites Enoch, Luke 11 speaks of all the murdered prophets, Matt. 2 cites a prophecy 'Out of Egypt have I called my son', Paul wrote to the Laodiceans a letter not in the canon); that heretics have interpolated some of the apocryphal documents; but that the spiritual and discerning reader can safely read even the interpolated texts, armed with the criterion that if an apocryphon teaches Christ to be God it is acceptable.

This position does not differ from that maintained by respected pillars of catholic orthodoxy. A decade or more before, Zeno of Verona is found defending the perpetual virginity of Mary by appealing to the story of the midwife in the Gospel of Pseudo-Matthew, and assumes all his hearers to know of St. Thecla.[2] Filastrius of Brescia never doubts that the apocryphal Acts of the apostles were genuinely written by immediate disciples of Andrew, John, Peter, and Paul. But because they have been interpolated by heretics, these books should be read for example of life and instruction of manners, especially as models for celibacy, but may not be applied to establish any doctrine.[3] As we shall

---

[1] *Tract.* ii, p. 42, 12.

[2] Zeno i. 54 (ii. 8), p. 129 Löfstedt; ii. 2 (i. 8), p. 152. Cf. the sixth Würzburg tractate (p. 74, 23–4) on Mary's perpetual virginity. For a close Greek parallel to Priscillian's list of non-canonical texts cited in scripture cf. the probably contemporary Joseph, *Hypomnesticon* 120–1 (*PG* 106. 121–4).

[3] Filastrius, 88 (*CSEL* 38. 48); below, p. 120. Cf. Jerome, *Ep.* 107. 12,

see, even Turibius of Astorga, whose fears of apocrypha went deep, does not doubt that the narratives and miracle-stories in the apocryphal Acts are wholly veracious and authentic, but interpolated with heretical teaching (below, p. 209).

Ambrosiaster's attitude is similar. In his Pauline commentary he refers freely to apocrypha, viz. the Acts of Paul and Thecla (on 2 Tim. 2: 18), the Acts of Peter (on Rom. 8, 39 and 16: 4), and the Penitence of Jannes and Mambres (2 Tim 3: 8). On 1 Thess. 5: 22 he emphasizes that claims to revelation are not to be rejected without scrutiny, and like Priscillian believes in the principle of reserve in the teaching of advanced truths (on 1 Thess. 2: 17 and 3: 10).

Even if the restraint and moderation of the canons of Saragossa did not invite the conjecture, it seems safe to deduce that the bishops were divided in counsel. The canons lay down that anyone, clerical or lay, excommunicated in one diocese may not be received by the bishop of another diocese, and any bishop contravening this ruling is to be excommunicate. As a statement of general principle nothing could be more reasonable for the prevention of scandals. The canon was, however, a potentially powerful weapon in the hands of any majority for coercing reluctant individuals among their colleagues. As the Priscillianists became stronger, the rule became harder to enforce; and as the controversy proceeded on its course, the lines became harder and sharper. The doves tended to lose out to the hawks. But at Saragossa the doves could make their presence felt.

Hyginus of Cordoba did not attend the council (above, p. 13). According to Sulpicius Severus, Hyginus was formally warned[1] about his reluctance to excommunicate the Priscillianists. The bishop of Cordoba may have judged that the extent of support for Priscillian in his region of Baetica had reached such proportions that abrupt and harsh action would simply make reconciliation impossible and the wound incurable. He had the misfortune to stand between the two extremes. Without ever being a Priscillianist, he refused to support Ithacius and Hydatius, which was to cost him dearly (below, pp. 134, 145).

Like Hyginus, Priscillian's known supporters among the bishops, Instantius and Salvianus, also stayed away from the

[1] Sulpicius Severus, *Chron.* ii. 47. 3 (*CSEL* 1. 100. 19). For the manuscript text 'communione faceret' read with Babut (*Priscillien*, p. 138, n. 2) 'commonefaceret'.

synod at Saragossa. The second tractate casts a shaft of light both on the reasons for this and also on the process of debate preceding the meeting when it says that before the council pope Damasus, who had evidently been consulted either by the Spanish or by the Aquitanian bishops, had formally forbidden any condemnation of absent persons without proper trial.[1] The principle was one that bitter experience during the Arian controversy had branded upon the consciousness of western bishops; in 382 Ambrose was able to make extensive use of it in dispute with the emperor Theodosius over the decisions of the council of Constantinople of 381.[2] The intervention of Damasus at this stage shows that a report on the Priscillianist affair had already been sent to Rome, which may explain why Damasus was later very cool towards the request of the Priscillianist bishops for an audience. He would have had reason to take interest in a Spanish controversy, not merely because of his patriarchal responsibilities in relation to the western provinces, but also because he was himself of Spanish origin.[3] The ruling that those not present to be heard should not be condemned will have encouraged Instantius and Salvianus to remain at home.

The Priscillianists, we may note in passing, regarded Damasus' letter to the council as more than a piece of brotherly advice (see below, p. 39). Moreover, it emerged that the Roman ruling had somehow been observed:

At the episcopal meeting which took place at Caesaraugusta none of our group was held to be liable to censure (*reus*), none was accused, none convicted, none condemned; no crime was charged against us in respect of our conduct and manner of life, none was put, I do not say

---

[1] Priscillian, *Tract.* ii, p. 35, 21 ff. He recurs to this point on four other occasions —ii, p. 39, 20; p. 40, 7–8; p. 42, 19–21; p. 43, 3–4. See below, p. 34. Behind Damasus' ruling there was some experience. The western bishops under Constantius had been pressed to condemn Athanasius who was not invited to defend himself. Lucifer of Cagliari's tract *De Sancto Athanasio* i is entitled by the manuscript tradition 'Quia absentem nemo debet judicare nec damnare' (*CSEL* 14. 66). The imperial law is not so absolute. A law of Gratian of December 384 (*Cod. Theod.* xi. 39. 9) says that accusations against an absent defendant should not be *at once* believed. Priscillian says that Damasus based his ruling on 'the commands of the Gospel' (p. 35, 23), but without indicating what text he has in mind. John 7 : 51 ? Since *Tract.* v, p. 62, 17, says Moses was 'in opus evangelicae dispositionis electus', 'evangelica iussa' may have a wide sense.

[2] Ambrose, *Ep.* 14. 4–5.

[3] 'natione Spanus': Duchesne, *Liber pontificalis* i. 212.

under the constraint of being summoned to answer, but even under the anxiety that this might occur.[1]

That no one had been condemned at Saragossa was an assurance explicitly given to the Priscillianist bishops after the council by Symposius, bishop of Asturica, who later appeared as a Priscillianist sympathizer.[2] Nevertheless the stridency with which the petition to Damasus repeatedly insists that no member of the group was put under censure at Saragossa is first-rate evidence that, already at the time of writing, the contrary story was widely circulated. In fact, Sulpicius Severus reports in exactly this sense, namely that at Saragossa judgement was expressly pronounced against Instantius and Salvianus whose absence was regarded as evidence of a heretical conscience.[3] In this conflict of evidence one is tempted to regard it as self-evident that the Priscillianist story is preferable.[4] However, the probability is high that, even if the formal *sententiae* unanimously agreed and signed at Saragossa did not actually condemn the Priscillianists by name, much was said at the council which was adverse to them. The minutes would have included attacks on named individuals, including Elpidius and Priscillian.

Clinching support for the view that this is the correct reading of the story may be found in the final verdict upon Symposius of Asturica and other Priscillianist bishops of Galicia pronounced by the council of Toledo in September 400. Their verdict is not composed or transmitted in lucid or incorrupt Latin, and there is room for debate about its meaning. But the sense of the council of Toledo seems to be this: the orthodox bishops have been required to exercise great patience in the

---

[1] *Tract.* ii, p. 35, 15–19; cf. p. 42, 19–23.

[2] *Tract.* ii, p. 40, 1–8. Symposius' support for Priscillianism appears in the records of the council of Toledo, 400 (see below).

[3] *Chron.* ii. 47. 2: 'verum haeretici committere se iudicio non ausi: in absentes tamen lata sententia damnatique Instantius et Salvianus episcopi.'

[4] This question is well discussed by A. García Conde, 'En el Concilio I de Zaragoza ¿fueron condenados nominalmente los jefes priscilianistas?', in *Cuadenos de estudios gallegos* ii (Santiago de Compostela, 1946), 223–30. But the illusion that there was a second council of Saragossa in the nineties prevents him using the clinching evidence of the council of Toledo of 400; and the suggestion that the conflict of evidence may be reconciled on the hypothesis of a provisional condemnation does not seem useful.

G. Cirot, 'Erreur d'historien ou mensonge d'hérétique', *Bulletin critique* 18 (1897), 350–7, has found no following with the notion that Priscillian simply told Damasus a lie and hoped to get away with it.

deliberations over a long period of time in dealing with the Priscillianists; for at the council of Saragossa, at which a sentence had been pronounced against certain particular individuals ('sententia in certos quosque dicta fuerat'), Symposius, who attended the proceedings of the council during only a single day, nevertheless later rejected the verdict and, though present at Saragossa, scorned to hear the matter mentioned. After the meeting at Saragossa Ambrose had written a letter to the Spanish bishops saying that the Priscillianists should be received back to communion ('pacem') provided that they renounced what they had been wrongly doing and submitted to the conditions laid down in his letter.[1] The consensus of opinion (Duchesne, Babut, Kidd, Batiffol, Caspar) has been that this passage in the Acts of Toledo refers not to the council held at Saragossa in 380, but to a later, otherwise unknown, second council of Saragossa, probably held about 395 or 396, perhaps after the death of Theodosius had given the signal for a renewed harassment of the Priscillianists in Galicia.[2] That such a second council could have occurred is not to be doubted. But the Latin text of the Acts of Toledo does not require to be interpreted as referring to a council other than that of 380, and councils of Saragossa should not be multiplied beyond necessity. That the reference is to the council of 380 is made probable by the bishops' insistence on the length of time ('diu') during which they have been exercising patience and, above all, by the explicit reference to a sharp division of opinion with Symposius whether at the council of Saragossa there had actually been an express condemnation of named individuals. Since the evidence both of Sulpicius Severus and of the second Würzburg tractate shows that this was a hotly contested point about the council of 380, the hypothesis that there was a second meeting at Saragossa in the mid nineties, at which the same issue was a matter of controversy, creates more problems than it solves.

The same piece of the Acts of Toledo, 400, mentions a bishop of Galicia named Vegetinus (see not given), whom the anti-

---

[1] For the verdict of the council of Toledo (400) on the Priscillianists see below, p. 182.

[2] L. Duchesne, *Histoire ancienne de l'église* ii. 542 (*ET* ii. 429); Babut, *Priscillien*, p. 172, n. 5, and p. 186; B. J. Kidd, *History of the Church to A.D. 461* ii (Oxford, 1922), 306; P. Batiffol, *Le Siège apostolique (359–451)* (Paris, 1924), p. 192; E. Caspar, *Geschichte des Papsttums*, i (Tübingen, 1930), 280. The correct view is in P. B. Gams, *Die Kirchengeschichte von Spanien* ii. 1 (1864 repr. 1956), 389, and B. Vollmann's article in *PW* Suppl. xiv (1974), 500–1.

Priscillianists at Toledo are ready to receive to communion, and whom they declare to have been made a bishop before the council of Saragossa. This, however, offers no obstacle to asserting that the council referred to was that of 380. Vegetinus could easily have held his see for more than twenty years, as Symposius did. Their contemporary Proculus held on to the see of Marseille (despite all the storms breaking upon him both at home and in correspondence from pope Zosimus) for nearly half a century.[1]

To return to the events of the council of Saragossa in 380, it has to be observed that it was not only the bishops who sympathized with Priscillian who are found to have stayed away, or to have attended, if at all, for a single day. Among the most striking features of the record of the council of Saragossa is the thin attendance. If there had been a general perturbation caused by the Priscillianists in several provinces of Spain, why did so few bishops come? No doubt allowance has to be made for lack of resources in the Spanish churches, for age and health, for weather, distance, and communications.[2] Even so, an attendance of not more than ten Spanish bishops amounts to a demonstration by the rest of intentional inertia. Either the majority of the bishops were not yet meeting a serious problem in their dioceses or they saw little reason for becoming excited about Priscillian's activities. Probably only those directly confronted by active Priscillianist cells thought the agenda sufficiently urgent to require their voice at the council.

The most prominent item in Priscillian's message to the churches was the demand for celibacy for all truly dedicated Christians, clerical or lay. Perhaps some bishops stayed away because they did not wish to attend an acrimonious debate on a controversial subject. Neglected light on the state of opinion is thrown by pope Siricius' letter of February 385 to Himerius, bishop of Tarraco, in reply to an inquiry sent to Rome by Himerius asking advice on some of the questions dividing the Spanish churches. Amazingly, Himerius can have said not a word overtly about Priscillianism, a silence which is deafening when one reflects on the situation in the late autumn of 384 when Himerius wrote to Rome. Although Saragossa was in his own

[1] The best, though incomplete, biography of Proculus is Ensslin's article in *PW* xxiii, 1 (1957), 81–2. See also Duchesne, *Fastes* i², 274, and Caspar, op. cit., i. 280 f., 385.
[2] On poor attendance at councils in Visigothic Spain see E. A. Thompson, *The Goths in Spain* (Oxford, 1969), pp. 276, 284–7.

province of Tarraconensis, Himerius did not go to the controversial council. Yet he was a bishop of such seniority that Siricius
can assume him to possess authority to distribute the papal
decretal throughout the Spanish provinces.[1] Perhaps if he had
attended at Saragossa, he might have had to preside. Himerius
has only one question explicitly relating to heresy, whether the
many converts from Arianism (i.e. signatories to the creed of
Ariminum now wishing to disown it) should be received as
penitents with no more than laying on of hands, or whether, as
some rigorist Spanish bishops thought, they should be baptized.[2]
Rigorism was represented no doubt by Gregory of Elvira for
whom all signatories to the general council of Ariminum were
rank heretics, incapable of valid orders and sacraments. Siricius
reaffirmed pope Liberius' ruling that, while the synod of Ariminum was null and void, the sacraments and orders of those who
had accepted it were not invalidated; therefore the ex-Arians
should be treated as reconciled schismatics, and must not be
rebaptized.[3]

On the other hand, Himerius also reported to Rome the divided
state of opinion in the Spanish churches in regard to clerical
celibacy. Many bishops, presbyters, and deacons have been
begetting children—and not merely the occasional bastard, but
legitimate offspring by their due and lawful wives, for the defence
of which they appeal to scripture. Against this view Siricius
rules that all clergy in major orders must be continent from the
day of their ordination, that they may be pure for the daily
offering of the mass. The rule of celibacy is here becoming a
part of the dedication and commitment inherent in ordination.
Siricius goes beyond the rule of the council of Elvira that the
clergy should abstain from conjugal intercourse before those
mornings on which they were on duty.[4]

---

[1] Siricius, *Ep.* i. 20 (PL 13. 1146B), 'pro antiquitate sacerdotii tui'. The phrase
indicates Siricius' awareness of the importance of seniority in Spanish notions of
authority where metropolitans, though not insignificant (cf. 15 (19), 1145B 'omnium
provinciarum summi antistes'), did not enjoy exalted primatial rights. Cf. above
p. 4, n. 1.

[2] Siricius, *Ep.* i. 2 (PL 13. 1133A).

[3] The old Spanish formula of reconciling by chrism and laying on of hands one
baptized in the Arian heresy is printed by Férotin, *Liber ordinum* 100–3. The Arian
Visigoths rebaptized all who joined their sect (Gregory of Tours, *Historia Francorum*
v. 28 (38)).

[4] Canon 33 'Placuit in totum prohibere episcopis, presbyteris et diaconibus vel

It appears from Priscillian's account[1] that after the council of Saragossa Hydatius of Emerita had worries. When he returned home, he found himself formally accused by one of his presbyters. If Himerius of Tarraco's letter to Rome is understood to refer even obliquely to the Priscillianist affair, then the charge can be expected to be that Hydatius had cohabited with his wife or even that she had secretly produced an infant, such evidence of conjugal acts being felt to be unsuitable in a bishop.

The nature of the charge Priscillian cannot bring himself to mention. But the document of accusation was widely circulated to other churches besides Emerita; and soon inspired *libelli* containing even graver charges against Hydatius were formally handed in at the churches of Salvianus and Instantius. At Emerita, meanwhile, a large group of clergy withdrew from communion with Hydatius, boldly declaring that they would not hold communion with him until he was cleared of the charge. If the conduct of the metropolitan was to be put in question, the responsibility for judgement necessarily lay in the hands of the other bishops of Lusitania. With foolish naïvety, Instantius and Salvianus tried to invoke the support of the sympathetic Symposius of Astorga and Hyginus of Cordoba. They then felt it to be their duty to go to Emerita and see Hydatius ostensibly to bring about 'peace' but in circumstances where they were sure to be suspected (probably rightly) of attempting to consecrate a successor to Hydatius and to extrude him from the see with the aid of the formal charges handed in. The result of their highly imprudent visit was the reverse of that intended. Hydatius evidently enjoyed a far larger measure of support in his city than Priscillian had expected. The visiting bishops were not merely excluded from the *praesbyterium* (the sanctuary of the church)[2] but were physically

---

omnibus clericis *positis in ministerio* abstinere se a coniugibus suis et non generare filios.' For the interpretation of this canon cf. R. Gryson, *Les Origines du célibat ecclésiastique* (1970), p. 39. I think it implausible to interpret it to mean that Elvira was abrogating a relaxation of normal rigour, previously allowed to clergy when not on duty (so E. Griffe in *Bulletin de littérature ecclésiastique* (Toulouse), 1973, pp. 142–5). The requirement of clerical celibacy is explained by Ambrosiaster on the ground of the frequency with which Christian clergy are on duty in comparison with the more numerous and underworked priests of the Old Testament (on 1 Tim. 3 : 9).

[1] *Tract.* ii, p. 39, 17 ff.
[2] This is the earliest example of the use of the word to mean 'presbytery'. For another instance see pope Gelasius, *Ep.* 14. 8, p. 366 Thiel. Priscillian's text is otherwise interpreted by W. Waldstein, art. 'Geisselung', *RAC* ii. 487 (1974). He thinks the

assaulted and beaten with rods by an excited crowd mustered by Hydatius. Outraged by this hostile reception, they took away a doctrinal manifesto by the laity of Emerita now dissenting from Hydatius, and distributed a circular letter 'to almost all our fellow-bishops', describing what had happened and the faith professed by the dissenting group, 'among whom there were many candidates put forward for the priesthood' ('nec hoc tacentes quod multi ex his post professionem ad sacerdotium peterentur').[1]
It is not clear here whether Priscillian means to say generally that the dissenting group of Emerita included an exceptional number of ordinands, or whether he is more specifically saying that in this particular group were several candidates being put forward to succeed Hydatius as bishop if he were to be deposed as unworthy of his sacred office. In favour of the former interpretation is a passage where Priscillian seems especially anxious to stress the readiness of members of his brotherhood to undertake the responsibilities of the pastoral office,[2] an assurance which seems designed to allay the kind of anxiety emerging in the canons of Valence and Saragossa deploring clergy withdrawing to become monks. The Priscillianists might have appeared in the past as if they wanted to set up within the church a quasi-independent *ecclesiola* with its own spiritual life fostered by unauthorised private teachers in spontaneous groups. Priscillian's supporters showed none of that ascetic reluctance to accept holy orders which had caused such hard feelings at the council of Valence in 374 (above, p. 14). They were only too anxious to carry through their reform of the church by putting forward members of their association for vacancies in the hierarchy, thereby acquiring the direct power to influence the normal life of the community. But a point telling in favour of the more specific interpretation is the word *sacerdotium* which is normally used to mean the episcopal office. If that is correct, the passage may well

presbyteral court of Mérida imposed a formal disciplinary flogging on Priscillian for his heresy. I take the scene to be less well ordered and to resemble the bloody affray in the sanctuary at Aix in 407 when, if we are to believe the hostile account of pope Zosimus (*Avell.* xxxvi. 5, *CSEL* 35. 104), the *defensor civitatis* resisted with futile force Lazarus' attempt to take possession of the see.

[1] *Tract.* ii, p. 40, 23.
[2] *Tract.* ii, p. 35, 3–5: 'Some of our group were already elected by God in the church, others were seeking to form our lives so that we might be elected.' The same contrast in iv, p. 60, 8–9; vi, p. 79, 19.

mean that Priscillian himself made a personal bid to be elected to the see of Emerita in the event of Hydatius' withdrawal under censure.

The conjecture that the manifesto produced by the dissenting laity of Emerita is identical with the first of the eleven Würzburg tractates, has something to be said in its favour, and enjoyed Babut's brilliant advocacy.[1] The first tractate bears all the marks of being a personal statement by an individual under attack, who uses the first-person plural because he is spokesman for a group; but the group stands or falls with his personal apologia. However, the situation and date of the first tractate is a complex problem needing special discussion (below, p. 47).

In any event it is certain that the bishops sympathetic to Priscillian's ascetic movement responded favourably. They approved the orthodoxy of the manifesto submitted by the dissenting group of Emerita, agreed that there was no bar in the decisions of Saragossa which might prevent any of this group from being proposed for the episcopate if the laity asked for them, and concurred in the request for a council to review the whole matter.

In 381, a few months after the council of Saragossa of October 380, the see of Abula (Avila) in Lusitania fell vacant. Instantius and Salvianus went there and with sufficient local support achieved the election and consecration of Priscillian.[2] The metropolitan Hydatius of Emerita, 160 miles away, took no part in the proceedings. Whether any bishop assisted Instantius and Salvianus in the consecration is not attested. Near the end of the petition to Damasus in the second tractate a contrast is drawn between the right of the people to elect and the right of the provincial bishops to consecrate (*Tract.* ii, p. 40, 26–7). The allusion may reflect controversy about the validity of the action at Avila. It is improbable that in Spain the Nicene rulings regarding the consent and power of veto of the metropolitan and the requirement of a minimum of three bishops for an episcopal consecration were understood to be in force, at least in the sense that failure to observe them could render invalid a consecration which the

---

[1] *Priscillien*, p. 143.

[2] Sulpicius Severus, *Chron.* ii. 47. 4. A bishopric at Avila is not previously attested, and does not reappear in the records until the synod of Toledo in 610 under Gundemar (*PL* 84. 484D).

local church desired. Nor, in the age when both Ambrose and Nectarius could be selected for the highest position in the church, though needing to be baptized before consecration, would anyone have been able to object to Priscillian's ordination *per saltum*, on the ground of the canon against this agreed by the western council of Serdica in 342. Those who distrusted Priscillian and regarded him as no true bishop are not recorded to have raised objections on such technical grounds of canon law. Their complaints, so far as known, were to be based on the argument that, at the time when Priscillian was still a layman, Instantius and Salvianus had been condemned together with him by the judgement of the bishops.[1]

The critics could well have appealed to the 51st canon of the council of Elvira, which expressly lays down that 'No layman coming from any heresy is to be promoted to the clergy; and those who have been ordained in the past, are to be deposed without hesitation'.

The character of the arguments used in the petition to Damasus shows that Priscillian's consecration to be bishop was rejected by his opponents because in the past he had been censured as a Manichee, which entailed the consequence that he was a pseudo-bishop. In other words, the answer to the anti-Priscillianists betrays the truth that the council of Saragossa really had adopted a critical resolution about Manichees, even if it did not particularly specify any named individuals.

The second tractate reveals more of the items in the anti-

---

[1] Sulpicius Severus, *Chron.* ii. 47. 4: 'Instantius et Salvianus damnati iudicio sacerdotum Priscillianum etiam laicum, sed principem malorum omnium, una secum Caesaraugustana synodo notatum . . . episcopum . . . constituunt.' Compare this with Priscillian's petition to Damasus, protesting that at Saragossa 'none of us was found guilty'. He continues: 'nemo etiam cum esset laicus obiecti criminis probatione damnatus est, licet noxio sacerdotium nihil prosit et possit sacerdos deponi qui laicus meruit ante damnari' (*Tract.* ii, p. 42, 20–3). That Priscillian's ordination was regarded as invalid by his opponents is evident from this reply; they regarded him as a pseudo-bishop (*Tract.* ii, p. 41, 1). But the objection (to judge from Priscillian's rejoinder) was based on the ground that he was a condemned heretic, a Manichee, not on more technical objections of canon law. Hence the Priscillianist insistence on the orthodoxy of the confession of faith professed at both baptism and ordination: p. 39, 13–16, 'Nobis enim Christus deus dei filius passus in carnem secundum fidem symboli baptizatis et electis ad sacerdotium in nomine patris et fili et spiritus sancti tota fides, tota vita, tota veneratio est.' For the opposite opinion, that Priscillian's opponents would have left no weapon of canon law unused, see an excellent paper by K. M. Girardet, 'Trier 385: der Prozess gegen die Priszillianer', *Chiron* 4 (1974), 577–608.

Priscillianist armoury. It contains answers to the following charges:

1. Denying hope of salvation to married Christians (p. 36, 1 ff.).
2. Holding Patripassian doctrines of the divine monarchy (p. 37, 23; p. 39, 15).
3. Holding a docetic notion of the incarnation which denies the reality of Christ's suffering in the flesh (p. 36, 23–4; p. 39, 13).
4. Studying heretical apocrypha (p. 41, 21 ff.).
5. Manicheism and magic (p. 39, 8–11).
6. Teaching wicked morals and indecency (p. 35, 26).

If the Priscillianist bishops needed to answer this list of accusations as early as the end of 381 or early in 382, it strengthens the case for concluding that words to much the same effect had been uttered at the council of Saragossa in October 380.

The second tractate disingenuously implies that these grave charges were first brought forward in consequence of the imprudent attempt by Instantius and Salvianus to intervene at Emerita, when bishop Hydatius resented their interfering hands and mobilized a rough reception for them. After the Priscillianists had reported the story to other bishops of the province, they received the reply that Hydatius' position should be examined at a council. According to the Priscillianist account, Hydatius was so alarmed at the threat of a council to scrutinize his conduct that he went behind and above the synod of the province: he quickly sent a report, which the Priscillianists regarded as thoroughly mendacious, to Ambrose of Milan and enlisted his support to obtain a rescript from the emperor Gratian which he could use to counter the opposition. He cleverly mentioned no names to the emperor, but complained of harassment by 'pseudo-bishops and Manichees', both categories being regarded by universal consent as socially undesirable and proper objects of state repression.[1] The emperor's rescript (presumably sent to the *vicarius*, the praetorian prefect's deputy administering the Spanish provinces) directed that the heretics must not only leave their churches and cities but be banished 'from all countries', a formula almost more reminiscent of a ritual curse than a legal definition

---

[1] *Tract.* ii (p. 40, 24–41, 4).

of their destination in exile.[1] Sulpicius Severus regards the action of Hydatius in thus turning to the secular arm as in principle mistaken. In practice the move seems to have been effective, and Sulpicius Severus notes that the Priscillianists had to scatter and conceal themselves.[2] Hydatius felt himself to be in so strong a position that he sent a letter round the Spanish churches formally indicting Hyginus of Cordoba of being a heretic together with the Priscillianists. The Priscillianists saw this as evidence that Hydatius was unable to attack them without bringing accusations against all true Christians.[3] But the threat of an inquisition under the authority of a secular tribunal, taking its lead from the emperor's rescript, made drastic action essential for the Priscillianist cause.

The appeal to Rome and Milan

At this point Sulpicius provides a circumstantial framework of narrative, with which the second tractate's statements cohere. According to Sulpicius' *Chronicle*, Instantius, Salvianus, and Priscillian decided that they must go to Rome and to Milan to plead their cause directly and obtain higher support. They travelled by Aquitania. On their way they were very favourably received at Elusa (Eauze), metropolis of the province of Novempopulana (the rough equivalent of southern Gascony, Béarn, and the Pyrenees departments). But in Aquitania the church was unfriendly: at Burdigala (Bordeaux) bishop Delphinus well recalled the proceedings at Saragossa in October 380 and drove them from his city. For a time they found hospitality on the near-by estate of well-disposed friends, Attius Tiro Delphidius, his wife Euchrotia and their daughter Procula. Delphidius was a prominent figure in Aquitanian society, a friend of the poet Ausonius (praetorian prefect of Gaul 377–8, consul 379). He taught rhetoric in Bordeaux and then became an advocate, in which role Ausonius

[1] Gothofredus' commentary on *Cod. Theod.* xvi. 2. 35 regards this as the legal equivalent of 'beyond the hundredth milestone', but he adduces no parallel in support. *Cod. Theod.* xvi. 5. 18 (17 June 389) banishes Manichees 'ex omni orbe terrarum sed quam maxime de hac urbe' (viz. Roma).
[2] *Chron.* ii. 47. 6.
[3] Priscillian, *Tract.* ii, p. 41, 3–7 '. . . cum relato sibi rescribto sub specie sectae quam nostrum nemo non damnat in omnes rueret Christianos, hereticum etiam Hyginum nobiscum vocans, sicut epistulae ipsius missae ad eclesias prolocuntur, agens scilicet ne iudices haberet si omnes diversis obtrectationibus infamasset. . .'.

says that he made many enemies.[1] He was a pagan,[2] but his wife Euchrotia was a Christian. He died in middle life,[3] in all probability about the time of Priscillian's arrival on his estate. So Euchrotia, accompanied by her daughter, made the journey with the three bishops to Rome as a widow, and her motives could have included a quest for consolation by making pilgrimage to the shrines of the apostles and martyrs of Rome.

Euchrotia and Procula were accompanied to Italy by other women, in addition to Priscillian, Instantius, and Salvianus. Severus represents the ladies as an abandoned company of loose females. Malicious tongues in Aquitaine even said that the young Procula had become pregnant by Priscillian and had disposed of the unwanted child by abortion. Since this piece of gossip is known to Ausonius as well as to Severus, it must have been widely diffused. Manichees were known to hold that procreation should be avoided, and horrified orthodox catholics by openly advising married couples to confine sexual intercourse to the 'safe period' of the menstrual cycle. They were naturally accused of justifying abortion.[4] This feminine company with the three bishops was a serious imprudence. But Priscillian had pronounced views on the equal capacity of both women and men to be vehicles of the Spirit, and his teaching attracted women round him.[5]

Jerome's letter to Ctesiphon (*Ep.* 133), on the other hand, simply regards Priscillian's entourage of aristocratic ladies as one more example of a general phenomenon of feminine patronage for deviationists. He gives a long list: Simon Magus and Helen, Montanus and Prisca and Maximilla, Donatus and Lucilla; and now (what he cannot bring himself to put into words) the great ladies of the *gens Anicia* are supporting Pelagius. In this catalogue Jerome inserts Agape and Elpidius (above, p. 20) and a

[1] Ausonius, *Prof.* vi. 21–2. Delphidius' career is traced in detail in *PLRE* i. 246. Babut (*Priscillien*, p. 51) conjectures the identity of Delphidius and Euchrotia with Helpidius and Agape whose gnostic doctrines (according to Sulpicius) influenced Priscillian. This conjecture is unsupported. Helpidius is not an uncommon name at this period, and there is no good reason to accept Babut's view.

[2] Jerome, *Ep.* 120, *praef.* (to Delphidius' descendant, Hedybia).

[3] Ausonius, *Prof.* vi. 36.

[4] Augustine, *De moribus Manichaeorum*, 18. 65; *Contra Faustum* 15. 7; 22. 30. The abortion charge in Titus of Bostra, *Adv. Manich.* ii. 56, p. 61, 25 Lagarde = ii. 33 (*PG* 18. 1197C). On Manichee doctrine see J. T. Noonan, *Contraception* (Harvard, 1965), pp. 107–26.

[5] *Tract.* i, p. 28, 14 ff.; Sulpicius Severus, *Chron.* ii. 46. 6.

Priscillianist lady named Galla, that being her name, he explains,
not her race. Jerome complains that a female relative of Galla
has been going about propagating another, similar heresy.
Unfortunately Galla is only mentioned in this letter of Jerome.
His phrase 'Galla non gente sed nomine' seems to discourage
identification with Euchrotia.[1]

Priscillian, Instantius, and Salvianus brought with them to
Rome letters of communion and support from their clergy and
people.[2] Their request was that Damasus should refer the accusations brought against them, and now indeed against Hyginus of
Cordoba, to a formal council of Bishops. Their preference for an
episcopal court did not mean, they explained, that they felt any
desire to run away from a secular tribunal if Hydatius preferred
to bring his case before that. But in a matter of faith their conviction was that the judgement of the saints should be preferred
to that of the world (a position forcefully put in Priscillian's
46th canon, 'quia ecclesiastici non debeant ob suam defensionem
publica adire iudicia sed tantum ecclesiastica', reflecting perhaps
Priscillian's reaction to Hydatius' success in obtaining an imperial rescript). Accordingly they had come to Rome not to be
a burden to anybody ('nulli graves'),[3] but because their petition
set out the true order of events and, above all, the catholic
orthodoxy by which they lived. If Hydatius has accused them of
studying apocrypha, let it be clear that their constant belief
is and always has been that all documents under the name of
apostles, prophets, or bishops (!),[4] if they agree with the canon
of scripture and proclaim Christ to be God, should not be condemned. At the council of Saragossa not one of them was censured, none was heard and put on trial, none was deposed. It is
agreed that a bishop may be lawfully deposed on the ground that
previously as a layman he deserved condemnation. But none of
them was condemned when a layman.

Accordingly (the petition continues) they have come to the
senior and first of all bishops, 'to the glory of the apostolic see'

---

[1] This obscure and allusive passage of Jerome has led to much speculation; see,
e.g. d'Alès, *Priscillien*, p. 185; F. Cavallera in *Bulletin de litt. ecclés.* (Toulouse), 38 (1937),
186–90; ibid. 39 (1938), 93–4. The notion that Galla's sister is Egeria is rejected,
e.g. by P. Devos, *Anal. Boll.* 85 (1967), 181.

[2] *Tract.* ii, p. 41, 7; 42, 17.

[3] p. 41, 17. Cf. the prologue to Priscillian's canons (p. 112, 8) 'nulli existens
inimicus'.   [4] e.g. I Clement.

which can speak with Petrine authority,[1] language which shows
that the Priscillianists (like the Pelagians in their appeal to pope
Zosimus in 417)[2] are taking pains to tell Damasus what he
liked to hear. Their request is for a proper formal inquiry ('audien-
tia'), either by Damasus summoning Hydatius to come to Rome
to prove his charges—'and if Hydatius is really confident of being
able to prove his case, he will not fail to present it to the crown of
eternal priesthood, if he has followed the zeal of the Lord to the
end'—or by Damasus remitting the matter to a council of Spanish
bishops. Before such a spiritual court Hydatius need have no
fear that, if he fails to prove his accusations, he will himself be
liable to judgement, as in a secular court: 'for if we are acquitted
we are very ready to forgive his sin against us.' The Priscillianists
have already on their record their tract against the Manichees
(possibly the first Würzburg tractate?) to prove their orthodoxy;
and they can rely on the supporting testimony of bishops who
were present at the council of Saragossa.

So runs the argument of the concluding pages of the Priscillianist petition to pope Damasus, and the skill with which the
case is presented compels admiration. It is clearly implied that
an imperial decree of exile against them was gravely improper
when their case had not yet been formally heard before a synod.
The procedure for which they ask is closely similar to, and perhaps modelled upon, that requested by the Roman synod of 378
in its letter asking the emperor Gratian to relieve Damasus of
liability to prosecution in the courts (below, p. 128).[3] The Priscillianists carefully frame their *libellus* to use language not only
about papal authority, but about the need to keep theological
disputes in the hands of episcopal synods, such as Rome is known
to find congenial.

Nevertheless, they were unable to submit their petition in a
personal interview.[4] The three bishops were refused an audience

---

[1] p. 34, 11; p. 42, 24–5. Cf. Batiffol, *Cathedra Petri* (Paris, 1938), p. 152.

[2] *Avell.* XLVI. 7 (*CSEL* 35. 104) where Zosimus tells the angry Africans, 'Ecce
Pelagius Caelestiusque apostolicae sedi in litteris suis et confessionibus praesto sunt',
ultramontane Pelagianism being held up as an example to transmarine Carthage. See
O. Wermelinger, *Rom und Pelagius* (Stuttgart, 1975).

[3] The Roman synod's letter *Et hoc gloriae* (PL 13. 575–84 = Labbe–Coleti,
Concilia ii. 1187). Gratian's rescript *Ordinariorum* (*Avell.* XIII) replies.

[4] Sulpicius Severus, *Chron.* ii. 48. 4 'Damaso se purgare cupientes, ne in conspec-
tum quidem eius admissi sunt'. Cf. *Tract.* ii, p. 41, 10, 'ad te qui potuimus venientes
voluimus quidem absentes supplicare.'

with Damasus, much as the ascetic Paulinus of Nola was to be
rebuffed by pope Siricius in 395,[1] and soon suffered the further
misfortune that bishop Salvianus died. Instantius and Priscillian went on to Milan,[2] no doubt hoping to get a hearing at
court by gaining the good offices of Ambrose the bishop. They
found Ambrose as unhelpful as Damasus. On presenting their
petition to the *quaestor* of the palace, they were encouraged to
think their request reasonable, but the *quaestor* was unaccountably
and ominously slow to reply.[3] However, they had money with
them (perhaps Priscillian's own, perhaps Euchrotia's), and by
coming to a satisfactory arrangement with the master of the
offices, Macedonius, well known to be jealous of Ambrose to
whom he once refused an interview,[4] they obtained an imperial
rescript restoring them to their churches. Armed with this they
returned to Spain. The rescript enabled them to turn the tables
on the opposition: the proconsul of Lusitania, Volventius,
summoned Ithacius to answer charges against him in a formal
trial. The charges against Ithacius will presumably have included
calumny, for which heavy penalties could be imposed.[5] Ithacius

---

[1] Paulinus of Nola, *Ep.* 5. 14, to Sulpicius Severus. But Ambrose, *Ep.* 58, to
bishop Sabinus of Placentia, was friendly on hearing of Paulinus' renunciation.
Babut's suggestion that at the time of his stay in Spain Paulinus was sympathetic to,
and associated with, the Priscillianist movement seems unlikely. But it is not to be
denied that there are affinities between the two Aquitanian and Spanish senators
who adopt the ascetic way and are then objects of censure. On Paulinus see W. H. C.
Frend in *Journal of Roman Studies* 60 (1969), 1–11, and in *Latin Literature of the Fourth
Century*, ed. J. W. Binns (1972), pp. 100–33; C. H. Coster, *Late Roman Studies*
(Harvard, 1968).

[2] Babut (*Priscillien*, p. 153) thinks Sulpicius reverses the order of the visits to
Rome and Milan. Priscillian mentions in his petition to Damasus that Ambrose 'your
brother' has received a mendacious account of the affair, which suggests to Babut
that Priscillian has already visited Milan to discover Ambrose prejudiced against
him. Babut's guess is possible, but nothing in Sulpicius' narrative order is improbable. Priscillian's need was for a powerful intercessor at court, and he may well
have judged correctly that his first task was to try to win Damasus. In the end he had
to 'short-circuit' episcopal support in his endeavours to have the rescript against
him qualified or withdrawn by the emperor.

[3] Priscillian, *Tract.* ii, p. 41, 15. For the duties of the quaestor of the imperial
palace, see *Notitia dignitatum, Or.* 12, *Occid.* 10; Symmachus, *Ep.* i. 23; and further
references in A. H. M. Jones, *Later Roman Empire*, ch. XII, n. 3, vol. iii, p. 74 (who
misses the Priscillian reference for petitions). Ambrose (*Expl. Ps.* 118. 22. 13, *CSEL*
62. 495) remarks on the complexities of protocol on presenting a petition. Priscillian
does not give the quaestor's name. He could be Proculus Gregorius, prefect of the
Gauls in 383, very possibly quaestor in 379. See *PLRE* i. 404; Matthews, *Western
Aristocracies*, pp. 71 f.

[4] Paulinus, *Vita Ambrosii* 37.   [5] *Cod. Theod.* ix. 39.

fled to Trier and there gained the ear of the praetorian prefect
Gregory (Proculus Gregorius). Gregory sent a report to Gratian
which was unfavourable to Priscillian. But Macedonius, the master
of the offices, intervened to see that the hearing was transferred
to the *vicarius* of the Spanish provinces, the deputy of the praetorian prefect at Trier to whom he was answerable.[1] Sulpicius
Severus' story evidently presupposes that the outcome of a
hearing in Spain was likely to be more favourable to the Priscillianists than one before the prefect in distant Trier. But one
cannot know whether this was because the extent of Priscillian's
popular support, not only in Galicia but generally in Spain, was
a social factor of which a prudent judge would need to take
account, or because of the accidental fact that the *vicarius Hispaniarum* at that moment happened to be a friend and protégé
of Macedonius, the master of the offices, and could therefore be
relied upon, in his own interests, to please a powerful patron at
court with direct access to the emperor. The latter hypothesis is a
safer conjecture; the transference of the affair to Spain is a wafer-
thin basis for asserting Priscillian's following in Lusitania and
Baetica to be too powerful to be safely resisted by a local governor; but certainly Priscillian had more friends, money, and influence in Spain than at Trier.

That the Priscillianists at Milan bribed Macedonius to help
them is likely enough:[2] at the imperial court all such assistance
carried the expectation of a suitable *douceur*, and the foul charge of
bribery was regularly brought in competitive situations by those
who found themselves outbid and disadvantaged.[3] It is probable
that the anti-Priscillianist faction had no very clean hands, and
that their mistake was to have brought insufficient financial

---

[1] The name of the *vicarius* was Marinianus, a friend and correspondent of the pagan
Symmachus (*Ep.* iii. 23–9), and attested as *vicarius Hispaniarum* on 27 May 383 by
Cod. Theod. ix. 1. 14. He was a native of Gallaecia (so read for 'Galatia' in Symm.
Ep. iii. 25). Cf. Matthews, *Western Aristocracies*, pp. 164–5, 169. Sulpicius (*Chron.* ii.
49. 3) notes that at this time the Spanish provinces ceased to be governed by pro-
consuls, who only lasted a short period.

[2] Even Babut (*Priscillien*, p. 158), who doubts the story as malicious slander origin-
ating with Ithacius, has to concede the inherent probability of the assertion. Explicit
testimony that nothing was achieved at the Milanese court of this time unless
officials were bribed is given by Paulinus, *Vita Ambrosii* 41, who goes on to complain that bishops are as bad as anyone in corrupting influential people to gain
privileges for their friends and relations.

[3] So, e.g., it was said by critics of pope Damasus, that he extricated himself from
the charge of homicide by bribing 'the entire palace' (*Avell.* I. 11; *CSEL.* 35. 4).

resources in comparison with Priscillian and Euchrotia or to have poor credit with the Milanese moneylenders.

Ithacius, having taken a leading role in moving against Priscillian and risking the potentially capital charge of sorcery, now found himself in an awkward situation. A guard of soldiers was instructed to conduct him from Trier to Spain. But in Trier he had acquired good friends, evaded his guards, and found asylum with the bishop of Trier, Britto.[1] No doubt he would have long stayed in retirement on the Mosel while Priscillian consolidated his position in Spain, had it not been for a sudden change in the political scene.

Magnus Maximus

The emperor Gratian, resident until 381 at Trier, then at Milan, was unpopular with his army officers because of his favours to his private bodyguard of barbarian Alans.[2] In 383, while he was on campaign in Raetia (Switzerland), a revolt was led by Magnus Maximus,[3] military commander in Britain, a soldier of Spanish origin like the emperor Theodosius, to whom he claimed to be related and whose success perhaps he sought to emulate. Just as Pannonians had done well under Valentinian I (or as in the next century Isaurians prospered under Zeno), so under Theodosius many high offices went to his Spanish friends.[4]

---

[1] Britto(n) of Trier attended the Council of Valence in 374 (Turner, *Eccl. occid. monumenta iuris ant.* i. 418, 423), and, since his name appears immediately after Damasus and Ambrose in the list of western bishops addressed in the synodal letter of Constantinople cited by Theodoret (*HE* 5. 9. 1), will have been present at Damasus' council of Rome (382) which adopted an unfriendly view of the acts of the council of Constantinople of 381. At Rome he would not have learnt to think well of Priscillian. Cf. L. Duchesne, *Fastes épiscopaux de l'ancienne Gaule* iii (1915), 36. The manuscript of Sulpicius gives *Britannium*, which should evidently be corrected to *Brittonium*. (In Latin *Britto* means a native of Britain; cf. Prosper, *Chron.* a. 413, *Chronica minora* i. 467 'Pelagius Britto'.)

[2] Zosimus iv. 35; *Epitome de Caesaribus* 47. 6. On the anti-barbarian tendency of the source here see J. Schlumberger, *Die Epitome de Caesaribus, Untersuchungen zur heidnischen Geschichtsschreibung des 4 Jhdts n. Chr.* (Vestigia 18, Munich, 1974), pp. 221–2.

[3] For Maximus' career see *PLRE* i. 588; W. Ensslin's article (1930) in *PW* xiv. 2546–55; J. R. Palanque, 'L'Empereur Maxime' in *Les Empereurs romains d'Espagne* (Madrid colloquium of 1964, Paris, 1965), a paper translated into English in *Classical Folia* 22 (1968), 85–104. On his religious policy see J. Ziegler, *Zur religiösen Haltung der Gegenkaiser im 4 Jh. n. Chr. (Frankfurter althistorische Studien* 4, 1970), pp. 74–85.

[4] See K. F. Stroheker's study in *Madrider Mitteilungen* 4 (1963), 107–32, reprinted in his *Germanentum und Spätantike* (Zürich, 1965), pp. 54–87; Matthews, *Western Aristocracies*, pp. 110–12. Orosius the Spaniard expresses regional pride in the Spanish emperors (*Hist.* 5. 23. 16).

Maximus might well assume that he would have room for one more. Acclaimed as Augustus by the troops, Maximus abandoned Britain and moved to the continent. At Paris his army met Gratian's. Gratian, abandoned by his own forces, had to flee. Pursued to Lugdunum (Lyon), he was captured by a trick at the Rhône crossing and at a feast on 25 August 383, at which he had been solemnly promised safety by an oath on the Gospels, was murdered by Maximus' cavalry commander.[1] Gratian's principal counsellors soon suffered, and not only in those provinces that fell immediately under Maximus' control. At Milan, then controlled by Valentinian II, his mother Justina, and the soldier Bauto, Gratian's death also brought revolution. Macedonius, the master of the offices, who had been on bad terms with Ambrose (above, p. 40), found himself in trouble, sought asylum in a church, but was arrested before he could find the door[2]—a story which implies that he was a pagan (like Symmachus in 388, below, p. 124) and invites the question whether Ambrose engineered his downfall.

Maximus was an orthodox Christian, anxious to win the support of the church. His desire to win recognition from Theodosius in the East would ensure that he gave no support to heresy. The sudden reversal of fortune's wheel brought revived hope to Ithacius of Ossonuba, who presented grave criminal charges against the Priscillianists before the new emperor at Trier. Britto, the bishop of Trier, had become a friend of Ithacius, and would have spoken in his favour to Maximus. Maximus directed that the affair be referred to a synod at Burdigala.[3] The choice of Delphinus' see as the location for the synod made it clear that the meeting was not intended to protect the Priscillianists. Letters were issed to the praetorian prefect and to the vicar of the Spanish provinces that all the Priscillianists were to be taken to Burdigala. Attendance on this occasion was not to be a matter of personal choice as it had been at Saragossa.

The Acts of the synod of Bordeaux are not preserved, being of

---

[1] On Gratian's death by treachery and perjury see Ambrose, *Expl. Ps.* 40. 23; 61. 23–6; below, p. 121.   [2] Paulinus, *Vita Ambrosii* 37.

[3] Sulpicius Severus, *Chron.* ii. 49. 5–6. For a sketch of the Christian history of ancient Burdigala in this period see R. Étienne, *Bordeaux antique* (Bordeaux, 1962), pp. 265–89, especially interesting on the archaeological remains of the fourth-century cathedral where the council was probably held. This church was on the site of the old church of St. Stephen, destroyed in 1787, about 400 m. south-west of the Roman amphitheatre.

no controversial or canonical interest to later generations in Gaul or Spain, and we have to rely on Sulpicius Severus' report. Bishop Instantius was first required to submit his defence. He failed to convince the council and was deposed from his see. Priscillian must have well understood that no meeting held in Bordeaux could be expected to be sympathetic to him. In Aquitaine dark rumours told of Priscillian's alleged affair with Procula and of nocturnal orgies on Euchrotia's estate (above, p. 37). Popular prejudice would be unfriendly. The point was driven home by an ugly incident. One adherent of Priscillian named Urbica, perhaps related to the poet and grammarian Urbicus whom Ausonius numbers among the intellectual lights of Bordeaux,[1] attracted the unpleasant attentions of bishop Delphinus' supporters. She was done to death with stones hurled by an angry mob, persuaded no doubt that she was a sorceress, not to be suffered to live.

Priscillian was convinced that at the hands of this synod he and his friends would see no justice. It was time to leave Bordeaux and to seek a more honest city. Like Athanasius after the council of Tyre he must appeal to Caesar and find his way under military escort to Trier, where perhaps Euchrotia and he could once again find the resources to gain powerful patrons, able to do at Trier what Macedonius had once done for them at Milan, and at least to have his case referred to a synod less packed with his avowed enemies. As the petition to Damasus had put it, he was content to stand trial with equal confidence before either an episcopal court or a secular tribunal.

Sulpicius Severus, sharing the opinion of his hero Martin of Tours that no ecclesiastical cause should ever be brought before a secular tribunal, reports with regret that the bishops in synod at Bordeaux raised no squeak of protest when Priscillian's refusal of their jurisdiction transferred the whole matter to the court at Trier. Perhaps this judgement was little more than the wisdom of hindsight. The tragic consequences seemed to vindicate the puritan and precisionist doctrine, for which, after all, Martin had secure support in the apostle Paul (1 Cor. 6: 1). Moreover, the

---

[1] Prosper, *Chronicon*, ann. 385 (Mommsen, *Chronica minora* i. 462; *PL* 51. 586B): 'Burdigalae quaedam Priscilliani discipula nomine Urbica ob impietatis pertinaciam per seditionem vulgi lapidibus extincta est.' Ausonius, *Prof.* 21. The possibility of kinship was observed by Bernays, *Über die Chronik des Sulpicius Severus* (Berlin, 1861), p. 7.

feelings generated by the outcome of Priscillian's trial made the question one that continued to divide the Gallic churches for many years after 385. Nevertheless the synod of Bordeaux did not behave strangely when it ignored Martin's voice (if, as seems likely, he was present at the council,[1] despite his prickly relations with his episcopal colleagues), and acquiesced in the reference of the case to the emperor's decision as a court of appeal from a judgement they had not been able formally to pronounce.

Martin's puritan doctrine was not universally held. Other bishops in trouble with their colleagues found it necessary to invoke the secular power. Pope Damasus himself could hardly have retained his august see if the prefect of Rome in 366 had not decided to support him rather than his rival Ursinus. An African bishop, Chronopius, was condemned in 368-9 by a council of seventy bishops, and appealed to the proconsul of Africa, Claudius Hermogenianus Caesarius (who became prefect of Rome in 374); a zealous pagan himself, Caesarius upheld the synodical censure, but remitted the case to the emperor for sentence—viz. fifty pounds of silver to be bestowed on poor relief.[2] The incident illustrates how natural it seemed to appeal from an episcopal council to secular authority, whatever prohibition or disapproval might be expressed in canon law.[3] On the other hand, as Maximus' decision to call the synod of

---

[1] The chronicle of Hydatius of Lemica (Ginzo de Lima, 40 km. south of Orense between Braga and Astorga), who became bishop probably of Aquae Flaviae (Chaves) in Galicia in 427 and wrote his chronicle in old age about 468 (see the introduction to the edition by A. Tranoy, *Sources chrétiennes* 218-19, 1974), records that in 385 in Gaul 'Priscillian was condemned as a heretic by St. Martin and other bishops and appealed to Caesar' (Mommsen, *Chronica minora* ii. 15; *PL* 51. 875B). Although Hydatius' text is deplorably transmitted (see C. Courtois in *Byzantion* 21 (1951), 23-54), the tradition seems correct here. Nevertheless this is no more than a deduction from Sulpicius Severus' writings and represents no necessarily independent information. There is, however, confirmation of a visit by Martin in the close vicinity to Bordeaux in a story of the saint told by Gregory of Tours, *Gloria confessorum* 45, where Martin is at Blaye on the shore of the Garonne. Attention to this text is drawn by J. Fontaine, 'L'Ascétisme chrétien dans la littérature gallo-romaine d'Hilaire à Cassien', Accademia Nazionale dei Lincei: Problemi attuali di scienza e di cultura, *La Gallia romana* (Rome, 1973), p. 104, n. 42. Hydatius may therefore be right that Martin was at Bordeaux for the council.
[2] *Cod. Theod.* xi. 36. 20 (369), where the recipient of the edict is given his later title 'prefect of the city'; his career in *PLRE* i. 171-2; A. Chastagnol, *Fastes de la préfecture de Rome au bas-empire* (1962), pp. 192-3.
[3] Appeals from a synod to the emperor were forbidden by canon 11 of the Greek

Bordeaux illustrates, it was a well-understood principle (even if acted on by governments merely from Gallio-like motives that they might not be troubled about 'trivial' internal disputes of faith and order that had no public consequence or were scarcely comprehensible to lay judges), that charges against a bishop should be remitted at least in the first instance to an episcopal synod of the relevant province.

The fact that the Spanish bishops were brought before a synod at Burdigala is at first sight a stumbling-block. The Priscillianists, as *Tract.* ii shows, were no simple innocents in matters of legal procedure, and could easily have pleaded that it was uncanonical for their case to come before a synod outside the Spanish provinces. The reason for the choice of Burdigala must lie in the decision of the prosecution to exploit the rumours of Priscillian getting Procula with child. Witnesses from Spain might be unreliable support for accusations of sexual orgies, but in Aquitaine public opinion was ready to believe anything said to have happened on Euchrotia's estate.

In the silence of the council of Burdigala about Priscillian's appeal to the emperor there is a more sinister possibility; namely, that Ithacius saw in Priscillian's summons to the synod an unacceptable recognition of the full validity of Priscillian's ordination to be bishop of Avila, and realized that the appeal to Maximus greatly facilitated his attack even if, simultaneously, it vastly raised the stakes so far as his own position was concerned. Ithacius had no good reason to put his trust in synods. The council of Saragossa had been weak and mealy-mouthed, and allowed itself to be swayed by the voices of moderation. But if Priscillian himself was so unwise as to take himself off to a secular tribunal, Ithacius was saved the trouble of persuading the synod to inquire into the truth of Priscillian's affinity with Manicheism. Ithacius had therefore no cause to regret the silence of the synod at Burdigala about the high question of principle. If there was regret, it would have been at the synod's failure even to proceed to any formal vote of censure upon Priscillian under canon law. But that weakness underlined the expediency of resting the case against him entirely on the civil law.

council of Antioch which met about 327-8 under Eusebius of Caesarea (the canons of which became attributed to the Dedication council of Antioch 341); text in Lauchert, *Kanones*, p. 46, or in Bruns i. 83.

The first tractate

The first of the eleven tractates in the Würzburg codex is the
longest and most important of the set. It is also the hardest to
place. Like the rest it is anonymous. The title 'Liber apologeticus'
assigned to it by its first editor Schepss, not by the manuscript,
correctly describes its purpose. It is an elaborate, full-length
vindication of the orthodoxy of the Priscillianists, and has the
nature of a very personal statement by a writer whose standing
is at stake. It is addressed to bishops, 'beatissimi sacerdotes',
probably an assembly of bishops, who have formally requested
a theological statement. The author clearly resents this demand,
saying that 'our faith has already been set out in several *libelli*
in which we have condemned the dogmas of all heretics, and in
the *libellus* of our brothers Tiberianus and Asarbius and others,
with whom we are of one faith and one mind'. Nevertheless as
the bishops have asked for a particularly detailed confession of
faith ('vultis nos ire per singula', pp. 6, 10; 23, 9; 38, 3), he
will set everything out in full, 'though our proper role is to be
attentive to you'. At the end the bishops are asked to consult
with their brother bishops, 'ad fratres vestros', a turn of phrase
that may imply that the author of the first tractate is not a bishop;
moreover, that the assembly of bishops addressed is small and
could naturally be asked to undertake wider consultations, or
(possibly) that the assembled bishops expect to have with them
representatives from another, neighbouring province perhaps as
independent assessors. That the author of the first tractate is not
a bishop is congruent with the tone and manner of the work,
but the matter is not indisputable. From the opening remarks
about numerous *libelli* that have already been issued it is certain
that the tractate does not belong to the early stages of the controversy; and the substance of the apologia and the painful
conscientiousness of its detail are incompatible with an early
date. Above all, the first tractate bitterly replies to an accusation
uttered 'in our ears' by Ithacius to the effect that the author has
been implicated in superstitious peasant magic. The nature of
the heresies disowned (below, p. 90) makes it evident that the
Priscillianists are accused of a Patripassian doctrine of God, a
docetic Christology, Manicheism, studies in heretical apocrypha,
and nocturnal orgies, whether magical or sexual.

If the bishops addressed in the first tractate are met in synod, then they must be either the combined Spanish and Aquitanian council of Saragossa in 380, at which date Priscillian was still a layman, or the similarly combined council of Bordeaux about 384, to which bishop Instantius presented an unsuccessful apologia for his association with Priscillian. J. Dierich (1897) and G. Morin (1913) thought that the first tractate was addressed to the synod of Bordeaux, which led Morin to the further proposal that its true author is Instantius. Morin accepted the case for attributing all eleven tractates to the same author, and therefore regarded Instantius as the writer of the complete set.[1]

The grounds on which a case for Instantius' authorship can be supported are varied. In the argument for regarding the first tractate as addressed to the council of Bordeaux much weight rests on the assumption that in October 380 at the time of the council of Saragossa the grave charge of magical activities had not yet been raised against the followers of Priscillian; as this charge is prominent in the first tractate, where Ithacius is specifically named as responsible for bringing it, the entire plea must be intended not for Saragossa but for Bordeaux. A second argument which moved Morin was the very unclassical Latinity of the tractates which he felt to be hard to reconcile with Sulpicius Severus' portrait of Priscillian as a man 'of keen intelligence,

---

[1] J. Dierich, *Die Quellen zur Geschichte Priscillians* (1897), pp. 35–40; G. Morin, 'Pro Instantio: contre l'attribution à Priscillien des opuscula du manuscrit de Würzburg', *Rev. Bénéd.* 30 (1913), 153–72. Morin's paper has acquired such a following that a list of his critics would be much shorter than one of his disciples. M. Hartberger, 'Instantius oder Priscillian?', *Theologische Quartalschrift* 95 (1913), 401–30, argued that *Tract.* i fits the synod of Saragossa just as well as that of Bordeaux, or, if not submitted to a sitting synod, may (as Babut thought) be the profession of the laity of Emerita. J. Martin, 'Priscillianus oder Instantius', *Historisches Jahrbuch* 47 (1927), 237–51, correctly observes that the author of *Tract.* i does not seem to write as a bishop addressing fellow bishops and yet, speaking as spokesman of a group, assumes that he is their recognized leader. U. Moricca, *Storia della letteratura latina cristiana* II. i (Turin, 1928), 613–16, similarly rejects Morin, and ascribes *Tract.* i to the time of the council of Saragossa (as Schepss and Hilgenfeld, *Z. wiss. Th.* 35 (1892), 77). H. Lietzmann, *Geschichte der alten Kirche* iv (1944), 62, notes that at p. 4, 8–14, the author of *Tract.* i speaks as a highborn, educated layman and of his conversion, which answers to Severus' description of Priscillian. Ramos y Loscertales, *Prisciliano* (1952), pp. 112–17, accepts that no charge of magic was brought until after 380, and thinks Priscillian wrote *Tract.* i after 381, as a personal profession of faith. Vollmann (*PW* Suppl. xiv. 557–8) denies *Tract.* i is by either Priscillian or Instantius, and attributes it to a Priscillianist layman or presbyter, perhaps for the council of Bordeaux.

wide study in books, quick in discussion and debate, and passing rich'. To ascribe the tractates to Instantius solves a further problem, namely, the marked difference in style between the eleven tractates and Priscillian's prologue to the Pauline canons which Peregrinus, the editor and bowdlerizer of the canons, reproduces at their head. If the tractates are the work of Priscillian, then it is necessary to assume that Peregrinus' activities included not merely the elimination of heresies but also the clarification of Priscillian's normal syntax, e.g. by putting main verbs into the indicative rather than using participles. If Instantius wrote the tractates, the admirably composed and lucid prologue to the canons becomes the one undoctored piece of Priscillian to come down to us.[1]

Against Morin, there is the strong self-consciousness of the author of the first tractate concerning his secular learning before his conversion, especially as reflected in p. 4, 8–14, where the author writes of his conversion and of his social position in society, 'although we ought not to boast of what we have been'. Moreover, whereas the petition to Damasus composed by Instantius, Salvianus, and Priscillian takes pains to stress the orthodoxy of the confession of faith which they made not only at their baptism but also at their consecration (ii, p. 39, 13–16), the author of the first tractate looks back only to his baptismal confession (i, p. 4, 19 ff.) and renunciation (p. 13, 15) as the moment of liberation (p. 26, 22). Thirdly, Priscillian played so central a role in the movement that the silence of the first tractate about him becomes a little surprising if it was written by one of his close friends and episcopal colleagues defending himself on a charge of being associated with him. Fourthly, it has already become clear from the previous discussion that there is illusion in the notion that the charges to which the first tractate seeks to reply had not been raised by the time of the council of Saragossa. The elimination of this illusion removes the linchpin of Morin's argument. Since the argument from the supposed silence of the bishops present at Saragossa about the accusations of magic, Manicheism, and Patripassianism is seen to lack cogency, it is

[1] J. Chapman, *Notes on the Early History of the Vulgate Gospels* (Oxford, 1908), p. 259: 'The Prologue to the canons he (Peregrinus) has evidently completely rewritten, for a comparison with the *Tractatus* of Priscillian shows that none of the peculiarities of Priscillian's style have been allowed to remain. The sentences are short and clear.'

not impossible to hold that the first tractate was sent to that council (cf. ii p. 35, 12); that the concluding request that the bishops will please consult with their brothers reflects an awareness that a large number of Spanish bishops were not at the council; and perhaps that the very softness and weakness of the canons of Saragossa become explicable if this eloquent apologia was read before them. The opening of the first tractate indicates that the controversy is already well developed with a pamphlet war of many *libelli*. But the fact that before the council of Saragossa pope Damasus was consulted about the council's procedure in dealing with the problem is an evident sign that the meeting in October 380 marked a decisive moment in a storm that had been gathering for some time past. The petition to Damasus says that the contention had arisen 'suddenly' (ii, p. 35, 5), but this certainly does not mean shortly before the council of Saragossa.

   If the first tractate was addressed, whether by Priscillian or Instantius or any other prominent Priscillianist, to the council of Bordeaux, one would expect it to contain more of the kind of argument found in the petition to Damasus, e.g. complaints on ground of legal procedure against the conduct of Hydatius of Emerita, or appeals to the lack of any specific condemnation of Priscillian by name at the council of Saragossa. Yet the first tractate contains no narrative of the *gesta rerum* and is concerned never with questions of order, but with a confession of faith, a disavowal of heresies and especially of Manicheism, a denial that the Priscillianists accept a fifth gospel and want to add to the sacred canon, a lie direct to Ithacius' accusation of compromise with peasant magical rites, and an implicit protest that the Priscillianists confess truly what they believe. The last sentence of the first tractate bitterly accuses the opposition of using religious issues to veil attacks motivated by private animosities (i, p. 33, 13; cf. ii, p. 43, 12). Otherwise the tractate is defensive. The petition to Damasus takes the offensive.

   There are other possibilities, perhaps, besides the two synods of Saragossa and Bordeaux. Ramos y Loscertales has suggested that the first tractate was a general manifesto put out by Priscillian not long after the débâcle at Emerita described in the petition to Damasus. Babut identified it with the confession of faith of the laity of Emerita dissentient from Hydatius their bishop. Both these suggestions take the document out of the context of a synod, which remains the most probable setting. After many doubts and hesitations, I am inclined to think the first tractate the work of Priscillian himself and a formal statement submitted to the council of Saragossa. It is easily identifiable with the 'tract against the Manichees' which is particularly mentioned at the end of the petition to Damasus in the context of the council of Saragossa (ii, p. 43, 9–11, '. . . tantum ut probata fide et vita nostra scribto quod contra Manichaeos datum est, dato testimonio sacerdotum qui interfuerint concilio, repugnemus . . .').

Ithacius' charges

To conclude this chapter, the charges brought by Ithacius will be considered in more detail, since only when they are understood can the road to Trier be clear.

Ithacius' main accusation is that peasant rites of weather magic have been employed. He charges the Priscillianists with pronouncing magical incantations over the first fruits of the crops and of consecrating an unguent with curses to the sun and moon, in sympathy with whose eclipses and wanings it diminishes. The unguent was evidently to be poured over some sacred stone in the countryside.[1]

That witchcraft should be practised at new moon and full moon, if the phases were to proceed in due order, was a truth

---

[1] *Tract.* i, p. 23, 22–p. 24, 3. At p. 24, 24, for the manuscript's *maledicti*, Schepss (introd., p. xxvi) rightly proposed *maledictis*. For the power of sorcery to stop the sun and to cause the moon to exude juices, cf. Apuleius, *Metam.* i. 3. The unguent evidently diminished with the planets by sympathetic magic. Varro (*Re rust.* i. 46) and Pliny (*NH* ii. 108) report that an olive tree turns its leaves at the solstice. Porphyry (ap. Eus. *PE* iii. 11. 32–4, p. 113CD) explains how the moon's phases control increase and decrease of crops. Cf. C. Préaux, *La Lune dans la pensée grecque* (Acad. Roy. Belg. Mémoires 61. 4, 1973), p. 94. For the sympathy of certain stones with the heavenly bodies see Proclus' tract 'On the Priestly art', edited by J. Bidez, *Catalogue des manuscrits alchimiques grecs* vi (1928), 149, 19 ff. For plants affected by the planets see the Hermetic tract in Pitra, *Analecta sacra* v. 2, pp. 279 ff. Pliny (*NH* 28. 77) reports the maleficent potency of menstrual fluid when sun or moon are in eclipse. (The moon controls menstrual flux: Aristotle, *Gen. an.* ii. 4, 738^{a}17; *Hist. an.* vii. 2, 582^a.) On sorcery producing eclipses cf. John Lydus, *De ostentis* 9, cataloguing different disasters that vary according to the sign of the zodiac under which the eclipse occurs.

generally known in antiquity.[1] Unguents were commonly used in solemn religious rituals of the pagan world for anointing holy stones and statues of the gods.[2] Country folk mouthed cursing and blasphemy as they sowed the fields in the belief that their imprecations had an apotropaic effect which would protect the crop from demonic blight, much as obscene songs were sung at weddings to avert infertility.[3] It was one thing for illiterate peasants to practise country magic,[4] another for this to be believed of a prominent teacher soon to be appointed bishop of Avila.[5] Priscillian's nocturnal meetings with women and going

[1] Cf. Martial xii. 57. 16; Juvenal, *Sat.* vi. 442–3; Lucian, *Philopseudes* 14. The principal passages are enumerated in W. H. Roscher's article 'Mondgöttin', in his *Ausführliches Lexikon der griech. und röm. Mythologie* ii/2 (1894–7), 3164–5. Mistletoe gathered at new moon, without the use of iron or touching the ground, was a cure for epilepsy, infertility, and sores: Pliny, *NH* 24. 11–12. For weather magic see Lucan vi. 461 ff.

[2] Oil was daily poured on the Omphalos at Delphi (Pausanias x. 24. 6). For the anointing of sacred stones or temple statues, cf. Cicero, *In Verrem* II. iv. 77; Tibullus ii. 2. 7; Lucian, *Alexander* 30; Minucius Felix, *Octavius* 3. 1; Arnobius i. 39; etc. Theocritus' sorceress melted wax with a spell to melt her lover's heart (*Idyll* ii. 28). In Christian usage holy oil, from lamps burning before an icon or the cross at Golgotha, was likewise of healing power: cf. *JTS*, N.S. 25 (1974), 54, n. 1.

[3] Theophrastus, *Hist. plant.* vii. 3. 3; ix. 8. 8 (mandragora). Horace (*Ep.* II. i. 145–6) says that farmers sing 'rustic insults' (*opprobria rustica*) to avert blight from their crops; similarly Livy vii. 2; Pliny, *NH* 19. 120; Plutarch, *Qu. conv.* vii. 2. 2 (701A); Palladius, *Opus agriculturae*, iv. 9. 14. With a similar purpose the Rhodian farmers of Lindos hurled stones and cursed Heracles; cf. Callimachus, ed. Pfeiffer, i. 31; Origen, *C. Cels.* vii. 54; Lactantius, *Div. inst.* i. 21. 31–6; Apollodorus ii. 5. 11. Cf. W. Speyer, article 'Fluch' in *RAC* vii. 1198; J. G. Frazer, *The Magic Art*[3] (1910) i. 281.

In the Near East seedtime was accompanied by lamentation, no doubt with the same intention; cf. Psalm 126: 6. For obscene songs at weddings see Ovid, *Fasti* iii. 675 and 695; and especially Joh. Chrys. *In ep. ad Col. hom.* xii. 6 (*PG* 62. 388–9), who deplores the custom. Most of the evidence for wedding ribaldry is Latin: see G. Wissowa in *PW* vi (1907), 2222–3, s.v. 'Fescennini versus'. The attachment of a phallic symbol to a general's chariot at his triumph was likewise intended to propitiate the envious goddess Fortune as well as to remind the successful of the low estate of their vile body (Pliny, *NH* 28. 39; Juvenal x. 41–2).

[4] The prevalence of peasant superstitions in sixth-century Spain was the subject of a tract by Martin of Braga, *De correctione rusticorum*. For north Italy see Maximus of Turin, *Sermo* 107 (pp. 420–1 Mutzenbecher), preached after 405.

[5] A number of fourth-century bishops were accused of magic or suspected of employing arcane arts. The Oriental synod of Serdica complains of Ossius of Cordoba that while staying in the East he had been in intimate relations with Paulinus bishop of Adana (read *adanae* for the MS. *daciae*, with Schwartz), 'a man who was accused of sorcery, was driven from his church, and to this day is publicly living in apostasy with concubines, whose magical books were burnt by Macedonius bishop and confessor of Mopsuestia' (*CSEL* 65. 66). Athanasius of Alexandria was believed to have powers of clairvoyance (Sozom. *HE* iv. 10; Ammian xv. 7. 8). Eusebius,

barefoot (if the anxieties of the council of Saragossa had foundation) suggest that already in 380 such superstitions were attributed to him—like Medea in Ovid's *Metamorphoses*, going in bare feet to bring down the moon and to concoct from herbs and other sources a rich brew in her cauldron which prefigures the weird sisters of Shakespeare's *Macbeth*.[1]

How deeply magic was feared in antiquity is attested by many texts; the fear arose from its maleficent potency.[2] It was harder to suppress white magic, amulets and peasant remedies believed to have therapeutic power or to grant long-desired pregnancy, or country rituals to bring good weather for the crops. A law of Constantine the Great, threatening the direst penalties against magicians, exempts those who use it to bring healing or to avert storms in country districts.[3] So if Ithacius' accusation against Priscillian is merely malicious invention, it is remarkable for its mildness. He has not suggested that Priscillian goes in for the black arts and is attempting by sorcery or requiem masses to bring about the sickness and death of his critics among the Spanish bishops; only that he has been a party to some age-old fertility rite in the countryside, where some farmer could easily have asked him to bless the fields by well-tried procedures. Andalucia has a low rainfall, and is often (as in 1974 when no rain

bishop of Emesa, was accused of addiction to astrology (Socrates, *HE* ii. 9. 8). For later evidence see E. Peterson, *Frühkirche, Judentum und Gnosis* (Freiburg, 1959), pp. 333–45 on Sophronius of Tella, accused at the council of Ephesus 449 of using cheese for divination (for cheese-magic cf. Aug. *De civ. Dei* 18. 18). *Act. Chalc.* xi. 73. 4 (*ACO* II. i. 383) records a deacon excommunicated for sorcery who, 'though liable to the death penalty', became bishop of Batnae.

[1] Ovid, *Metam.* vii. 180–293. For 'bringing down' the moon, cf. Aristophanes, *Clouds* 749–55; Lucan vi. 499–506, etc. D. E. Hill, 'The Thessalian Trick' in *Rhein. Mus.* 116 (1973), 221–38, argues against the rationalist view that it means an eclipse.

[2] See A. A. Barb's chapter in *The Conflict between Paganism and Christianity in the Fourth Century*, ed. A. Momigliano (Oxford, 1963), pp. 100–25, many of whose references are drawn from Ammianus Marcellinus and so speak for Priscillian's generation. Ammianus' accounts of sorcery trials under Valens and Valentinian, leading to the torture and execution of many notable pagans (xxviii. 1; xxix. 1), afford a striking parallel to the Priscillianist affair. Ammianus regarded the penalty for dabbling in black arts as cruel, while not denying that the accusations were in substance true (xxix. 1. 22). It is clear from his narrative that there was a close association between sorcery and treason. See below, p. 142.

[3] *Cod. Theod.* ix. 16. 3. A law of 371 speaks of divination and augury as tolerable (ix. 16. 9). But necromancy and nocturnal rites are intolerable (ix. 16. 5 and 7), and horrible tortures are prescribed even for those of the highest social rank if they indulge in sorcery (ix. 16. 6, of 357–8 under Constantius II); cf. Ammian xxviii. 1. 10–11. On storm demons cf. below, p. 195.

fell in Seville between early spring and 15 November) afflicted by severe drought killing the cattle, burning the crops, and threatening the water supply of cities. No measure to ensure survival can be neglected.

Ithacius' complaint then is that Priscillian has at some time compromised with popular beliefs about magic and superstition. The earliest church held magic in abhorrence, and came into the world with a message of the conquest of evil powers. But plentiful evidence for the late fourth century, especially in John Chrysostom and Augustine, shows how difficult it was for authority to wean the half-converted from their favourite ways of ensuring survival and success. In the end there was no alternative but to tolerate amulets with Christian symbols in place of the old amulets with pagan inscriptions.[1] So the old peasant magic would gradually be replaced by protection which at least looked Christian. About 400 the Latin Christian poet Severus Endelechius, orator of Rome and friend of Paulinus of Nola, wrote a poem 'De mortibus boum', describing how a herd of cows was preserved from plague because there had been branded on them 'the sign of the cross of God, Christ who alone is worshipped in great cities'.[2] The poem reflects the endeavour of this period to extend the Christian mission, so successful among the urban societies, into a simpler and more rural setting by seeing Christ as the protector of the crops and the beasts. Remembering the evidence of the council of Elvira (above, p. 2) concerning the tendency of Spanish farmers to invite others beside the clergy to bless their fields, it seems easy to imagine an incident at which Priscillian may have been present, when some farmer, who felt that one could not be too careful, combined the blessing of the clergy with older rites. At least Ithacius' charge does not look wild or extravagant.

This reading of the charge is supported by a passage in the first tractate boldly defending the possession of an amulet

[1] For the tracing of this development see N. Brox, 'Magie und Aberglaube an den Anfängen des Christentums', *Trierer theologische Zeitschrift* 83 (1974), 157–80; C. D. G. Müller, art. 'Geister: Volksglaube', *RAC* ix. 761–97 (1975).

[2] C. Riese, *Anth. Lat.* II. ii. 338. On Endelechius see F. J. Dölger, *Antike und Christentum* 3 (1932), 25; W. Schmid in *RAC* v. 1–3 (1960); J. F. Matthews in *Class. Rev.*, n.s. 24 (1974), 102. The presence of a holy man was a talisman: farms near Sens were protected from hail by Martin of Tours, as was deduced from the damage done in a storm soon after his death (Sulp. Sev. *Dial.* iii. 7).

inscribed with the name of God in Hebrew, Latin, and Greek and 'King of kings and Lord of lords', and apparently bearing a picture of a lion.[1]

Priscillian nevertheless sees great danger in Ithacius' charge, which his nocturnal meetings could make plausible. He protests that such practices are to him unheard of. But according to Orosius (writing about 415) the Priscillianists were using an apocryphal book entitled 'Memoria Apostolorum', containing theosophical mysteries about the rulers of wetness and of fire. The book taught that God is not directly responsible for all good things in this world, since there exists a Light-Virgin whom God shows to the Prince of Wetness when he wishes to give rain to man; by the sight of her the Prince of Wetness is so aroused to desire that his sweat produces rain and his groans thunder.[2] It later became a standing orthodox complaint against Priscillian that according to his alleged teaching the devil on his own independent authority causes thunder, lightning, and drought.[3] The Manichee notion that rain comes from devils is denounced in the first tractate (p. 24, 14).

The second tractate shows that the accusations of practising magic and holding near-Manichee beliefs have already been made by (or very soon after) the year 380. The first tractate is an elaborate protestation of orthodoxy, together with a detailed disclaimer of a string of heresies (below, p. 90), among which a prominent place is occupied by the Manichees (p. 17, 29 ff.; p. 22, 13 ff.), the licentious Nicolaitans, and the Docetists who deny the reality of the Incarnation (p. 7, 19-26, cf. p. 23, 4 ff.). The Priscillianists are evidently being accused by Ithacius of grave moral enormities based on a radical gnostic dualism. (Cf. i, p. 17, 16 f., we renounce the *turpitudines* of Venus, as also (p. 22, 14) of Mani.) Moreover the charges include disingenuousness: Priscillian protests that he has nothing to hide, and that he does not say one thing and mean another (p. 4, 2-8; cf. p. 13, 22). Ithacius must therefore have made a pre-emptive strike, not only accusing Priscillian of vice and heresy but also insisting that the disavowals about to be offered by so unscrupulous a

[1] *Tract.* i, p. 26.

[2] Orosius, *Commonitorium de errore Priscillianistarum et Origenistarum*, 2 (*CSEL* 18. 158. 12-14). See below, p. 194.

[3] The proposition is condemned at the first council of Braga of 561 (C. W. Barlow, *Martini Bracarensis opera*, p. 108); below, p. 225.

man cannot be believed. Nothing is so damaging as a total denial.

In bringing a charge of lack of integrity Ithacius is insinuating that Priscillian is behaving as the Manichees are generally expected to act. The common attitude to the sect in Priscillian's time can be seen in Ambrosiaster's commentary on 2 Tim. 3 : 6–7, where he cites Diocletian's edict against the Manichees. Ambrosiaster reports that they say one thing in public, another in private; forbid marriage while privately indulging in vice; assert that the world is to be despised while taking care for their personal advancement; boast of fasting while being stuffed with food; get hold of women and persuade them to do 'foul and illicit things'. Other hostile evidence similarly treats the Manichees as people to whom oaths mean nothing and truth is negligible.[1]

The first tractate also defends the reading of apocryphal texts. From the fact that heretics have forged or interpolated such texts, it does not follow that the only apostolic documents to come down to us must necessarily be contained in the canon. The test is whether the texts are orthodox, whether Christ our God is preached (p. 30, 11 ff.).

Finally, the vigour with which Priscillian (p. 5, 10) attacks the 'Binionites' (that is, those whose doctrine of God is not strictly monotheist and monarchian) suggests that his own Trinitarianism was under fire from critics.

Accordingly, Ithacius' charges are that Priscillian holds a heretical doctrine of the Trinity, studies heretical apocrypha, practices magic, teaches the radical dualism of the Manichees, which explains his overt propagation of the celibate ideal while indulging in sexual orgies, and above all feels at liberty in conscience to deny anything whatever.

---

[1] Ambrosiaster on 2 Tim. 3 : 6–7 (*PL* 17. 493; *CSEL* 81. 3. 312). Cf. the ninth-century formula of renunciation prescribed for recanting Manichees (*PG*. 1. 1469–72 = Adam, *Texte zum Manichäismus*[2], p. 103), especially: 'Anathema to those who never tell the truth on oath . . .', and the council of Toledo's condemning of recalcitrant Priscillianists who refused to admit that their teacher was a Manichee, on the charge of 'lying perjury' (below, ch. IV, p. 185). On Augustine's accusation that Priscillianists felt free to commit perjury (*Ep.* 237. 3), see ch. III, p. 156, n. 1; on Bachiarius, ch. III, p. 168.

II

THE TEACHING OF PRISCILLIAN

To this point the narrative has reflected the success of Priscillian's accusers in portraying him as a crypto-Manichee, implicated in sorcery and sexual orgies. In this chapter the narrative
must break, in order to allow Priscillian and his circle to speak for
themselves concerning their real beliefs and teachings. It is time
to question the documents of directly Priscillianist origin.
Difficulties of different kinds attend upon the critical evaluation
of all these documents, but need not be felt to be of such magni-
tude as to induce despair. The texts that emerge directly from the
Priscillianist circle are fivefold: (*a*) Priscillian's canons on the
fourteen Pauline epistles, edited by Peregrinus; (*b*) a fragment of
a letter by Priscillian cited by Orosius in his *Commonitorium*
(discussed in detail below, p. 192); (*c*) the anonymous Würzburg
tracts; (*d*) an anonymous treatise on the doctrine of the Trinity
edited by Morin from a Carolingian manuscript at Laon; (*e*) the
Monarchian prologues to the four Gospels contained in numerous
manuscripts of the Vulgate. Several other documents recommending celibacy and citing apocrypha have also been conjectured to
be of Priscillianist origin, but none of these can be used with
confidence for our purposes. Not everyone who preached asceticism or read apocryphal texts was necessarily Priscillianist.

Among the five texts or groups of texts listed above, only the
Würzburg tractates provide a wholly secure criterion by which
the doctrine of the movement can be assessed; but the degree of
uncertainty will not appear to be uncomfortably high in relation
to the canons or Orosius' fragment (even though its authenticity
has often been doubted). The treatise on the doctrine of the
Trinity and the Monarchian prologues have such strong affinities
with the doctrines of the Würzburg tracts that it seems reasonable
to place them with confidence in the catalogue of Priscillianist
documents, though here again this judgement cannot be regarded
as indisputable and the degree of uncertainty is obviously higher

than in the case of Peregrinus' recension of the canons and the fragment gleefully copied by Orosius. Only the canons and Orosius' fragment are expressly transmitted under Priscillian's name.

Priscillian's Pauline Canons

The canons on the fourteen Pauline epistles (Priscillian's prologue is insistent on the number fourteen, that is on the inclusion of the epistle to the Hebrews in the corpus)[1] are extant in many manuscripts of the Vulgate. They are printed by Schepss (*CSEL* 18) and in Wordsworth and White's Vulgate, vol. ii. They have a substantial preface by Priscillian himself, dedicating them to an unnamed male friend and correspondent who had asked him for a refutation of interpretations placed upon the apostle by unidentified heretics. His friend has desired not a lengthy argument, but a summary for quick reference. Priscillian welcomes the suggestion, for heretics must be answered on scriptural authority, not with the sophistical subtleties of dialectic and syllogism on which some rely. So will be seen the 'spiritual and innocuous Christian faith' which this world's wisdom counts foolishness. The method of the compilation is further explained, and Priscillian concludes by assuring his readers that his purpose is simply to correct minds in error, not to indulge in personal polemic ('nulli existens inimicus'). It is safe to deduce that Priscillian has already become a controversial figure.

Accordingly the canons consist of groups of Pauline texts, referred to by a system of divisions which is Priscillian's own, comparable, but not identical, with those in a number of manuscripts of the Latin Bible.[2] The texts are put together under

[1] Priscillian's prologue to the canons (*CSEL* 18. 111. 2 = Oxford Vulgate, II. 18. 16). Schepss (p. xli) argued from the acceptance of the apocryphal letter of Paul to the Laodiceans in *Tract*. iii (p. 55, 12 ff.) that Priscillian's canons also included this letter, and that Peregrinus altered XV to XIIII. This seems unlikely in view of the implicit numerological mysticism in *Tract*. iii about the number fourteen (below, p. 82), particularly in relation to the canon of scripture.

Tract. iii, p. 45, 4, quotes 'Paulus in epistola ad Hebreos'. As will emerge, it will be essential to Priscillian's argument that although fifteen letters of Paul survive, the canon includes only fourteen.

[2] [Donatien de Bruyne], *Sommaires, divisions et rubriques de la Bible latine* (Namur, 1914), pp. 527–49, places Priscillian's divisions in parallel columns with those in various Vulgate manuscripts. See also Wordsworth and White's Oxford Vulgate, ii. 45–61.

A similar work in which the teaching of the Gospels was organized under *tituli* had been composed in the 350s by Fortunatian of Aquileia (Jerome, *Vir. inl.* 97).

theological headings designed to give the reader a coherent picture of what Priscillian thinks central in Pauline theology and to provide terse signposts to tell him where to find speedily what he may need for polemical purposes.

The canons survive, however, only in a recension corrected by a 'bishop Peregrinus', whose identity is not further specified in the manuscripts, but who seems to have been editor of a recension of a Vulgate text of St. Paul, to which he appended this expurgated text of Priscillian's canons. Peregrinus prefixes to Priscillian's dedicatory letter his own prefatory note explaining that these canons are not Jerome's work but Priscillian's, that for Bible study the work is an indispensable aid, and that he has corrected away any heretical language in the original canons.

The identity and date of this Peregrinus are mysterious. The name appears in colophons in early manuscripts of the Vulgate, as in a notable Irish manuscript of about 800, the Stowe St. John bound up with the Stowe Missal (that is, the Ashburnham manuscript given by the British Government to the Royal Irish Academy—Lowe, *CLA* ii. 267);[1] or in the codex Gothicus in S. Isidoro at León, a Vulgate Bible written near Burgos in 960, where the final note reads 'et Peregrini fratris o karissimi memento'; or in a group of Vulgate manuscripts which prefix to the Sapiential books Jerome's preface and conclude: 'Ideo et de graeco et de hebraeo praefatiuncula utraque in hoc libro praemissa est quia nonnulla de graeco, ob inluminationem sensus et legentis aedificationem, vel inserta hebraicae translationi vel extrinsecus iuncta sunt. et idcirco qui legis semper Peregrini memento.'[2]

It has sometimes been suggested that Peregrinus was a pseudonym, meaning an ascetic wanderer choosing physical homelessness to express the spiritual attitude that to him this world is foreign. Such language occurs in the Galician writer Bachiarius

[1] B. MacCarthy in *Transactions of the Royal Irish Academy* 27 (1886), 139; S. Berger, *Histoire de la Vulgate* (1893), p. 42. At the end of the Gospel (fol. 11) appears this note: 'Rogo quicumque hunc librum legeris ut memineris mei peccatoris scriptoris i(d est) *Sonid* [written in ogamic script] peregrinus. Amen. Sanus sit qui scripsit et cui scriptum est. Amen.' Sonid was perhaps a Gothic name.

[2] de Bruyne, *Préfaces de la Bible latine* (Namur, 1920), p. 119; Schepss, *CSEL* 18, p. xxxiii. See B. Fischer, 'Bibelausgaben der frühen Mittelalter', in *Settimane di Studio, Centro Italiano sull'alto medioevo, Spoleto* 10 (1963), 532–40, who thinks Peregrinus worked in fifth-century Spain, using an Italian codex of the Vulgate. J. Chapman, *Notes on the Early History of the Vulgate Gospels* (1908), pp. 258–61.

early in the fifth century.[1] Above all, in 434 Vincent of Lérins published his *Commonitorium*, not under his own name, but as the work of 'Peregrinus', and the identity of the author is known from Gennadius of Marseille.[2] Schepss thought the editor of Priscillian's canons might be Bachiarius himself, which must be considered a possibility. Whoever Peregrinus was, he was a dedicated editor of holy scripture, and evidently felt that Priscillian's canons were much too good to lose. That he was not without sympathy for Priscillian may be deduced from the way in which he insists on giving Priscillian credit for their authorship; only he has to allay suspicion by assuring his readers that he has expurgated the canons of all ill.

A reading of the ninety canons shows that Peregrinus corrected well; the text contains nothing heretical. At the same time the veil concealing the original Priscillian often seems diaphanous. A face with the same outlines as will meet us in the Würzburg tracts peers at us through the medium of Peregrinus' revision. The main themes of the canons may be summarized: a sharp dualism, moral at least and possibly metaphysical, between God and the world or the devil (canons 2–6); the enmity of the flesh with God (28–9); a defence of vegetarianism and teetotalism (35); requests for celibacy (33–4), voluntary poverty (37), and almsgiving (60), while recognizing the propriety of marriage for the incontinent (57); the 'freedom' of the heavenly Jerusalem (20), and the immunity of the spiritual man from criticism because he possesses power to know even the deep things of God (21); the abolition of slavery and sexual difference in Christ (55); the distribution of charismatic gifts to the saints (44; cf. 9) and the high value set upon the Christian service of the laity (61); the importance of the ministry exercised by teachers within the Church ('doctores' 39, 'magistri' 48); scorn for the foolishness of this world's wisdom (89; cf. 4 and the prologue) and joy in persecution (81, 85, 89); the exalted nature of the elect (24) as sons of God (72)

[1] Bachiarius, *Professio fidei*, 1 (PL 20. 1019); cf. Gennadius, *Vir. inl.* 24, briefly discussed by H. von Campenhausen, *Tradition and Life in the Church* (London, 1968), p. 240. The suggestion that Peregrinus might be a pseudonym was made by Arévalo in his edition of Isidore of Seville (i. 307). Identification with Bachiarius, proposed by Schepss, *CSEL* 18. 179, is favoured by O. F. Fritzsche, 'Über Bachiarius und Peregrinus', *Zeits. f. Kirchengeschichte* 17 (1897), 210–15, evidently writing without awareness of Schepss's suggestion.

[2] See R. S. Moxon's edition of Vincent (Cambridge, 1915); Gennadius, *Vir. inl.* 65.

whose inward man is new, a heavenly image, reformed by the grace of God and the light of knowledge (31) in contrast with the ignorance of the sons of darkness (23); the redemptive work of Christ whom the apostle calls God and Lord (17). By his cross Christ has abolished the bond or 'chirographum' (18) and has saved us from the curse of the Old Testament (66). In him are riches and many-sided wisdom (10). All things are of God and are in God (8 and 25).

The work of the Christian teacher and evangelist must continue not only by day but also by night (39). He should imitate the apostle in being all things to all men (41). To sing psalms, hymns, and spiritual songs and to attend prayers are essential obligations (40). Merely nominal Christians are rejected (58). The righteous are engaged in a spiritual war with evil powers (38), and are an élite called to share in a mystery to which God has predestinated them (15 and 24). But they must be on their guard against heretics and false prophets (52–3), against those whose god is their belly (50), and against unworthy reception of the eucharist (42).

A stern canon (46) lays down that churchmen ought not to litigate in civil courts to defend themselves but only before ecclesiastical tribunals, words that read like tragic irony to the reader knowing the outcome, but very possibly reflecting Priscillian's attitude when Hydatius and Ithacius, frustrated by the mildness of the council of Saragossa and infuriated by Priscillian's election to be bishop of Avila, turned to the court of Gratian to obtain a rescript of repression against the Priscillianists (above, p. 35). It is hard not to discern a bow of gratitude to Euchrotia in canon 63: 'That some have laid down their necks for the apostle, to whom gratitude is due not only from him but from every church which they have received into their own houses.'[1] Awareness of critics who may be accusing him of separating married couples and of encouraging a too active, prophetic role for women within the church may lie behind canon 56: 'That he orders the people to be subject to the powers and to work with their own hands, wives to love their sons and slaves, and slaves to love their masters, and women to keep silence in church and not to presume to teach.'

The last eight of the ninety canons disclose the urgency of Priscillian's apocalyptic expectation. 'Before the day of judgement

---

[1] Cf. Babut, *Priscillien*, p. 212.

will come the son of sin who is understood to be Antichrist'
(87). Accordingly the felicity of this present world is not merely
to be despised as short-lived but hated as harmful and evil (89).
The resurrection of the body is affirmed: the bodies of the saints
will be endued with varying brilliance, and flesh and blood, that
is the appetites of the flesh, will not be in control (82). Likewise
there will be judgement (85), heaven (90), and hell (50).

The Würzburg tractates

The codex Mp. th. Q. 3 in the University Library at Würzburg,
written in uncial letters during the fifth or sixth century,[1] without
punctuation or spacing between words, contains a collection of
eleven pieces which internal evidence shows to be certainly
Priscillianist. A colophon at the foot of fol. 74ᵛ, at the end of the
third tractate (but after the words 'incipit tractatus paschae'
announcing the fourth tractate with which the next fol. 75
begins), reads:

Lege felix Amantia [this name erased but legible] cum tuis in xр̄o iħu
dñо nosī.

Although the name Amantia has suffered erasure, the letters NTIA
are beyond doubt, and the scribe also recorded the name in a
shorthand note. Why the name Amantia was judged so dangerous
as to merit erasure cannot be easily guessed. Amantia might be the
name of some noble lady for whom this codex was written, or
of the lady for whom the original collection was made. Perhaps
she was the person for whom the paschal cycle of tractates iv–
xi was compiled. The position of the colophon at the end of the
third tractate, which deals with the right and duty of studying
non-canonical texts, makes it a particularly plausible hypothesis
that she was the person for whom that tractate was originally
written. In that event, Amantia was a contemporary of Priscillian rather than a lady of A.D. 500, and like Euchrotia she may
have been one of the devout women attracted to Priscillianist
teaching and to the master's personality. Since she has associates
('cum tuis'), perhaps she was a prominent member of one of
Priscillian's sororities. Amantius and Amantia were common
names well attested at this period. There is not the least justification for dallying with the romantic but extravagant notion

[1] Lowe, *CLA* ix. 1431, concurs with Schepss that the codex could be as early as
the fifth century.

that Amantia was Priscillian's term of endearment for Euchrotia's daughter Procula.

To the provenance of the codex there is no clue except that it is well written (and carefully corrected). E. A. Lowe expressed the tentative opinion that 'to judge from the script' it was written in Italy. Lowe's intuition in such matters was remarkable and, although the contents can only have been put together in Galicia, no doubt the original model could have travelled to north Italy in the fifth century, and been copied for devotional use there. Be that as it may, by the eighth century the codex had found its way north into the Anglo-Saxon world (and later came to Würzburg cathedral). A note in an eighth-century hand on the first leaf mentions the name 'bilihilt', perhaps St. Bilihild, widow of the duke of Thuringia, Heden or Hetan; she lived in the eighth century and became abbess of Altmünster at Mainz.[1] The codex may have been hers.

The codex now consists of eighteen quaternions, but once had more which were lost at an early date. After the second tractate (the petition to Damasus) the scribe left the verso of fol. 55 blank, and the third tractate, which begins on fol. 56, has lost its first part. The blank leaf suggests that there was a lacuna confronting the original scribe, and that the start of the third tractate was missing in his model. After fol. 121 the loss of a quaternion has removed the end of the eighth and the beginning of the ninth tractates. The losses probably had merely accidental causes. There is no particular reason to think that the lost sections contained such explosive matter as to lead to their deliberate excision, except for the erasing of Amantia's name in the colophon at the end of the third tractate; one may speculate that she was mentioned by name in the lost opening section, which was therefore destroyed by someone to whom her patronage of Priscillian had become an embarrassment. But this is merely to record a possibility.

The eleven tractates are anonymous, and the codex has no title at the beginning. Priscillian's name never occurs at any point. Nevertheless the discoverer and first editor, Georg Schepss, felt certain not only that the tractates are Priscillianist (which is non-controversial) but that all eleven come from a

[1] M. Stimming, 'Die heilige Bilhildis', *Mitt. Inst. österr. Geschichtsforschung* 37 (1916–17), 234–55.

single pen which can be identified as Priscillian's. This opinion
has not passed unchallenged. Critics have doubted whether
there is good reason to assert a single author.[1] On the other
hand, Dom Morin, while not questioning the arguments for
unitary authorship, urged the claims of bishop Instantius (above,
p. 48).

The first three tractates stand on their own. The first is the long
vindication of the orthodoxy of the group and of their acknowledged leader who writes in their name. The second is the joint
petition submitted in Rome to pope Damasus. The third, of
which the opening has been lost, is entitled 'de fide de apocryphis';
it skilfully and elegantly defends the right of instructed Christians
to read apocryphal texts with discretion. While the second
contains essential information about the course of events, the
third has few historical references to events or people.

The remaining tractates are a Lenten set which do not reflect
the heated controversies of 380–5,[2] except rather distantly and
indirectly in alluding to persecution. The fourth (*Tractatus Paschae*)
is a Lenten exhortation to prepare for Easter by continence,
fasting, and voluntary poverty. The fifth (*Tractatus Genesis*)
defends the allegorical interpretation of the Old Testament,
attacks heretics who deny the creation of God, ascribe the
human body to the devil, and venerate sun and moon as gods,
and asserts Christ, who is God's Name, to be present in all
things. The sixth (*Tractatus Exodi*) is again concerned to defend
the spiritual interpretation of the Old Testament and to affirm
that both Old Testament and New come from one God. It
includes an elaborate Christological passage and exciting flights of
numerological mysticism. The seventh is a short sermon on the
first psalm, exhorting the hearers not to allow the body's desires
to weigh down the soul. The eighth expounds the third psalm
to speak of the renewal of the inner man;[3] its ending is lost with

---

[1] e.g. E. Michael in *Zeitschrift für katholische Theologie* 16 (1892), 692–706; K. Sittl
in *Bursian* 59 (1890), 44 f.; 68 (1892), 267–9. The attack on unitary authorship of the
tractates has lately been reopened by Vollmann in *PW* Suppl. xiv (1974), 554–8.
Schepss replied to his critics in his article 'Pro Priscilliano', *Wiener Studien* 15 (1893),
128–47, his main arguments being common groupings of biblical citations and
above all similar diction and turns of phrase shared by different tractates.

[2] Vollmann, *PW* Suppl. xiv. 553–4, notes the structural parallels in the fragmentary cycles of Lenten discourses given by Zeno of Verona (see the capitula in
Löfstedt's edition, pp. 5–7).

[3] This theme of the inner man is obscured by a corruption in the text. At p. 87, 3,

the falling out of a quaternion, which has also removed the start of the very short ninth tractate which looks like an exposition of Psalm 14 (15) and concerns the alms of the rich. The tenth tractate, on the holy war against persecution, demonic powers, and the downward pull of worldly goods, reflects upon Psalm 59 (60). The last is incomplete at the end, but probably not much is missing; it is an elaborate and beautiful prayer of blessing upon the faithful,[1] evidently written for liturgical use with great care and conscious echoes of Hilary of Poitiers, *De Trinitate*, whose influence is pervasive in the majority of the tractates.

The diction and style of the tractates impose considerable strain on the reader.[2] That their idioms are those of late Latin is no ground for surprise or complaint, but their sense is in places a struggle to discover. This is partly because of the love for long periods, inflated by concessive clauses (introduced by *etsi*, *quia*, *dum*, etc.), often by clauses beginning with *ut*. The use of participles is typical of late Latin; they often float as nominative absolutes without any clear construction. Asyndeton is particularly frequent (see Schepss's index, p. 185). Nevertheless none of the tractates reads like the work of a simple or half-educated person. There is no lack of confidence about using neologisms or highly individual constructions, and through the contorted prose there emerges a profound sense of religious passion, especially in searching out the inner meaning of holy scripture.

In attempting to decide the question whether one author is responsible for all eleven tractates, it is necessary to remember that the word *tractatus* (meaning a homily or exposition of scripture) is not applied in the manuscript to the first three pieces, nor to the liturgical 'Benedictio super fideles' at the end. We have various genres to deal with here, and the style may have been varied accordingly. The form appropriate for a profession of faith submitted to Spanish bishops or for a petition to the pope differs from that of an exegetical homily. Moreover, among the homilies themselves there are evident differences of atmosphere and construction. The reader of the fourth, sixth, and

for 'qui iunctus est' read 'qui intus est', as the allusion to 2 Cor. 4: 16 requires; cf. p. 20, 26, 'qui intus est renovatur'.

[1] The 'Benedictio super fideles' has been re-edited by P. Siffrin in Mohlberg's edition of the *Missale Gallicanum Vetus* (1958), pp. 103–5.

[2] Schepss, 'Die Sprache Priscillians', *Archiv. f. lat. Lexicographie* 3 (1886), 309–28, is good on Priscillian's diction.

tenth tractates is bound to feel that in these the same person is addressing him.

Vollmann has lately proposed to see iv, vi, ix, and x as the work of a single author, v and vii of a second; while viii stands apart and contains nothing distinctively or even characteristically Priscillianist.[1] In view of the explicit interest of Priscillian's 31st canon in the renewal of the inner man (an interest which also appears in the first tractate, p. 20, 26), this judgement of viii seems an overstatement. It seems preferable to say simply that the eighth tractate, of which we have only the beginning anyway, betrays neither the elegance of the third and eleventh nor the pietistic tone of the fourth, sixth, and tenth. But it contains much matter that in content is paralleled elsewhere either in the canons or in the tractates: the insight that discerns typological meaning in the Old Testament (p. 86, 13); the contrast between sons of light and sons of darkness (p. 87, 1); the renewal of the inner man (p. 87, 3–4); the exhortation to study night and day to know the secrets of the celestial precepts while there is yet time (p. 87, 14–15); the special significance seen in the third psalm being David's words when he fled from his third son Absalom, symbolic of the third stage in man's fall into sin after the stages of desire and consent and also of the fact that we ourselves produce the forces that oppose us (p. 88, 18 ff.). The fifth tractate (p. 63, 13) also stresses man's responsibility.

The case for asserting unitary authorship of all eleven pieces cannot depend simply on the occurrence of repeated ideas (Monarchianism, celibacy, ascetic voluntary poverty, etc.), though in such respects the tractates tell a mutually consistent story. It is not in dispute that all the tractates emerge from a close, tightly knit community in Galicia, and coherence is to be expected. Nor can the case depend only on the repetition of the same vocabulary. But some repetitions are of the kind that strongly suggest a single mind at work. A few examples can be given to illustrate links between i–iii and the rest.

(1) i, p. 5, 4: (Christum) qui peccatorum remissione concessa passus ipse pro nobis:

    iv, p. 60, 17: liberi a peccatis esse non possumus, nisi remissione baptismatis et divinae crucis redemptione salvemur. (Repeated verbatim in x, p. 100, 4.)

[1] *PW* Suppl. xiv. 555–6.

(2) i, p. 5, 10: attacks 'Binionitae' as iii, p. 49, 8.

(3) i, p. 6, 2: the use of *totus* here is characteristic of several of the tractates (see Schepss's index).

(4) i, p. 13, 15: scimus nos credidisse quod credimus deo et renuntiasse quod renuntiavimus zabulo.

    cf. vii, p. 83, 16–17: ... ut nec cui renuntiavimus inveniamur participes nec cui credimus infideles.

    x, p. 99, 9: illud (sc. quod saeculi est) renuntiamus, hoc (sc. quod dei est) credimus.

(5) i, p. 5, 22: qui fuit est et futurus est; cf. iii, p. 49, 6: quod fuit est et futurum erat.

(6) i, p. 22, 20: attacking those who say sun and moon, the rulers of this world, are gods, citing Sirach 17: 30; cf. v, p. 63, 25–p. 64, 1, and vi, p. 78, 7.

(7) ii, p. 35, 3–4: alii nostrum iam in eclesiis electi deo, alii vita elaborantes et eligeremur;

    cf. iv, p. 60, 8–9: alteri consepulti in mortem in baptismum sumus, alteri ut commoriamur et consepeliamur optamus.

    vi, p. 79, 19: iam alii cognovistis, alii ut cognoscatis optatis.

(8) iii, p. 49, 10: deus unus non divisus; cf. x, p. 93, 17: unus et indifferens sibi deus.

The fourth and tenth tractates have several verbal parallels, sometimes making identical borrowings from Hilary of Poitiers; e.g. iv, p. 58, 7, with x, p. 94, 20–4. Both iv, p. 57, 3, and x, p. 94, 25, have 'ipsa natura nos docet', and what follows in iv, p. 57, 3, is paralleled in x, p. 92, 16. Likewise there are parallels between the fourth and the sixth (iv, p. 60, 3, with vi, p. 77, 15, sharing nine consecutive words), and, most spectacular of all, a precise correspondence between iv, p. 57, 13–14 = x, p. 94, 13–14 = xi, p. 104, 3–4. One link is striking for the author's sense of responsibility and authority as a teacher in the apostolic succession of St. Paul: iv, p. 60, 16, 'ego testis sum'; vi, p. 80, 26, 'et ego testis vester habeor'. Cf. iii, p. 53, 20, 'ego ... debitor sum' (Rom. 1: 14).

Similarly there are close links between the sixth and the tenth: vi, p. 72, 15 ff. on the two Testaments, as x, p. 98, 18 ff.; vi, p. 73, 7, on humanity the 'divinum genus', with x, p. 93, 16, and 98, 16. The eleventh piece, the liturgical 'Blessing over the faithful', is an exalted prose-poem, owing not a little to Hilary, but un-hesitating in its Monarchian theology. The thesis that 'although men journey to your tabernacle by various ways of callings, yet all find entrance to you by one ingress of Christ who brings it about, that he whom Christ had shut out, should not have access to you, because he had not known the Father of the Son in the Son and the Son of the Father in the Father' (xi, p. 103, 12–15) is in its conclusion reminiscent of the third tractate (p. 49, 7), and of the protest in the first tractate that there is salvation only through Christ (p. 29, 11 ff.). Two further detailed verbal parallels between the Blessing and the tenth tractate point to a common mind: x, p. 95, 15, '(David sanctus) divinae intellegentiae opus moliens et . . . humanae inbecillitatis respueret errores' with xi, p. 104, 1, 'mens nostra inexplicabilis intellegentiae opus moliens intra humanae inbecillitatis claudatur errore . . .' (echoing Hilary, as in iv, p. 57, 10, 'sensuus . . . captivi intra humanae inbecillitatis clauduntur errorem'). The second is uncertain because of damage to the last leaf of the codex: xi, p. 105, 8, has '. . . bulacra (?) statutum (?)' which is close to x, p. 93, 4, 'inter divinorum deambulacra verborum'.

The absence from the catalogue above of the eighth and ninth tractates calls for comment. The eighth, and especially the ninth, are merely brief fragments, their end and beginning lost respectively, and neither of great moment. The debt to Hilary in the eighth is extensive. The ninth exhorts to poverty and almsgiving with a row of favourite biblical citations used in other trac-tates.

The seventh, apart from the parallel with the first and tenth already noted above, has one tell-tale link with the sixth at p. 83, 9, 'evidentior poena peccati eundem cotidianum testem habere quem iudicem illique debere mortem quem vitae intellegimus auctorem'; cf. vi, p. 70, 16 'aut certe deum in homine cottidianum sui testem passum pro nobis et nostri iudicem monstrat.'

The tractate that, in view of its length (six pages of Latin text), surprises by the relative paucity of its links with the others is the fifth, expounding Genesis on creation. Its doctrines (the contingent status of the world and its elements upheld against doctrines of the eternity of the world and of fate, Monarchianism, the need for chastity to 'rise above' the cycle of sexual reproduc-tion, three stages of spiritual progress) do not stand in contrast to other tractates, but perhaps it is the work of a different member of the Priscillianist confraternity. The link between the fifth and the eighth in their common insistence on free will and responsibility for sin has been noticed already (above, p. 66).

Support for the opinion that the main body of the tractates comes from Priscillian himself may be found in the external attestation. Both Jerome and Vincent of Lérins know about *opuscula* circulating under Priscillian's name (see pp. 152, 208, below). Moreover, the accusation that Priscillian called the Son 'unbegettable', 'innascibilis', is based on the sixth tractate (below, p. 88). That doctrine, together with all heretical writings of Priscillian personally, was disowned at the council of Toledo in 400 by Symposius of Astorga and his son Dictinius (below, p. 182). The language of the council of Toledo is intelligible only if there was a group of writings ascribed to Priscillian which were being used to justify the requirement imposed on the Galician bishops that they condemn Priscillian as a heretic. This group of writings need not be precisely identified with the eleven Würzburg tracts, the original collection of which is likely to have been put together in Galicia between 385 and 400 to provide a vindication of the Galician view that Priscillian was an orthodox martyr brought to his death by worldly bishops pursuing a private vendetta. But the probability is high that there will have been a substantial overlap between the extant tractates and the *opuscula* known to Jerome and exploited by the inquisitors at Toledo in 400.

Accordingly, it is not unreasonable to think Priscillian himself the principal author of the tractates, the fifth being granted as a likely exception. But in any event all eleven are committed Priscillianist texts, and the state of the evidence simply does not allow us to begin trying to distinguish between Priscillian and the -ism associated with his name. The distinction that can be critically carried through is that between doctrines directly attested by works of Priscillianist origin and doctrines attributed to the group by their opponents. In what follows an attempt is made to provide a synthetic statement of the main doctrines found in the Würzburg tractates taken as a set. The validity of this statement as a portrait of the group's concerns should remain unimpaired by nagging critical doubt whether or not a particular treatise in the Würzburg codex (or even any of them) should be confidently attributed to Priscillian of Avila himself.

The teaching of the tractates

'Make your souls chaste for the obedience of faith.' The text
(1 Pet. 1 : 22) is cited in the tractates more frequently than any
other. Christians are called to follow their Master on a journey
(*iter* is a favourite word) towards perfection. In St. Paul's phrase,
which Priscillian seems specially to have liked, they must seek
'to apprehend that for which they have been apprehended'
(i, p. 7, 15; the formula is twice echoed in the Monarchian prologues).[1] This ladder of ascent requires an end to all compro-
mises with the world, the flesh, and the devil. Avarice and envious
quarrels are to be put away (iv, p. 59), and worldly goods
renounced (i, p. 17, 3–16; x, p. 99), a demand which the ninth
tractate interprets of income rather than of capital at least at
the level of precept (ix, p. 91). The essential step is to realize that
friendship with this world is enmity with God (iv, p. 57, 7;
ix, p. 90, 16; x, p. 94, 15). For the entire world lies in the hand of
Satan (v, p. 57) who originated in a lie (p. 64, 19), and man has
fallen to become the son of perdition (viii, p. 89, 2–3; canon 87,
p. 146, 2). But this does not mean that humanity is so far gone
from original righteousness that there is no ray of light at all.
Man retains free will and must never ascribe responsibility for
his sins to the devil (v, p. 63, 13–14; viii, p. 88, 5 and 21 ff.).[2]
Man is a mixture of divine and earthly elements (x, p. 98, 14 ff.),
and because of this mixture redemption is possible by baptism
and the redeeming sacrifice of Christ (ix, p. 60, 17 = x, p. 100, 4).
There the divine pity offers a harbour in the storm (iv, p. 57,
13; cf. i, p. 4, 14).[3] But it is easier to be sorry about one's sinful
state than positively to desire the holiness which is God's will
(x, p. 100, 13). The believer is called to make the temple of God
pure within him (vii, p. 83). But there is a downward drag which
can be countered only by serious conflict. To conquer sins of the
body and sins of the soul are two distinct tasks (x, p. 95, 11–24).
Though made by God, the body is 'figura mundi' and the 'old

---

[1] The formula appears in the prologues to St. Matthew and St. Luke (p. 13, 7, and
p. 15, 5, ed. Lietzmann, *Kleine Texte*, 1).

[2] Hilary, *In Ps.* 118, Nun 20, p. 486: some wrongly say, to excuse their own un-
belief, that dedication to good works is God's own gift.

[3] The image of a harbour may be borrowed by Priscillian from Cyprian (*Mort.* 3,
p. 299, 7 Hartel) or Hilary (*De Trin.* 1. 3; 12. 1). But Ambrose (*Expl. Ps.* 47. 13,
CSEL 64. 355, 13; *Expl. Ps.* 118. 11, 9, *CSEL*, 62. 239, 5) shows that it had become
a cliché. Campbell Bonner in *HTR* 34 (1941), 49–67, collects many instances.

man' (vi, p. 73, 3–4). Our bodily appetites are not of diabolical creation (v, p. 63, 20); but they are exploited by the wiles of the devil (vii, p. 84), and a particular cause of corruption is sexual desire (x, p. 101, 26).

The summons to practise continence is prominent in the Priscillianist discourses (v, p. 65, 18 ff.; iv, p. 58, 12; especially vi, p. 81). At Lent and at Easter Christians have a particular duty and opportunity to strengthen the resolve of their will in this respect (iv, p. 58). If such preaching upsets some and causes offence, that must be accepted as inescapable; words capable of producing in some the response of faith are sure to scandalize others (v, p. 66, 14). It is right to affirm that God not only created Adam and Eve but also willed their possession of reproductive powers (v, p. 63, 18, and p. 65, 25). Yet there is a moral progress from the Old Testament to the New, a gradual divine education of the human race (vi, p. 77) which means that higher things are now expected. In the divine dispensation that governs history, we have now passed beyond the six days of the created order and are called to enter the sabbath rest of the people of God (v, p. 66, 2–3).

This higher spirituality, however, does not rest on a gnostic dualism. Both Old and New Testaments come from one and the same God (vi, p. 72, 4). The Old Testament is an allegory for our edification (v, p. 62, x, p. 93) rather than a norm with validity now. (The Pauline conception of the superseding of the Mosaic dispensation is the theme of canons 65–70.) The sixth tractate accepts the doctrine, ultimately derived from Origen, perhaps mediated through Hilary of Poitiers, that in scripture there is a threefold sense corresponding to St. Paul's threefold division of man into body, soul, and spirit (vi, p. 70).[1] But they are three levels of spiritual interpretation on top of the basic literal and historical sense. They indicate three grades of sanctification up which believers are to climb (p. 70, 8 ff.; p. 76, 4; p. 78, 11). At the first grade we are to learn to discipline the flesh. At the second stage we direct the soul, which is 'divine', away from the cultic observances of days, months, seasons, and from the

---

[1] By what line of theological influence did this doctrine reach Priscillian? Nothing of Origen was available in Latin for him. One would expect Hilary of Poitiers to provide the link. The Pauline trichotomy used by Origen as an exegetical principle is not found in Hilary.

idolatry associated with earthly birth ('idolicis terrenae nativitatis vitiis', p. 70, 14). It seems clear, here and elsewhere in the tractates, that 'earthly birth' puts one somehow under the power of destiny, under 'the wheel of becoming' of which St. James speaks (i, p. 26, 21–2). At the third stage we walk in the spirit since God has willed us to be partakers of the divine nature (2 Pet. 1 : 4, cited in vi, p. 70, 18). And God transcends all sexual differentiation (i, p. 28, 16).

Priscillian does not deny the possibility of salvation to ordinary Christians living with their wives in a normal married life. Those who wish to pursue their ambitions in this world, or to retain high secular office,[1] or prefer to ignore Christ's stern call for an abandonment of family ties, may indeed hope for pardon, provided always that their orthodoxy remains intact. For the apostle gives precepts to some, pardon to others, and unmandatory counsel to others still, in hope of gaining for all eventual salvation of an appropriate kind and class. In heaven there are many mansions (ii, p. 36, 1 ff.). Renunciation of the world is the high and truly Christian way; but this does not mean the loss of all hope by those who want to belong to the Church and still retain their family property to bring up their children. Jesus' words to the rich young ruler or his parable of Dives and Lazarus do not mean that hell is unconditionally the destiny of all rich men. Almsgiving and a good life are beginnings which set them on the road to the Lord. Little by little we may advance to the things which are highest (ix, pp. 90–1).

Priscillian's ascetic demands do not make him desire to be associated with the rigorist Novatianists who seem to delight in the thought that the elect are such a tiny minority. His message is not, he protests, intended to induce despair in ordinary Christians with family ties that they may feel unable to sever (ii, p. 36, 3;

---

[1] Cf. Hilary, *In Ps.* 1. 10, pp. 25 f: Christians ambitious for worldly success cannot escape defilement, even though they bring a religious intention to their secular duties. Hilary speaks sadly of half-Christians (1. 22, p. 35; cf. Zeno of Verona, i. 35 (= ii. 21), p. 90 Löfstedt), who only profess their faith from fear, not love (118, Mem 2, p. 467; cf. Koph 6, p. 525), of bishops occupied with secular business, commercial and family cares, and feastings (138. 34, p. 768); of the hatred irreligious men feel towards the devout (118, Lamed 13, p. 464). Ambrose complains of cases where bishoprics have been used for financial gain by men as corrupt as Eli's sons (*Expl. Ps.* 1. 23, *CSEL* 64. 17, 22). In Spain cases of scandalous secularity among the bishops are complained of by pope Innocent I, *Ep.* 3. 7 (*PL* 20. 491A); below, p. 186.

ix, p. 91, 4).[1] But the danger for the Spanish churches is on the other side, that they have become complacent and comfortable, conformed to this world. Christians seem unaware of the holy war against the hidden forces of evil, whose power within the very citadel of the Church itself is demonstrated by the persecution and hostility being experienced by Priscillian's followers upon the ascetic path (x, pp. 92–102, an exposition of Psalm 59 (60)).[2] Like Christ whose physical body was fixed to the cross, the believer must mortify the flesh to set free the 'impassible divine element' within himself (vi, p. 76, 1–3).

Bible study is central to the ascent up the way of sanctification (i, p. 8, 16 ff.). To apprehend the higher truth, search the scriptures (iii, p. 47, 25; p. 51, 13), night and day (viii, p. 87, 10). How noble were the Jews of Beroea who searched the scriptures to see whether the things that Paul taught them were indeed so (Acts 17: 11, cited iii, p. 53, 8). Scripture invites its readers to stretch their minds by containing so many hard sayings and parables which the prayerful exegete will be granted grace to interpret (i, p. 28, 9). Scripture is full of secrets (viii, p. 87, 14). 'To us learning is to understand scripture' (i, p. 28, 25).[3] The key is given by the God Christ, 'Deus Christus', who himself interprets the scriptures for true believers (i, p. 9, 27 f.).

The burden of care upon the Christian interpreter is a heavy one. The Priscillianist teacher feels himself to stand in a special relationship both of grace to Christ and of responsibility to his followers: 'I the Lord's servant' (iii, p. 56, 25). 'I am held as your witness in Christ Jesus' (vi, p. 80, 26). The author of the first tractate is also conscious of a certain social position and high education, no doubt also of birth and rank; he writes as if he expected to be treated with respect and attention, explaining that, without wishing to boast of his past career, he was not at the time of his conversion in an undistinguished position or lacking in wisdom. But at baptism he had wholly renounced all his past life (i, p. 4, 8–14). He looks back penitently on the delight that once he had in worldly wisdom (i, p. 14, 9; cf. canon 89 on

---

[1] Priscillian's position is indistinguishable from that of Augustine, *Contra Faustum* 5. 9.

[2] That this tract is based on Psalm 59 was pointed out by G. Mercati, *Note di letteratura biblica e cristiana antica, Studi e testi* 5 (1901), 125 ff.

[3] Cf. Hilary, *In Ps.* 125. 2, p. 605 (no arrogance in the Christian claim to be able to interpret scripture).

'sapientia saecularis'). But now all his studies are self-consciously directed towards scripture (i, p. 8, 12). His mother is the Church (i, p. 17, 20), not the philosophy of this world.

Priscillian's exegesis often follows the Origenist tradition found in Hilary where numbers and animals are of deep allegorical significance. The very order in which the psalms occur in the psalter is symbolic (viii, pp. 87–8), a doctrine almost certainly derived from Hilary who explains, following Origen, that originally the psalms were unnumbered but were gathered together in one volume by Ezra and received their numbering from the seventy translators of the Greek Old Testament according to their spiritual meaning.[1] The third tractate observes that everyone knows Ezra to be responsible for the rewriting of the Old Testament after it had been burnt; that the burning is recorded in canonical scripture, but the rewriting only in the non-canonical 4 Esd. 14 (iii, p. 52)—a book known to other Spanish writers such as Isidore of Seville and Vigilantius (for which Jerome insinuates that he is touched by Priscillianism: *Adv. Vigilantium* 6).

Although Priscillian attaches deep importance to number-mysticism as a hermeneutic key to scriptural mysteries, number is associated for him with the successiveness and disintegrated nature of our earthly condition. Days, times, seasons, and places are of intense importance in polytheistic cult because in his fallen state the natural man is brought down to a low level of experience where special times and particular places are all-important to him (vi, p. 76, 15 ff.).

If this last judgement is accepted as a principle, the Priscillianists have a problem on their hands with the Christian calendar, especially with the annually recurring Easter festival whose date is fixed in accordance with sun and moon, being assigned to the Sunday following the first full moon after the spring equinox. The sixth tractate explains (after Ambrosiaster, whose *Questions*, here as elsewhere in the tractates, seem to have had an influence)[2]

---

[1] Hilary, *Instructio Psalmorum* 8 (*CSEL* 22. 9), from Origen, *In Ps.*, *PG* 12. 1076. Cf. E. Goffinet, *L'Utilisation d'Origène dans le commentaire des Psaumes de S. Hilaire de Poitiers*, *Studia Hellenistica* 14 (Louvain, 1965), 26–30. M. R. James thought it possible that to Priscillian may be due the existence of the Spanish text of 4 Esdras (in his edition of R. L. Bensly, *The Fourth Book of Ezra*, *Texts and Studies* iii. 2 (1895), p. xxxvi).

[2] Ambrosiaster, *Quaestiones* 84 (*CSEL* 50), similarly explains that the lunar

that the moon's role in calculating Easter does nothing to justify lunar cult. It is the Creator's way to recognize that 'man is tied down by attachment to visible objects and that, being flesh akin to the elements and bound to days and times, he supposes the rulers of this world to be gods'. But God used the moon, which, by waxing and waning, shows itself not to be possessed of freedom, to demonstrate that the heavenly bodies are not divine and sovereign (vi, p. 78, 3–27). The presuppositions of the argument may be illustrated from the Greek Apocalypse of Baruch where the moon's waxing and waning is a consequence of the Fall.[1]

The observance of special days was highly characteristic of paganism. Ammianus Marcellinus speaks unkindly of Roman aristocrats 'without any belief in the gods' who would not go out of doors or eat a meal or take a bath until they had examined the calendar and studied the location of the stars.[2] The elder Pliny remarks on the use of astrological calendars by physicians.[3] Suetonius reports that the emperor Augustus thought the nones unlucky for any activity and never travelled on days following *nundinae*.[4] The fact that these writers thought these superstitious practices noteworthy presupposes that such scrupulosity was not universal. That they were widespread is not to be doubted.

According to the doctrine of the sixth tractate, to be counted and countable is to be finite and creaturely; so Christ is uncountable ('innumerabilis', vi, p. 79, 5), but the 'saeculum

computation of the date of Easter is wholly different from pagan veneration of the moon and from superstitious observances of what may or may not be done at various phases of the moon's course. Cf. above p. 52, n. 1. Augustine's fifty-fifth letter (to Januarius) argues at length that the dependence of the date of Easter on the full moon gives no ground for astrology or magic.

Parallels between Ambrosiaster and the tractates are noted by Hugo Koch in *Zeitschrift für Kirchengeschichte* 47 (1928), 1–10.

[1] Greek Apocalypse of Baruch 9, a work which was apparently circulating in Latin in seventh-century Galicia, to judge from the vision of Baldarius described by Valerius of Vierzo (*PL* 87. 431); see M. R. James in *JTS* 16 (1915), 413.

[2] Amm. Marc. 28. 4. 24.

[3] Pliny, *NH* 29. 9.

[4] Suetonius, *Aug.* 92. 2. On lucky days cf. Vergil, *Georg.* i. 276 ff., or the fragments of the Orphic poem collected by O. Kern, frr. 271–9. Augustine (*Exp. ep. ad Gal.* 35, *PL* 35. 2139) says that while there would be a riot if a Christian were detected keeping the Jewish sabbath, yet the churches are full of people whose decisions are ruled by astrologers' almanacs, who begin no new undertakings on *dies Aegyptiaci*, and who openly declare 'I never start a journey on the day after the Kalends.' Astrology in Christian epitaphs: Diehl, *ILCV* 4377–79.

numerabile' (vi, p. 77, 19). This language for expressing divine transcendence is derived from Hilary of Poitiers, for whom the Son of God is 'not limited by time, not subject to number';[1] for 'God is eternal, without measure of times'.[2] Ambrose can likewise be quoted to illustrate how the Arian controversy had made the orthodox insistent upon the transcendence of Christ over the temporal process.[3] The first, second, and fifth tractates all contain attacks inveighing against the cult of sun and moon (which the first tractate strangely represents as the specific heresy of the Manichees, i, p. 22, 20), against astrology, and against the Platonic belief that the cosmos is an eternal cycle rather than a created order dependent for its beginning on the will of its Creator, and therefore capable of ending (cf. v, p. 63, 9 ff.; p. 64, 12). But in the sixth tractate more than one sentence could be taken to imply that the higher Christian should be liberated from all calendrical observances which are in principle expressions of the unredeemed experience of natural earthbound man. As in Ambrosiaster's commentary on Romans 5 : 7, the time-process itself is part of this fallen world from which we need to be redeemed to be with God, who is beyond time (vi, p. 78, 22, 'intemporabilis') and is the One beyond all multiplicity and division (iii, p. 49, 10; x, p. 93, 17). To distinguish temporal from eternal is parallel to the distinction of false from true (x, p. 93, 15).

All division is inherently inferior to unity. The successiveness of temporal experience in seasons and days belongs to the contingent and transitory condition of finite and fallen beings, so that redemption means the destruction of 'opera divisa aut mundi opus' (vi, p. 70, 9; cf. p. 72, 8; p. 76, 16–17). Sin is defined, therefore, as 'man dividing himself' (vi, p. 75, 21). All created natures beneath the sun are 'vitiorum divisa' (vi, p. 73, 7).

Christ, on the other hand, is the very principle of unity : 'He is one in all things and desires man to be one in him' (vi, p. 75, 9). It follows that any pluralistic language about differentiation and multiplicity within the being of God himself is dangerous heresy. The cardinal error of the Arians is to 'divide that which is one'

---

[1] *In Ps.* 2. 23 (*CSEL* 22. 55), 'non definitus in tempore, non subjectus in numerum'.
[2] *In Matt.* 31. 2 (PL 9. 1066c) 'Deus sine mensura temporum semper est, et qualis est talis aeternus est.'
[3] *Expl. Ps.* 118. 18. 41; 19. 16–17.

(ii, p. 38, 9), and similarly the complaint against the 'Binionites' (that is, those who distinguish between the Father and the Son) is that they 'divide' and must therefore be in error (i, p. 5, 9; cf. below, p. 87).

Detachment from all that is narrow and limited is an essential constituent in Priscillian's message to the torpid Spanish churches of his time. Here his devotion to celibacy joined forces with liberal convictions about the wideness of God's mercy to stimulate him to deep interest in apocryphal Gospels and Acts; for why should the overflowing bounty of the apostolic message be confined to books that have been accepted in the lectionaries of the churches? Admittedly these apocryphal documents need to be handled with care by wise and experienced men of the Spirit, especially because they have suffered interpolation from heretics (i, p. 22, 10–12; iii, p. 46, 23; p. 51, 25; p. 56, 7). But the gift of faith brings with it an intuitive power of discernment between sound and unsound, and Priscillian feels sufficiently confident of the correctness of his own faith, in both will and deed, to have no hesitations or fears of being personally misled. The claim would not have seemed unreasonable to Priscillian's contemporaries. In the controversy whether one could safely read Origen, those sympathetic to Origen, like Rufinus, similarly claimed that his writings had been interpolated by heretics but that spiritual men could discern good from bad.[1] Moreover, adds the first tractate (p. 23, 11), heresy can be based on canonical scripture as well as on apocrypha.

The apocryphal Gospels and Acts, particularly the Acts, found their way to Priscillian's heart because with one voice they proclaimed the specific content of the message of Jesus to consist in the call to give up sexual intercourse.[2] The mission of Thomas or John or Paul or Peter or Andrew was none other than a zealous advocacy of the encratite ideal of virginity. The apocryphal Acts had other features as well which found a responsive echo in Priscillian. Together with their strong emphasis on celibacy, the Acts spoke of the wanderings of the homeless apostles, of their detachment from the fixed rigidities and the conventional life of settled churches, of their sufferings in the course of their itinerant

---

[1] Cf. Sulpicius Severus, *Dial.* i. 6. 2, borrowing from Rufinus, *De adulteratione librorum Origenis.*

[2] I have collected the main references in *RAC* v. 355, s.v. 'Enkrateia' (1962).

mission.[1] Moreover, the Acts of John have a militantly Monarchian Christology, according to which Father and Son are just two among a number of names that finite human beings use to describe the one God.[2] In the Acts the names are equipollent: 'we glorify thy name that was spoken by the Father; we glorify thy name that was spoken through the Son.'[3]

Naturally Priscillian is aware that apocryphal texts are frowned upon by the official clergy because of their popularity among the Manichees. For the Manichees, the apocryphal Acts of Peter, Paul, John, Thomas, and Andrew constituted an additional corpus among their canon of sacred texts. Augustine's opponent Faustus the Manichee says expressly that the Manichees appeal to these five books to vindicate their celibate ideals for the Elect;[4] and his evidence of their status is supported by the Coptic Manichean Psalm-book. That these Acts circulated in the fourth century in Latin is evident not only from Priscillian and from Faustus but also from Filastrius of Brescia, though he omits the Acts of Thomas from his list of Manichean texts.[5] If relatively little of them has been transmitted in Latin, that is probably in consequence of the Priscillianist controversy. The Acts of Thomas are attested as current among the Priscillianists of Galicia in a letter of Turibius, bishop of Astorga, written about 445 (below, p. 209).[6] Turibius expresses the characteristic episcopal fear that

[1] This is the theme in a striking passage, with allusions to episodes of apocryphal Acts that have not otherwise come down to us, in the *Manichaean Psalm-Book* (ed. C. R. C. Allberry, 1938), pp. 142–3.

[2] *Acta Johannis* 98: 'For your sakes the cross of light is sometimes called by me Logos, sometimes mind, sometimes Jesus, sometimes Christ, sometimes a door, sometimes a way, sometimes bread, sometimes seed, sometimes resurrection, sometimes Son, sometimes Father, sometimes Spirit [om. cod. C], sometimes life, sometimes truth, sometimes faith, sometimes grace. These names are given with regard to men's understanding.'

[3] *Acta Joh.* 109. A list of titles of Christ follows which is closely akin to the fifth tractate, p. 66, 15 ff., where the context is also strongly Monarchian. C. L. Sturhahn, *Die Christologie der ältesten apokryphen Apostelakten* (Diss. Heidelberg, 1951), seeks to show that the Monarchianism of the Acts of John derives from a gnostic conception of revelation. He is criticized by K. Schäferdiek in E. Hennecke and W. Schneemelcher, *New Testament Apocrypha*, ii. 213.

[4] Aug. *C. Faust.* 30. 4; cf. 22. 79. Discussion in P. Nagel, 'Die apokryphen Apostelakten des 2. und 3. Jh. in der manichäischen Literatur', in K. W. Tröger (ed.), *Gnosis und Neues Testament* (Gütersloh, 1973), pp. 149–82.

[5] Filastrius 88 (*CSEL* 38. 48).

[6] *PL* 54. 694C. No trace of the form of the Acts of Thomas familiar in Greek and Syriac now survives in Latin, in which tongue the extant Thomas-apocrypha are the book of Miracles probably by Gregory of Tours and the *Passio*, both edited by Max

these Acts will infiltrate heretical fantasies into the flock. In Priscillian's eyes such fears are a cloak for unworthier motives, namely a hunger for domination over the freedom of the laity and a jealous attitude of distrust towards the possibility of learning truth from an unusual source. Towards apocrypha the right attitude is illustrated by Joshua's readiness to recognize the angel as captain of the Lord's host, because he knew that 'there is nothing outside God' (i, p. 31, 11).

As a lay teacher Priscillian feels himself called to exercise a prophetic and teaching ministry, the authority for which is found in the immediate grace of Christ his God, not in a mediated commission transmitted through the normal and official authorities of the Church. In strong contrast to his Italian contemporary Filastrius, in whose eyes it is gravely heretical to suppose that prophecy has not come to an end with Christ and that live prophets may still be around in the Church,[1] Priscillian is persuaded that the gift of charismatic prophecy remains among the people of God. The mark of a prophetic ministry is freedom ('libertas'); and the Spirit's activity is not confined to the episcopate and the clergy on whom they laid hands in ordination, but is found in all who aspire to holiness and to an understanding of the deeper meaning of scripture.

The need to be ready to receive the immediate inspiration of the Spirit probably explains the Priscillianist demand for vegetarianism which, though not mentioned specifically in the tractates, is well attested as the practice of the movement (see below, pp. 208 and 223–5). Filastrius devotes his 154th chapter to certain 'heretics' who think Elijah the prophet to have been fed by the ravens with meat in the evening and bread in the morning. He complains that a holy prophet would never eat meat at any time,

---

Bonnet (*Acta Thomae*, Leipzig, 1883; not in the Lipsius–Bonnet corpus). These are discussed by K. Zelzer in *Wiener Studien* 84 (1971), 161–79, and 85 (1972), 185–212. For an echo of the Manichee doctrine of twelve virtues in the *Passio* and perhaps in Priscillianism see below, p. 114 n. 2. F. C. Burkitt romantically but improbably conjectured that the Acts of Thomas were first brought to the West by the pilgrim Egeria after her visit to St. Thomas' shrine at Edessa, where she read 'something of St. Thomas himself' (*Itin.* 19); see C. H. Turner in *JTS* 7 (1906), 603–5. K. A. D. Smelik (*Vig. Chr.* 28 (1974), 290–4) thinks she read the Nag-Hammadi Gospel of Thomas; a work perhaps available in Latin since G. Quispel finds *Ev. Thomae* 3 cited by Augustine (*Serm. dom. in monte* 2. 17); see *Mélanges H.-C. Puech* (Paris, 1974), pp. 375–8.

[1] Filastrius 78 (*CSEL* 38. 40).

and suggests that Elijah's abstinence from meat was the cause of his assumption to heaven in a chariot of fire. Bread he thinks acceptable, but meat 'unsuitable'. Filastrius regards it as self-evident that a charismatic figure would at no time weigh down his soul with meat.

Accordingly, Priscillian's asceticism is intended to enable the inward man to rise above earthly bonds and to be prepared for the wings of the Spirit. To despise prophesyings is characteristic of the worldly (i, p. 29, 6; iii, p. 54, 29). Moreover, both men and women may receive the gift. The Holy Spirit is in male and female equally (i, p. 28, 16) and in the realm of the Spirit sexual differentiation is left behind—'there is neither male nor female, but we are all one in Christ Jesus' (p. 28, 23), a very different conception from that of the hell-bent heretics who imagine that God is bisexual (p. 28, 15). The Lord promised to pour out his Spirit on all flesh, so that sons and daughters would prophesy, young men see visions, and old men dream dreams (Acts 2: 17–21 from Joel 2: 28–32); and the words 'super servos et ancillas meas' show that both sexes equally would become recipients of this charismatic outpouring. Under this influence Zacharias uttered the Benedictus, and Tobit declared to his son 'We are sons of the prophets; Noah was a prophet, as Abraham, Isaac, and Jacob and all our fathers who prophesied from the beginning of the world.'[1] The authority of non-canonical prophecy is proved by the epistle of Jude, whom Priscillian takes to be Judas Thomas, the Lord's identical twin; for Jude quotes Enoch as uttering prophecy.[2] Likewise in writing to the Corinthians St. Paul 'shuts the way to no one to speak about God' (i, p. 33, 1). There is no evidence that the Priscillianists spoke with tongues, however. Prophecy is understood to mean inspired insight into the sense of scripture, much as Ambrosiaster in commenting on Eph. 4: 11, holds that, parallel to the continuation of the apostolic ministry by bishops, the prophetic ministry is carried on by biblical exegetes.

---

[1] Tobit 4. 12–13 Old Latin (not Vulgate).

[2] See *Tract.* iii, p. 44, 12. Priscillian's belief in the Lord's twin did not prevent him from affirming the perpetual virginity of Mary; below, p. 86. The identification of Jude the Lord's brother with the apostle Thomas is otherwise found only in Syria. At John 14: 22 for 'Judas not Iscariot' the Curetonian Old Syriac version has 'Judas Thomas', the Sinaitic Syriac 'Thomas'. See T. Zahn, *Forschungen zur Geschichte des neutestamentlichen Kanons* vi (1900), 347.

The presence in the scriptures of quotations from non-canonical writings was felt by some contemporaries of Priscillian to be a source of embarrassment. The newly printed Pauline commentary edited by H. J. Frede comments (with Origen and Ambrosiaster) that at 1 Cor. 2 : 9 the apostle quotes from the Apocalypse of Elias, but adds, as Ambrosiaster also implies, that the words also occur in the Hebrew text of the canonical Isaiah, a solution clearly dictated by the desire to avoid attributing to the apostle a quotation from an unauthorized apocryphon.

According to the third tractate, when the apostle tells the Colossians to read the letter that he has sent to the church of the Laodiceans, he thereby relaxes 'their liberty to read the things written about Christ' (iii, p. 55, 14). The argument presupposes that Priscillian is familiar with the apocryphal letter to the Laodiceans. Filastrius mentions some who want the letter to the Laodiceans admitted to the lectionary, but, he explains, it is not so read because it has been interpolated by heretics, and is therefore confined to private study. In the same context Filastrius vigorously defends the position of the epistle to the Hebrews, though speaking with a hesitant voice about its authorship; on the one hand, he regards the opinion which ascribes Hebrews to another author than Paul as deviationist, while on the other hand his formula for the Pauline canon is 'the thirteen epistles of Paul and the epistle to the Hebrews as well' (*interdum*).[1] The fact that by the first half of the sixth century the letter to the Laodiceans was being included in manuscripts of the Vulgate shows that it quickly achieved wide acceptance despite Jerome's confident condemnation ('although some read the letter to the Laodiceans, yet *ab omnibus exploditur*').[2] Priscillian's argument simply proceeds from the presupposition that the apocryphal letter is authentically Pauline and is generally recognized as such by his readers.

Priscillian explains that 'Peter' (he or the scribe no doubt meant to say Paul)[3] knew well the reason why the canon of scripture was

[1] Filastrius 89. 2. In this writer *interdum* (see Marx's index in *CSEL* 38) can have a qualifying, almost adversative force, in some respects analogous to the English use of 'at the same time' in a non-temporal, contrasting sense. Ambrosiaster's Pauline commentary omits Hebrews, though that epistle is part of his New Testament (see on 1 Tim. 1 : 3). To Jerome it is uncanonical but Pauline.

[2] *Vir. inl.* 5. For a collection of evidence concerning the epistle to the Laodiceans see Zahn, *Geschichte des neutestamentlichen Kanons* ii (1890), 566–85.

[3] Jacob is confused with Moses in iii, p. 46, 15, so that the carelessness is probably the author's.

limited to a particular number of books. The argument remains submerged in obscurity because Priscillian is not good enough to give a clear hint what the reason might be. However, he has said immediately before that the number of books in the sacred canon is indicated by the genealogy of Jesus in the Gospels (iii, p. 55, 7), a notion that surfaces for a passing appearance also in the first tractate (i, p. 32, 4). Probably, therefore, Priscillian's argument is that fourteen is a sacred number. The genealogy of Jesus in Matthew is arranged in three groups of fourteen generations. Quite a number in the line are omitted in order to achieve this end, from which it is fair to conclude that for the evangelist the number was a riddle. The numerical value of the Hebrew letters of the name David adds up to fourteen, which may be the solution.[1] Priscillian did not know that, but was right in discerning high significance in the number for the first evangelist.

A clue to Priscillian's meaning may be found in the last book of Gregory the Great's *Moralia* on the book of Job where he comments on Job surviving 140 years after his troubles. Fourteen, he explains, is symbolic of Law and Gospel together, ten for the ten commandments, four for the gospel makers. Moreover, on the same ground the Church accepts only fourteen Pauline epistles in the canon, though the apostle wrote fifteen, to symbolize the truth that St. Paul understood the secrets of both Law and Gospel.[2]

In his treatise on the numbers found in the scriptures Isidore of Seville devotes a chapter to the symbolism of the number fourteen, twice the sacred number seven. It occurs in the gospel genealogy; in the passover on the fourteenth day of the month; in the measurements of the heavenly altar in Ezekiel (43 : 17); in the years of Jacob's service to Laban; in the years of plenty

---

[1] A. F. Gfrörer, *Die heilige Sage* (1838), ii. 9; G. H. Box, *Interpreter*, Jan. 1906, p. 199. A. Finkel, *The Pharisees and the Teacher of Nazareth*, p. 104, points out the close analogy with Exodus Rabbah xv. 26 on Exod. 12 : 2, where the Midrash links the fifteen generations from Abraham to Solomon with the passover full moon. Priscillian's contemporary Ambrosiaster is well aware that St. Matthew omits some ancestors in Jesus' genealogy to achieve the symbolic figure (*Quaest.* 85, *CSEL* 50. 146; cf. Appendix, *Qu.* 6–7).

[2] *Moralia in Iob* 35. 20. Priscillian's contemporary, the anonymous commentator on St. Paul lately edited by H. J. Frede (*Ein neuer Paulustext und Kommentar*, ii, 1974, prol. 47 ff., p. 16), says that Paul wrote ten letters to churches to correspond to the ten commandments and to show Old and New Testaments to be in agreement. The new commentary shares with Priscillian the belief that Hebrews is Pauline (prol. 57 ff.).

in Egypt in the time of Joseph; in the interval of fourteen years before Paul's second visit to Jerusalem; in the number of epistles in which he expressed all his preaching; and so on.[1] In his work on the prefaces to the books of the Bible Isidore remarks that Paul wrote fourteen letters, but to only seven churches to symbolize the sevenfold gift of the Spirit.[2]

Priscillian vehemently rejects the suggestion that he could admit a fifth Gospel, by the argument that the sacred number of four Gospels corresponds to the three immersions and one font of baptism (i, p. 31, 28).

Accordingly, Priscillian's point is that the New Testament canon, because its limits are determined by mystical principles, cannot be regarded as a rigid limit of divine tradition outside which no authentic apostolic teaching may be found. This is not to ask for the canon to be enlarged by the addition of new pieces. The very belief that the limits of the canon have been fixed simply and solely by esoteric numerological considerations constitutes compulsive evidence that truth may also be found beyond the canon of holy scripture. In logic the argument runs closely parallel to the Montanist argument with which Tertullian begins his tract on the Veiling of Virgins: the absolute immutability of the propositions contained in the apostolic Rule of Faith proves that one is at liberty to change anything not so contained.

A tantalizing scrap of evidence for further speculation on this topic within the Priscillianist community appears in Leo the Great's letter to Turibius of Astorga (*Ep.* 15) replying to a memorandum in which Turibius listed dangerous Priscillianist propositions. The thirteenth heretical proposition ascribed to the Priscillianists is that the entire body of the canonical scriptures is to be received under the names of the twelve patriarchs (below: p. 212). Nothing quite to this effect occurs in the surviving Würzburg tractates.[3] Nevertheless the proposition is akin to the number-mysticism of the tractates in determining the limits of the Pauline canon. Here again Isidore of Seville's treatise on the

[1] *Liber numerorum* 23. 97–9 (PL 83. 197–8). The authenticity is disputed.
[2] *In lib. vet. et nov. Testam. prooemia* 92 (PL 83. 176). On Isidore's numerology see J. Fontaine, *Isidore de Séville et la culture classique dans l'Espagne wisigothique* (Paris, 1959), pp. 369–91.
[3] The end of the sixth tractate speculates on the 12,000 sealed from the twelve tribes of Israel in Apoc. 7.

numbers in holy scripture may throw light on the problem. Isidore remarks that twelve is the number of the patriarchs, apostles, minor prophets, stones on the high priest's breast, stones for Elijah's altar, baskets after the feeding of the multitude, stars above the head of the Lamb, gates into the heavenly Jerusalem, months, winds, hours of the day and of the night, etc.[1] It would not be hard to see how the correspondence between Old and New Testaments (and the natural order) could be made the basis of the Priscillianist thesis. In Turibius, however, there is no hint that duodecimal mysticism is being used to show how arbitrary the limits of the canon really are.

Although Priscillian clothes his question in bizarre covering, it is clear that his question is a real one. In another form other ancient Christians were also raising the same issue when they pressed for the reading of the Acts of the Martyrs in public worship. The prologue to the Passion of Saints Perpetua and Felicity presents the text of their martyrdom expressly as a supplement to the biblical canon. Fear of what might then be smuggled into the official teaching of the Church led to the rigorist exclusiveness of the pseudo-Gelasian Decree, the author of which (according to von Dobschütz, a private individual working at Rome in the sixth century) says that 'with a singular caution' the Roman church does not read such Acts in the liturgy.[2] Perhaps in reply, the prologue to the contemporary Passion of St. Anastasia has a vigorous defence of the right to read the Acts of the Martyrs in church.[3]

Priscillian never has recourse to this weak argument from the supplementary services which the Church found it necessary to have in order to control the popular cult of the martyrs. For him the concept of revelation is essentially wider than the biblical canon. In short, Priscillian's strong thesis is that the stress which Christian theology of his time has come to place upon the unique

---

[1] *Liber numerorum* 13 (PL 83. 192–3).

[2] A. Thiel, *Epistolae romanorum pontificum* (1868), p. 458; von Dobschütz's edition in *TU* 38. 4 (1912).

[3] See the text in H. Delehaye, *Étude sur le legendier romain* (1936), p. 221. It is seen as a deliberate retort to the *Decretum Gelasianum* by B. de Gaiffier, *Anal. Boll.* 82 (1964), 341–53.

The wide acceptability of orthodox apocrypha in ascetic circles may be seen from the familiarity with the *Visio Pauli* shown both in the *Regula Magistri* and by Caesarius of Arles; see B. Fischer in *Vigiliae Christianae* 5 (1951), 84–7. *Reg. Mag.* 72 also assumes knowledge of the Acts of Andrew and the Acts of John.

and the particular, in consequence of its defensive understanding of the incarnation, has led the Church into exclusiveness and rigidity and has blinded it to the universal elements in the Gospel. He gives this thesis a sharp polemical thrust. He believes that only a bigoted clericalism can treat revelation as cabined and confined within the constricting borders of the canonical books admitted to the lectionary: 'Who would not rejoice to know Christ has been spoken of not by a few prophets but by all? Or who is so narrow and sterile that, while he believes the incredible miracle of the virginal birth both in conception and in parturition, yet he does not think the divine secrets are proclaimed to all the world and to every man.' Such a man's attitude is like that of the Pharisees trying to silence the cries of Hosanna (iii, p. 53, 22 ff.). The truth is that Christ is the subject of all prophecy without exception. 'I boldly declare the truth that the devil so dislikes: every man knew that God would come in the flesh, not to mention those whom God put in the family tree (*dispositio*) of his genealogy' (iii, p. 55, 3 ff.). We meet again here Priscillian's conviction that the gospel genealogies of Jesus are rich in theological significance. Hilary's commentary on St. Matthew anticipates Priscillian in seeing the genealogies as showing the way to faith in the divinity of Christ; and the same idea reappears in the Monarchian prologues.[1] But the third tractate finds in the genealogies a radical universalism which looks beyond the exclusiveness and particularity of the Old Testament for evidence of the expectation of the incarnation. The first tractate mentions the genealogy of Jesus in the context of the theme of universal prophecy (i, p. 32, 2 ff.), and the tenth tractate specially mentions Ruth the Moabitess who 'meruit divinum genus in conceptibus' (x, p. 101, 17). The God who came into flesh and showed his name to be Jesus was in divers ways and at divers times saving his people from the very beginning and showing himself to our fathers (i, p. 28, 11–13). Ambrosiaster has the point:[2] 'ex multis et diversis incarnatio Christi consistit ut, quia ex uno diversi esse coeperunt, de omnibus corpulentiam traheret, de Iudaeis et gentibus et de dignis et indignis . . .'

Hilary taught that salvation hangs on the confession of Christ's

---

[1] Hilary, *In Matt.* 1–2 (*PL* 9. 919–21). On the Monarchian prologues see below p. 102.

[2] *CSEL* 50. 431. Likewise Jerome, *in Ezech.* xiii p. 529.

deity, and that to deny Christ to be divine is the unpardonable sin.[1] Priscillian has one simple criterion for judging the acceptability of an apocryphal document, namely, whether it is found to teach the divinity of Christ (i, p. 30, 13; ii, p. 41, 25). 'He who does not love Christ is anathema maranatha' (iii, p. 56, 25). One must confess the God Christ; 'Christus deus' is a formula repeated some thirty times in the tracts.[2] He is 'God coming in the flesh', 'God suffering in the flesh', 'deus in carne' (p. 28, 12–13; p. 60, 4; p. 61, 8; p. 75, 3; p. 102, 7), 'passus in carne' (p. 39, 13; p. 49, 4; p. 71, 8; p. 72, 3), 'passurus deus' (p. 48, 10; p. 71, 15). But he is also 'homo hominum' (i, p. 24, 13; cf. vii, p. 82, 18).

The 'Christus deus' formula is not distinctive to Priscillian. Several instances of the same way of speaking occur in his Italian contemporary Filastrius of Brescia.[3] In the travel diary of Egeria the usual formula is 'deus noster Iesus'.[4]

The Christian confession for the Priscillianists is that Christ is God and man. 'Our God assumes flesh taking to himself the form of God and man, that is of divine soul and earthly flesh' (vi, p. 74, 8–9). The phrase reminds one of Hilary's censure of heretics who say that God the Word became soul to the physical body of Jesus.[5] Christ does some things as God—rising again, declaring that he will sit at God's right hand, promising paradise to the dying thief. Other things he does as man—fearing in Gethsemane, complaining of dereliction in his passion. He is called son; yet Joseph is not his father. Mary his mother remains a virgin not only before and in conception but in and after the process of birth.[6] How paradoxical and contrary to human intelligence is the conjunction of virginity and birth, death and eternity, fear and liberty (vi, p. 74, 14 ff.).

In the petition to pope Damasus the Priscillianist bishops set out their baptismal creed, farced with biblical citations to justify and illustrate each clause. As a creed it has the special interest of

[1] Hilary, *De Trin.* 6. 24; *In Matt.* 5. 15; 12. 17.
[2] i, pp. 8, 18; 9, 27; 13, 16–17; 16, 20 and 28; 21, 12; 22, 1; 23, 16; 25, 13; 27, 12; 30, 13–16; 32, 1; 33, 5; ii, pp. 35, 7; 38, 13–16; 39, 13; iii, pp. 49, 4; 51, 19; 55, 22; 56, 14; iv, p. 61, 8; vi, p. 74, 8; vii, pp. 82, 16; 83, 3; x, pp. 92, 13; 93, 3.
[3] Filastrius 50. 1; 64. 2; 91. 2; 122. 3; 128. 3 and 9.
[4] Egeria, *Itin.* 3. 2; 10. 2; 18. 1; 19. 2.
[5] *De Trinitate* 10. 50 f.
[6] For Hilary's insistence on Mary's perpetual virginity see *In Matt.* 1. 3.

being the earliest Spanish example, but has marked affinities with later Spanish creeds preserved from the Visigothic period,[1] so that it is safe to assume that it is far from a private invention of Priscillian himself. But the creed as a whole is interpreted to mean that Christ, who is all in all, is one God with threefold power (ii, p. 37, 23–4). The third tractate, while principally concerned with defending the study of apocryphal texts, likewise affirms the Christian faith in Father, Son, and Spirit to be belief in one God Christ: he is God, Son of God, Saviour, was born in the flesh, suffered and rose for the love of mankind. Moreover, 'when giving to his apostles the creed ('symbolum'), which was, is and was to be in the future, in himself and in his creed he showed the name of the Father to be Son and of the Son to be Father, lest the error of the Binionites should prevail' (iii, p. 49, 5–8). The abusive term 'Binionitae' occurs also in the first tractate (i, p. 5, 10). It is Priscillian's rejoinder to a charge of being a 'Unionita', a term applied to Sabellius by one source which shows signs of having drawn upon Ithacius' book.[2] The proposition that the name of the Father is Son and of the Son Father recalls the Monarchian language of the apocryphal Acts of John (above, p. 78). The anonymous treatise *De Trinitate fidei catholicae*, edited by Morin (below, p. 100), actually includes the words as a quotation from 'the apostle': 'Ait enim apostolus, Nomen patris est filius, itemque filii pater.'[3] It is very possible that the sentence is a quotation from a part of the Acts of John which has not been otherwise transmitted, in which the risen Lord imparted to the apostles the word of a creed.

For Priscillian the distinction between God and Christ is like the distinction between mind and speech ('sensus' and 'sermo').[4] The incarnation means that God is 'seen on earth' (Baruch 3 : 38, cited in the first three and fifth tractates, and as the opening sentence of *De Trinitate fidei catholicae*).

Priscillian's emphatic language about the simple identity of Christ as God goes with a rejection of a restrictively Christocentric

[1] See Hahn, *Bibliothek der Symbole und Glaubensregeln der alten Kirche* (3rd edn., 1897), pp. 64–9.
[2] Pseudo-Jerome, *Indiculus de haeresibus*, a work of about 400 which drew on Ithacius' apologia (below, p. 203). Here the thirty-ninth heretic is 'Sabellius qui et Patripassianus, idem et Unionita' (*PL* 81. 642B).
[3] Morin, *Études, textes, découvertes* (1913), p. 193, line 25; *PL Suppl.* ii. 1499.
[4] vi, p. 75, 3–4; x, p. 94, 5–6.

view of divine activity which treats the incarnation, with the specifically biblical revelation that leads up to it and follows on from it, as unique because exclusive. Christ, he affirms repeatedly, is in all creation. 'Nothing is outside of him, he is one in all things' (vi, p. 75, 8). Such language is shared with contemporary writers like Ambrosiaster.[1] Priscillian wants to say that Christ is the divine force in the cosmos as a whole (ii, p. 37, 23–4; v, p. 66, 18–22; vi, p. 71, 21 ff.; p. 77, 20), at work in all the energy and vitality of nature (xi, p. 104, 29). Christ has been 'made all things for us' (vi, p. 71, 3 ff.). He is the first principle ('principium', i, p. 16, 11) and first cause of all things, 'origo omnium', who at the same time can be affirmed to be himself without beginning ('sine principio', vi, p. 71, 23). Accordingly, the sixth tractate declares that 'the unbegettable is born'— 'innascibilis nascitur' (p. 74, 13).

The term 'unbegettable' or 'unbegotten' had been made a matter of technical dispute in the Arian controversy by Eunomius' radical thesis that, if the Father is unbegotten and the Son begotten, this is a fundamental unlikeness between them which must be the starting-point of serious theology. Hilary of Poitiers had wrestled with the question. He criticizes the term 'innascibilis' as being unscriptural and therefore no substitute for 'Father'. He concedes that the Son does not share in the supreme majesty of being unbegotten, but affirms that this does not constitute a difference of nature.[2]

Priscillian is not interested in the distinctions within the Holy Trinity which both Eunomius and Hilary, in different ways, wish to bring out. He has a passing and quite unimportant attack on Arianism, on which his information seems short (i, p. 23, 14). But he does not stand to affirm the 'equality' of the Son to the Father in the manner and terminology of Hilary (see especially *De synodis* 72) or Ambrosiaster.[3] Arianism is a distant cloud on his horizon. To Priscillian, or at least the author of the sixth tractate, 'innascibilis' is simply God who is without beginning by definition. The term is as true of the Son as of the Father. Indeed, the Old Latin version of 1 Pet. 1 : 20 expressly says of

[1] *Quaest.* 1. 2 (*CSEL* 50. 13): 'est deus . . . spiritus natura simplex, lux inaccessibilis . . . . extra quem nihil est, immo in quo sunt omnia . . . . nihil est quod non eius est.'

[2] *Contra Constantium* 16 (PL 10. 594); *De Trinitate* 9. 56–7.

[3] *Quaest.* 97. 2 and 11.

Christ 'sine initio manens in patre'.[1] The sixth tractate emphasizes that Christ is without either beginning or end (p. 72, 1). Questions about time and eternity do not enter the discussion. In the 'innascibilis' of the sixth tractate only a hostile inquisitor would seriously find fault with the thought being expressed. Nevertheless, it may be noted that in the gnostic tract from Nag-Hammadi, entitled by its editors *De supernis*, the Son is said to be without beginning and unbegotten.[2]

Christian doctrine is for Priscillian a matter of authority. It has a sure and solid foundation in holy scripture which is not a book that man has chosen because he happens to like it but one given by God (iii, p. 48, 18). The characteristic of heresy is to prefer one's individual preference to the authority of God. So heretics love to debate and dispute. Echoing Tertullian, Priscillian affirms that if they knew what faith is, they would hold nothing beyond the creed. To dispute about the creed rather than simply to believe it is to violate its seal ('designare symbolum').[3] The 27th canon likewise proclaims that 'questions and contentions subvert rather than edify'. The prologue to the canons contrasts the logic-chopping of the controversialists with the simple truth conveyed by the authority of scripture.

It does not occur to Priscillian that there might be controversy in his own interpretation of the creed. He is confidently and stridently assertive that it means one God, totally present throughout creation, wholly present as incarnate Lord. The oneness of the Father in the Son and of the Son in the Father means one God, 'transcendent and immanent, enfolding and pervading' ('supereminens et internus et circumfusus et infusus in omnia'), invisible in the Father, visible in the Son and the Holy Spirit united for the work of the two ('unitus in opus duorum'): xi, p. 103, 14–20. Here the terms for transcendence and immanence are borrowed from Hilary, *De Trinitate*, 1. 6. It is remarkable that a theologian so deeply indebted to Hilary should have ended with so strong a Monarchianism.

---

[1] See the Oxford Vulgate, ed. Wordsworth and White, iii. 279, or the Beuron *Vetus Latina*, ed. Thiele.

[2] *Tractatus tripartitus, pars I De supernis*, ed. R. Kasser, M. Malinine, H.-C. Puech, G. Quispel, J. Zandee (Bern, 1973), p. 58, 7–8. I know no evidence that the Manichees used such language.

[3] 'designare' or 'dissignare' meaning 'corrupt' is also found in the Mozarabic *Liber ordinum*, col. 74 Férotin.

In the passage of the first tractate where the Binionites are attacked, monotheism is underpinned not only by texts from the Old Testament but also by the *Comma Johanneum*, the interpolation of the three heavenly witnesses in the first epistle of John (5 : 7–8). Priscillian is the first writer to provide certain attestation of the interpolated text which, in the form cited by him, ended 'and these three are one in Christ Jesus'. However, the case for thinking Priscillian himself the author of the interpolation carries no conviction.[1] It is surely older (Cyprian, *De Unitate* 6, comes close to it), a modification of the text made in the West at a time when the Monarchian controversy was raging during the third century.

The first tractate disowns a long list of heresies (above, p. 55), and it is a fair presumption that Ithacius was accusing Priscillian of several of them. It is important that the Patripassians are the first to be put under anathema (i, p. 6, 19 ff.). The Luciferians were suspected of this, and Gregory of Elvira disowns the heresy.[2] Indeed the Patripassians appear as conventional figures in a number of lists of heretics of this period.[3] Nevertheless, Priscillian does not condemn them on the ground that impassibility expresses transcendence but for the reason that Peter said, 'You are the Christ, Son of the living God,' and John said 'He who has the Son has life and he who has not the Son has not life', and Jesus himself says 'I and the Father are one' and 'I in the Father and the Father in me', and the devil in the Gospel confesses 'You are Christ the Son of God.' As a list of proof texts, this catena does not do much to establish the point. All seem relevant to establishing the unity of Father and Son rather than to refuting

---

[1] K. Künstle, *Das comma Johanneum* (1905), argued for this. See the adverse review by Jülicher in *Göttinger gelehrte Anzeigen* 1905, pp. 930 ff., and Harnack's note in the Berlin Academy *Sitzungsberichte* 1915, pp. 572 f. reprinted in *Studien zur Geschichte des Neuen Testaments und der alten Kirche* i (1931), 151–2.

[2] See the confession of faith submitted to the emperor Theodosius by the Luciferian presbyter Faustinus (ed. M. Simonetti, *Corpus Christianorum* 69. 357 = *PL* 13. 79); Gregory of Elvira, *Tract. de libris ss. script.* iii. 33 (p. 27 Bulhart) and especially *De fide* 9 f., on the two editions of which work see now M. Simonetti, 'La doppia redazione del De fide di Gregorio di Elvira', in *Forma Futuri: Studi in onore del Cardinale Michele Pellegrino* (Turin, 1975), pp. 1022–40.

[3] For lists of heretics including Patripassians, cf. Cyprian, *Ep.* 73. 4; the Arian Auxentius' letter on the faith, life, and death of Ulfila, preserved in Maximin, *Contra Ambrosium*, ed. Kauffmann, *Aus der Schule des Wulfila* (1899), p. 74 = *PL Suppl.* i. 704. Patripassians also appear in Optatus 5. 1 (*CSEL* 26. 121) and in the recently printed commentary on St. Paul edited by Frede, *Ein neuer Paulustext und Kommentar* ii (1974), 62, where Rom. 9 : 32 is 'contra patripassianos'.

Patripassianism. The reader is left with the feeling that the author of the first tractate could not easily explain why the Patripassians are wrong. The style is that of a self-taught amateur with a few strongly fixed ideas.

Next follow the puritan followers of Novatian whose error is to think post-baptismal sin can be purged only by repeating baptism, which is agreed to be impossible; the Docetists who deny Jesus Christ has come in the flesh; and the licentious Nicolaitans.

Fifth on Priscillian's list is a surprising item: the man who, or sect which, in expounding the scriptures takes griffins, eagles, asses, elephants, and serpents as symbols of divine worship ('religio') when a correct exegesis must understand them as demonic forces. Priscillian seems to have a rooted objection to those who fail to interpret wild beasts in a sufficiently hateful way. The depth of his feelings may be measured by the extraordinary length of the rambling disquisition that he devotes to the subject, extending to nearly seven pages of print in Schepss. The matter looms larger than anything else in his mind, and he recurs to the subject later (i, p. 26, 13 'nobis leo non est deus').

One possible and, if true, sufficient explanation is that the right exegesis of beasts happened to be a private obsession of a theological autodidact with a lonely mind and an axe to grind, much like those fierce attacks on mistaken interpretations of scripture that enliven the later chapters of the book against heretics by Filastrius, and which led Augustine to comment that Filastrius confused heresies with mere errors from which even the most orthodox are not immune.[1] However, if Priscillian had a particular sect in mind, then it is not likely to have been Manicheism. According to Filastrius, the Manichees take beasts and snakes to be rational beings like men;[2] and they certainly believed in the transmigration of souls into animal bodies.[3] But that can make no sense as the background of Priscillianist polemic in the first tractate. A rather more possible background might be offered by the Barbelognostic text, the *Apocryphon of John* (ch. 41), where the

[1] Augustine, *De haeresibus* 80, 'et alias quidem ipse (Philaster) commemorat, sed mihi appellandae haereses non videntur'. Cf. praef., 'non enim omnis error haeresis est'.
[2] Filastrius 100.
[3] *Acta Archelai* 10, p. 15 Beeson. Cf. Augustine, *C. Faustum* 22. 72, 'the Manichees think that not only pigs but the lowest insects have souls like men'.

mighty Rulers of the seven heavens have zoomorphic faces and
semitic names (Iaoth—lion, Eloaios—ass, Astaphaios—hyena,
Iao—seven-headed serpent, Adonaios—dragon, Adoni—ape,
Sabbataios—flaming fire) parallel to the Ophite scheme described
by Origen.[1] Theodore bar Konai, writing late in the eighth
century but using good sources, describes the Ophite system as
having ten heavens controlled by angels, eight of whom have
animal shapes (pig, lion, panther, camel, weasel, goat, dog, hare).[2]

Another source for the doctrine which the tractate disowns
might be sought in the titleless tract on the origin of the world in
Nag-Hammadi codex II, where various Egyptian animals (phoenix, water-snakes, 'the two bulls', the worm engendered by the
phoenix) are given a gnostic interpretation (codex, p. 122 =
p. 170). But the text is not sufficiently close to Priscillian to be
likely and is not more than an illustration of the gnostic interest
in spiritual bestiaries. Priscillian makes nothing of the phoenix
despite its reputation as model of continence since it reproduces
itself only by its own death and without a partner. Ambrose holds
it up as a model to his flock.[3]

The Origenist ascetic tradition interpreted wild beasts in scripture as devils; e.g. John Cassian's seventh conference (ch. 32).

There is one extant text which supplies an almost exact illustration of the doctrine which Priscillian so elaborately disowns,
and that is the *Physiologus*. This strange work has a complex
textual history.[4] It passed through many recensions. Possibly an
early form of the work may go back to the third or even second
century. The oldest extant Greek recensions do not look earlier

---

[1] Origen, *C. Cels.* vi. 30–1.

[2] H. Pognon, *Inscriptions mandaites des coupes de Khouabir* (1898), pp. 212–14.

[3] *Expl. Ps.* 118. 19. 13 (*CSEL* 62. 428, 18) 'phoenix coitus corporeos ignorat,
libidinis nescit inlecebras.' For a monograph on the work on the origin of the world
see M. Tardieu, *Trois mythes gnostiques* (Paris, 1974); the text is edited by A. Böhlig
and P. Labib, *Deutsche Akademie der Wissenschaften zu Berlin, Institut für Orient-
forschung* 58 (1962), to be used with *The Facsimile Edition of the Nag-Hammadi Codices,
Codex II* (Leiden, 1974), pp. 97–127.

[4] The Greek recensions of the *Physiologus* are edited by F. Sbordone (Milan,
1936). The text of the oldest recension is edited by D. Offermanns, *Beiträge zur
klassische Philologie* 22 (1966), and by D. Kaimakis, ibid. 63 (1974). For an early date
see U. Treu in *ZNW* 57 (1966), 101–4, and R. Riedinger in *Byz. Z.* 66 (1973), 273–307.
One of three Latin recensions is printed by F. J. Carmody, *Physiologus latinus* (Paris,
1939). For a guide to the labyrinthine literature see F. McCulloch, *Mediaeval Latin
and French Bestiaries* (University of N. Carolina Studies in the Romance languages and
literature 33, 1960).

than the fourth century. The first attestation of the Latin version appears at the end of the fourth century. Shortly after Priscillian's time the *Physiologus* is cited by name in Rufinus' tract 'On the Benedictions of the Patriarchs'.[1] In Ambrose's *Hexaemeron* there is a sentence that appears in almost identical wording in one of the Latin recensions; the dependence probably lies on Ambrose's side.[2] The Latin translation is censured in the 'Gelasian Decree' as a heretical production circulating in Ambrose's name.[3] The many spiritual lessons drawn from animals in the *Hexaemeron* would make Ambrose a natural candidate for authorship, but the work also became current under other august names.

According to the plan of the work a succession of beasts (lions, eagles, snakes, lizards, plovers, elephants, etc.) are interpreted as symbols of God, Christ, the Spirit, and of the ascetic conflict with temptation, especially sexual desire (see chapters 9–10, 33, and 41, where this theme is prominent). Not only is the *Physiologus* strongly in favour of celibacy. Its spirituality is one of inward experience to which sacraments appear secondary, in a manner that recalls Messalianism. Moreover, the author used several apocrypha: the Ascension of Isaiah (ch. 1), a Life of Adam and Eve (40), the Acts of Paul and Thecla (17 and 40), possibly also the Acts of John (31) and the Apocalypse of Peter (25).[4] The author believes that in his descent to this world Christ became all things to all dependent beings: an archangel to archangels, an angel to angels, and so down the hierarchy of creation (1). His universalist view of the divine presence immanent in the created order goes with a conviction that in the Church there are many who have only the form of piety without the inward power (13 and 21). Twice he protests against critics who deny that animals declared in the Law to be unclean can be symbols of high spiritual realities (3 and 5). In short, the character of the book would have made it popular reading at Priscillian's nocturnal conventicles for deeper

---

[1] *De bened. patr.* 1. 6 (*PL* 21. 302 = *PG* 12. 257A; ed. Simonetti, *Corpus Christianorum* 20 (1961), 193).

[2] Ambrose, *Hexaem.* xi. 3. 13 (*CSEL* 32. 211, 5 ff.), parallel to *Physiol. lat.* 25, ed. Carmody.

[3] 'Liber Physiologus ab haereticis conscriptus et beati Ambrosii nomine praesignatus, apocryphus' (Thiel, p. 466). Cf. Nicephorus Constant. in Pitra, *Spicilegium Solesm.* iv. 390; but his reference is more probably to a work on the zodiac.

[4] See E. Peterson, 'Die Spiritualität des griechischen Physiologus', repr. from *Byz. Z.* 1954 in his *Frühkirche, Judentum und Gnosis* (1959), pp. 236–53, especially 250–2.

spiritual study. The conjecture may be ventured that the long discussion in the first tractate replies to malicious caricatures based upon the book's currency in Priscillianist circles.

Priscillian's collection of Old Testament texts mentioning wild animals includes an Old Latin mistranslation of Job 38 : 39–40 'Will you hunt out food for lions ?' Priscillian's Latin Bible transliterates the Greek words meaning 'food for lions' to produce a monster, Leosibora (i, p. 11, 19). Augustine's *Annotations on Job* are not parallel to Priscillian's biblical text but interpret the words to refer to the devil. It is possible that Priscillian found the name as title of some mythological figure in an apocryphon.

The last group of heretics to be disavowed are the Manichees. How much the author of the first tractate really knew about them it is hard to say. He is strangely silent about the Manichee doctrine that evil is an ultimate principle of things or that this created world is a confused mixture of good and evil in consequence of primordial conflict between equally balanced light and darkness. The first tractate represents them as those who venerate the sun[1] (i, p. 8, 12; p. 22, 20; cf. ii, p. 39, 9; v, p. 63, 25 ff.), are given to astrology (i, p. 14, 5 ff., p. 26, 19 ff.; cf. v, p. 63, 25 ff.), and offer cultic acts to demons with strange names: Saclas, Nebroel, Samael, Belzebuth, Nasbodeus, Belial (i, p. 17, 9). These names Priscillian treats as different ways of describing one and the same devil (p. 18, 5) who, like God in the title on the cross, is all the same person whether named in Hebrew, Latin, or Greek (p. 18, 6; cf. 26, 4). A second list of mythological gnostic names occurs towards the end of the first tractate (p. 29, 14 ff.). Here appear Armaziel, Mariame, Ioel, Balsamus, Barbilon. It looks as if all these names appeared somewhere in Ithacius' *libellus* of accusation. In every case the names are elsewhere attested in gnostic or magical texts.

The first list of names takes us into the world of the *Apocryphon of John* and a prominent theme in Manichee cosmology where Adam and Eve are the offspring of Saclas and his female consort Nebroel.[2] Saclas is also called Ialdabaoth in the *Hypostasis of the*

---

[1] For the Manichee doctrine of the cult of the sun see the Coptic *Kephalaia* 65, p. 169; Augustine, *Contra Faustum* 20. 1.

[2] *Apocr. Joh.* 41–2; Coptic *Kephalaia* 56, p. 137; Epiphanius, *Panarion* 26. 10; Augustine, *Haer.* 46; Theodoret, *Haer. fab.* i. 26 (*PG* 83. 3770); Theodore bar Konai, p. 191 Pognon; the ninth-century formula for recanting Manichees in *PG* 1. 1464B = Adam, *Texte zum Manichäismus*, 2nd edn., 1969, no. 64, lines 48–9. In the Peratic

Archons and other places such as the *Apocalypse of Adam*.[1] In the
Nag-Hammadi tract entitled the 'Protennoia Trimorphos' we
meet 'Sakla that is Samael Ialdabaoth'.[2] The name Saclas is
derived from the Aramaic *sakla* meaning 'fool'. Samael is commonly found in Jewish and Rabbinic texts as a name for Satan,
e.g. in the *Ascension of Isaiah* i. 8, or the Angel of Death in Targum
Jonathan on Gen. 3 : 6.[3] Saclas–Ialdabaoth–Samael becomes in
gnosticism the arrogant and ignorant Archon who imagines
himself to be supreme, unaware that there is a transcendent power
higher than he is. His female consort Nebroel is also called
Namrael or Nebrod or Nembroth or Nebroe. 'Nebrod' could be
the title of the second document in codex V from Nag-Hammadi
with the sub-title 'the Perfect Nous'.[4] Among the Mandeans her
name becomes Namrus, the world-mother.[5] The co-operation of
Saclas and Nebroel is well attested as part of the Manichee
creation-myth. Ambrosiaster observes that the figure of Saclas as
world-creator comes from an Egyptian cosmogony, and distinguishes this from the Manichee form of the myth in which
Saclas is creator not of the world but of man.[6] (Even into 1975
Saclas survives as the proprietary name of an Italian rat-poison.)

The other names in the first list raise no problems. Belzebuth is
obviously Beelzebul, with a part in Valentinian myth.[7] Nasbodeus
is an evident by-form of the familiar Asmodeus, the demon of
Tobit iii. 8 and 17 and also of the *Testament of Solomon* 5. In the
form Nasmodeus he appears in an old Spanish formula of exorcism in the Mozarabic *Liber ordinum* (Férotin, 80, 9). Belial appears
in the *Apocryphon of John* 40 and in the gnostic book of Baruch,[8]

gnosis described by Hippolytus (*Refut.* 5. 14. 6) Soklas is archon of midnight and a
name of Osiris, and Nebroe has a minor role in the system (5. 14. 3).

[1] *Hypostasis of the Archons* 95. 7; *Apoc. Adae* 41. 6; 42. 10.
[2] Nag-Hammadi codex XIII, p. 39, 27, edited by Y. Janssens in *Le Muséon* 87
(1974), 368–9. There is now a fine paper by G. Scholem, 'Ialdabaoth Reconsidered',
in *Mélanges H.-C. Puech* (Paris, 1974), pp. 405–22. On Saclas' ignorance see *Hypostasis
of the Archons* 86. 20 ff. (English tr. in W. Foerster, *Gnosis*, ed. R. M. Wilson, ii
(1974), 44–5).
[3] On Samael see Scholem's article in *Encylopaedia Judaica* xiv (1972), 719–22.
[4] This is remarked by H. M. Schenke, *Orientalische Literaturzeitung* 69 (1974), 231.
His interpretation is strongly rejected by M. Tardieu in *Le Muséon* 87 (1974),
523–30.
[5] K. Rudolph, *Das Mandäerproblem* i (1960), 184, n. 5.
[6] *Quaestiones* 3. 1 (*CSEL* 50. 21) cf. *Qu.* 106. 1.
[7] Hippolytus, *Refut.* 6. 34. 1.
[8] Hippolytus 5. 26. 4. Cf. J. Maier in *RAC* ix. 633–5 (1974).

besides many occurrences in the Qumran texts and the Testaments of the Twelve Patriarchs.

All the names of the second list are met elsewhere. Armaziel is an angel of light called Harmozel in the *Apocryphon of John*, Armedon in Nag-Hammadi codex XIII, p. 38, 25 (edited by Y. Janssens in *Le Muséon* 87, 1974), and Armages in Irenaeus i. 29. 2 f. (I. 223 Harvey). No doubt the name is ultimately derived from Ahura Mazda. Mariame appears in the Coptic Gospel of Mary and in the Naassene system,[1] and is the only human name in Priscillian's list, the rest being angelic agencies. Ioel, mentioned in Theodoret's important account of the Manichees,[2] is the 'daughter of light' through whom Eve, at first lifeless and motionless, came to share in life and light. In a prayer ascribed to St. Gregory Nazianzen printed by Reitzenstein from the fifteenth-century codex Paris. gr. 2316, Ioel is the angel presiding over sleep.[3] The name may be related to Jobel (meaning in Hebrew a ram, and so a sign of the zodiac) who is a power in the *Apocryphon of John* 40. One manuscript of the *Testament of Solomon* 18. 6 gives a power Ioelet.

Barbelo is a familiar figure in the *Apocryphon of John*. in Irenaeus' account of the Barbelo-gnostics, and in some Nag-Hammadi texts (codex XIII, p. 38, 9). Balsamus is a power invoked in the Greek magical papyri.[4] 'Beelsamen' is Lord of Heaven in the Phoenician mythology of Sanchuniathon as given by Philo of Byblus in Eusebius.[5] Augustine explains that the Punic for Lord is Baal, for heaven Samen, so that in Punic or Phoenician they say Baalsamen for 'Lord of heaven'.[6] Perhaps it is relevant that in a medieval Hebrew text Balsan is the angel who watches over the month Siwan.[7]

The tractates leave no doubt on two major points. They make it quite certain that Priscillian is *not* a member of the Manichee

[1] *Ev. Mariae*, ed. W. Till in *TU* 60 (1955).

[2] *Haer. fab.* 1. 26 (*PG* 83. 380A). On Ioel see A. Böhlig and F. Wisse's edition of the *Gospel of the Egyptians* (Nag-Hammadi Studies iv, 1975), p. 47.

[3] R. Reitzenstein, *Poimandres* (1904, repr. 1922), p. 297.

[4] K. Preisendanz, *PGM* iv. 1019; xii. 494.

[5] Eusebius, *Praep. evang.* i. 10. 7. See Klauser's article 'Baal' in *RAC* i. 1078 and 1106 (recording this passage of Priscillian).

[6] *Locutiones in Heptateuchum, Quaest. jud.* 16 (*Corpus Christianorum* 33, p. 341, ed. Fraipont). Cf. Plautus, *Poen.* 1027: 'Balsamem'.

[7] M. Schwab, 'Vocabulaire de l'angélologie', in *Mémoires de l'Académie des Inscriptions* x. 2 (1897), 196. At p. 294 Schwab notes Nibrael, an angel watching over the month Adar; cf. Mani's Nebroel.

confraternity and indeed regards the Manichees with deep abhorrence. The Manichees are associated with black magic and moral enormity—'turpitudines'—for which they deserve to be 'persecuted with the sword' and, if it were in Priscillian's power, 'sent to Hell' (i, p. 22, 13–17; p. 24, 5), for scripture says 'you shall not suffer magicians to live' (Exod. 22 : 18). In view of the outcome of the trial at Trier there is terrible meaning in these words; and it is even possible that the wretched man wrote his own death-warrant by these two fierce anti-Manichee sentences. At the same time it is also clear that Priscillian is informed about, and interested in, demonology. In one place he seems to feel that his cabbalistic investigations into such occult mysteries require a little justification. He appeals to an acknowledged principle (also stated by Ambrose)[1] when he says that we need to know about darkness that we may desire the Lord's light (i, p. 15, 13)—'ut intellegentes tenebras desideremus lucem domini'. 'We study the scriptures to understand the depth of Satan' (i, p. 13, 24). Priscillian's primary and driving impulse is to discover and share a deeper religious experience than ordinary church services are providing. The impulse seems undoubtedly to have led him into occultism, principally through the quest for mysteries in apocryphal texts, his defence of which is so extended and heartfelt that they are certainly not of peripheral or academic interest in his mind.

Priscillian's disavowal of Manicheism is passionate and surely sincere. Yet his emphatic protest against narrow constriction of the area of God's providential care is in spirit and tone remarkably akin to the language used by Mani, whose claim to present a universal gospel valid for both East and West depends on a generous recognition of the validity of 'prophecy' in the various religious traditions of mankind. To Mani not only the Old Testament but Buddha and Zoroaster are inspired teachers in the advancing religious experience of the human race.[2] In the book Mani dedicated to the king Shapur, son of Ardashir, he lays down his principles :

Wisdom and deeds have always from time to time been brought to mankind by God's messengers. So in one age they have been brought by the messenger called Buddha to India, in another by Zarādusht to

[1] Ambrose, *Expl. Ps.* 35. 1 (*CSEL* 64. 48–9), 'neque enim possumus cognoscere quae sit forma iustitiae, nisi cognoscamus quae sit iniquitatis effigies'.
[2] See *Kephalaia*, introduction, pp. 7–8 and 12 (ed. Polotsky and Böhlig).

Persia, in another by Jesus in the West. Thereupon this revelation
has come down, this prophecy in this last age, through me, Mani,
messenger of the God of truth to Babylonia.[1]

Ephraem Syrus similarly reports that the Manichees 'say about
Hermes in Egypt, and about Plato among the Greeks, and about
Jesus who appeared in Judaea, that "they are Heralds of that
Good One to the world"'.[2] Augustine's account of the Manichee
interpretation of human religious history likewise says that Mani
is held to give the final interpretation of the divine mysteries
taught in symbols in ancient books.[3] His opponent Faustus the
Manichee expresses deeper sympathy for Buddha, Zoroaster, or
Plato than for the Old Testament, which troubles him by its
incompatibility with the teaching of Jesus.[4]

To sum up, the Würzburg tractates leave no doubt that Priscillian, although he has a sombre view of the earthbound fallen
condition of man, disclaims Manicheism with great vehemence;
and there is not the slightest hint to suggest that behind the mask
of the anathemas there lies a secret radical dualist putting up a
smokescreen of verbiage to conceal his real beliefs. Yet at the
same time he betrays interest in several topics that bring him
strangely and disturbingly close to his heretical opponents.
He is deeply interested in the war of the sons of light against the
sons of darkness. He shares to the full the Manichee enthusiasm
for the apocryphal Acts, in which the apostles preach the urgent
gospel of conversion to continence. He makes, as the Manichees
made, a demand for virginity which can nevertheless look toler-
antly on married members enjoying association with the society
in a supporting but inferior role.[5] But it is not difficult to per-
ceive that the apocryphal Acts mean more to Priscillian than a
convenient authority for the ideal of sexual abstinence, a thesis
for which he could surely have found all the authority he wanted
in 1 Cor. 7 without needing to go outside the catholic canon. His

[1] Mani, *Shābūhragān*, cited by Al-Biruni, *Chronology of Ancient Nations* (a work of
c. A.D. 1000), transl. E. Sachau (London, 1879), p. 190; Adam, *Texte*[2], no. 3a.
[2] C. W. Mitchell, *S. Ephrem's Prose Refutations* ii (1921, repr. 1969), p. xcviii.
[3] Augustine, *Contra epistulam Fundamenti* 23 (*CSEL* 25. 221, 2 ff.)
[4] See Faustus in Aug. *C. Faustum* 4. 1; 12. 1 (no prophecies in O.T.); esp. 13. 1
(the Sibyl, Hermes Trismegistus, or Orpheus more helpful than the Hebrew
prophets). But Enoch and Seth are held in high regard (*C. Faust.* 19. 3). 'Sethel'
(= Seth) is an important power for good in the *Kephalaia*.
[5] Augustine, *C. Faustum* 15. 7; esp. 30. 6. For the Manichee call for renunciation
see Faustus in 5. 1 and 5.

defence of his use of apocrypha is not merely a debating point (in which, on the merits of his case, in logic he certainly defeats his critics). Priscillian's heart is involved in this issue, not just his head. In short, everything falls into place if the apocryphal Acts have become not only an inspiration to adepts of the ascetic ideal but also the prime symbol of the principle that divine truth can be found outside the exclusive, narrow limits of the official documents which, for excellent and undisputed reasons of numerological mysticism, have been accepted as the scriptures read in the lectionary. That principle mattered to Priscillian at least as much as virginity.

There can be no doubt that Priscillian comes very close to the generous universalism of Mani when, with the strong consciousness of proclaiming an unpopular truth that Satan is straining every nerve to suppress, he declares twice over that 'every man knew that God would come in the flesh' (iii, p. 55, 3 ff. cf. iii, p. 54, 2–3). As against the catholic insistence on authority, the Manichees claimed to represent liberty (Aug. *C. Faust.* 22. 15). It appears from Augustine's *Contra Faustum* (20. 4) that the Manichees were critical of calendrical observances. They also believed Christ to be immanent in all the natural order (*C. Faust.* 2. 5). The mortal Jesus, declared Faustus, hangs from every tree; orthodox Christianity, with its characteristic insistence on the particular and exclusive, attaches to eucharistic bread and wine the sacredness that Manichees find in everything (20. 2).

These striking parallels do not add up to a demonstration that Priscillian is a crypto-Manichee. They show how genuinely vulnerable he is to orthodox anxieties about his position.

The evidence suggests, in short, that while Priscillian was not a Manichee, his doctrine is not, as has been suggested by W. Schatz and others, explicable simply in terms of ascetic influences from the Egyptian desert. He has a place in the long line of Christians who have sought for hidden mysteries in the Bible or in nature, anticipating writers like Vincent of Beauvais or St. Albert the Great (among many great names) who have sought to reconcile alchemy with their faith or even, as in the case of the French bishop Jean-Albert Bélin (1659), assimilating alchemy with the liturgy of the mass.[1]

---

[1] Cf. Michel Noize, 'Le Grand Œuvre: liturgie de l'alchimie chrétienne', *Revue de l'histoire des religions* 186 (1974), 149–83.

For the fascination of Priscillian's age with the occult there is an explicit testimony in the *Consultationes Zacchaei et Apollonii* 2. 19, where the Christian Zacchaeus tells his philosophical interlocutor Apollonius to resist the temptation of curiosity and to be content with what is revealed in the canonical scriptures; those whom the devil cannot deceive by sins of the flesh he trips up by 'occulta scientia', urging on learned men 'to inquire into the stone that lies under the stone—that they may discover a serpent.'[1] The extent to which a highly placed and educated man of this age could be absorbed in occultism and peasant magic is illustrated on almost any page of the long treatise *De medicamentis* by the Christian writer Marcellus of Bordeaux, master of the offices under Theodosius I, whose work abounds in healing recipes dependent for their power on magical words and the observance of days assigned to particular planets. In comparison with Marcellus Priscillian seems an austere rationalist.

The treatise on the Trinity

In a ninth-century manuscript at Laon (cod. 113) C. H. Turner found an unprinted tract on the doctrine of the Trinity entitled 'De Trinitate fidei catholicae', and drew the attention of Dom Germain Morin to the text as worthy of printing among his anecdota. At first little interested in the content, in 1908 Morin sent a transcript to Theodor Zahn, who pointed out its affinities with the Würzburg tractates and suggested a Priscillianist origin. Morin printed it with an introduction in 1913, and it was reprinted by A. Hamman in 1962.[2] Morin decisively agreed with Zahn that the treatise must be Priscillianist, and argued from some close resemblances in thought and diction with the Würzburg tractates that the treatise could be by the same writer as the author of those documents, whom Morin at first believed to be Priscillian but then thought to be bishop Instantius (above, p. 48). The transmission of the treatise by a solitary manuscript is indifferent. Cardinal Mercati made some suggestions, mainly

---

[1] *PL* 20. 1145C.

[2] G. Morin, *Études, textes, découvertes* (1913), pp. 151–205; 'Un traité priscillianiste inédit sur la Trinité', *Revue Bénéd.* 26 (1909), 255–80. *PL Suppl.* ii. 1487–1507. Discussion by J. Pérez de Urbel, 'La teología trinitaria en la contienda priscilianista', *Revista española de Teología* 6 (1946), 589–606, and especially A. Orbe, 'Doctrina trinitaria del anónimo priscilianista De trinitate fidei catholicae', *Gregorianum* 49 (1968), 510–62. Vollmann, *Studien*, p. 71, doubts the Priscillianist origin of the tract, surely mistakenly.

good, for the amelioration of the corrupt text.[1] The general
sense, however, is usually not doubtful.

The treatise begins with one of the favourite texts of the tractates in reference to the Monarchian understanding of the incarnation, Baruch 3 : 38 'in terris visus est et inter homines conver-
satus est'. In Christ the Father is known. God is invisible; none
has seen him at any time. So he came in name and form such that
he could make himself known. He comes as Son of the Father and
as firstborn among brothers. He says in Ps. 21 : 23, 'I will proclaim your name to my brothers', but in Isa. 8 : 18 'Behold, I
and the sons whom God gave me'. The same person cannot have
both sons and brothers unless he is a father and a son. Accordingly,
Father and Son are names for the same person. Again the Johannine prologue says God is Word. 'Word' implies unity, the unity
of mind and uttered speech. *Sensus* and *verbum* cannot be separated.
The Father is mind, the Son word.[2]

The analogy for the Trinity is throughout psychological rather
than social. We are will, *virtus*, wisdom, speech, life; many things
in one person.

All that has come from God remains in God, because God is
life, without beginning and without end. It is mere secular
sophistry to say that life, which is in God and is made from
God, once was not in God. The life of the Father and the Son is
the Holy Spirit. That means, the life coming from the Father is
known in the Son. So Father and Son are one God.

There is no distinction between Father and Son as impassible
and passible. The Son too is impassible. He says, 'I am in the
Father and the Father in me'. This does not mean that they are
like two vessels the contents of which are poured from one into
the other. There are those who preach two. They teach equality
and the sharing of divinity in two. But they do not give both
the same rank and power.

There is a mystery of the name of the Father and of the name of
the Son. 'The apostle says, "The name of the Father is Son and
the name of the Son is Father"' (above, p. 87). This secret name
is 'Principium', Beginning, for it is applied to both Father and
Son. The Son reveals every secret of the name of God.

---

[1] G. Mercati, *Opere minori* iii (*Studi e testi* 78, 1937), pp. 502–10.
[2] This is exactly the doctrine which in the second edition of his *De fide* Gregory of
Elvira had to disown (above p. 90, n. 2).

The consistently Monarchian tendency of the treatise and its contacts with the Würzburg tracts in idea and language make it highly probable that it should be ascribed to the Priscillianist circle. It need not be ascribed to Priscillian himself, but may belong to a stage in the controversy where the group's Trinitarian doctrine continues to be under fire and requires defence.

The Monarchian prologues to the four Gospels

Many manuscripts of the Vulgate, including early codices, include a prologue to each of the four Gospels which is certainly not the work of Jerome. In fact the prologues presuppose a pre-Hieronymian text and, as the prologue to St. John shows, were composed for an Old Latin edition in which the gospels stood in their normal Old Latin order, Matthew, John, Luke, Mark. A critical edition of the prologues was given by John Wordsworth in the Oxford Vulgate, volume I (1889–98),[1] and the first serious essays in their historical evaluation were made by E. von Dobschütz, *Studien zur Textkritik der Vulgata* (Leipzig, 1894), and P. Corssen, *Monarchianische Prologe zu den vier Evangelien* (Leipzig, 1896), both of whom thought the prologues originated at the time of the Monarchian controversy about A.D. 200. Von Dobschütz thought them a poor translation of a Greek original, but Corssen saw (correctly) that they were first composed in Latin. Samuel Berger dissented from this dating, and ascribed them to the fourth century.[2] In a review of Corssen in 1897 Adolf Hilgenfeld noticed in passing, but without drawing any further conclusions, that the prologues had parallels in the Priscillianist tractates.[3] Nevertheless, in 1908 it was virtually thunder from a clear sky when Dom John Chapman's *Notes on the Early History of the Vulgate Gospels* amazed the learned world with

---

[1] A critical edition is also given by Corssen and Chapman, and in D. de Bruyne, *Préfaces de la Bible latine* (Namur, 1920), pp. 170–4; a convenient cheap text in H. Lietzmann, *Das Muratorische Fragment und die monarchianischen Prologe zu den Evangelien, Kleine Texte* I (1902), often reprinted. K. Aland, *Synopsis Quattuor Evangeliorum* (Stuttgart, 1964), pp. 547–8, prints Wordsworth's text, from which Chapman diverges. The prologues are also extant in an Arabic version made in Spain: see K. Vollers and E. von Dobschütz in *ZDMG* 56 (1902), 633–46; F. Taeschner in *Oriens Christianus* 32 (1933), 80–99.

[2] S. Berger, *Les Préfaces jointes aux livres de la Bible dans les manuscrits de la Vulgate*, Mémoire Posthume, Mémoires présentés à l'Académie des Inscriptions et Belles-Lettres, 1er série, xi. 2 (1902), 9–10.

[3] *Z. wiss. Theol.* 40 (1897), 439, n. 1.

a virtually mathematical demonstration that the prologues come from a Priscillianist milieu and have the closest parallels in thought and diction with the Würzburg tractates.[1] While Chapman's book failed to carry conviction in his account of the transmission of the Vulgate, the chapters on the prologues and Priscillian compelled the assent of almost all his readers.[2] At first sight the prologues appear nothing but inspissated darkness, so opaque to the understanding that no tolerable sense can be extracted from them (hence superfluous theories of a bad Latin translator trying to interpret a Greek original). Chapman saw that in the light of the Würzburg tractates the prologues can be made to yield a consistent and, for the most part, satisfactory sense, even if that sense is at times oracular. The author of the prologues had a strongly Monarchian theology which is unambiguous. At the same time he did not wish to be too comprehensible.

The prologue to St. Matthew has an interpretation of the genealogy of Jesus which is parallel to that in the Würzburg tractates (especially iii, p. 55) and indeed makes it possible to see what the author of the third tractate was driving at. The prologue explains that Christ's birth has two aspects, first as a physical Jew—'of fleshly circumcision'—and secondly of the election that is according to the heart. In either case Christ is in the fathers ('in patribus').

The doctrine here is akin to that of the third tractate (p. 52, 19–20) where the non-canonical 4 Esdras is authority for the view that 'the Holy Spirit from the beginning of the world has entered the heart of the elect man'. The 67th canon shows Priscillian's interest in the argument of Romans 2 concerning true circumcision of the heart replacing that of the Mosaic law. A passage near the end of the first tractate also makes an allusion

---

[1] Chapman published a preliminary statement of his conclusion in *Rev. Bénéd.* July 1906, pp. 335–49.

[2] e.g. F. C. Burkitt, *JTS* 10 (1909), 282. Harnack, who had accepted the view that the prologues belong to the early third century (*Die Chronologie der altchristlichen Litteratur bis Eusebius* ii (1904), 204–6), capitulated to Chapman's argument (*Sitzungsberichte der preussische Akademie der Wissenschaften* 1928, phil. hist. Kl., p. 322). D. de Bruyne, at first unconvinced (*Rev. Bénéd.* 26 (1909), 113–14), became a strong supporter (ibid. 40 (1928), 210). A judicious survey by J. Regul, *Die antimarcionitische Evangelienprologe* (Freiburg i.B., 1969), pp. 207 ff., concludes in favour of Priscillianist origin. Babut (*Priscillien*, pp. 294–308) argued for a later, fifth-century Priscillianist, so preserving the picture of his hero as a simple evangelical.

(of marvellous obscurity) to the gospel genealogy as being in some way related to the Lord's predestination of his elect from the beginning of the world and to the universal outpouring of the prophetic Spirit (i, p. 32, 2 ff.).

The prologue continues that the gospel genealogy, based on the sacred number fourteen, both showed what Christ was and also witnessed to his working from the beginning. This helps to explain the thesis of the third tractate that the genealogy not only fixes the number of the canon but also gives evidence of faith in the divine nature (of Jesus) iii, p. 55, 8 (above, p. 85).

Christ ('deus Christus') is the time, order, number, arrangement ('dispositio') and reason of all things. The word 'dispositio' and the asyndeton are highly characteristic of the tractates. So also is the belief in the immanence of Christ throughout the created order.

There follows a passage of rare obscurity, in which the author of the prologue evidently took high delight. The redemptive incarnation and atonement, in which Christ 'affixed all things to the cross', was undertaken 'that he might restore the name of Father in the fathers to the Son, and the name of Son to the Father in the sons, without beginning, without end, showing himself to be one with the Father, because he is One ('unus')'. Chapman's interpretation rises to the occasion:

In the genealogy each name is that of a son, but is repeated as the name of a father: . . . *genuit Isaac, Isaac autem genuit* . . .' etc., except in the case of the first name and the last. . . . The genealogy is a sort of tunnel; what comes out at the end was what was put in at the beginning: Christ was *in His fathers, in patribus Christus*, and at His resurrection He, who was the last term of the genealogy, identified himself with the first term, the Father. Thus the list began with God, who is then in all the succession of fathers as a father. It ends in Christ, who was in all the succession of sons as a son. But when His resurrection identifies Him with the Father, he 'restores the name of Father to Himself, the Son, in the whole line of fathers, and the name of Son to the Father in the whole line of sons.' . . . It could not be said that the Father was in all the fathers, and the Son in all the sons, without identifying Father and Son, for in the list the same persons are successively named son and father.

The doctrine that Christ wrought redemption by 'fixing all things to the cross' is characteristic of the Würzburg tractates (i, p. 16, 23; especially iv, p. 60, 1–7; vi, p. 77, 16; and Orosius' fragment on the *chirographum*, below, p. 192).

The prologue concludes that the Gospel helps seekers to know the 'beginning, middle, and end' by understanding 'the apostle's calling, the work of the Gospel, the love of God born in the flesh'. It has not been the author's intention to be too clear in this prologue, but to spur seekers to be diligent in observing the plan to which God works.

The formula 'beginning, middle, and end' is a cliché in the tractates on several occasions (ii, p. 36, 4–5; v, p. 67, 19–24; vi, p. 78, 19–20; p. 81, 3; x, p. 93, 13).

The prologue to St. John stands next in the normal order of the Old Latin Bible. The transmission of the prologues with the Vulgate, where Jerome gave the Gospels in the familiar order, led to some alteration of the text at this point, since the author of the prologue saw deep significance in the placing of John in the second place, though chronologically the last, much as the eighth and tenth tractates see significance in the special order of the Psalms (viii, pp. 87–8; x, p. 100). In the appendix to Ambrosiaster's *Quaestiones* (*CSEL* 50. 430. 19) it is explained that the order of the canonical Gospels is theological rather than chronological.

The principal theme of the Johannine prologue is celibacy. The story of the marriage at Cana is retold to justify not the sanctification of marriage by Christ's presence and first miracle that he wrought but virginity. The apostle John turns out to have been the bridegroom at the wedding at Cana, but the Lord called him away to virginity (a tradition known also to Jerome, *Adv. Iovin.* i. 26, 'Ioannes apostolus, maritus et virgo'). The wine at the wedding ran out because Christ was invited. The new wine that he miraculously created is symbol of the new life of celibacy to which the higher Christian is called. Probably this retelling of the marriage feast is derived from the apocryphal Acts of John. At least that is certainly the source of a later part of the prologue which tells how John, on the approach of his death, descended into his grave and prayed (an episode from the Acts of John also mentioned by Augustine, *Tr. Jo.* 124. 2). The thesis that the newness of the Gospel and the passing away of the old signify the call to celibacy is found in the sixth tractate (pp. 72 and 79).

Because John was a virgin, he was the disciple whom God

loved more than the others. Moreover, when he went to the cross God commended his mother to him, that the Virgin might be guarded by a virgin. He wrote his Gospel in Asia after having written the Apocalypse on Patmos, so that the virgin author in the Apocalypse, where Christ says 'I am Alpha and Omega', might attribute the incorruptible end to the same God to whom the incorruptible beginning is attributed in Genesis. In other words, Christ is the Creator, and God is one.

The prologue concludes by reflecting on the significance of the Gospel being placed second, this being a special honour to reward virginity, but tantalizingly adding that no detailed explanation of the order of the canonical books is given here, to stimulate the seeker to research and to leave the path clear for God himself to teach him.

The proposition that John's virginity was the reason why Christ loved him more than the others and also entrusted to him his Virgin Mother is one of the more provocative and characteristic Priscillianist ideas which came to have a history. For it achieved admission to the Latin liturgy,[1] becoming the basis of the Responsory at mattins on the feast of St. John the Evangelist on 27 December, where it may be read in the Roman Breviary:

R. Diligebat autem eum Jesus, quoniam specialis praerogativa castitatis ampliori dilectione fecerat dignum: Quia virgo electus ab ipso, virgo in aevum permansit.

V. In cruce denique moriturus, huic Matrem suam virginem virgini commendavit.

St. Luke was likewise unmarried. He is strangely said to have died in Bithynia.[2] (The usual tradition would be Boeotia.) He wrote after Matthew and Mark for three reasons: first, because of his place (not further explained) in the order of the Old Latin canon; secondly, to keep Greek Christians from Judaism and from heresy (so he writes for Theophilus); thirdly, to manifest the perfection of God of whom prophecy declared that he would come into flesh. The particular purpose of the Gospel is conveyed by the genealogy. Unlike Matthew, who began from Abraham and traced the line through David to Christ, Luke starts from the perfection of the generation fulfilled in Christ and runs back to

---

[1] Cf. A. Baumstark in *Jahrbuch für Liturgiewissenschaft* 12 (1932), 194–7.

[2] There is a good note on this variant by T. Zahn, *Kommentar zum Neuen Testament* iii, *Das Evangelium des Lucas* (1913), p. 17, n. 3.

God through David's son Nathan. From pondering on the symbolism of this, seekers may discern what the evangelist had apprehended, namely that the indivisible God ('indispartibilis deus'), to proclaim his Christ among men, made the work of the perfect man return to himself by David's son, and also by David the father, offered in Christ a way to those who come to him (language reminiscent of *Tract*. xi, p. 103, 9–11).

The prologue's meaning is less than clear. The contrast between the Matthaean and Lucan genealogies seems to be the starting-point of the author's speculation. In Matthew the line is traced through David's son Solomon, who does not appear in Luke's tree. The return back to God through David's son Nathan may signify the role of the Son as mediator and pioneer, through whom the perfect man may ascend to the Father. David, on the other hand, symbolizes the initiative of the Father in opening a path through Christ the Son. Whatever speculative extravagance may be hidden here is less important to discover than the truth the prologue chiefly derives from the genealogy, namely the Monarchian doctrine of God, the mutual interchangeability of the symbolic titles Father and Son.

The prologue continues with a reference to Luke's authorship of the Acts. After the Ascension, 'God being full into God' ('deo in deum pleno') and the son of perdition dead, the elect number of apostles was completed by the lot of the Lord, and Paul's conversion brought the consummation of the Acts of the Apostles. On these topics much more might be said for seekers, but they can find it out for themselves. 'We avoid public curiosity less we should seem not so much to show God to willing inquirers as to betray him to scorners.'

The reference to the Ascension is reminiscent of the first tractate (p. 6) 'et ascendens in caelos venientibus ad se iter construit, totus in patre et pater in ipso'. The last sentence of the prologue is the author's strongest statement that he regards his doctrine as in part esoteric because liable to provoke hostile reaction.

The prologue to St. Mark, 'the evangelist of God', explains that he was Peter's son by baptism, and before his conversion a Levite (being cousin to the Levite Barnabas, Acts 4: 36; Col. 4: 10) and a priest in Israel. He begins his Gospel with the prophet's cry. He put first John the Baptist, son of Zacharias the priest, to show his own Levitical order. He speaks of the 'cry' ('vox') to show not merely 'the Word made flesh' but 'the body of the Lord in all things ensouled by the word of the divine voice' ('corpus domini in omnia per verbum divinae vocis animatum').

The implied doctrine here looks close to the Christology of the seventh tractate (p. 74, 9) where 'our God assumed flesh, taking to himself the form of God and man, that is of a divine soul and earthly flesh'. Except in a loose and generalized sense, it is not quite precise to label the doctrine 'Apollinarian', though no doubt what is meant is precisely that the divine nature is the animating principle of the body derived from Mary. The Christology here is an archaic survival from the third century, paralleled in the utterances ascribed to pope Callistus by Hippolytus,[1] and comes close to the notions formulated by the manifesto of the western council of Serdica in 342, preserved by Theodoret.[2]

What follows in the prologue is the hardest nut of all to crack. Sedulius Scotus described it as an 'inextricabilis nodus', a knot none could untie.[3]

Mark put John the Baptist's prophetical voice first so that 'the reader may know to whom flesh owes the beginning of flesh in the Lord and the tabernacle [*habitaculum*, a favourite word in the tractates] of God's coming, and may find in himself the word of the voice which in the consonants he had lost'.

John Chapman thought this meant 'The reader's own soul being a part of God, he himself is a word, but he has probably not perceived this, through paying attention to the fleshly part, the consonants, and not to the soul which makes them vocal, and so forms a word'.[4] Sedulius Scotus thought the 'consonantes' were the other two Synoptists, a conjecture rightly regarded by Chapman as brilliant but impossible. I am tempted to suspect a quasi-cabbalistic flight of speculation, that the consonantal text of the Hebrew Old Testament is given its fulfilment and true meaning by a vocalization which the coming of Christ supplies.

The prologue continues that thereafter Mark wrote a perfect gospel, omitting the birth of the flesh (at Bethlehem) which he had surpassed ('vicerat') in what preceded, but after the

[1] Hippolytus, *Refut.* 9. 12. 17–18.

[2] Theodoret, *HE* 2. 8. 48–52.

[3] *PL* 103. 283A. Sedulius is frank about the author's exasperatingly abstruse style, e.g. 281D.

[4] Chapman, *Notes*, p. 234.

Baptism wholly ('totus', again a favourite idiom in the tractates) devoting himself to the expulsion into the desert, the fast for a mystical number of days, the temptation, the keeping company with beasts, and the ministry of angels.

The prologue ends by the story that to disqualify himself from the ministry, Mark cut off his thumb; nevertheless, he became bishop of Alexandria, appropriately enough since a bishop's task is to know each detail, the sayings of both Gospel and Law, and to understand the divine nature of the Lord in the flesh.

The impassioned Monarchianism, the free use of apocryphal Acts to illustrate and enforce the demand for celibacy, the numerology and far-fetched biblical exegesis, the many contacts in diction and style with the Würzburg tractates, the archaic Christology, and the awareness of the need to use great reserve and oracular obscurity in formulating theological statement, combine to make it virtually certain that the prologues emerge from the Priscillianist milieu, perhaps from the master himself. The extent of his success in concealing his meaning by his involuted style and dark sayings may be seen in the acceptance of the prologues into the manuscripts of the Vulgate Gospels written in the sixth century, with the exception of those written in north Italy.[1]

The 'Letter of Titus' and the 'Apocalypse of Thomas'

Chapman's discovery that anonymous texts can be identified as Priscillianist led to a series of over-adventurous proposals especially by Donatien de Bruyne in a paper in *Revue Bénédictine* 24 (1907), 318–35. Of de Bruyne's Priscillianist discoveries the most interesting (and perhaps the only reasonably plausible suggestion) is the so-called 'Letter of Titus' concerning celibacy, contained in an eighth-century manuscript at Würzburg University Library (Mp. th. f. 28). de Bruyne first printed the text in *Revue Bénédictine* 37 (1925), 47–72, and it is reprinted in *PL Suppl.* ii. 1522–42. An English translation with introduction by A. de Santos Otero is included in the second volume of Hennecke/Schneemelcher, *New Testament Apocrypha*, edited by R. McL. Wilson (1965). The 'Letter of Titus' is an extraordinary work, with an abundance of citations from apocryphal Gospels and

[1] Chapman, *Notes*, p. 274.

Acts and other pseudepigrapha. However, its allegedly Priscillianist character is reducible to its enthusiasm for virginity and its exploitation of apocryphal texts. Other characteristically Priscillianist themes are not found in it. Not everyone who appealed to apocrypha to justify the demand for celibacy was a Priscillianist. The work is too marginal to be examined in detail in this study, and its connection with the history of the Priscillianist group may well be nil.

Also marginal is the 'Apocalypse of Thomas', though this work combines advocacy of celibacy with a strongly Monarchian theology and has therefore closer links with doctrines found in Priscillianist material. The work begins 'Audi Thomas, quia ego sum filius dei patris et ego sum pater omnium spirituum . . .' which is flying a Monarchian flag from the beginning. However, it is not possible to say more than that the work may well have been favoured among Priscillianists. The work is put on the index of prohibited books in the Gelasian Decree.[1]

Both of these apocryphal documents belong to the late fourth or early fifth century, and therefore illustrate the same tendencies as are found in Priscillianism. But they cannot be made the basis of confident assertions about the literature read by the Galicians.

---

[1] English translation with introduction by A. de Santos Otero in Hennecke/ Schneemelcher, op. cit. ii. 798–803. Text edited by P. Bihlmeyer in *Rev. Bénéd.* 28 (1911), 270–82.

III

PRISCILLIAN'S END AND ITS CONSEQUENCES

The pressures on Maximus

PRISCILLIAN'S decision not to appear at the unfriendly synod of Bordeaux but to lay his case directly before the emperor began a fateful train of events. In the light of his past experience the decision is intelligible. The Priscillianist bishops had successfully stayed away from the synod at Saragossa in 380; and after initial difficulty he, with Instantius, had negotiated remarkable favour from Gratian's court at Milan. Perhaps it could be done again. . . . But history did not repeat itself, mainly because Maximus was in a different political situation from Gratian.

It is hard to imagine that Priscillian's arrival at Trier can have been welcome. To Maximus here was a tiresome complication that the synod of Bordeaux had failed to settle, tediously filling the ante-rooms of his great palace at Trier with factious clergymen from Spain and Aquitaine. The newly victorious emperor already had sufficient problems in the effort to establish his power and to decide whether to be conciliatory or vindictive towards high officials who admired Gratian and had supported his vain resistance to Maximus' rebellion.[1] Moreover, Maximus wanted but failed to gain control of the western provinces other than Britain, Gaul, and Spain. When in September 383 the news of Gratian's death reached Milan, the widow of Valentinian I, Justina,[2] whose son, in 383 only twelve years old, had been acclaimed Augustus

---

[1] The count Valio committed suicide (Ambrose, *Ep.* 24 (30). 11; Pacatus, *Paneg.* xii. 28). From Sulpicius Severus (*Dial.* iii. 11. 8) it is clear that Maximus won over the great majority of Gratian's officials but had to threaten death to a recalcitrant minority, including the count Narses and the *praeses* Leucadius, for whose life Martin of Tours pleaded. Severus tantalizingly observes that they had been more obstinate than others 'for reasons which this is not the time to explain'.

[2] See the article 'Justina' by Seeck in *PW* x (1919), 1337–8, and *PLRE*.

in 375, took control as regent with the support (more realistically, as the tool)[1] of the Frankish general Bauto, Gratian's *magister militum*, an eminent representative of the Germanic group whose influence Maximus had risen up to reduce. From Milan Valentinian II would be sovereign over Italy, Africa, and Illyricum if Maximus could be kept at bay.

In the autumn of 383 Maximus was very powerful. He sent an embassy to Theodosius demanding recognition as Augustus and offering no word of explanation for his revolt against Gratian.[2] He sent to Milan a count named Victor[3] to bring Valentinian II to Trier, 'as a son to his father'. The perjury and treachery that had brought Gratian to his death cannot have encouraged consent to the proposal. Justina played for time. She had anticipated the crisis by sending bishop Ambrose to assure Maximus of Valentinian's innocuousness; the little boy could not be expected at Trier till the winter was past and travel easier. Justina's wise choice of the strictly catholic Ambrose as legate to the equally devout Maximus shows that the Milanese court was well informed about the new emperor's position in this regard. Without explicitly making false promises Ambrose succeeded in deceiving Maximus about Justina's intentions, an act which he felt to be justified when done on behalf of a defenceless, orphan boy.[4] Maximus received the impression that Valentinian would come to Trier in the spring. Meanwhile, Bauto did not wish to see Milan absorbed by Trier. Both sides made use of barbarian forces to harass the other. Maximus tried to tie Bauto down by instigating an invasion of Raetia by the Juthungi. Bauto moved the Huns and Alans to attack the Alemanni and to pursue them so close to the Rhine that Maximus had to stand to the protection of the frontier and could not move into northern Italy. In any event, his brother Marcellinus, who under Gratian had apparently held some post in Italy, was being detained at Milan as a

---

[1] As Maximus told Ambrose at Trier (*Ep.* 24 (30). 4).

[2] Zosimus iv. 37. 10.

[3] Maximus' son with whom he hoped to share power was also 'count Victor' (Sulpicius Severus, *V. Martini* 20. 4; Orosius vii. 35. 10; Zosimus iv. 47. 1), but he was too young to be hazarded as legate if Aurelius Victor (*Epitome De Caesaribus* 48. 6 'intra infantiae annos') is right. The *Epitome* is supported by a fragment of Sulpicius Alexander cited by Gregory of Tours, *Hist. Franc.* ii. 8 (9).

[4] Ambrose, *Ep.* 40. 8. The main source is Ambrose's report on his second mission to Trier, on which occasion Maximus accused him of deceiving him at the time of his first embassy: *Ep.* 24 (= 30 Faller); cf. *Ep.* 20. 23; 21. 20.

hostage.[1] So Maximus missed his hour of opportunity, and some time late in 384 had to be content to make a pact with Theodosius by which he would leave the young Valentinian in possession of Italy, western Illyricum, and North Africa.[2] This concession was probably imposed on Maximus by Theodosius, who sent a legation to Valentinian II in the summer of 384.[3]

It does not seem that the pact between Valentinian and Maximus went as far as a formal and full mutual recognition. Maximus wanted to be regarded as Valentinian's protector and superior. He resented the fact, which he attributed to the influence of Ambrose, that Valentinian's advisers had looked towards Theodosius for help rather than to himself.[4] That the pact was much less than a full recognition is evident from Ambrose's account of his second mission to Trier (the date of which is to be discussed shortly). Maximus consistently refused to acknowledge Valentinian as an equal,[5] whereupon Ambrose openly described Maximus to his face as a usurper,[6] directly challenging the legitimacy of his rebellion against Gratian. So at least Ambrose reported to Milan. Even if it might be doubted perhaps whether Ambrose's account of his embassy may not be exaggerating, and if one wonders whether he actually used quite such strong words to Maximus, it is certain that 'usurpation' was precisely the language that Valentinian wanted to hear, and which must have been in current use at the court of Milan. It follows that at the time of Ambrose's second mission to Trier neither Valentinian nor Maximus had formally and publicly conceded the right of the other to reign. It is coherent with this that the reports (*relationes*)

[1] Ambrose does not name Maximus' brother, but he is mentioned in Pacatus, *Paneg.* xii. 35. 1, and Sulpicius Severus, *V. Martini* 20. 4. He was recipient of the law, *C. Theod.* ix. 27. 5 of 4 Apr. 383.
[2] *Chronica minora* (ed. Mommsen, *MGH*) i. 646. 11; 648. 16.
[3] Themistius, *Or.* 18. p. 221. *C. Theod.* xii. 1. 107 (31 Aug. 384), is dated from 'Verona' which Seeck took to show that Theodosius himself came to north Italy, but Gothofredus' commentary acutely suggested that *Veronae* is a corruption of *Beroeae*. See Matthews, *Western Aristocracies*, p. 178.
[4] Ambrose, *Ep.* 24 (30). 11.
[5] There may be an echo of this in Ambrose, *Expl. Ps.* 38. 2 (*CSEL* 64. 185, 6–9): 'One claiming equality is told by the insolent, You are a conquered man and have not the power you claim'. These sermons on the psalms contain many indirect allusions to the politics of the time. Cf. L. F. Pizzolato, *La Explanatio Psalmorum XII*, Archivio Ambrosiano 17 (Milan, 1965).
[6] Ambrose, *Ep.* 24 (30). 10 'Nisi fallor, usurpator bellum infert, imperator ius suum tuetur' (cited as his words to Maximus); cf. 24 (30). 3.

submitted to Milan by Symmachus during his time as prefect of Rome, from June 384 to February 385, are addressed to Valentinian and Theodosius only, omitting all mention of Maximus, whose name must surely have been included had he been admitted by Valentinian to be a legitimate emperor.[1] As we shall see, it is hardly possible to put this second mission to Trier earlier than the autumn of 384, and this, the earliest possible date, is not likely; a later dating is altogether more probable.

Maximus' threat to Italy and to the survival of the court of Valentinian II at Milan would be directly increased in proportion as he became able to win the general loyalty of the Italian churches. In the western provinces Gratian had done much to foster and favour the church, especially after the death of Valens and the disaster at Adrianople in 378;[2] and his decisions not to accept the ancient pagan title of 'Pontifex Maximus' and to remove the Altar of Victory from the senate house in Rome were public and dramatic symbols of his commitment to an uncompromising break with polytheism and the old gods of Rome. Pagans thought Gratian's attitude to the old gods a cause of his fall before Maximus, and Zosimus reports pagans as prophesying 'The pontifex will soon be Maximus'.[3] As late as the composition of the fifth book of Augustine's *City of God* in 413, the fall of so devout a catholic to a usurper raised painful questions for Christians about the way in which God cared for his own.[4] The existence of this pagan reading of the work of providence in history explains both why the Christians felt emotionally committed to the memory of Gratian long after he had left the scene and why Maximus, particularly interested in gaining the confidence of the churches, faced an uphill task. As the soldier directly responsible for the orthodox emperor's fall and, at least indirectly, for his death by treachery, Maximus needed to reassure the western bishops, embarrassed to discover the ineffectiveness of their prayers for Gratian's prosperity and victory.

---

[1] The relevance of this evidence from Symmachus is noted by A. Chastagnol in the discussion following on the paper by J. R. Palanque in *Les Empereurs romains d'Espagne* (1965), p. 264.

[2] Cf. G. Gottlieb, *Ambrosius von Mailand und Kaiser Gratian* (Göttingen, 1973).

[3] Zosimus iv. 36. Alan Cameron has suggested that Gratian's disavowal of the title was in 383 at the time of Maximus' revolt: 'Gratian's repudiation of the pontifical robe', *Journal of Roman Studies* 58 (1968), 96–102.

[4] Augustine, *De civ. Dei* 5. 25.

The charge of illegal usurpation was not wholly unanswerable. Maximus could claim that there was a spontaneous revolt against Gratian's policy of favouring the Germanic and Alan soldiers, and that he had been forced by the army into the civil war and the seizure of power.[1] He was, he said, a man with a mission who had been clothed with the purple and acclaimed as he ascended from the baptismal font.[2] Moreover, it was not, he protested, by his command that Gratian had been killed,[3] even though he could not risk the step of degrading or censuring the officer who had done the deed, since he owed power to those who disliked Gratian.

The bishops naturally cared also for other matters beside legitimacy and clean hands. In the atmosphere of high tension between Christian and pagan, between orthodox and heretic, characteristic of this period of the fourth century, nothing would do more to give reassurance to the churches, as also to the emperor Theodosius at Constantinople, than an unyielding stand on the question of orthodoxy. A weak indifferentism towards heresy, schism, or paganism, would be politically damaging even if compatible with Maximus' personal convictions (which was not the case).

The pagan prophecy of Maximus' victory in 383, if reported by Zosimus in anything like a correct form, suggests that the overthrow of Gratian may have temporarily raised hopes in the hearts of the defenders of the old polytheism that perhaps the new emperor might treat them with greater consideration than Gratian had done. Disillusion must have come quickly. On this point clear indications of the reality of the situation at least by the summer of 384 are provided by a passage in the contemporary correspondence of Ambrose. In his letter to Valentinian II in the summer of 384 attempting to counter Symmachus' elegant plea for the restoration of the Altar of Victory in the senate house and the continued toleration of the old religion—'for by one road only one cannot attain to so great a mystery'—Ambrose directly warns the young

---

[1] Sulpicius Severus, *V. Martini* 20; *Dial.* ii. 6. 1 (Postumianus); Orosius vii. 34. 9. This argument was conventional; it appears in Julian's letter to Constantius of 360 (Ammianus xx. 8. 8 ff.), and in the apologia of the British usurper Constantine to the emperor Honorius in 407 (Zosimus v. 43. 1).

[2] See Maximus' letter to pope Siricius, *Avell.* XL. 1 (*CSEL* 35); below, p. 147.

[3] Ambrose, *Ep.* 24 (30). 10. The Milanese court thought otherwise: see Ambrose, *Expl. Ps.* 61. 24–5 (*CSEL* 64. 393); Zosimus iv. 43. The usurper Constantine likewise apologized to Honorius that his kinsmen had been killed contrary to Constantine's instructions: Zosimus vi. 1, 5.

emperor that, if he gives way to the great pagan aristocrats, he will be abrogating his brother Gratian's edicts on religion which Maximus is being inflexible in maintaining. The implication is evident that the churches in Italy will immediately begin to look towards Maximus as their protector if Valentinian concedes toleration, even though that toleration would be precisely what Valentinian I had maintained to his death and what Gratian himself had certainly adhered to until at least 380.[1] Ambrose forestalls the argument that toleration would only be a return to the religious neutrality of Valentinian II's father by claiming that if Valentinian I had ever visited Rome and discovered the existence of the Altar of Victory, he would surely have abolished it.

Maximus was certainly not a man with any reputation for compromise with polytheism. Zosimus reports that when Theodosius eventually decided to give formal and official recognition to Maximus, he linked the public manifestation of this with the campaign of Cynegius against pagan cult in Egypt. Cynegius simultaneously closed the temples of the gods and erected in Alexandria statues and pictures of Maximus.[2] The link is unlikely to have been merely fortuitous. The two orthodox Spanish emperors were united in their view that there could be no concessions to the old paganism, and it would therefore be politically disadvantageous to Valentinian, leaving him isolated between the two more strictly orthodox Augusti, if he yielded to Symmachus over the Altar of Victory.

Maximus' coins minted at Trier meanwhile proclaimed the CONCORDIA AUGG, the agreement of both emperors, Valentinian

---

[1] Ambrose, *Ep.* 17. 16. For the texts, with translation and brief notes, concerning the controversy about the Altar of Victory see J. Wytzes, *Der Streit um den Altar der Viktoria* (Amsterdam, 1936); R. Klein, *Der Streit um den Victoriaaltar* (Darmstadt, 1972), well reviewed by O. Zwierlein, *Gnomon* 46 (1974), 768–75. Latin text and translation of Symmachus' third *Relatio* in R. H. Barrow, *Prefect and Emperor* (Oxford, 1973), pp. 34–47. J. F. Matthews, 'Symmachus and the Oriental cults', *Journal of Roman Studies* 63 (1973), 175–95, and in *Western Aristocracies*, p. 208, stresses the formal and diplomatic nature of Symmachus' third *Relatio*, i.e. its incompleteness as a statement of his personal beliefs. On Symmachus' idea of toleration, see R. Klein, *Symmachus* (1971), pp. 83–92; thereon W. R. Misgeld in *Jahrbuch für Antike und Christentum* 14 (1971), 157–62. The relativistic epistemology underlying Symmachus' plea for toleration is found in Porphyry (ap. Aug. *De civ. Dei* 10. 32), but was not the unanimous late pagan view. On the moral and legal presuppositions of the controversy see A. Dihle in *Romanitas et Christianitas: Studia J. H. Waszink oblata* (1973), 81–98.
[2] Zosimus, iv. 37. Cf. Libanius, *Orat.* xix. 14.

being ignored. The coins struck by Valentinian never give any recognition to Maximus.[1]

As Justina's confidence grew that the Milanese court would be upheld by Theodosius and therefore left in peace by Maximus, she became increasingly open about her personal allegiance to Arianism, as formulated by the broad terms of the general council of Ariminum of 359, in preference to the Nicene orthodoxy of Ambrose whom she found discourteous and domineering, too prone to preach sermons to the young Valentinian II on the prior duty to obey God rather than one's parents or even on Herodias and Jezebel.[2] Although Justina's Arian sympathy was evidently known, it seems first to have affected her public policies from early 385 onwards. By Lent 385 Ambrose was being asked to allow the Arian Goths, that is, the circle of like-minded friends that Justina had brought with her from Illyricum, to use one of the basilicas of the city. During Lent 386 after a formal edict in favour of toleration this issue boiled up into a fierce confrontation between the court and the bishop, Ambrose's passive resistance being vigorously supported by the guild of city merchants who cordially disliked the Arian foreigners from Pannonia.[3]

Justina's breach with Ambrose was a huge political risk to take. Its imprudence was eloquently pointed out in lapidary terms by none other than Magnus Maximus himself in a letter to Valentinian II probably written shortly after Easter 386 when reports of the troubles in Milan were reaching Trier.[4] Maximus observes

---

[1] H. Mattingly, C. H. V. Sutherland, R. A. G. Carson, *The Roman Imperial Coinage* ix: *Valentinian I–Theodosius I*, by J. W. E. Pearce (London, 1951), p. xxi.

[2] Sozomen, *HE* vii. 13. 3, says that Justina complained of being publicly insulted by Ambrose, perhaps because of some allusion by him to Herodias or Jezebel (cf. *Ep.* 20. 18 and Gaudentius' dedication to Benivolus, *PL* 20. 830A: 'regina Iezabel Arianae perfidiae patrona'). For the charge that Ambrose was tyrannically assuming powers he did not rightly possess, cf. *Ep.* 20. 22–3 and 27 (Ambrose's report to his sister Marcellina). For duty to God preceding parents see *Expos. in Lucam* 7. 201; 8. 79; *Expl. Ps.* 118. 15. 20.

[3] Ambrose, *Epp.* 20–1; *Sermo contra Auxentium*; Paulinus, *Vita Ambrosii* 12–13; Augustine, *Conf.* ix. 15; Rufinus, *HE* ix. 15–16. Justina had lived for some time in Illyricum at Sirmium where about 376 Ambrose had forced the election of an anti-Arian metropolitan, Anemius, to whose appointment Justina took exception (Paulinus, *Vita Ambrosii* 11). Anemius asserted metropolitan rights in the province, evidently with difficulty to judge from the stridency with which he blows his trumpet on the subject at the council of Aquileia of 381 (*PL* 16. 921A: 'Caput Illyrici non nisi civitas est Sirmiensis; ego igitur episcopus illius civitatis sum'). Cf. Sulpicius Severus, *Dial.* ii. 5. 5; Socrates, *HE* 5. 11. 4.

[4] *Avell.* xxxix (*CSEL* 35. 88). The undated document falls about Easter 386. It

that nothing could be more favourable to his interest than that Valentinian should be in conflict with the church and put himself out of step with the faith of all provinces except Illyricum, where pockets of Arianism still remained and where divine vengeance had lately obliterated the old Arian stronghold of Mursa (Osijek in Yugoslavia). Nevertheless (Maximus continues) religion is too serious a matter to be cynically treated as a mere means of undermining the loyalty of Valentinian's subjects. He is therefore writing an admonition to prove the sincerity of his professions of friendship which Valentinian has persisted in scorning as mere pretence.[1]

The date and authors of this destruction of Mursa, famous as the see of the long-lived Arian leader Valens who survived into the seventies, are not known. Maximus does not further specify, and the event is not elsewhere recorded. Pannonia was wide open to barbarian raids after the upheavals in the Balkans following the Hun migration and the battle of Adrianople with the Goths (378). Goths were freely ravaging Pannonia in 380–1;[2] John Chrysostom says that the barbarians laughed at the Empire and danced rather than fought, one barbarian chief being amazed at the cowardice of the legions. About a decade later Jerome hyperbolically describes the utter obliteration of towns in Thrace and Illyricum, including his own birth-place Stridon.[3] Maximus' thesis that the

cannot belong to 385 as it alludes to the edict of toleration of 23 Jan. 386 (*C. Theod.* xi. 1. 4 = 4. 1) and the siege of the basilicas: 'Audio enim (nam fama non patitur occultari, praesertim quod agatur in populos) novis clementiae tuae edictis ecclesiis catholicis vim illatam fuisse obsideri in basilicis sacerdotes, multam esse propositam, poenam capitis adiectam et legem sanctissimam sub nomine nescio cuius legis everti.'

[1] Rufinus (*HE* xi. 15) attributes pretence to both Maximus and Valentinian, which is no doubt correct. Ambrose's report to Valentinian on his second mission to Trier concludes that when Maximus uses the word 'peace' he means 'war' (*Ep.* 24 (30). 13).

[2] Jordanes, *Getica* 27. 140; Zosimus iv. 34. John Chrysostom, *Ad viduam iuniorem* 4 (*PG* 47. 606 = *Sources chrétiennes* 138, ed. G. H. Ettlinger, 1968, p. 140).

[3] Jerome, *In Osee* i p. 35; *In Sophon.* i p. 676; *Vir. inl.* 135. Cf. Ambrosiaster, *Quaest.* 115. 49 (*CSEL* 50. 334, 16), 'quid dicemus de Pannonia quae sic erasa est ut remedium habere non possit?' Disruption probably varied in degree in different regions of the province. The peaceful coexistence of Goths and Romans at Jovia in Pannonia is attested, with admiration and astonishment, in the epitaph of bishop Amantius (*CIL* v. 1623 = Bücheler, *Carmina latina epigraphica* ii. 1350 = Diehl, *ILCV* 1061a), if, as is probable, he is rightly identified with the Amantius of Jovia present as an ally of Ambrose at the council of Aquileia, 381, which tried to uproot Arianism in Illyricum (see F. Kauffmann, *Aus dem Schule des Wulfila* (1899), p. 61 a 17). See R. Egger in *Jahresheft d. österr. arch. Inst.* 21–2 (1922), Beiblatt, pp. 327–41, approved by A. Alföldi, *Der Untergang der Römerherrschaft in Pannonien* ii (1926),

barbarians' depredations in Illyricum are a divine punishment for the prevalence of Arianism in the churches of that region is a direct restatement of a theme once urged upon Gratian by Ambrose, who liked to draw a contrast between Arian Illyricum under its Gothic masters and the unwaveringly orthodox, so unravaged, land of Italy.[1] Provinces have the government they deserve.

Moreover, Maximus could have reason to think that the churches in Italy generally were not predisposed towards the Priscillianists. Apart from the evidence of Ambrose, opinion can be assessed from Filastrius of Brescia (above, p. 9). Some time between 380 and 390 the bishop of Brescia (Brixia) in the province of Milan wrote his guidebook to heresies which on this issue may be taken to reflect the accepted attitudes of Italian churchmen. Filastrius' account of the Manichees concludes with the observation that 'they are said to hide both in Spain and the five provinces [i.e. Aquitaine], and daily to capture many by this deceit'.[2] The reference is likely to be to the Priscillianists. In another chapter he says:

There are others in the Gauls, Spain, and Aquitania who are as if abstinent, who follow the pernicious doctrine of the Gnostics and Manichees and do not hesitate to preach this, persuading married couples to separate and requiring abstinence from foods, which is a grace allowed by Christ to individual human choice for the sake of gaining heavenly reward and dignity, not a precept of the law.[3]

Filastrius adds that he particularly fears the infiltration by Manichees of apocryphal texts, especially the Acts of Andrew, John, Peter, and Paul; but he allows (above, p. 24) that such documents may be studied by the perfect for their ethical (rather than

---

61–2; L. Varady, *Das letzte Jahrhundert Pannoniens 376–476* (Budapest, 1969), p. 37; A. Mocsy, *Pannonia* (London, 1975), pp. 347–8.

On Illyrian Arianism see M. Meslin, *Les Ariens d'occident* (Paris, 1967).

[1] Ambrose, *De fide* ii. 139–42. Gunther Gottlieb, *Ambrosius von Mailand und Kaiser Gratian* (1973), argues that *De fide* i–ii were written in 379–80. Against this, P. Nautin holds that these two books fall in Dec. 378 or Jan. 379: 'Les premières relations d'Ambroise avec l'empereur Gratien', in *Ambroise de Milan, XVIᵉ centénaire de son élection épiscopale* (Paris, 1974), pp. 229–44.

[2] Filastrius 61 (*CSEL* 38. 32). Filastrius may have written his book after Priscillian's death, but this does not affect the relevance of his evidence.

[3] Ibid. 84. Augustine (*Haeres.* 70) takes Filastrius to be referring here to the Priscillianists.

dogmatic) content.[1] On this last point, at least, Filastrius was not in disagreement with Priscillian.

Maximus was not mistaken, therefore, in assuming that in Italy an anti-Priscillianist policy could expect favour.

Despite its protestation of high-mindedness and disinterested amity, Maximus' letter could not have been more ingeniously designed to appeal to the churches in Italy and to drive a wedge between Valentinian and his Christian subjects. The more effective for not containing a single minatory word, the letter was by implication a claim to justify a holy war to protect the church in Italy now being threatened by active persecution, perhaps also to intervene in Illyricum to restore simultaneously both orthodoxy and the integrity of the Empire. Maximus was orchestrating with trumpets a theme that Ambrose himself had gently and tentatively voiced in soft flute-like tones in his own protest to Valentinian of 386, boldly affirming his readiness to die for that faith professed not only by Valentinian I and Theodosius, but also by 'the provinces of Gaul and Spain'[2]—in other words by Magnus Maximus, well known to be an upholder of the Nicene creed. In 387 Theodosius himself remonstrated with Valentinian, contrasting his toleration of heresy with Maximus' ardent orthodoxy which earned heaven's gift of victory.[3]

In this tense political and religious situation of the years 384–6 nothing would be less likely than an act of generosity by Maximus towards a Spanish bishop known to be regarded as heretical in both Rome and Milan. Moreover Priscillian could hardly expect Maximus to feel committed to the policy in his favour adopted (or at any rate rubber-stamped) by Gratian. Accordingly if Priscillian went to Trier in hope of finding in a fellow Spaniard a friendly or even impartial protector free to judge without fear or favour, he misjudged both the man and the situation. Whatever imperial favour Priscillian had obtained in the past he owed to the emperor that Maximus had risen up to overthrow, the very mention of whose name raised awkward questions about the legitimacy of Maximus' rule. That Maximus had a skin sensitive to those pricking questions of legitimacy is evident from the picture

---

[1] Filastrius 88. [2] Ambrose, *Ep.* 21. 14.

[3] Theodoret, *HE* 5. 15. 1; cf. Suda, s.v. 'Valentinianos' (Adler iii. 574); Zonaras xiii. 18. The Gallic chronicle of 452 says that Maximus' protest at the persecution of the church gave him excuse to break the pact he had formed with Valentinian (Mommsen, *Chronica minora* i. 648. 16).

of him in Sulpicius Severus' *Life of St. Martin* (20). Orthodox
Christians felt Gratian to be the Lord's Anointed, whom it was
a sin to touch.[1] The more sensitive Maximus felt on this delicate
matter, the more he would be on the defensive, and therefore not
well able to face out accusations that he had been tolerant of
Spanish semi-Manichees believed to be actively interested in
occult sciences. His authority, which had already laboured under
the difficulty of getting recognition from Valentinian and Theodosius, would be seriously vulnerable if he could be represented
as soft with sorcerers. Accordingly a hard line on orthodoxy was
politically necessary to Maximus if he were to retain the confidence
of the church. Priscillianism was a godsend to him since he would
be easily able to represent its occultism and freedom for women
as a dreadful pollution which Gratian had done much to encourage, but which God had now specially raised him up to check.[2]
In an entirely different context Ambrose once remarks that in
general the clergy are conservative supporters of peace and established order unless they feel that there is some offence against
God or his Church against which they must protest.[3] Maximus'
task was to convince Christian opinion that under Gratian's regime
there was a grave offence against God which he had a divine
mission to rectify. Priscillian simplified this task for him.

The impact on church opinion of Maximus' propaganda
achieved at least a measure of success, despite the relatively short
time for which he reigned and the massive Theodosian propaganda against him in 388, as can be seen in the generally favourable
estimates of his character preserved in retrospect by the Aquitanian Sulpicius Severus, for whom he was 'a good man, only led
astray by his episcopal advisers',[4] and by the Spaniard Orosius

---

[1] Ambrose, *Apologia prophetae David* 27 (*CSEL* 32. 316)—an impressive protest
against the disastrous civil wars leaving the empire at the mercy of the barbarians.
Expl. Ps. 61. 17–26 develops at length the theme of Gratian as a Christlike figure
betrayed to death, with Maximus washing his hands like Pilate.

[2] Maximus so argues in his letter to pope Siricius (*Avell.* XL).

[3] *Ep.* 40. 6.

[4] *Dial.* iii. 11. 2 (Gallus). Partly to make a contrast with his hero Martin Sulpicius
Severus gives a consistently sombre estimate of the Gallic bishops of this period,
which is no doubt unfair (above, p. 5). According to *Chron.* i. 23 the bishops are
better at caring for their estates than for their flocks or, if poor, are constantly
begging for gifts. Jerome (*Ep.* 69. 9 to Oceanus) astringently comments that too
many bishops buy the favour of the people at a high price like charioteers, or are so
cordially hated that even their money fails to extort the applause that actors win by
their performances.

who looked back on him as 'a man of energy and honesty, but for his usurpation worthy of being Augustus'.[1] The simple Ambrosian picture of Maximus as a wicked tyrant and usurper, who murdered the good Gratian, and added to the blood on his hands by the execution of Priscillian, is far from the truth as seen by most of those who lived under his rule.[2] The attack on the legitimacy of his rule has left a deep mark on the ancient sources, and modern textbooks faithfully echo the propaganda of Valentinian and Theodosius in simply labelling him 'the usurper'. But that is partly because of the disproportionate dimensions of Ambrose among the available sources, partly because it was this issue that Theodosius used to justify the blitzkrieg attack on Maximus in north Italy and Pannonia which eliminated him from the scene on 28 July 388.[3] At the time Theodosius was universally understood to have recognized Maximus, probably since the end of 384 after they had made their pact. The emphatic denials of recognition in Pacatus' *Panegyric* must imply that everyone supposed the opposite to be the case. In 386 Maximus' praetorian prefect Euodius was fully acknowledged in the Greek East as one of the two consuls of the year.

   Zosimus cynically but plausibly explains Theodosius' change of tune by the story that in 388 Theodosius' decision to support the weak, refugee Valentinian and to attack the strong Maximus was motivated not (as his propaganda claimed) by high-minded loyalty to Gratian's memory but by the sudden passion he had

---

[1] *Historia adversus paganos* vii. 34. 9: 'vir quidem strenuus et probus atque Augusto dignus nisi contra sacramenti fidem per tyrannidem emersisset.' The pagan historian Zosimus (iv. 37. 2) records that Maximus refused to employ eunuchs as palace officials; this is incompatible with Ambrose (*Ep.* 24 (30). 2) who says he was received at Trier by a court eunuch; but in view of the venomous anti-Maximus bias in Ambrose's letter it has to be considered possible that Zosimus is correct, and that by 'eunuch' Ambrose is merely employing a disparaging term like 'lackey'.

[2] Cf. J. R. Palanque, 'Sur l'usurpation de Maxime', *Revue des études anciennes* 31 (1929), 33–6.

[3] The date of Maximus' death is differently given as 28 July by some chroniclers (*Chron. min.* i. 245, ii. 15), 28 Aug. by others (Socrates, *HE* 5. 14. 1; *Chron. min.* i. 298; the Alexandrian world-chronicle, *Denkschr. Wien* 51 (1906), 59). Seeck (*Regesten,* p. 275, *Untergang* 5, p. 525) opts for 28 Aug. That 28 July is correct is argued by O. Perler, 'Augustinus und das Todesdatum des Augustus Magnus Maximus von Trier', *Festschrift Alois Thomas* (Trier, 1967), pp. 289–96, from Augustine, *C. litt. Petiliani* iii. 25. 30: 'I left Rome for Africa after the death of the tyrant Maximus', and from the evidence of Possidius (*Vita Augustini,* 3 f.) that Augustine was at Carthage, then at Thagaste probably in September; so he left Rome during August. Perler restates his argument in *Les Voyages de S. Augustin* (Paris, 1969), pp. 197–203.

formed for Valentinian's sister Galla, who had been carefully presented to him, groomed for the kill, by her mother Justina.[1] Although as an ardent pagan Zosimus had no liking or respect for Theodosius, his story is evidently not mere gossip: the wedding took place in the autumn of 387. Even before he fell in love as a merry widower, Theodosius' relations with Valentinian were close and friendly,[2] very unlike those between Valentinian and Maximus, where soft speeches about friendship were understood otherwise on both sides. But until 388 Theodosius did not actually dispute the legitimacy of Maximus' rule over Britain, Gaul, and Spain. The area of doubt lay in a theoretical claim, which Maximus did not formally withdraw, to be a supreme Augustus over Italy as well. In 388 Theodosius may reasonably have thought it dangerous for Maximus to be the actual controller of so large an area of the West as his invasion of Italy and western Illyricum had brought to him.[3]

Questioning the legitimacy of government is ineffective and useless if not carried on in public, and usually autocratic emperors are not publicly called 'usurpers' within their dominions as long as they remain in power. It is a term for the unsuccessful or unacknowledged. Admittedly the attested behaviour of every one during the five years of Maximus' reign is unintelligible unless it was only in the circle of Valentinian's court (where Justina no doubt stayed silent about her own first marriage to the 'usurper'

---

[1] Zosimus iv. 44. S. I. Oost, *Galla Placidia Augusta* (Chicago, 1968), p. 47, prefers the kinder view of Augustine, *De civ. Dei* 5. 26 (cf. Socrates, *HE* 5. 12) that Theodosius was answering the call of duty, unselfishly caring for the defenceless boy Valentinian against the evil Maximus. Augustine, be it noted, was in Milan at the time when Valentinian II was under pressure from Trier; on 1 Jan. 385 he delivered the panegyric when Bauto entered on his consulship (*Conf.* vi. 6. 9; *C. litt. Petil.* iii. 25. 30; Possidius, *Vita* 1). This would have coloured his view of Maximus. On Augustine's knowledge of Priscillian's trial at Trier, see below, p. 206.

It is unnecessary to explain Theodosius' relation with Maximus until 388 on the conjectural hypothesis that Theodosius distrusted Justina and Valentinian II and placed agents in the West to spy on, and undermine, their rule (see (e.g.) J. W. E. Pearce in *The Roman Imperial Coinage* ix, pp. xx f.). Of anti-Milanese collusion between Trier and Constantinople the sources give no serious evidence other than the shared Spanish background of Maximus and Theodosius, perhaps their blood-relationship (above, p. 42, n. 3), and their common attitude to Nicene orthodoxy. These factors may have helped Theodosius to take Maximus by surprise, since Maximus may have felt himself secure on his eastern front. They can hardly be the basis of more elaborate speculations.

[2] Ambrose, *Ep.* 17. 12, writes to Valentinian: 'You have consulted Theodosius on all important matters of politics; do so on religion also.'

[3] Oost, op. cit., p. 47, suggests this.

Magnentius), that men openly declared Maximus to be an illegal *tyrannus*, until after he had surrendered and suffered execution, probably to please Justina, in July 388.[1] The unexpectedness of his fall before Theodosius is revealed by the extreme embarrassment endured by the great pagan aristocrat Symmachus: in 388 he delivered a fervent panegyric on Maximus, and then found that overnight the government had changed, that he was charged with treason, and that he, of all people, was under the humiliating necessity of seeking asylum in a church; at which the Christians failed to conceal their pleasure.[2] When Theophilus, bishop of Alexandria, whose intelligence service was superior to that of the emperor Maximus, learnt that Theodosius was intending war against Maximus, he sent to Italy his presbyter Isidore with a reader carrying gifts and two letters of congratulation, instructed to deliver the appropriate letter to whichever turned out victor. Isidore was betrayed by the accompanying reader, and Theophilus' stock fell sharply with Theodosius.[3]

The analysis here suggested of the way in which interlocking

[1] By immediately capitulating at Aquileia Maximus saved many lives. Except for the execution of Maximus and his son Victor, and the suicide of the officer responsible for Gratian's death, there was hardly any Roman blood shed. Theodosius was generous to Maximus' mother and daughter (Ambrose, *Ep.* 40. 32). Paulinus (*Vita Ambrosii* 19) shows that the instant surrender was represented as Maximus' admission of the illegitimacy of his rule. The cheerful, insensitive Orosius (*Hist. adv. paganos* vii. 35. 6) sees in the loss of only two Roman lives a striking demonstration of the happy manner in which, under the new order of Christian emperors, civil wars were settled. Of Theodosius' civil war with Eugenius he comments that it cost merely the lives of 10,000 expendable Goths, whose removal from the scene a loyal Roman would not regret. On Orosius' inconsistencies in regard to the barbarians see A. Lippold, 'Orosius, christlicher Apologet und römischer Bürger', *Philologus* 113 (1969), 92–105. In the war of 388 both Theodosius and Maximus used mainly barbarian troops, who fought hard engagements in Pannonia at Siscia and Poetovio (Ambrose, *Ep.* 40. 22–3; Pacatus, *Paneg.* xii. 34–6). Ambrose's funerary panegyric on Theodosius (*Obit. Theod.* 39) couples Maximus and Eugenius as instances of the retribution that comes on rebels against the Lord's Anointed.

[2] Symmachus, *Ep.* ii. 12 and 30, 31; Socrates, *HE* 5. 14. 5–6; John of Antioch, frag. 186 (C. Müller, *Fragmenta Historicorum Graecorum* iv. 608).

[3] Socrates, *HE* 6. 2. 6–9. Theophilus' discomfiture would have been recalled by John Chrysostom's supporters. Before attacking Maximus Theodosius had sent a confidential inquiry to the charismatic Egyptian hermit, John of Lycopolis, in whose prediction of victory the emperor had more confidence than had the bishop of Alexandria. The oracle's response was evidently leaked to the patriarch. See Rufinus, *HE* vi. 19 and 32; Palladius, *Historia Lausiaca* 35; *Historia monachorum in Aegypto* i. 1; Augustine, *De cura pro mortuis* 21; *De civ. Dei* 5. 26; John Cassian, *Inst.* iv. 23; *Coll.* xxiv. 26; Prosper, *Chron.* a. 394 (*Chron. min.* i. 463).

According to Sulpicius Severus (*Vita Martini* 20) Maximus consulted Martin of Tours on the outcome of his expedition into Italy.

pressures of religion and politics determined Maximus' attitude
to the Priscillianists in 384-5 can be further illustrated by a passage
in one of Ambrose's letters written after Maximus' fall in 388.
Ambrose's fortieth letter is addressed from Aquileia (where
Ambrose had gone to elect a new bishop) to the emperor Theodosius, now in Italy after the defeat of Maximus, and expostulates
against the emperor's order, reinforced by an oath,[1] that the local
church at Callinicon, a fortified trading post on the Euphrates,
must pay restitution to the Jews for the burning down of a synagogue at the hands of zealous monks incited by the local bishop.
One of Ambrose's strongest arguments is that if Theodosius
implements this order, he will be following the example of Maximus who in Italy in 388 had commanded full restitution from the
church in Rome where a synagogue had been burnt down. No
doubt by 388, when at last he had control of all the western provinces and when Valentinian was a refugee at Thessalonica,
Maximus felt so much stronger than in 385, that he was able to
enforce just treatment to the Jews in face of the intolerance of
much Christian opinion of the time. Politically he did not now
have the same need to make a striking gesture to gain loyalty.
But Ambrose revealingly comments that the enforcement of
restitution did Maximus fatal political harm: men began to say
'This emperor is a Jew', and Ambrose thought that the conse-
quent erosion of support had contributed to Maximus' downfall.[2]

Priscillian was followed to Trier by his principal Spanish
accusers, Hydatius of Mérida and especially Ithacius. A passing
reference in Ambrose attests the presence in Trier of Hyginus of
Cordoba.[3] Probably several other bishops came on from the un-
completed synod at Bordeaux. At any rate in his *Life of St. Martin*
Sulpicius Severus paints a scene, admittedly stylized, in which
among a great gathering of fawning bishops at Maximus' court,
Martin of Tours alone treated the usurper without flattery or
indeed any special courtesy.[4] The Priscillianist affair would be
a natural context for the calling of a large episcopal assembly.

---

[1] In accordance with the best ancient moralists, Ambrose explains to Theodosius
that no promise or oath in an evil cause is binding.

[2] *Ep.* 40. 23. Ambrose shared what he revealingly calls 'the majority view' among
Christians of his time that pagans, Jews, and heretics will not get to heaven; see
Expos. Luc. 7. 197-200.

[3] Ambrose, *Ep.* 24 (30), 12; see below, p. 134.

[4] *Vita* 20.

Maximus seems to have taken the opportunity to ensure their loyal support for his regime. Maximus gave the bishops good dinners (after all he needed them as much as they him); and once even Martin accepted an invitation, though making it very clear that he would not kotow to his host." At Trier Ithacius had the evident advantage over Priscillian that during his previous residence there he had acquired friends in the city, especially the bishop Britto.[1] Moreover, he had the sense to see that the ecclesiastical questions (of the kind reflected in the canons of Saragossa) had become secondary. The emperor would not be greatly interested in disputes about Advent, or bare feet, or even clerical celibacy. But Ithacius could bring charges against Priscillian before the imperial tribunal that were under imperial edict criminal and capital, viz. Manicheism and the employment of magic arts. Priscillian had appealed to Caesar: to Caesar must he go, and find that the secular arm wielded blunter and bloodier instruments than mere synods had at their disposal.

The appearance of the bishop of Avila before a secular tribunal raised an awkward question of first principles, irrespective of the charge. Was it right that a bishop primarily on a charge of heresy should be heard and judged by anybody other than an episcopal synod? Intermittently, since Constantine the Great, both bishops and emperors had from time to time asserted the principle that ecclesiastical causes should be heard solely before ecclesiastical tribunals, not before emperors and prefects, whose duty was to preserve public order but not to interfere in technical dogmatic or disciplinary issues.[2] Admittedly bishops and emperors had

---

[1] On the occasion of his first mission to Maximus in 383 Ambrose also had stayed at Trier for many weeks (the count Victor had time to travel to Milan and back while he was detained). Ambrose therefore knew Britto well, but unfortunately never says a word about him. Ambrose's friends among the Gallic bishops include Constantius of Orange (present at Milan in 389–90, *Ep.* 42. 15), Justus of Lyon (at Valence, 374), Domninus, first bishop of Gratianopolis (Grenoble), and the long-lived Proculus of Massilia, all of whom attended the council of Aquileia (381). On his journey to Trier on his first mission he passed by Mainz (*Ep.* 24 (30). 6), as by Valence on the way back (ib. 7); but he does not mention the bishops there. Accordingly, Ambrose was well acquainted with several of the Gallic bishops, and his opinion on the Priscillianist affair is certain to have had some influence in Gaul, though he did not command enough authority to settle the keen debate for and against Britto's successor at Trier, Felix (below, p. 158).

[2] According to Ambrose (*Ep.* 40. 11) even the preservation of public order should yield before violent demonstrations in favour of orthodoxy against heresy: the rightness of the end justifies the unfortunate means used.

made such assertions from different motives: bishops because they thought it unfitting for the people of God to be in litigation with one another before worldly judges; emperors because they wanted to keep their hands free and not to take sides too soon in the partisanship of a heated controversy on abstruse matters. Valentinian I, who, though himself an adherent of Nicene orthodoxy as a matter of personal belief, made toleration and conscious refusal to interfere in religious controversy matters of stated imperial policy, found the principle an invaluable way of preserving his own detachment. In a rescript he declared: 'It is not for me to judge between bishops'.[1] On the other hand, bishops would urge their exclusive right to judge because they felt it their pastoral responsibility, inherent in the power of the keys, to decide matters of correct doctrine and discipline. They did not believe the laity to possess authority so to judge.

This distinction between priestly and lay responsibility gradually became fused with the very different Pauline instruction that Christians should never carry their disagreements to litigation before pagan magistrates, a principle that came to lay on bishops a heavy burden of arbitration in property disputes.[2] The consequence of this fusion was to begin to foster the notion that clergy ought not to be brought before lay tribunals and had the right of immunity. Rufinus reports Constantine the Great as ordering the bishops, who arrived at Nicaea in 325 full of mutual suspicions and accusations, to hand him their *libelli* of complaint, which he then ordered to be burnt unread, saying: 'God appointed you his priests and gave you power to judge us, and so we are rightly judged by you, but you cannot be judged by men. . . . To us you are given by God as gods and it is unfitting that man should

---

[1] Ambrose, *Ep.* 21. 5. Cf. Sozomen, *HE* vi. 7. 2. Ambrose (*Ep.* 21) is objecting to the Arian Auxentius' opinion that a disputation between orthodox and Arian should be decided by lay judges. The Acts of the council of Aquileia (381) show that the two Arian bishops from Illyricum, Palladius and Secundianus, came to Aquileia under the impression that they were to dispute, (as they had requested) at a full council of both eastern and western bishops before lay *auditores* (*Acta Aquil.* 37 and 47, PL 16. 927C and 930C; also edited from Paris. lat. 8907 by Kauffmann, *Aus der Schule der Wulfila* (1899), pp. 53*b* and 57*b*). But the meeting was transformed by Ambrose into an Italian episcopal council for putting heretics on trial, the distinction between prosecutor and judge being thereby submerged. Ambrose, *Ep.* 21, to Valentinian II, is a brilliantly formulated refusal to dispute with the Arian bishop Auxentius before lay arbiters or indeed before a boy emperor who is only a catechumen.

[2] See (e.g.) Ambrose, *Ep.* 82, for a case transferred by the emperor from a civil court to his arbitration; or canon 9 of Chalcedon, 451.

judge gods. . . .'¹ The passage, gratefully quoted by pope Gregory the Great,² came to be important in the armoury of medieval canonists. In a law of 7 October 355 the emperor Constantius exempted bishops from private prosecution in the courts, but one wonders how long it remained in force; it was certainly not being enforced in Africa at the end of the century.³

In 367 Gratian began his reign with an instruction, arising out of the disruption and disturbance caused by the antipope Ursinus, that a bishop should be tried by competent judges, i.e. by bishops, not by an inexpert profane court.⁴ In 372 Valentinian I's rescript to the prefect of Rome, Ampelius, instructed the prefect to coerce Ursinus' followers with severe penalties, and to treat him 'not as a Christian but as deprived of the benefit of both law and religion'.⁵ At the same time a parallel rescript to the vicarius of Rome, Maximin, declares that Ursinus shall be treated not as a Christian seeing that his unquiet mind has separated him from the communion of religion, but as a factious person and a disturber of the public peace, an enemy of the laws and of religion.⁶ The rescript strikingly illustrates the way in which the high principle that ecclesiastical causes should be judged exclusively by ecclesiastical courts would lead to a dreadful corollary, that a person agitating for religious motives could come to be treated as an outlaw enjoying not merely no benefit of clergy but not even ordinary rights as a citizen. Once the church had put the man outside the pale he could be treated by the secular arm as if mere vermin.

The Roman synod of 378 set out to defend pope Damasus from the unpleasant charge of homicide by seeking to exempt all bishops, and above all the bishops of Rome, from being answerable to a secular court of law. The synod appeals to Gratian's instruction of the beginning of his reign that in matters of religion the charges should come before expert judges and, like Ambrose (who may have contributed much to the drafting of the letter), takes this to mean that bishops alone may be judges of accused

¹ Rufinus, *HE* x. 2. Socrates (i. 8. 18–19) and Sozomen (i. 17. 3–6) omit the second sentence cited above.
² Gregorius Mag. *Reg.* 5. 6 (*MGH* edn., i. 318), to the Byzantine emperor Maurice.
³ *C. Theod.* xvi. 2. 12; the *Hippo Breviary* (of 393), Canon 9 (ed. C. Munier, *Concilia Africae*, p. 36).
⁴ See the letter of the Roman synod of 378, *Et hoc gloriae*, Labbe–Coleti, *Concilia*, ii. 1187D = *PL* 13. 577B; Ambrose, *Ep.* 21. 2.
⁵ *Avell.* xi. 3 (*CSEL* 35).
⁶ *Avell.* xii. 2.

bishops. The continuation is quite remarkable. The bishop, the synod claims, has a higher moral standing as a judge because he is bound by his conscience to acquit the innocent and to condemn the guilty; he will not need to tear the flesh of innocent witnesses under judicial torture because his charismatic office enables him to judge the moral character of the defendant.[1] How often bishops have found to be guilty persons mistakenly acquitted by secular courts, and have been able to pronounce innocent those sentenced by profane judges!

The synod probably had in mind a law of Gratian of 17 May 376 addressed to four (probably Gallic) bishops, directing that theological dissensions and minor offences shall be decided by episcopal synods, but that criminal charges shall be heard in the secular courts.[2]

From all this evidence it seems clear that Maximus would have been thought to be infringing church principles if he admitted a bishop as defendant before his tribunal where the charge was one of doctrine or church discipline. But in the case of a charge of criminal acts of sorcery, it would be far from clear that Maximus had erred in fundamental juristic theory. Nothing would have been easier than to see a precedent in the outlawing of Ursinus, against which Milan and Rome had raised no protest. It may be simply the result of accident in the nature of the sources preserved that the debate about Priscillian's trial seems never to have included this point. To both Ambrose and Martin of Tours the Priscillianists were simply heretics who, as such, should not have been tried before the praetorian prefect. Neither Ambrose nor Martin consider the question whether recourse to black magic is outside the jurisdiction of a lay court of law. It would have seemed an implausible assertion.

For Ambrose and Martin there was a central offence in the trial. A bishop, set apart by consecration to be a vessel of divine mercy, was a self-chosen instrument of wrath.

---

[1] Augustine (*De civ. Dei* 19. 6) observes that because judges cannot discern the thoughts of defendants they have to torture innocent men. Agobard of Lyon (*De grandine et tonitruis* 16, PL 104. 158) remarks how under torture men confess to crimes which they cannot possibly have done. On Gregory the Great, see below, p. 139, n. 3. For the power of holy men to discern guilt and innocence cf. *Historia Monachorum* 16 (18) on Eulogius.

[2] *C. Theod.* xvi. 2. 23, dated from Trier, addressed to Artemius, Eurydicus, Appius, Gerasimus, and all other bishops. A bishop Artemius was at the council of Valence. 374.

The accusing of one bishop by another on a capital charge raised acute questions of conscience. The consistent Christian tradition was to regard capital punishment as in all circumstances unacceptable. Athenagoras declares that the death penalty is intolerable even if in accordance with the code of justice.[1] The *Apostolic Tradition* of Hippolytus forbids any Christian in authority to order an execution.[2] The council of Elvira forbids a Christian magistrate to attend church services during his term of office, which betrays some modification of rigour.[3] Lactantius says that no Christian may cause death either in war or *by accusing anyone of a capital offence* or by exposing an unwanted child.[4] So, unfortunately for Ithacius, there were bishops who thought it wrong in principle for a bishop to be the accuser of a colleague on a capital charge, quite apart from the question of making a heretical bishop the defendant in a lay court. It was one thing for a heretical or schismatic bishop, after canonical deposition by a synod, to be exiled from his city by the government, since to allow him freedom to stay would surely lead to breaches of the peace and the division of the city into factions.[5] It was quite another thing for a bishop accused of heresy to be liable to execution at the hands of the civil authority. Capital punishment was inherently offensive to Ambrose of Milan, as to Augustine, because its exclusively retributory and deterrent character eliminated any possibility of remedial effect upon the criminal. Neither Ambrose nor Augustine goes so far as to say that capital punishment or even torture is in all conceivable circumstances an outrage; but both think a wise justice should forgo their use. Ambrose's twenty-fifth letter replies to a Christian governor Studius who has asked his advice about the death penalty. Ambrose feels unable to agree with the strict Novatianists who excommunicate those who pass sentence of death, but thinks a Christian judge should avoid it. Moreover 'even pagan governors commonly boast of having never executed a man'.[6]

---

[1] *Legatio* 35.   [2] *Ap. trad.* 16. 17.   [3] Canon 56.

[4] Lactantius, *Div. inst.* vi. 20. 15–20. Elsewhere (*Ira Dei* 17) he is inconsistent with this.

[5] So, for example, Ambrose, *Ep.* 10. 8 (the council of Aquileia) on the Arians of Illyricum.

[6] For Augustine see *Sermo* 13. 8; *Ep.* 91. 7; *Ep.* 153. 10 (*CSEL* 44. 407, 17–18) to Macedonius. See F. Homes Dudden, *The Life and Times of St. Ambrose* (Oxford, 1935), i. 121, n. 2; H. A. Deane, *The Political and Social Ideas of St. Augustine* (New York, 1963), p. 329, n. 133. Pope Innocent I is a little less rigorist against capital

Nevertheless Ambrose interprets Phineas' zeal in killing the
Israelite who had a Midianite wife (Num. 25 : 8) as a model for
bishops to imitate in crushing heresy. During the fourth century
the use of the sword by the secular arm in defence of the prevailing
orthodoxy had not been unknown. If Christians could allow the
possibility of a just war, in logic they should come to allow that
there can be a justified exercise of capital punishment. In the
forties of the fourth century when Constantius sent Macarius to
Numidia to coerce the Donatists, a few died as martyrs. Optatus
defended Macarius' severity by appealing to the Old Testament
precedents of Moses ordering the execution of 3,000 (Exod. 32 :
28) immediately after descending from Sinai with the command-
ment, 'Thou shalt not kill,' or Elijah slaying 450 priests of Baal
at the brook Kishon (1 Kings 18 : 40).[1] The application of drastic
penalties was no doubt defended on the ground that the Donatists
were sources of division frequently leading to riot and disorder.
In 366 the Arian population of Sirmium wanted the Nicene layman Heraclian tried before the governor and put to death for
causing sedition and schism by his rejection of the great council
of Ariminum.[2] Their demand is a reminder that when in a majority
Arianism was no more tolerant than orthodoxy.

   In the Greek East the extrusion of Arianism after the council of
Constantinople (381) was not such as to produce Arian martyrs,
and the Christological controversies, though from time to time
producing vehement crowd reaction which led to loss of life,
were not marred by actual executions of those deemed heretical.
The language of total intolerance first begins to be met in the
dark passions of the Byzantine iconoclastic controversy. In the
sixth century Symeon Stylites the younger, from his column on the
Wonderful Mountain near Antioch on the Orontes, encouraged
the emperor Justin II to kill the rebellious Samaritans. His letter

punishment (*Ep.* 6. 3–5; below, p. 187). Leo I (*Ep.* 118. 2 to Julian of Cos) hopes the
emperor, while dealing severely with turbulent heretical monks, will avoid capital
punishment. On the other hand, of the Priscillianist executions at Trier Leo writes
that their 'severity was for long a help to the gentleness of the Church; for although
it is content with episcopal judgement and flees from acts of cruel retribution, yet
it is assisted by the severe edicts of Christian princes, since those who fear bodily
punishment often run to seek a spiritual remedy' (*Ep.* 15, praef.); below, p. 215.

   [1] Ambrose, *Expl. Ps.* 118. 18. 10–11; Optatus iii. 7.
   [2] *Altercatio Heracliani laici cum Germinio episcopo Sirmiensi*, ed. C. P. Caspari,
Kirchenhistorische Anecdota i (1883), 146–7 (= PL Suppl. i. 349). Cf. M. Meslin, *Les
Ariens d'occident*, pp. 69–70, 294–6.

was to become a fatal document to justify executions in the quarrels of the iconoclastic struggle. Even then the great iconophile Theodore of Studios protested to Theophilus, bishop of Ephesus 824–33, that iconoclast heretics must be taught, not killed. On the authority of Dionysius the Areopagite Theodore rejects the validity of appeals to the executions carried out by Moses and Elijah. If the emperor took arms against the Samaritans, that can be justified if they rebelled with force against his government, but not because of religious dissent.[1]

The date of Priscillian's end

The date of Priscillian's trial and execution is assigned to the year 385 in the chronicle of Prosper of Aquitaine, first produced in 433 and particularly interested in Gallic affairs.[2] The same date is assigned to it in the anonymous Gallic chronicle of 452, which places Justina's quarrel with Ambrose over the basilicas *after* the trial at Trier.[3] On the other hand the chronicle of Hydatius, written in 468 or 469, seems to put Priscillian's appeal in 385, his trial and execution in 387.[4] Sulpicius Severus says that after the condemnation of Priscillian discord among the Gallic bishops continued for fifteen years.[5] While he notes that he has written his work in the first consulship of Stilicho (400),[6] yet passages in the *Chronicle* about the Jewish revolt under Hadrian and Helena's pilgrimage to the holy places have been adapted with borrowings from a letter to Severus from Paulinus of Nola written in 402 or more probably 403.[7] So the *Chronicle* is likely to have been written in or about 400, but to have undergone revisions before publication in 403. It is therefore reasonably probable that Severus dated Priscillian's condemnation about 385;

[1] Theod. Studita, *Ep.* ii. 152 (*PG* 99. 1481–5). Symeon's letter survives by citation in the Acts of the Second Council of Nicaea, 787, actio V (Labbe–Coleti viii. 1000 f.).
[2] Mommsen, *Chronica minora* i. 462.
[3] Ibid. i. 646. Paulinus (*Vita Ambrosii*) completes the narrative of Justina's persecution before referring to Ambrose's second embassy to Trier.
[4] Ibid. ii. 15. Since Maximus invaded Italy in 387, this seems too late to be credible unless the trial fell early in the year.
[5] Sulpicius Severus, *Chron.* ii. 51. 8. The approximate period may run from the trial at Trier to the council of Turin, the date of which is also contested, but is most simply assigned to 398 (below, p. 164).
[6] *Chron.* ii. 9. 7.
[7] Paulinus, *Ep.* 31, probably written in 402 or 403 (see P. Fabre, *Essai sur la chronologie de l'œuvre de S. Paulin de Nole* (Paris, 1948), p. 40), used in *Chron.* ii. 31. 3 and 33–5.

but this is not a certainty, and he cannot be made to give an exact answer.

In his dialogue 'Gallus' Sulpicius Severus declares (according to the text of the Verona manuscript of A.D. 517) that after the synod held at Trier as the trial was ending, when Felix was consecrated to succeed Britto as bishop of Trier, Martin of Tours lived for a further sixteen years.[1] Gregory of Tours, however, states with precision that Martin died aged eighty-one at Candes (a village in his diocese) on a Sunday night in the year 397.[2] Since Priscillian's trial cannot be put back to 382, either Severus or Gregory must be wrong. Martin's feast day is 11 November, which fell on a Sunday in 400 but not in 397. On the other hand, 11 November 397 could be the date on which he was buried at Tours. It would be unusual for the feast day to be other than the day of death. But the bishops who assembled in synod at Tours in November 461 explain that they have come together for the feast of the 'reception' of Martin.[3] Accordingly, since Tillemont[4] the majority of scholars have favoured 397 for Martin's death rather than 400, although the latter date is easily reconcilable with Sulpicius Severus and would give 385 as the date of Priscillian's trial. If Gregory of Tours's date 397 is accepted (and the balance of probability favours its correctness), then Severus' 'sixteen' must be a transcriptional error. The simplest conjecture, made recently by Vollmann,[5] is to regard XVI as an error for XIV, giving 384 as the year both of the trial and of the consecration of Felix. However, this discussion makes it clear that neither Severus nor Gregory of Tours can bring us certainty.

Since the date of the trial at Trier depends on the date assigned to Ambrose's second mission to Maximus on behalf of Valentinian, the possibility of achieving greater precision depends directly on the interpretation of Ambrose's text in the setting of his biography. *Ep.* 24 (30 in Faller's edition in *CSEL*) is a careful but undated report on this mission, which ends with a description of his dismissal by Maximus when he had refused to hold

[1] *Dial.* iii. 13. 6 'sedecim [sedicem V] postea vixit annos'.

[2] *Historia Francorum* i. 48; x. 31.

[3] See the Acts in C. Munier's critical edition, *Concilia Galliae a. 314–a. 506* (*Corpus Christianorum* 148, 1963), p. 143, or in Bruns ii. 139 (not in Lauchert).

[4] *Mémoires* x (1705), 776–81, a masterly discussion. 397 is accepted by Babut, *St. Martin de Tours* (1912), and Duchesne, *Fastes épiscopaux de l'ancienne Gaule*, ii (1910), 302.   [5] *Studien*, pp. 4–5.

communion with bishops 'who were seeking the death of anyone though heretical in faith'.[1] He was sad, he adds, to see the aged bishop Hyginus (of Cordoba) being roughly sent off into exile at his last gasp without any cushion or covering. From this conclusion of the letter it is evident that the second mission to Maximus coincided with the conclusion of the Priscillianist process; it would be tempting to add that the concern for Hyginus' warmth points to a date other than high summer, if the climate in the Mosel valley were, as it is not, consistently warm in summer.

Ambrose's report on his second mission to Trier has odd features that have not been noticed by all readers. Ambrose seems at first sight to be representing himself as an ostentatious and offensive boor, indifferent to the most elementary considerations of courtesy. He emphasizes at every possible point what an arctic reception he was given by Maximus and what an abysmal failure he has been as Valentinian's legate. The ostensible purposes of his journey were to put the record straight about the deception which Maximus was accusing him of practising at the time of his first mission in 383 and to beg for the remains of Valentinian's brother Gratian for worthy burial at Milan.[2] On his arrival at the palace Ambrose was refused a private audience and was received with ceremonious formality in the consistory. As he entered, he refused with studied offensiveness the emperor's customary kiss of greeting.[3] In the ensuing dialogue bishop and emperor exchanged a succession of abrasive discourtesies so that there was not the least hope of gaining co-operation from Maximus on anything, and the sole ascertainable objective appears to have been to achieve a resounding failure, even if only to be able to represent Maximus as an inhuman monster refusing Gratian

[1] Paulinus, *Vita Ambrosii* 19, transforms Maximus' brusque dismissal of Ambrose into an initiative taken by Ambrose censuring Maximus for shedding the blood of the innocent Gratian. But the distortion is not perhaps so great as may appear. Ambrose's refusal of communion with Britto of Trier was automatically a refusal of Maximus as well.

[2] Similarly Ambrose, *Obit. Val.* 28: 'I went twice as your legate to the Gauls, and it was my sweet duty first to act for your safety, then for peace and for piety in that you were asking for your brother's remains.' *Expos. Ps.* 61. 24 (*CSEL* 64. 393).

When Valentinian II was murdered, Ambrose wrote to offer burial in the porphyry sarcophagus made for Maximian, colleague of Diocletian (*Ep.* 53. 4). Something similar was probably in view for Gratian.

[3] Other evidence on the imperial kiss of greeting is collected by A. Alföldi, *Die monarchische Repräsentation im römischen Kaiserreiche* (Darmstadt, 1970), p. 41, reprinted from *Römische Mitteilungen*, 1934.

decent burial and a tyrant worse than Pontius Pilate.[1] In the
dialogue Ambrose directly accuses Maximus of illegal usurpation;
and in reply Maximus explicitly refuses to recognize that equality
of imperial status which Ambrose claims for his master Valentinian.[2] The entire conduct of the embassy is indeed a bizarre
affair if any actual success in negotiation was really hoped for.
Moreover, it seems so strange not to have begged for Gratian's
corpse on the first mission of 383, that one is tempted to think
there was more to the mission's motives than Ambrose quite
openly reveals. Ambrose travelled with Valentinian's commission,
and emphasizes that he wasted no time at Trier on arrival but at
once presented himself at the palace. Yet it is hard not to wonder
whether in Ambrose's mind a principal motive for the journey
was to be able to observe closely the course of the Priscillianist
trial, the outcome of which was of vital interest to the church in
Milan and Rome.

The manner in which Ambrose delights in reporting his fracas
with Maximus and his anxiety lest rumours of close accord should
get about are intelligible only if his own relations with Valentinian and Justina are already under a black cloud. The report on
the second mission is designed to clear away all suspicion of being
in secret collusion with Maximus. He sends on the report ahead
of him, post-haste, lest Valentinian should first receive from
someone else a slanted or malicious account of Ambrose's dis-
charge of duty. Accordingly at the time of the second mission
Ambrose's personal situation at Milan is already that he is and is
known to be distrusted by the court. He must on no account
represent himself as having enjoyed a friendly and successful
negotiation, since the more friendly he was with Maximus the
more exposed he would be to suggestions of high treason.[3]

[1] *Expos. Ps.* 61. 25, perhaps preached to Valentinian II at Milan soon after
Ambrose's return, again with the motive of denying any compact or understanding
between himself and Maximus.   [2] *Ep.* 24 (30). 3 and 10.
  [3] The old date of spring 387 for Ambrose's second visit (Baronius, Tillemont)
has been rejected in favour of the autumn of 384 by many German scholars in this
century; e.g. Rauschen, *Jahrbücher der christlichen Kirche unter den Kaiser Theodosius*
(1897), p. 487; H. von Campenhausen, *Ambrosius von Mailand als Kirchenpolitiker*
(1929), pp. 183 f.; H. J. Diesner, *Kirche und Staat im spätrömischen Reich* (1964), p. 27.
O. Seeck, *Untergang* 5, pp. 510, 515, opts for spring 384; W. Ensslin, art. 'Valentinianus II', in *PW* viiA. 2210–11, for midsummer 384, and likewise V. Grumel,
'La Deuxième Mission de St. Ambroise auprès de Maxime', *Revue des études byzantines*
9 (1951), 154–60.
  J. R. Palanque, *S. Ambroise et l'empire romain* (1932), pp. 516–18, and Homes

It cannot be insignificant, in the light of Maximus' endeavours to steal the hearts of the Italian bishops, that the dispute with Maximus is not merely about Gratian's burial or his own disingenuous winks and nods at the time of his first mission to Trier. He and Maximus finally parted brass-rags not on a political question but on a specifically ecclesiastical and moral issue. Valentinian must not think that Maximus and Ambrose are in intimate agreement even on church policy. The ordinary reader of *Ep.* 24 (30) is likely to think that Ambrose protests too much; so much as to make it very possible that Maximus had made some indirect bid to win over Ambrose to his support. If he expressed quiet sympathy with Ambrose in regard to the Altar of Victory or the basilicas, it would be the last matter that Ambrose could mention.

If this analysis is correct, or even near the truth, it follows that the second mission of Ambrose to Trier falls not only after the first emergence of a sense of estrangement and suspicion between Ambrose and Justina, but also after some consciousness of Maximus' propaganda on the religious question of toleration for pagans and heretics has penetrated the Milanese court. The earliest possible date for supposing such a situation to exist is the late autumn of 384, after the confrontation over the Altar of Victory in which Ambrose was successful. A date in the late summer or autumn of 385 is more likely; by this time the question of toleration in Milan for Arian worship has been raised, even if it has not yet become the red-hot issue that it becomes during Lent 386. There are two considerations that make the summer of 386 the most plausible date. First, Ambrose's report says that on arrival

Dudden, *Saint Ambrose* (1935), i. 346, saw correctly that *Ep.* 24 presupposes deep distrust of Ambrose at the Milanese court. Palanque mistakenly argued that the visit should be put after Easter 386 on the basis of Paulinus (*Vita* 12–19) who first speaks of the mission after completing his narrative of the Arian crisis in Milan. This untenable argument he has abandoned. Palanque is now content to affirm that the embassy may fall between September 384 and Valentinian's flight in 387 (*Les Empereurs romains d'Espagne*, 1965, p. 259). Within this area of possibility, probability still favours 386, with 385 as less probable, but more so than 384 or 387. The date 386 for which Palanque argued in 1932 is generally accepted by most French scholars, e.g. A. d'Alès, *Priscillien*, p. 60; A. Piganiol, *L'Empire chrétien*, 1st edn. (1947), p. 243 = 2nd edn. (1972), p. 268; J. Fontaine in *Studia Anselmiana* 46 (1961), 195, n. 16; also by J. Matthews, *Western Aristocracies* (1975), p. 180. A. Paredi, *St. Ambrose* (Notre-Dame, 1964), pp. 237, 239, puts Ambrose's second mission in Oct.–Nov. 384, but defers Priscillian's condemnation to spring 385. Vollmann, *Studien*, p. 4, n. 6, follows Ensslin in putting the second embassy in summer 384, but allows that the execution could have been early in 385; in *PW* Suppl. xiv. 513 he opts for the end of 384 for the date of execution.

at the palace in Trier he was asked if he had brought with him
Valentinian's 'rescript'; that is, his reply to a letter from Maximus.
It is possible that the letter from Maximus to which this word
contains an implicit reference is the extant letter contained in the
Avellana collection, in which Maximus warns Valentinian of
the disastrous political consequences for him of persecuting the
orthodox. Secondly, the entire manner of Ambrose's report
strongly suggests that he regarded his mission as a dangerous trap,
designed to discredit him at Milan by suggesting that, if he succeeded with Maximus, that must be evidence of treasonable conspiracy. The mission to Trier cannot have been one that Ambrose
would have undertaken of his own choice; on the other hand,
he could not possibly have refused to go if asked. Therefore,
without ruling out 385 as actually unlikely in any way, the summer
of 386 is the date that looks most probable from a careful consideration of Ambrose's report on his embassy.

There is one scrap of evidence which at first sight seems to tell
against this conclusion, and to point to the late autumn of 384.
In the letter to his sister Marcellina describing his first skirmish
in regard to the basilicas, written about Easter 385, Ambrose says
that Maximus has been complaining that his (first) embassy
hindered him from invading Italy.[1] Since this is precisely the
charge levelled against Ambrose at his second embassy before
the consistory at Trier, it seems an almost irresistible temptation
to suppose that Ambrose is here reporting to Marcellina a complaint of which he came to learn at the time of his second expedition to see Maximus.[2] The argument is not, however, decisive,
and the temptation can be resisted. One of the explicit motives
which led Ambrose to make his second visit to Trier was his
awareness that Maximus was accusing him of duplicity and deceit;
that is to say, he knew of this complaint before going again to
Trier and so could easily have mentioned it in a letter to his sister
written before the journey.[3]

One other allusion has to be placed in the scales of judgement.
There is a nettled, reproachful sentence in the letter written by
Ambrose to Valentinian at the height of the crisis over the sur-
render of the basilicas: 'I have not learnt how to stand in the

---

[1] Ambrose, *Ep.* 20. 23, parallel to 24. 6.
[2] So Ensslin in *PW* viiA, 2210–11 (s.v. 'Valentinianus II').
[3] So rightly V. Grumel in *Revue des études byzantines* 9 (1951), 156.

consistory except as your representative.'[1] The reference can only be to Maximus' insistence on receiving him at Trier, both on his first and on his second embassies, in full consistory[2] rather than in the private audience which Ambrose claims to be the normal protocol for a bishop, and which he would particularly have preferred on his second visit when the discussion was partly concerned with his personal integrity. On his first visit Ambrose uttered no protest against being received in consistory; on the second visit he tried to make an issue of it, and Maximus was able to point out that he had uttered no word of dissatisfaction on the occasion of his first reception in full consistory. It must be concluded that the sentence from the letter to Valentinian is indecisive. While it would be tempting to think it written after the second mission to Trier, it could just as well have been written with reference to the first.

The Trial

The arrival of Ambrose at Trier while the Priscillianist process was in train is never mentioned by Sulpicius Severus, for whom the moral issue of a bishop prosecuting on a capital charge was raised solely by his hero Martin of Tours. From his Dialogue 'Gallus' it emerges that another Gallic bishop Theognitus, whose see is not mentioned, had already refused to join the other bishops by withholding his assent before Martin came to Trier to make his protest to Maximus.[3] In Sulpicius Severus Martin used language on which Ambrose could not have improved to raise three complaints: firstly, that it was morally wrong for a bishop to be prosecuting anyone on a capital charge; secondly, that since the Priscillianists had been synodically censured as heretics and declared excommunicate it was enough now for the secular arm to expel them from their churches for the preservation of public order; thirdly, that charges against a bishop should be heard by bishops, not before a secular tribunal. This last complaint presupposed that Priscillian was a bishop, a proposition denied by Ithacius and

[1] *Ep.* 21. 20.
[2] On the role of the consistory see A. H. M. Jones, *Later Roman Empire* i. 333–41, 504–7; W. Kunkel in *Jahrbuch für Antike und Christentum* 11/12 (1968/9), 230–48 = *Kleine Schriften* (Weimar, 1974), pp. 405–40. Jones's brief account of Ambrose's interview with Maximus treats *Ep.* 24 (30) too much at face value; i.e. as additional evidence that Ambrose was a dislikeable bully.
[3] Sulpicius Severus, *Dial.* iii. 12. 1.

Hydatius of Mérida. At first (Severus explains) Maximus was influenced by Martin; but later was misled by Magnus and Rufus,[1] of whose role and identity Severus says nothing to satisfy curiosity, and so concluded by entrusting the hearing of the case to his praetorian prefect Euodius, a man with a reputation for severity. On a charge of employing malignant witchcraft severe torture could be, and normally was used. Ambrose's biography mentions the torturing of a sorcerer at Milan,[2] and it was the expected procedure in all such cases. Sorcery was closely associated with suspicions of high treason, and in such an atmosphere of fear the Roman judicial system took little account of the virtual certainty that some of those tortured would be innocent citizens who had done nothing to deserve hooks lacerating their sides and their limbs torn out on the rack. Augustine observed that it is a melancholy duty to be a judge who, being human, cannot penetrate the thoughts of defendants and witnesses and so uses torture under which many innocent men confess to crimes they have not committed, or from which they emerge with mangled bodies if they do not die.[3]

Under judicial examination Priscillian confessed to his interest in magical studies, to having held nocturnal gatherings of (loose) women, and to having prayed naked. The juxtaposition of the charges was surely intended to insinuate the suggestion that, in what was believed to be Manichee fashion, these activities had gone on at one and the same time and place. The most orthodox nocturnal vigils were always vulnerable to suggestions of improper conduct. Vigilantius attacked them as highly dangerous

---

[1] The bishop of Metz about this time was named Rufus (Duchesne, *Fastes* iii. 54). This is a more likely identification than the Spanish bishop Rufus of Sulpicius Severus, *Vita Martini* 24, deposed for accepting the claims of a young Spaniard that he was Elijah or even Christ at his second Advent (above, p. 10).

[2] Paulinus, *Vita Ambrosii* 20. 1.

[3] Augustine, *De civ. Dei* 19. 6. On torture in the ancient judicial system see the articles by G. Thür and J. Vergote in *RAC* viii, s.v. 'Folter' and 'Folterwerkzeuge' (1969). Under later canon law clergy were forbidden to be present at torture (canon 33 of Auxerre, between 573 and 603; canon 19 of Mâcon II, 585; canon 6 of Toledo XI, 675, 'his a quibus domini sacramenta tractanda sunt, iudicium sanguinis agitare non licet'). Gregory the Great told Constantius of Milan that, since torture often made innocent men confess to crimes they had not committed, no confession extorted by violence should be accepted (*Ep.* x. 11 (29), May 600). Pope Nicolas I tells the Bulgar king in 866 that torture is contrary to divine and human law (*Ep.* 97. 86, PL 119. 1010). The use of torture to uncover heresy from Innocent IV (1252) onwards was a sharp break with past tradition.

to pure morals.[1] As we have already seen (above, p. 18), the accusation of praying naked is probably linked with belief in the magical potency of nakedness, and with the anxieties of the council of Saragossa about Priscillian's followers going about with unshod feet. The ascetic movement of the fourth century seems to have held strong views on the inappropriateness of praying naked even in private and alone.[2] Palestinian rabbis certainly regarded the practice with abhorrence.[3] Jerome could mock Vigilantius because once during an earthquake at Bethlehem he had prayed for safety without stopping to clothe himself decently.[4] Nevertheless in the context of the charge of *maleficium*, Priscillian's nakedness is less indecent than magical.

A law of Valentinian I of 364 expressly forbade anyone during the hours of the night offering malignant prayers or using magical preparations or celebrating sinister ('funesta') sacrifices.[5] The reaction after the death of Julian had seen many trials of distinguished pagans on charges of sorcery which had involved harsh torture and had ended in executions.[6] Under Julian Christian holy men with charismatic powers had been open to like treatment.[7] Something of the atmosphere of tense hatred is revealed by the decision of Julian's successor Jovian to burn a library that Julian had installed in a temple built by Hadrian at Antioch.[8]

---

[1] Jerome, *Contra Vigilantium* 1; *Ep.* 109. 3. Cf. canon 35 of the council of Elvira: 'Women are not to keep vigil at the cemetery, for the reason that often under the excuse of prayer they secretly commit sins.'
The Manichees were believed to have meetings for worship at which men and women prayed together naked: Anastasius Sinaita, *In Hexaemeron* 7 (*PG* 89. 963D). For similar reports of the Adamites see Epiphanius, *Panarion* 52. 2. The question was raised among the Messalians, but Macarius/Symeon held that such worship was possible only after the resurrection (*Hom.* 34. 2).

[2] Sulpicius Severus, *Dial.* iii. 14. 8–9.   [3] Mishnah, *Berakhoth* 3. 5.

[4] Jerome, *Contra Vigilantium* 11.

[5] *Cod. Theod.* ix. 16. 7 (9 Sept. 364). Zosimus (iv. 3) explains that Praetextatus was able to obtain exemption for the Eleusinian mysteries on the ground that, though nocturnal, they were hallowed by ancient custom.

[6] Ammian xxviii. 1; xxix. 1–2; Zosimus iv. 13–16. E. A. Thompson says that, though Ammian was horrified by the trials, he nowhere asserts the innocence of the defendants (*The Historical Work of Ammianus Marcellinus*, 1947, p. 102). See below, p. 142, n. 3.

[7] Jerome, *Vita Hilarionis* 33 (*PL* 23. 48): 'Gazenses . . . loquebantur, Nonne vera sunt quae audivimus? magus est et futura cognoscit. Urbs enim Gaza, postquam, profecto de Palaestina Hilarione, Julianus in imperium successerat, destructo monasterio eius, precibus ad imperatorem datis, et Hilarionis et Hesychii mortem impetraverat; amboque ut quaererentur toto orbe scriptum erat.'

[8] Joh. Antioch. fr. 181 (*FHG* iv. 607); Suda, s.v. 'Jovianus' (Adler, ii. 638).

The fear of sorcery was ubiquitous in the ancient world.[1] Some Platonists claimed that immunity from its effects was granted to those who devoted themselves to philosophy.[2] But other Platonists thought nothing so important as the correct ritual of 'theurgy', and in the middle of the fourth century this school, following the influential teaching of Iamblichus (who died about 325–30), became very prominent.[3] The young Julian was led to abandon Christianity because fascinated by Maximus of Ephesus, who could make a statue of Hecate smile by appropriate rites.[4] The Julianic revival of militant polytheism greatly stimulated the fear of divination and magic among the Christians. But even before Julian, under Constantius II, accusations of using sorcery were touching figures of high pagan society. The characteristic feature of this fourth-century obsession with sorcery is not the belief in its effectiveness for evil (which was not stronger in the fourth century than at other times), but the social prominence of the persons accused of resorting to it and the atmosphere of hysteria in which the trials were conducted. As at Salem in 1692, panic deprived men of the power and the will to distinguish between innocent and guilty.

Why this was so is a question hard to answer with confidence. One can speculate on the rivalries created by the power conflicts between the old senatorial families and the rising new men, usually Christians, who had more direct access to the ear of a Christian emperor. In situations of harsh rivalry resort to sorcery is perhaps instinctive.[5] Or one can turn for more particular explanation to the modest success in continual wars against Persia enjoyed by the Roman armies in the fourth century. Persia was the very home of magic,[6] and it was well known that the magi wickedly assisted

---

[1] Pliny, *NH* 28. 10 and 18, says that it is a great and unanswerable question whether spells take effect, but 'no one is without fear of being bewitched by dire curses'.

[2] Celsus in Origen, *C. Cels.* vi. 41; Plotinus, iv. 4. 43–4.

[3] Iamblichus' *De mysteriis*, Julian's discourses, and Sallustius' treatise 'On the gods' are the classic documents of this development.

[4] Eunapius, *V. Soph.* 475 Boissonade (p. 44 edn. Giangrande).

[5] See an instructive, generalising essay by Peter Brown, *Religion and Society in the age of St. Augustine* (1972), pp. 119–46, first printed in the monograph, *Witchcraft, confessions, and accusations* (Association of Social Anthropologists, 1970). In the trial of Priscillian episcopal rivalry is clearly a *vera causa* of the accusation but cannot be seen to motivate recourse to magic.

[6] Diocletian's edict against the Manichees (of 297) execrates them because they come from 'Persia with whom we are at enmity' and declares that they are to be

the Persian troops by all manner of hocus pocus.[1] After Julian's death on the Persian campaign in June 363, the sense of misfortune was strong. Julian's death and the defeat of his army was to the Christians a vindication of their faith and a refutation of Julian's. Yet the *Schadenfreude*, which the Christians took no pains to hide, can only have been mingled with gloom at the reality of the military catastrophe involving the ignominious surrender of Nisibis and Singara.[2] The Christians had once looked forward with confidence to the day when a Christian emperor would reign gloriously and at peace. Not only was the Persian army in control of Mesopotamia, Valentinian I had hard campaigning on the Rhine. From 375 onwards the Hun migration was producing chaos on the Danube and in the Balkan peninsula. It was natural for Christians to extricate themselves from the embarrassment of military failures by asking if the displeasure of heaven was caused by pagan theurgy and sorcery. The emperors Constantius II, Valentinian I, and Valens were all terrified of magic, and the rigorous tortures with which men were examined under their rule touched many eminent figures who vainly protested their innocence of all treasonable thoughts.[3]

hunted out under the laws against sorcerers; any *honorati* found associated with this disgusting sect ('turpem sectam') are to have their property confiscated and be sent to the mines of Phaeno or Proconnesus. (The text, from *Mosaicarum et Romanorum legum collatio* xv. 3, is in Adam, *Texte zum Manichäismus*[2] (1969), pp. 82–3. The passage on Persia is cited by Ambrosiaster on 2 Tim. 3: 6–7.) For studies of the extent to which in the fourth and fifth centuries Manicheism was objectionable because Persian, see Peter Brown, *Religion and Society in the Age of St. Augustine*, pp. 94–118 (from *JRS* 1969), and L. J. van der Lof, 'Mani as the danger from Persia in the Roman Empire', *Augustiniana* 24 (1974), 75–84.

[1] John of Nikiu, *Chronicle* 96. 17 (p. 156, tr. R. H. Charles). Nisibis was three times under siege, in 337, 346, and 350; and in 359 the Persians captured successively Amida and Singara. For a summary see Festus, *Breviarium* 27, with J. W. Eadie's notes (London, 1967) for parallel sources.

[2] Of the wretched fate of the citizens of Nisibis, Malalas reports that they were resettled in an unprotected shanty town outside the walls of Amida (xiii. 336 Bonn). On the extent of the surrender see Ammian xxv. 19. 9. The line of the new frontier is discussed by E. Honigmann, *Die Ostgrenze des byzantinischen Reiches* (Brussels, 1961), pp. 5–8. In 383–4 the western pilgrim Egeria, who had special interest in Mesopotamian monasticism (below, p. 166), found to her disappointment that she could not visit Nisibis and Ur of the Chaldees, because 'the Romans now have no access there, and all this region is in Persian hands' (*Itin.* 20. 12). The difficulty of crossing the Romano-Persian frontier by Nisibis is attested also by Jerome, *Vita Malchi* 3.

[3] See Ammian xix. 12. 8–15 on the purge at Scythopolis in 359. Ammian xiv. 1. 2 reports that Gallus (Julian's brother) and his wife eliminated innocent victims with false accusations of 'ambition to be emperor and black arts'. For the sorcery trials and Ammian's attitude to them see H. Funke, 'Majestäts- und Magieprozesse bei

The primary charge on which the prefect Euodius found Priscillian guilty was that of sorcery and, since the edict of Diocletian, sorcery and Manicheism were associated. Nevertheless, it does not seem that merely being a Manichee at this time was in itself a grave hazard to one's life. Manichees lay low, as Augustine remarks,[1] but until the time of Anastasius and Justinian they were not hounded to actual execution. In a law of 8 May 381 Theodosius imposed civil disabilities on Manichees, depriving them of legal rights, confiscating their property, prohibiting their assemblies.[2] Admittedly a further law of 31 March 382 went so far as to impose the death penalty on certain extreme sects in Asia Minor of Manichee sympathy—the Encratites, Saccophoroi, and Hydroparastatae—encouraging informers to report all such persons to special inquisitors. But this degree of severity seems to have been temporary and purely local.[3] Manichees were disliked and distrusted, generally supposed to be guilty of enormity.[4] Ithacius' accusation that Priscillian was a secret Manichee, combined with the admitted fact that he believed in exceptional freedom for women, would quickly lead to suggestions of improper conduct unfitting in a bishop. Hence no doubt the gossip that Priscillian got Procula with child (above, p. 37). Accusations of moral pollution confirmed, however, the substantive capital charge of witchcraft. Priscillian was eventually executed for sorcery rather

Ammianus Marcellinus', *Jahrbuch für Antike und Christentum* 10 (1967), 145–75; R. C. Blockley, *Ammianus Marcellinus* (Coll. Latomus 141, Brussels, 1975), pp. 105–22.

[1] Aug. *Conf.* 5. 10. 19 'plures enim eos Roma *occultat*'. Capital punishment for Manichees was enacted under the emperor Anastasius (*C. Just.* i. 5. 11). Justinian's edicts (ibid. 12 and 16) require relentless extermination. On the repression of Manichees there is a useful provisional note by F. Decret, *Aspects du Manichéisme dans l'Afrique romaine* (Paris, 1970), pp. 331–2.

[2] *Cod. Theod.* xvi. 5. 7.

[3] Ibid. xvi. 5. 9, dated from Constantinople. Theodosius' law of 17 June 389 (*Cod. Theod.* xvi. 5. 18, to which the council of Milan in 390 gratefully refers: Ambrose, *Ep.* 42. 13) exiles Manichees.

[4] See, e.g. Ambrose, *Ep.* 50. 14 (Manichees combine sacrilege with *turpitudo*). Augustine (*De moribus* ii. 19–20, 67–75) tells of incidents of sexual immorality among the Manichees, endeavouring (rather unconvincingly) to suggest that they were typical rather than exceptional. He mentions one of the Manichee Elect in his time at Rome (when Augustine was a Manichee himself) who resented the popular image of the sect as given to sexual orgies and tried unsuccessfully to form an ascetic Manichee community in his own house. An inquisition at Carthage (reported by Augustine, *De haeresibus* 46) uncovered sordid erotic practices with a girl Margarita not yet twelve years old and with an older Manichean nun. See also the text of Ambrosiaster, summarized above, p. 56.

than heresy; but it was the taint of Manichean heresy that made the graver charge easy to believe.

After the first trial Priscillian was imprisoned and the question of sentence was referred to the emperor. Meanwhile, Ithacius had become aware of the depth of resentment against himself as accuser of a brother bishop on a capital charge. He was allowed to withdraw from the prosecution, presumably by the emperor himself. His withdrawal at this late stage is not likely to have been the result of loss of confidence on his part, in view of the fact that to bring a capital charge unsuccessfully was to risk one's own head.[1] His withdrawal, however, necessitated a second hearing of the case. He was replaced as prosecutor by Patricius, a treasury advocate (*fisci patronus*). The interest of the state treasury in the trial is underlined by a passing comment in Sulpicius Severus' dialogue 'Gallus' that Maximus 'wanted the heretics' property'. Large confiscations would help to provide the sinews of the coming civil war to gain control of Italy.[2]

When Maximus condemned Priscillian to be executed on the charge of *maleficium*, sorcery, there died with him two clergy, Felicissimus and Armenius; his wealthy friend Euchrotia, widow of Delphidius;[3] and Latronianus, a Christian poet of sufficient note to receive an entry in Jerome's *Lives of Illustrious Men*, where the name of Julianus is also given as one of those who died.

Tribunes were sent to Spain to carry out a further inquisition there,[4] which resulted in the beheading of Asarivus (or Asarbus) and a deacon named Aurelius. Tiberianus lost all his property by confiscation and was exiled to the island of 'Sylinancis beyond Britain' (the earliest reference to the Scilly Isles).[5] Jerome likewise

---

[1] Ambrose, *Expl. Ps.* 118. 8. 25 (*CSEL* 62. 165, 14). Under the law a prosecutor was not allowed to withdraw if he realized things were going badly for him.
[2] The office of the *patronus fisci* appears several times in the Theodosian Code (e.g. x. 15; xi. 30. 41). For a treasury official being responsible for a prosecution for sorcery cf. Zosimus iv. 14. Sulpicius Severus (*Dial.* iii. 11. 10–11) mentions the emptiness of the chest as one of two possible explanations for Maximus' deplorable handling of the case, the other being the excessive influence of bishops upon him. Under a law of 8 May 381 Manichees' property was liable to confiscation (*C. Theod.* xvi. 5. 7). Of Maximus' confiscations Pacatus' *Panegyric* on Theodosius (26 ff.) draws a lurid picture.
[3] *Vir. inl.* 122. The execution of Euchrotia, as widow of a distinguished rhetor of Bordeaux, receives notice from Ausonius, v. 5 (*Prof.*), 37–8, as well as from Pacatus, *Paneg.* xii. 29.
[4] Sulpicius Severus, *Dial.* iii. 11.
[5] *Chronicon* ii. 51. The first of the Würzburg tractates mentions a libellus composed

records him as a writer, because he wrote a (lost) vindication of his beliefs as a Priscillianist, to which *Tract.* i, p. 3, 9, may refer, but sadly adds that in exile he pressed his daughter, who had taken the veil, to marry.[1] Three others from Spain, Tertullus, Potamius, and John, made a free confession before the threat of trial and torture; they were treated mildly with a sentence of exile in Gaul. Bishop Instantius was sent with Tiberianus to the Scilly Isles.

The exile of Hyginus of Cordoba has already been noted. He had first expressed alarm about the spread of the Priscillianist movement in Spain, but consistently played the part of a dove rather than a hawk, refusing to join in the excommunication threatened in 380 by the council of Saragossa, hoping to retain the devotion of the Priscillianists within the church, while correcting their exaggerations (above, ch. I, pp. 25 and 36). When the axe fell at Trier, Hyginus paid the price for his tenacious refusal to join Ithacius and Hydatius of Mérida. It is noteworthy, perhaps puzzling, that we hear no word of any move to call Symposius of Astorga to Trier.

The great majority of Gallic bishops obediently supported Ithacius, who published an 'apologia pro vita sua', painting a lurid picture of Priscillian's occultism and lecherous morals, asserting him to be an indirect imbiber of the Manichee doctrines of Mark of Memphis.[2] A synod was held in Trier (probably in the year after Priscillian's death), which formally pronounced Ithacius innocent of fault for the part he played as accuser in the trial. The same synod had to replace bishop Britto of Trier, who died about this time, and chose a virtuous man named Felix. To Felix's personal character there was no objection, but a bishop may be judged not only by his personal character but also by that of the bishops who take part in his consecration. (The general principle

by 'Tiberianus, Asarbus and others'. Early Christian archaeological remains on the Scilly Isles are undatable, but unlikely to be of the fourth century; for a summary see Paul Ashbee, *Ancient Scilly* (London, 1974), pp. 221–30.

[1] *Vir. inl.* 123. The marriage was probably a symbol of his own disenchantment and detachment from Priscillian's ideals, and therefore a request for release.

[2] Isidore of Seville, *Vir. inl.* 15 (PL 83. 1092). It is as good as certain that this work was a major source used by Sulpicius Severus for the account of Priscillian's origins in his *Chronicle*, where the same filiation is asserted (above, ch. I, p. 20), and probable that from the same source come the attributions to Priscillian of theosophical speculations (e.g. Orosius on the *Memoria apostolorum* and on the zodiac: below, p. 194).

is stated in Priscillian's 51st canon: 'Assuredly they who in some way consent to sinful men share in their sin.') At first Martin of Tours refused to hold communion with the bishops who accepted Ithacius and Hydatius as brothers; because it would mean associating in a sacred act with men who had blood on their hands, he declined to have anything to do with the consecration of Felix. He was brought to another view. According to Sulpicius Severus, in the Dialogue 'Gallus',[1] Martin went to petition Maximus to call off the inquisition already sent to Spain to hunt out the adherents of Priscillian. Severus defensively explains that Martin was not so much anxious to defend the Priscillianists as fearful of the indiscriminate nature of the inquiries, which would almost certainly catch not merely guilty men but innocent ascetics. Anyone with a pale face and shabby clothing would be liable to be arraigned without the least discrimination between orthodox and heretic.[2] The same fear had long since been expressed by Priscillian himself when he observed that Ithacius and Hydatius were ending by attacking not merely his own group but 'all Christians', as was proved by their attack on Hyginus of Cordoba.[3]

Martin's intervention with Maximus led to the prompt and natural accusation that he was a secret sympathizer with Priscillian. Nevertheless Maximus was determined to win Martin over. He received him not in consistory, as he had done with Ambrose, but in a private interview, and argued that Martin had no good reason to refuse communion with the bishops at Trier; for the sentence against the heretics had been pronounced not by malicious or jealous rivals but by a fair-minded, properly constituted court of justice. If it would enable Martin to take part in the

---

[1] *Dial.* iii. 12–13.
[2] Sulpicius Severus, *Chron.* ii. 50. 4. That ascetics in Aquitaine continued in the fifth century to be objects of obloquy appears in pseudo-Jerome, *Ep.* 6. 9 (PL 30. 93A), a work ascribed by Courcelle (*Revue des études anciennes* 56 (1954), 377–90) to the Aquitanian presbyter Eutropius noticed by Gennadius, *Vir. inl.* 50. Cf. also the anonymous *Consultationes Zacchaei et Apollonii* 3. 3 (PL 20. 1151–4) on odium against monks; on the placing of this work see G. M. Colombás, 'Sobre el autor de las Consultationes Zacchaei et Apollonii', *Studia monastica* 14 (1972), 7–15. Jerome complains that at this time any grave and pale ascetic was likely to be labelled a Manichee: *Ep.* 22. 14; *Adv. Iovin.* i. 3. For 'Manichee' as an imprecise term of general abuse, many examples occur in Greeks of this period; e.g. Athanasius, *Ad episc. Aeg.* 16 (of Arians); Nestorius, *Ep. ad Cyrillum*, PG 77. 56c = *ACO* I. i. 1, p. 32, 11 (of Cyril); Cyril's memorandum to Posidonius, *ACO* I. i. 7, p. 171, 33 (of Nestorius); etc.
[3] Priscillian, *Tract.* ii, p. 41, 4–5.

consecration of Felix, Maximus would be willing to order the recall of the tribunes from Spain. Martin accepted the bargain, but the compromise of his moral principles brought him sharp twinges of conscience which were allayed only by a private revelation that he had in fact done the right thing in the circumstances. It had been an unpleasant experience, and he never again attended a synod of bishops, even when its business was of deep concern to him. He used sadly to confess that since the day when he had felt forced to join with those polluted men in laying hands on Felix of Trier, he had suffered a loss of charismatic and healing powers.[1]

The Trier trial was condemned not only by Martin and Ambrose but also by pope Siricius, who wrote a formal letter to Maximus to protest. The letter is lost, but its content can be largely deduced from Maximus' extant reply. It is as good as certain that Siricius' complaints were at the bringing of a bishop for trial before a secular tribunal instead of before a synod and at the role played by bishop Ithacius in bringing an accusation on a capital charge. Siricius also took the opportunity to express anxiety about a Gallic cleric named Agroecius who had been improperly advanced to the presbyterate; unfortunately it is impossible to say what the objection to his promotion was, but in view of Siricius' interest in clerical celibacy it would not be implausible to speculate that Agroecius had acquired notoriety by refusing to put his wife into a convent.

Maximus' reply to Siricius survives in the *Avellana* collection. He courteously thanks the pope for his letter, and claims that his call by God to power was a religious vocation which came immediately following his ascent from the baptismal font. Two questions had been raised by Siricius. That of Agroecius' promotion would be referred entirely to the expert judgement of a coming council of all Gallic and Aquitanian bishops to be held in a city

---

[1] Babut, *S. Martin de Tours*, pp. 163–4, hazarded that Sulpicius Severus attributes his own anti-Felician stance to Martin, who in reality was contentedly in communion with Trier and all other Gallic bishops. The speculation is unsupported by considerations of general probability.

With the reserve towards the polluted Felix, compare the Donatists' argument, which embarrassed Augustine at the Carthage conference of 411, that the entire catholic church of North Africa was implicated in a transmitted taint because, a hundred years before, Caecilian of Carthage had been consecrated by bishops who had compromised the faith as *traditores*. Augustine denies that pollution can be so transmitted (*Gesta Coll. Carthag.* iii. 187 and 233).

of their choice, and Siricius could rest assured that nothing lay nearer to Maximus' heart than the unity of the church. On the second question, what vile pollution Maximus' advent to power had averted Siricius could see for himself by reading the records of the trial. He would see from their perusal that 'the Manichees were convicted not by circumstantial inferences nor by doubtful suspicions but by their own confession under judicial examination'. Indeed, Maximus has found the records so disgusting that he cannot summarize them without a blush and must leave Siricius to read the report of the trial for himself.[1]

It is clear that Martin of Tours was not the only Gallic bishop to object to the Priscillianist executions. Probably he was supported by others besides Theognitus in refusing to have anything to do with Felix of Trier or with anyone in communion with him. In this situation of incipient schism the scene was suddenly changed in the summer of 388 by the unexpected fall of Maximus before the lightning thrust of Theodosius. Maximus was declared a tyrannical usurper, whose acts had been illegitimate. All statues and pictures of him were to be destroyed.[2]

The martyrs of Trier

The fall of Maximus spelt a reversal of policy which was golden news for the Spanish Priscillianists. Ithacius was canonically deposed from his see, the complaint against him being the bringing of an accusation on a capital charge. The location of the synod is never mentioned. It was probably in Spain; but it could also have been on the agenda at the synod held in Milan in 390,[3] since the Italian churches led by Ambrose disapproved of Ithacius as much as anyone did. Ithacius' friend Hydatius of Mérida saw trouble coming and resigned of his own free choice. But both he and Ithacius shared excommunication and a sentence of exile.[4]

---

[1] *Avell.* xl (*CSEL* 35). The collector did not include the *gesta* sent to Rome by Maximus. Maximus' coyness is conventional polemic against Manichees. Cyril of Jerusalem (*Cat.* vi. 33) says he cannot describe Manichee baptism before a mixed audience, but then proceeds to scatological detail.

[2] Ambrose, *Expl. Ps.* 38. 27 (*CSEL* 64. 204): 'hic si quis tyranni imagines habeat, qui iam victus interiit, iure damnatur.' *De interpellatione Iob et David* iii. 8. 24 (*CSEL* 32, 2. 262): 'vide quemadmodum in civitatibus bonorum principum imagines perseverent, deleantur imagines tyrannorum' (probably contrasting Gratian and Maximus). A similar allusion in Jerome, *In Abacuc* ii p. 659.

[3] Ambrose, *Ep.* 51. 6. A Spanish council is altogether more probable.

[4] Prosper, *Chron.* ad ann. 389 (*Chron. min.* i. 462) 'Itacius et Ursacius episcopi ob

Their place of exile is not known. The belief that they were
condemned to exile in Naples (which would be an unusually comfortable place for such a penitential discipline) depends on ascrib-
ing to Ithacius the anti-Arian work written at Naples 'Against
Varimadus',[1] an ascription which certainly appeared in one (lost)
manuscript of that work used by Sichard in 1528, but which is
now recognized to be impossible since the unknown author used
both Jerome and Augustine.[2] The recent discussion by Schwank
suggests plausibly enough that the *Contra Varimadum* was written
by one of the North African refugees who went from Carthage
to settle at Naples after the Vandal capture of Carthage in 439.[3]

Ithacius is not easy to judge. His role in the trial was repugnant
to the majority of the western church, and the portrait of him in
Sulpicius Severus is of a man 'without weight, without any touch
of holiness; rash, talkative, impudent, given to high living, much
enjoying the pleasures of the stomach and a gormandizer', so
stupid as to accuse all saintly men dedicated to Bible reading and
fasting of being fellow travellers with Priscillian.[4]

But Severus takes a melancholy view of the standards of discipline generally in the episcopate of his time, and does not actually
suggest that Ithacius was seriously worse than most other contemporary bishops. It was rather that circumstances thrust him
into prominence. Ithacius' apologia expressed his conviction, of
which the Priscillianists appeared to him to offer striking confirmation, that the ascetic movement was not free of dangerous
penetration by Manichee influences. Even Sulpicius Severus does
not take his dislike of Ithacius to the length of denying the truth
of this thesis so far as the Priscillianists were concerned, and his
objection is rather that Ithacius failed to distinguish between
orthodox and heretical asceticism. Ithacius' admission to Isidore

necem Priscilliani, cuius accusatores exstiterant, ecclesiae communione privantur'.
Isidore of Seville (*Vir. inl.* 15, PL 83. 1092) says Ithacius died in exile during the
reigns of Theodosius I and Valentinian II (died 15 May 392: Epiphanius, *Mens et
pond.* 20, ed. Moutsoulas (Athens, 1971), p. 168).

[1] *PL* 62. 351 = *Corpus Christianorum* 90, ed. B. Schwank (1961): *Clavis* 364. The
ascription to Ithacius is accepted by Duchesne, *Hist. anc.* ii. 538 f. (*ET* ii. 427), and
Kidd ii. 305.

[2] B. Fischer in *Biblica* 23 (1942), 154.

[3] Victor of Vita i. 12. See B. Schwank in *Sacris erudiri* 12 (1961), 112–96, at 145–6.

[4] *Chron.* ii. 50, 2–3. If we are to believe Jerome (*Ep.* 69. 9), the episcopal duty of
hospitality led to some danger of alcoholism among bishops of his time. On Roman
ladies fond of the bottle see Ambrosiaster on Col. 3 : 11.

of Seville's catalogue of illustrious men shows that the later orthodox tradition in Spain remained aware of his censure and exile for acting as accuser in a capital charge, but did not think that he had judged Priscillianism wrongly. Yet in 380 Ithacius failed to convince the council of Saragossa. If he convinced Maximus, that is easily explained by the political situation which made Maximus wish to be convinced. The truth is probably that Ithacius was hysterically fearful of sorcery and Manicheism, and was led into exaggeration from which he became unable to retreat.

In parts of Spain, especially in Galicia, Priscillian was jubilantly celebrated as a martyr. The bodies of all those executed at Trier were lovingly recovered and taken to Spain for burial. They became deeply valued as relics of holy men. Oaths were solemnly sworn at Priscillian's shrine,[1] which seems to have been somewhere in Galicia rather than at his own church of Avila in Lusitania. Prosper of Aquitaine writing about 455 believed Priscillian's see to have been in Galicia.[2] Feeling in other parts of Spain, especially in the south in Baetica, is likely to have been less sympathetic to this posthumous rehabilitation. But in the reaction immediately after Maximus' fall the general opinion of lay observers was that Priscillian and his friends had been the victims of a judicial murder.

The imperial panegyrist, Pacatus Drepanius, who in 389–90 congratulated Theodosius in a speech in the Roman senate upon his victory over the wicked usurper, speaks of the miserable men and women tortured and killed by this new Phalaris, 'on a charge of excessive religion and too diligent a worship of the deity', which had been offensively brought by (of all people) delating bishops;

---

[1] Sulpicius Severus, *Chron.* ii. 51. 5–8. The Acts of the council of Toledo, 400, complain of the 'recitatio eorum quos [quae M] dicebant martyres'; see below, p. 237. Cf. Augustine, *Contra mendacium* 9: 'Priscillianistarum falsa martyria'. Professor Peter Brown draws my attention to Optatus ii. 22: Donatist oaths invoking their martyrs imply power to grant rain. For the potency of oaths if taken at particular shrines see Augustine, *Ep.* 78. 3, deciding to send two quarrelling men, one of whom must be lying, from Hippo to Nola in Campania to swear before St. Felix, such oaths not being effective at African shrines. (It is noteworthy that the saint is here no advocate of mercy but a vessel of wrath.) Gregory of Tours required oaths at St. Martin's tomb (*Hist. Franc.* 5. 48–9). Philostratus (*V. Apoll. Tyan.* i. 6) says a Cilician spring could detect perjurers.

[2] Prosper, *Chron. min.* i. 460. This text supports the conjecture that Priscillian was originally a native of Galicia, advanced with a touch of regional patriotism by A. Quintana Prieto in *Legio VII Gemina* (León, 1970), 446, n. 90.

moreover, these bishops had not been content to see the wretches' property confiscated, but took cruel pleasure in watching their victims writhing and screaming under torture before going off to conduct sacred ceremonies with polluted hands.[1] In a letter written about this time Ambrose writes of 'the bloody triumphs of bishops' as a cause of passionate division of opinion.[2] In his commentary on Ps. 118 (119) written about 388–90 Ambrose comes to verse 92: 'Unless thy law were my meditation, then I had perished in my humiliation', and comments how those words could be echoed 'today' by him who in martyrdom has endured repeated beatings and has been examined on the rack and with hooks, leaden weights, red-hot rods, and the sword; for he could have perished unless he had meditated in the law and had believed that future punishments would be worse than the present.[3] When this sermon was preached at Milan, many of his hearers must have turned their minds to the recent news from Trier. A passage in Ambrose's twenty-sixth letter even compares Priscillian's accusers to the Jewish high priests handing Jesus over for execution to Pilate. Not surprisingly, some of the Priscillianist martyrs succeeded in finding their way into medieval calendars.[4]

[1] Pacatus, *Paneg.* xii. 29.

[2] Ambrose, *Ep.* 26. 3. Cf. Paulinus, *Vita Ambrosii* 39, on Ambrose's ideal that a bishop should intercede for sinners before God rather than accuse them before men (an ideal akin to Cicero's as cited by Ammian 19. 12. 18).

[3] Ambrose, *Expos. Ps.* 118. 12. 20 (*CSEL* 62. 269) 'Quam grate hoc dicit *hodie* qui in martyrio plurima flagella sustinuit, eculeo et ungulis, plumbo, lamminis ardentibus, gladio comprobatus'. Ambrose continues by expatiating on Joseph's heroism when hated by his brothers and on an apocryphal story of Isaiah in prison, tempted by Satan to deny that his prophecies were given him by the Lord. Emotive descriptions of torture are part of Ambrose's rhetorical armoury: cf. *Expos. Ps.* 118. 20. 10 and 21. 8 (*CSEL* 62. 449 and 477), the latter passage being notable for its reference to hell as God's torture chamber. Elsewhere Ambrose talks of the 'fables' of punishment in Hades and says that we should fear not death but a guilty conscience: cf. *De bono mortis* 8. 33.

On the date of the commentary on Ps. 118 see M. Ihm, *Studia Ambrosiana* (Leipzig, 1889), p. 24, for 387–8; Palanque, pp. 524–5, and Dudden, p. 691, prefer 389–90.

[4] Tillemont, *Mémoires* viii, 2nd edn., 1713, p. 517, drew attention to the bizarre entry in the fourteenth-century Venetian hagiographer Petrus de Natalibus, *Catalogus sanctorum* (first printed at Vicenza, 1493, many later editions), xi. 89, recording the martyrdom in Gaul of the Spaniard Latrocinianus, a learned author of Christian poetry which survived to the times of Jerome; but under a certain Maximian, a tyrant who under the first Theodosius had seized the Gauls, through the faction of some he was executed at Trier for the truth and defence of the catholic faith, together with Priscillian 'Bapille episcopo'; their bodies are buried in the church at Trier.

This was the kind of entry Baronius purged for his Roman Martyrology. On Petrus de Natalibus see A. Poncelet in *Anal. Boll.* 29 (1910), 34–6.

Nevertheless Ambrose ultimately remained negative towards Priscillian's doctrines. In his second sermon on the Prayer of Job and David he invites his hearers to 'consider a heretic intent on bodily abstinence and the study of heavenly mysteries' as a transitory flash, like Lucifer falling as lightning from heaven, without permanence.[1]

Writing in 392 or 393 Jerome records Priscillian in his catalogue of illustrious Christian writers, saying that he was the author of certain tracts which have reached Jerome in Bethlehem. By some, Jerome adds, he is accused of the gnostic heresy of Basilides or of Mark; but by others he is defended as holding no such opinion.[2]

It is a remarkably neutral notice, not taking sides between the two factions in Spain, and certainly implying that in the tracts which have come to his notice there is nothing to cause alarm. Later Jerome's allusions to Priscillian and to his tracts were to become less benevolent, and the change of attitude is evidence of a general shift in opinion after 400 which hardened in the western church against Priscillian. But in 393 Jerome was not certain how to assess him, and hedged his bets.

Schism in Spain

Nevertheless the division of opinion so neutrally recorded by Jerome was not in Spain a matter of cool academic interest but one which was rending the church into two embittered factions. Some time in the nineties, perhaps about 396, the bishops of the Spanish provinces other than Galicia invited their colleagues of the north-west to come to a synod at Toledo[3] there to give an

[1] *De interpellatione Iob et David* ii. 5. 16 (*CSEL* 32, 2. 242): 'considera haereticum aliquem intentum abstinentiae corporis et cognitioni caelestium sacramentorum.' Dudden, p. 687, dates this work 388–9, and thinks an allusion to Priscillian here possible.

[2] *Vir. inl.* 121. Jerome identifies Mark of Memphis with the second-century gnostic of Irenaeus (above, p. 22). From *Ep.* 75. 3 (after 398) and *Adv. Vigilantium* 6 (of 406), it is certain that Jerome had read at least the first of the Würzburg tractates; and this passage of *De viris inlustribus* shows that he regarded Priscillian as their reputed author. That Priscillian himself is author of the sixth tractate is taken for granted by both the Priscillianists and their opponents at the council of Toledo in 400 (Labbe–Coleti ii. 1477; Vives, *Concilios*, p. 11); below, p. 182.

[3] The only reference to this abortive council of Toledo is contained in the Acts of Toledo, 400 (text below, p. 237). The same passage discloses Symposius' journey to Milan. Florez, *España sagrada* vi (Madrid, 1751), 53, pointed out that there was a council called at Toledo about 396; little attention has been paid to his views, but they were sympathetically regarded by Catalani in his re-edition of Aguirre's *Concilia Hispaniae* (Rome, 1753), iii. 39.

undertaking no longer to commemorate the Priscillianists as martyrs. The Galicians refused. Their leader was now the old Symposius, bishop of Astorga, who had played the part of a moderate, gently sympathetic to Priscillian, since the first beginnings of the controversy at the council of Saragossa in 380. But Symposius was no schismatic; he was not a man to think that there could be a separate community in Galicia indifferent to the opinion of catholic Christendom. He realized the weakness of the Galicians' isolation, and travelled to Milan to ask for communion with Ambrose. Ambrose laid down conditions for the restoration of peace, consistent with the position that he had adopted after the council of Saragossa of 380, but now adding that the Galicians must abandon the commemoration of the Priscillianists as holy martyrs, whether at their tombs or in the *Memento* of the liturgy. There was also a practical question which was less than one of principle, namely whether it was fitting for Symposius to consecrate his own son Dictinius to be coadjutor bishop of Astorga where the people were vocal in asking for him. Ambrose advised that Dictinius, who was an advowed admirer of Priscillian's tracts, should remain a presbyter 'for the sake of peace'. That there was any objection at this time to a son being consecrated by his father, with the expectation of the reversion of the see, does not appear, though this could have played some part. In Rome in 401 Innocent I succeeded his father Anastasius in the papacy;[1] but Anastasius had not pre-emptively consecrated him. Ambrose's words 'for the sake of peace' suggest that Dictinius was objectionable because he was known to be a particularly controversial figure.

On both matters Symposius' hopes of reaching a settlement on the terms proposed by Ambrose were dashed by the hard reaction of the clergy and laity at home. He found it a simple impossibility to discontinue the commemoration of the Priscillianists as holy

---

[1] Jerome, *Ep.* 130. 16. The later *Liber pontificalis* (i. 220 Duchesne) says that he was 'ex patre Innocentio'. The practice of a bishop consecrating (or at least designating) his successor, was commoner in the West than in the East. In Ambrose's time (*Ep.* 15. 9) Acholius of Thessalonica consecrated his successor Anysius. Augustine designated his successor at Hippo with a formal act recorded by stenographers, hoping to avert riots on his death (*Ep.* 213), but apparently did not consecrate; and his candidate did not have the reversion of the post. The 23rd canon of Antioch (*c.* 328, but ascribed to the council of 341; Lauchert, *Kanones*, p. 49) declared all pre-consecrations illicit; this canon was included in Martin of Braga's canons from eastern synods (p. 126 edn. Barlow). In 530 pope Felix IV formally designated his successor: Duchesne, *Liber pontificalis*, i. 282.

martyrs. The attachment of the clergy and people in the province was unbreakable, a fact which may suggest that miraculous healings were being granted to those who prayed at Priscillian's tomb, though our anti-Priscillianist sources naturally never mention it. The cult of the martyrs was always a matter in which official authority found itself vainly trying to put a brake on the enthusiasm of private devotion. Whatever Symposius had agreed to in Ambrose's presence at Milan, he rapidly found to be quite unacceptable to his flock in Astorga. Similarly he found that popular demand was irresistible for the consecration of his son Dictinius to be coadjutor bishop of Astorga.

Dictinius was not, like his father Symposius, a moderate. He was a known enthusiast for Priscillian's memory. Moreover he was author of a book defending the right to study esoteric books and advanced doctrines. His book dealt with twelve questions and, since an ancient pound contained twelve ounces, he entitled his work *Libra*, 'A Pound'. Perhaps the title carried other overtones.[1] The Latin word also means 'Balance', and is one of the signs of the zodiac, in which (if Orosius may be believed) the Priscillianists had some interest (below, p. 194). Our knowledge of Dictinius' book is derived entirely from the hostile account of its argument given by Augustine in his *Contra mendacium* written for his Spanish correspondent Consentius probably of the Balearic islands (above, p. 11). Consentius had sent Augustine his own voluminous anti-Priscillianist writings; he had learnt something about the group from an ascetic named Fronto, and was particularly interested in Dictinius' argument because he himself wanted to justify the use of deceit to gain the confidence of the Priscillianists and so to discover their esoteric doctrines of which Fronto had been unable to tell him anything reliable. The

---

[1] A. Lezius, 'Die Libra des Priszillianisten Dictinius von Astorga', *Abhandlungen A. von Oettingen gewidmet* (Munich, 1898), pp. 113–24, observed that the title *Libra* might have been influenced by a passage in the *Passio S. Thomae* where the apostle describes twelve virtues as 'integra libra aequitatis' (Max Bonnet, *Acta Thomae*, Supplementum codicis apocryphi, Leipzig, 1883, p. 147). Lezius fails to note a possible source of support for this in Leo, *Ep.* 15. 13 ad Turibium (*PL* 54. 687A), quoting from Turibius' memorandum the attribution to the Priscillianists of the doctrine that 'all the body of canonical scripture under the names of the patriarchs is to be accepted because they symbolize the twelve virtues that reform the inner man' (below, p. 114).

There is a good discussion of Dictinius by Babut, *Priscillien*, pp. 283–90. For truth-telling cf. Jerome, *In Gal.* ii. 7–14; iv. 20; Cassian, *Coll.* 17. 20. 9.

argument that one is not obliged to deal truthfully with heretics shocked Augustine. There is no evidence that Augustine had before him a copy of Dictinius' *Libra*. He was working from Consentius' hostile account. All that is certain is that Dictinius discussed what circumstances might qualify the requirement to tell the whole truth and that, like Jerome and John Cassian among other church fathers who observe that on occasion to say all that is in one's heart may do harm, Dictinius did not think that no such circumstances could exist.

Dictinius saw that to assert with Priscillian the Church's possession of doctrines and documents suitable for some believers, unsuitable for others, implies that one is morally justified in concealing or darkly hinting at doctrines unfitted for the ears of the unworthy. Dictinius therefore set out to show that the Bible provided precedents for not telling all that is in one's heart. The apostle could be a deceiver and yet true. Jehu pretended to be a worshipper of Baal to discover the identity of those unfaithful to Yahweh. Abraham pretended to be Sarah's brother. Jacob deceived his father, Joseph his brethren. David feigned madness. Rahab the harlot lied about the spies. The Hebrew midwives played false with Pharaoh. Peter and Barnabas dissembled at Antioch. Paul avowed his policy to be all things to all men. Jesus himself asked a question as if not knowing the answer. In every case the lack of total candour was practised for highly edifying reasons. It must be concluded that unreserved declaration of the whole truth is not necessarily that highest virtue which overrides all others in a situation of conflicting values.

Dictinius' defence of reserve in communicating religious knowledge was no doubt intended to justify the expert study of apocrypha. It ended by giving the unfortunate impression, or at least making it easy for hostile critics to say, that he lacked integrity. His book therefore served to confirm the worst suspicions of those who accused the Priscillianists of accepting all the enormities attributed to their master while believing themselves fully justified in denying on oath that they held any such thing. To assert the possibility of reserve left Dictinius defenceless before the suspicion that his esoteric doctrine was heretical. So Augustine could retail a report from converts from Priscillianism to the effect that it was a maxim among members of the sect: 'Swear, perjure yourself, but never betray a secret' ('Iura, periura, secretum

prode noli').[1] This is not quoted from Dictinius' book, but is
hearsay evidence from a hostile witness. Converts are seldom
a reliable source of fair-minded information about the group they
have come to renounce, a point sufficiently illustrated by the
extent to which Augustine, though a Manichee hearer for nine
years, gives incomplete and distorted accounts of Manicheism
in his polemical writings.[2] The charge that Priscillianists held
themselves free, without loss of integrity, to deny their deepest
convictions goes back to an early stage in the controversy, when
Ithacius skilfully asserted that no denial of Manichee beliefs could
be believed from a man whose principles allowed him to lie with
a good conscience (above, p. 56). The proposition made it
easy confidently to attribute to Priscillian and his followers all
manner of moral enormity and deviationist doctrine whether or
not the charges were true, simply because from men of such principles, or lack of them, absolute denial was only to be expected
and should always be construed as an admission of the worst.
Nothing so clearly proved for Augustine the diabolical nature of
the Priscillianist heresy than the strictness of orthodoxy with
which they interpreted their beloved apocrypha. That they should
give an utterly innocuous exegesis of the hymn in the Acts of John
just showed how clever and double-faced they were.[3] Their
orthodoxy in accepting the entire canon of scripture made them
worse than the Manichees who rejected the Old Testament.[4] The
heretics were therefore put in the position that no one seemed
willing to listen to what they had to say. Dictinius' book made it
even less likely that they would listen.

There is other evidence that in the nineties the Spanish churches
outside Galicia again became openly unsympathetic to the cause
of Priscillian, after the temporary rehabilitation following Maximus' fall. Sulpicius Severus has a tantalizing note in the last
chapter of his *Chronicle* that at a certain stage Hydatius of Mérida,
who with some instinct for self-preservation had withdrawn from

[1] Augustine, *Ep.* 237. 3 (*CSEL* 57. 528), to Ceretius, probably a Spanish bishop,
unless he is to be identified with the bishop of Grenoble (Gratianopolis) present at
the council of Orange in 441 (Munier, *Concilia Galliae*, p. 87) and correspondent of
pope Leo the Great (*Ep.* 68 of A.D. 450).
[2] See F. Decret, *Aspects du manichéisme dans l'Afrique romaine* (Paris, 1970).
[3] Augustine, *Ep.* 237. 4–9.
[4] Orosius, *Commonitorium de errore Priscillianistarum*, 2 (*CSEL* 18. 153), followed
by Augustine, *De haeresibus* 70.

the prosecution at Trier long before Ithacius had done so, and who had voluntarily resigned his see in 388 without tarrying for a synod to declare him deposed, found it possible to return to Mérida to seek reinstatement. No doubt he still had friends there among those muscular supporters who had once given Priscillian and his episcopal colleagues so warm a reception in the presbytery (above, p. 31). However, Hydatius cannot have lasted long as a revenant, since by 400 at the council of Toledo the presidency of that council was in the hands of Patruinus who is mentioned in the correspondence of pope Innocent I as bishop of Mérida.[1] (Ithacius died in exile and never found his way home.)[2]

Just as some sympathy for Priscillian could be found outside Galicia, so Galicia was not quite monolithic in its adherence to Priscillianism. But the price of dissent had to be paid by those who openly failed to approve of their colleague's enthusiasm for the martyrs of Trier. Ortygius, bishop of Aquis Celenis (probably Cuntis, 29 km. north of Pontevedra), was driven from his see by the synod of the province. The man who replaced him, Exuperantius, signed at Toledo as bishop of the *municipium* Celenis in the region of Lugo; he succeeded in quietly surviving without conforming to the will of the Priscillianist majority, or at least by quickly disassociating himself from them in 400.[3]

Schism in Gaul

The division of opinion that embittered relations in Spain also affected the churches in Gaul and Aquitaine, where the divisive question remained whether one could be in communion with

[1] Innocent I, *Ep.* 3.

[2] Above, p. 148, n. 4.

[3] Both Ortygius and Exuperantius appear in the list of bishops present at the council of Toledo, 400. The see of Ortygius is identified as Aquis Celenis in the chronicle of Hydatius, ad ann. 399 (*Chron. min.* ii. 16), not in the Acts of Toledo. The site of Aquis Celenis is not certain, but the itineraries (ed. Cuntz) make it clear that it was one of the places with hot springs between Pontevedra and Santiago. The case for Cuntis is argued by M. Estafania Alvarez, 'Vias romanas de Galicia', *Zephyrus* 11 (1960), 5–103 at pp. 55–61. Exuperantius is said in the Acts of Toledo to be 'de Gallicia Lucensis conventus municipii Celenis'. The words 'de Gallicia conventus Lucensis' look like a (correct) marginal gloss on Celenis which has crept into the text. 'Conventus Lucensis' (cf. Pliny, *NH* iv. 111) is the region of north-west Spain whose chief centre was Lucus Augusti (Lugo) in the area inhabited by the Celeni. After Ortygius' reinstatement perhaps Exuperantius acted as coadjutor, unless the council put him into one of the hot seats, viz. the sees of the Priscillianist bishops whom they deposed.

Felix of Trier when he had been consecrated by bishops who
included Ithacius and Hydatius of Mérida and who had declared
the hands of these two to be free of all stain. The issue generated
the most painful quarrel. In 392 Ambrose travelled to Gaul to
baptize Valentinian II; but he was later to protest that his reason
for visiting Gaul was exclusively the emperor's baptism, not to
attend 'any synod of Gallic bishops whose frequent dissensions
have often led me to excuse myself'.[1] In October of either 394 or
(more probably) 396 a synod of twenty-one bishops met at Nîmes
'to remove scandals from the churches and to settle the schism
(*discessio*) and to restore peace'.[2] Martin of Tours refused to attend,
though the business on the agenda was of such passionate concern
to him that, according to Sulpicius Severus, he received special
intelligence of its decisions by the message of an angel.[3] Among
the signatories of the canons of Nîmes stands the name of Felix,
no doubt the bishop of Trier whose consecration was the central
bone of contention. Unfortunately to agree upon his personal
virtues was irrelevant to those who thought that the bloody
hands laid upon him at his consecration had involved him in
indelible pollution.

The decisions of the council of Nîmes come accordingly from
the Felician party, holding its own in Gaul against a small puritan
party, but not accepted by Rome and Milan. The six disciplinary
canons of the council do not seem very relevant to the problem
of Priscillian or his trial. They reiterate that bishops should respect
the excommunications decreed by their colleagues (canon 3) and
should not judge clergy from dioceses other than their own (4).
Those undertaking journeys abroad should not look to the church
chest for their travelling expenses (5), and no ecclesiastical pass-
port shall be valid unless bearing the diocesan bishop's personal

---

[1] *Obit. Val.* 25. It seems that Ambrose was suspected of having visited Gaul on
imperial affairs when his real interests lay in ecclesiastical matters; cf. above, p. 135.

[2] The Acts of the council of Nîmes, preserved by a single codex written in France
during the pontificate of Gregory the Great (590–604) and now at the cathedral
library of Cologne (Dombibl. 212, s. vi/vii), are best edited by C. Munier, *Concilia
Galliae a. 314–a. 506* (1963), pp. 49–51. For the codex see F. Maassen, *Geschichte der
Quellen und Literatur des canonischen Rechtes* (1870), pp. 574–85; E. A. Lowe, *CLA* vii.
1162.

[3] Sulpicius Severus, *Dial.* ii. 13. 8 'apud Nemausum episcoporum synodus habe-
batur ad quam quidem ire noluerat (Martinus), sed quid gestum esset scire
cupiebat . . .' Severus records the synod only because of his interest in Martin's
angelic pigeon-post, not because its decisions, of which no word is said, were
important for either Severus or his readers.

signature (6). The first two canons have been taken to have some bearing on the Priscillianist affair: the first complains of many coming from the most distant parts of the East who pretend to be presbyters and deacons, bringing letters of communion whose signatures and authenticity cannot be checked; such persons are not to be admitted to ministerial duty at the altar. That 'those coming from the East' are Manichees, i.e. Priscillianists, is surely most improbable since under the canon they are debarred not from communion but only from celebrating. The second canon of Nîmes discloses that in some places (the bishops pretend not to know where) women have been admitted to the diaconate. The synod declares that such ordination, because contrary to reason, is invalid ('contra rationem facta talis ordinatio distruatur'). Priscillian had expressed some strong opinions about the admissibility of women to equal ministry with men, and at the same time had not wished to see his movement grow into a separatist group apart from the regular ecclesiastical hierarchy. It is therefore possible that this might be an allusion to an originally Priscillianist practice.[1] On the other hand, if so, the bishops at Nîmes might well have been expected to mention the fact as an additional argument (besides the plain deliverances of reason) for discrediting the practice. More probably therefore it is a further reference to migrants from the Greek East where female deacons normally received formal ordination by laying on of hands.[2]

This canon of Nîmes is the first of several protests uttered by Gallic councils against female deacons, but like many episcopal prohibitions it was in practice ineffective. Bishop Remigius of Reims (died 530) left by will a servant 'for my blessed daughter Hilaria the deaconess'.[3] A few years later bishop Médard of Noyon

[1] The second canon of Nîmes is understood as attacking a Priscillianist position by R. Gryson, *Le Ministère des femmes dans l'église ancienne* (Gembloux, 1972), pp. 162 f., and by P. H. Lafontaine, *Les Conditions positives de l'accession aux ordres dans la première législation ecclésiastique (300–492)* (Ottawa, 1963), p. 21. It is worth recalling that the 56th of Priscillian's canons (perhaps as revised by Peregrinus?) insists on the silence of women in church and forbids them to teach.

[2] Goar, *Euchologion* (edn. 1730), p. 218, preserves the prayers of the rite. For discussion see C. Vagaggini, 'L'ordinazione delle diaconisse nella tradizione grece e bizantina', *Orientalia Christiana Periodica* 40 (1974), 145–89. The Mozarabic *Ordo ad ordinandam abbatissam* (Férotin, *Liber ordinum*, 66–8) is an investiture with mitre, episcopal kiss, rule-book, and rod, not an ordination rite.

[3] PL 65. 973. The legislation of later Gallic councils is well surveyed by Gryson, op. cit., pp. 164 ff.; Lafontaine, op. cit., pp. 27–55.

ordained Rhadegund deaconess by laying on of hands.[1] Peter
Abelard was sure that male and female deacons share in one and
the same diaconate, even if they may have different duties to
perform.[2]

The contention in the Gallic churches about the possibility of
being in communion with the bishop of Trier was a matter of
profound concern to the churches in Italy. The firm stand adopted
by Ambrose (and Siricius) against Felix was an obstacle to any
relaxation of the tension, but after his death and that of Martin
of Tours in 397 the way looked open for the possibility of a compromise. The whole question came before a council held at Turin
not long after the death of Ambrose in response to a request from
the Gallic bishops for independent help in bringing peace to their
quarrelling churches. The unusual choice of Turin for the convening of the council of the province of Milan is probably
explained by its closer proximity to the Aquitanian and Gallic
churches. Perhaps also the atmosphere might be rather more open
in a city where the memory of Ambrose was less vivid than in
Milan, and where a synod might therefore feel less sense of being
unfaithful to the policy of so great a man if they took a more
moderate stance.

The synod of Turin[3] was well attended by bishops from Aquitaine, where they were divided not merely about Felix of Trier
but also by disputes arising from the first moves towards establishing some kind of metropolitan authority, in place of the older
tradition of the western provinces whereby the presiding bishop
was simply whoever was senior by date of consecration. Proculus,
bishop of Massilia (Marseille), who had gone as a legate of the
Gallic churches to the anti-Arian council of Aquileia under
Ambrose in 381, and by the end of the fourth century must have
had considerable seniority, was anxious to keep or assert ordination rights in Narbonensis II (to the east of Massilia), which were
unwelcome to the bishops in that province. Since Massilia was

---

[1] *PL* 88. 502.

[2] *Sermo* 31, *In natali S. Stephani* i. 553–6 Cousin.

[3] The Acts of the council of Turin are critically edited by C. Munier, *Concilia
Galliae*, pp. 54–8. The list of bishops present has not been preserved, and the name
of its president is unknown. But the 21st sermon of Maximus of Turin (= *Sermo* 96,
PL 57. 726) speaks of hospitality to visiting bishops. If, as is possible, Maximus was
already bishop at this time, then this could well be a reference to the council. See A.
Mutzenbecher's introduction to the edition of Maximus in *Corpus Christianorum* 23
(1962), p. xxxiv. F. Savio, *Gli antichi vescovi d'Italia: Il Piemonte* (1899), p. 291.

in Viennensis and not even metropolis of that province, the claim can have rested only on his seniority and on past precedents, that is, on the system now in process of passing away before the new order which gave a more centralizing authority to the bishop of the civil metropolis. The same shift was simultaneously producing tension between Vienne and Arles, cities which were secular rivals; both bishops were making claims to be metropolitan.

The precise date and circumstances of the council of Turin have been hotly contested questions and require a brief digression. The main evidence for the council consists of (*a*) the eight disciplinary canons preserved in Latin canonical manuscripts, where the council is dated on 22 September but without any year being specified;[1] the main topics of these canons are the disputed claim by Proculus of Massilia to consecrate bishops in Narbonensis II, rivalry between Arles and Vienne, and the question of Gallic bishops in communion with Felix of Trier; (*b*) some allusions to the council, and to Proculus of Massilia mentioned in the canons, found in the correspondence of pope Zosimus in 417. Zosimus there angrily attacks Proculus for declining to accept the papal grant of special privileges to Patroclus of Arles, made on the ground of St. Trophimus' alleged mission there from Rome, and for appealing to the council of Turin as authorizing him to ordain bishops in the province of Narbonensis II (his own see being in Viennensis).

From these documents taken together it is certain that the council of Turin fell after the deaths of both Ambrose (397) and Martin of Tours (probably 397, possibly 400). The sixth canon of Turin speaks of Felix of Trier as still alive and in office; but the length of Felix's episcopate is not reliably known. A hagiographical life of Felix,[2] written after the Norman sack of Trier (882) and designed to fill the gap resulting from the destruction of the books and records, says that Felix resigned after twelve years as bishop and died on 26 March. The date in March, being of immediate liturgical relevance for the Calendar, is likely to be correct. What of the 'twelve years'? The hagiographer makes use of Sulpicius Severus' Dialogues on the Life of St. Martin, a fact which shows his interest in using historical material where it was available.

---

[1] The canons, which are not accompanied by a list of the bishops present or signing, are edited by C. Munier, *Concilia Galliae a. 314–a. 506*, pp. 52–60.

[2] Printed in *Acta Sanctorum*, March, vol. iii, at p. 624.

He also knew where Felix's tomb was in the church at Trier, and it is therefore conceivable that he derived his information about the length of Felix's episcopate from an epitaph, especially since the story of resignation is not a mere hagiographical cliché. If so, Felix resigned about 398–9. But this can be affirmed as probable only if it fully coheres with all the other evidence. Judgement about the likely length of Felix's tenure of office hangs on an independent estimate of the date of the council of Turin.

If 398 is the earliest possible date for the council, 407 is the latest. According to pope Zosimus, Lazarus, who was 'many years later' consecrated bishop of Aix by Proculus of Massilia, had been censured after lengthy debates at the council of Turin for bringing false accusations against Britius (Brice), Martin's successor as bishop of Tours.[1] (It appears from Gregory of Tours that the calumny was a charge of being father to his washer-woman's bastard.)[2] Zosimus adds that Lazarus owed his elevation to be bishop of Aix to the favour of the usurper Constantine, who ruled Gaul from 407 until his death in 411, with his capital at Arles. After Constantine was killed, Lazarus resigned, his position having become untenable in a city where he had few friends. Together with Heros of Arles, who was extruded to make room for Patroclus, he went to Palestine where he won his way to the favour of Jerome and Orosius by becoming a plaintiff against Pelagius in the action which led to the council of Diospolis.[3] One of Zosimus' main complaints against Proculus is that he consecrated Lazarus a bishop when many years previously at Turin he had joined in condemning him for calumny. It therefore seems probable that within the available dates the council of Turin ought to be dated within 398 and 407, but nearer to 398.

Babut believed in two councils of Turin, one about 405–7 at which Lazarus was censured, a second in September 417 to which we are to ascribe the eight disciplinary canons. Babut's thesis met with astringent criticism from Duchesne and has enjoyed only occasional support.[4] Its plausibility depends on three points, all

---

[1] Zosimus, *Ep. Posteaquam* 5 (*Avell.* XLVI, *CSEL* 35. 104) '. . . ab eodem Proculo fit post multos annos sacerdos tyrannici iudicii'.   [2] *Hist. Franc.* ii. 1.

[3] Probably Lazarus returned to Gaul, perhaps with John Cassian about 415–16. For his career and the surviving inscription on his tombstone, see H. I. Marrou in *Revue de moyen âge latin* i (1945), 22–3.

[4] Babut, *Le Concile de Turin* (Paris, 1904), criticized by L. Duchesne in *Revue*

highly disputable, and all load-bearing in Babut's construction, viz. (*a*) the correctness of his interpretation of Zosimus' letter *Multa* of 29 September 417—an exegesis possible if the letter stood alone, but irreconcilable with the other evidence;[1] (*b*) the conjectural insertion of a negative ('haud') in Zosimus' statement that 'many years' elapsed between Lazarus' censure at Turin and his consecration as bishop; (*c*) the assertion that the letter (ascribed to Zosimus) to Simplicius of Vienne, *Revelatum* of 1 October 417, is genuine and not, as Gundlach thought, one of a group of medieval forgeries in the interest of Vienne in association with which the letter is transmitted.[2]

historique 87 (1905), 278–302. Babut replied in the same journal, 88 (1905), 57–82 and 324–6. He was supported by E. Stein in the first edition of his *Geschichte des spätrömischen Reiches*; the second edition in French, revised by J. R. Palanque, has corrected this away. More surprisingly Babut is supported by A. Chastagnol in *Revue historique* 249 (1973), at pp. 36–40, justly criticized by E. Griffe in *Bulletin de littérature ecclés.* (Toulouse), 1973, pp. 289–95. Chastagnol is right in affirming that there is no necessary connection between the claims of Proculus of Massilia (attested in Turin, canon 1) and the principal theme of his paper, viz. the date of the transfer of the prefecture of the Gauls from Trier to Arles. The date of this transfer falls after 395. While the first certain evidence of the prefect's residence at Arles is in Honorius' edict of 17 Apr. 418 to Agricola (*MGH Epist.* III. i, pp. 13–15), the move was probably earlier. Trier fell to barbarians early in 407 (Salvian, *Gub. Dei* vi. 8. 39; 13. 74), and Arles was the seat of Constantine's government 407–11.

[1] Zosimus' letter *Multa*, to the bishops of Viennensis and Narbonensis II, explains that at Rome recently a well-attended inquiry has been held into Proculus' usurpation of ordination rights in Narbonensis II. Proculus refused to attend when summoned. Zosimus has been specially angered that Proculus presumed to appeal to the synod of Turin against the authority of the apostolic see, and gained the support of Simplicius, bishop of Vienne, who claims ordination rights in Viennensis (i.e. over against Patroclus of Arles whom Zosimus has appointed papal vicar). They are agitating for a council. But Proculus' indecent boldness can be non-suited from the start ('in ipso vestibulo'): no council, indeed not even the authority of the pope himself, can stand against the sacrosanct ruling of St. Trophimus first metropolitan of Arles. Text in *MGH Epist.* III. i p. 11.

For Babut (and Chastagnol) 'in ipso vestibulo' shows that the council of Turin occurred a mere week before Zosimus' letter, 22 Sept. 417. But the more probable meaning is that, since all was settled by St. Trophimus and a sacred tradition of immemorial antiquity, the premisses that might justify appeal to a council are lacking. Griffe (art. cit., p. 295, n. 8) justly observes that Zosimus utters no criticism of the council of Turin, which, on Babut's hypothesis, needs explanation.

[2] The letter, transmitted with other Vienne forgeries, is printed in *PL* 20. 704 and critically edited by W. Gundlach, *MGH Epist.* III. i (1892), p. 90. The Vienne forgeries were assigned by Gundlach to the eleventh or twelfth century, the date of the oldest manuscripts; see his paper, 'Der Streit der Bistümer Arles und Vienne um den Primatus Galliarum', *Neues Archiv* 15 (1889), 9–102. But they are certainly earlier. The letter *Revelatum* ascribed to Zosimus is alluded to in canon 8 of the council of

The deep quarrels in the Gallic churches resulting from the Priscillianist executions and their immediate consequences did not come before the Italian bishops for the first time at the council of Turin; for the council explains that their ruling is a refusal to modify a position adopted long before ('dudum') in letters sent by 'Ambrose of venerable memory', and by the bishop of Rome who is unnamed in the canon.[1] The fact that Ambrose is dead, while the bishop of Rome who gave the ruling is apparently still living at the time of the council, suggests the virtual certainty that the unnamed bishop of Rome is Siricius, who died on 26 November 399. Accordingly the years 398 or 399 remain the only reasonable options for the council of Turin, and 398 is the more probable.[2]

The council of Turin reaffirmed the opinion that those who wished to separate themselves from Felix of Trier should be accepted into the communion of Milan and Rome. The text transmitted by all the extant manuscripts says that the council was attended by legates sent to Turin by Gallic bishops in communion with Felix, evidently (if the text is correct) asking Milan and Rome to moderate their twelve-year refusal to have any contact with the defiled bishop of Trier. However, in the text given by the sixteenth-century printed editions of Crabbe (1538) and Surius (1567), whose conjecture is preferred by Babut (1904), the Gallic legates sent to Turin were from the bishops *not* in communion with Felix. As the manuscript reading gives good sense, there is no good reason to emend it.[3] The question of the reading does

Francfort of 794 (*MGH Leges* III, *Concilia* II. i, p. 169), to which Babut appealed as if it proved the document's authenticity. It proves only that the forgery is earlier than Gundlach supposed.

[1] Canon 6 reads: 'Illud praeterea decrevit sancta synodus ut, quoniam legatos episcopi Galliarum qui Felici communicant destinarunt, ut si quis ab eius communione se voluerit sequestrare in nostrae pacis consortio suscipiatur, iuxta litteras venerabilis memoriae Ambrosii episcopi vel Romanae ecclesiae sacerdotis dudum latas, quae in concilio legatis praesentibus recitatae sunt.'

[2] The great influence of Hefele's history of the councils long made the textbooks assert the council to have taken place in 401. That the correct year is 398 was argued by Tillemont, viii. 516, and by Fedele Savio, *Gli antichi vescovi d'Italia: Il Piemonte* (1899), pp. 554–66. The case for 398 is fully set out by J. R. Palanque, 'Les Dissensions des églises des Gaules à la fin du IV⁺ siècle et la date du concile de Turin', *Revue d'histoire de l'église de France* 21 (1935), 481–501, a paper that has convinced many who have not seen Savio. Cf., e.g. G. Langgärtner, *Die Gallienpolitik der Päpste im 5. und 6. Jahrhundert* (Bonn, 1964), pp. 22–4.

[3] Duchesne's criticism that '(non) communicant' gives no satisfactory sense (*Revue historique* 87 (1905), 295) is overstated. But the rest of the canon suggests that

not affect the date of the synod at Turin, and makes only a modest difference to the resultant narrative: on either text the Gallic episcopate is divided between those in communion with Trier and those in communion with Rome and Milan, who may have been a minority in Gaul and Aquitaine.

The bishops at Turin concluded by ruling that clergy who beget children while on duty ('in ministerio') are not to be promoted (canon 8). Perhaps to avoid embarrassing proceedings against bishops who had not rigorously conformed to the celibate ideal, the canon does not formally legislate for those who have already become bishops—'summi sacerdotes'[1]—but no doubt it is hoped that they will observe abstinence from conjugal relations and have wives as though they had not. The council therefore adopted a position which on the celibacy question was sympathetic towards the ideals of the ascetic movement. In 417 pope Zosimus could even accuse Proculus of Massilia of having consecrated as one of his suffragans, or country bishops, Tuentius, an ex-Priscillianist.[2] On the other hand, the decisions of Turin represent an attempt by moderate men to recover peace in Gaul, and the actions of moderate men seldom please the strict extremes. Hence no doubt the silence of Sulpicius Severus about the conciliatory proposals of Turin.

If the medieval Life of Felix of Trier is correct in saying that he resigned his see, this would have been Felix's personal contribution to the ending of the troubles. But Sulpicius Severus ends his *Chronicle* with the sombre opinion that even after fifteen years of quarrelling the Gallic dissensions were not appeased.

the council of Turin's decision to reaffirm Ambrose's policy towards the Felicians will have been in response to a move by the Felician bishops rather than by their opponents. If so, the insertion of the negative is a misunderstanding.

[1] 'Summus sacerdos' is regular in this period for a bishop, e.g. Council of Turin, canon 1; Ambrose, *Expl. Ps.* 118. 2. 23 (*CSEL* 62. 33. 22). Innocent I, *Ep.* 3. 7 (*PL* 20. 491A); Gaudentius of Brixia, 16. 3 (*PL* 20. 956A = *CSEL* 68. 138. 2). An alternative title is 'pontifex': e.g. the Roman synod of 378, *Et hoc gloriae* (Labbe–Coleti II 1187D = *PL* 13. 577B), and Jerome, *Ep.* 64. 5. Not until Renaissance times could the popes take the title 'pontifex maximus' which in the time of Damasus or Siricius had the strongest pagan associations; but 'summus pontifex' for a bishop occurs in Montanus of Toledo, 522–31 (*PL* 65. 52A = *PL* 84. 338B), and *Sacr. Leon.* 986. Augustine calls Ambrose 'pontifex magnus': *C. Jul. op. impf.* ii. 8.

[2] *MGH Epist.* III. i, p. 8 = *PL* 20. 664A. The bishop in question had the additional disadvantage of having been entrusted by Proculus with a region falling within the jurisdiction of Arles. He was a poacher. See Duchesne, *Fastes* i. 98–100.

Galicia as a Priscillianist province

A retrospect on the consequences of Priscillian's execution must judge that even in merely political terms it was a tragedy for the Church in both Gaul and Spain. Galicia, a remote mountainous province, had become entrenched in its separate life. Two Galician Christians of the period are known to us, and in both cases there appears to have been contact with the Priscillianist movement. The aristocratic pilgrim Egeria made her way to Sinai, Palestine, and Mesopotamia in all probability during the period 381–4.[1] The Galician monk Valerius of Bergidum (Vierzo, north-west of Ponferrada) in the seventh century wrote for his fellow monks an account of her pilgrimage which says that she came from 'the extreme coast of the western ocean'. This is a common way of referring to Galicia in texts of this time,[2] and Egeria's Galician origin is probable. Her date and place of origin make it worth putting the question whether she had direct contact with Priscillian's movement. Four points point to a positive answer to this question: (*a*) Egeria writes for the members of a religious sorority, of the type that Priscillian encouraged. (*b*) She has an eye for apocryphal texts; e.g. 'at home', she says, she has the correspondence between Jesus and Abgar (*Itiner.* 19. 19). At Edessa she is interested to hear 'something of St. Thomas himself' read at his shrine (17). She prizes the shrine of St. Thecla (23). (*c*) She notes that in Palestine they do not fast on Saturday or Sunday (44). The manner of her comment here implies that in her native land she is accustomed to occasions when there may be fasts on both of these days. Sunday fasting was one of the Priscillianist practices to which specific exception was taken at the council of Saragossa in 380 (above, p. 14). (*d*) Egeria has a special interest in ascetics, in discovering that in the East the *apotactitae* include both men and women (23. 6; 24. 1; 28. 3). After her visit to Jerusalem she even goes off on a lengthy detour to the north-west to visit the monks of Mesopotamia of whom she will have heard something that especially attracts her.

[1] P. Devos, 'La Date du voyage d'Égérie', *Anal. Boll.* 85 (1967), 165–94; id. 'Égérie à Édesse', ibid. 381–400.
[2] Hydatius, *Chron.* 49 (*Chronica minora* ii. 18) 'Gallaecia . . . sita in extremitate oceani maris occidua.' *Conc. Bracar.* i. 5 (p. 110 Barlow) 'in huius extremitate provinciae'. *Vita S. Fructuosi* 1 'huius occiduae plagae extremitas'. Valerius Bergidensis, *Epistula de beata Egeria*, PL 87. 424B (critical edition by Z. García in *Anal. Boll.* 29 (1910), 393–9): 'extremo occidui maris oceani littore . . . exorta.'

It is tempting to ask if the attraction is the Messalian movement, at that moment spreading through the Mesopotamian monasteries like a forest fire. Although a comparison between Priscillianism and Messalianism would include a long list of dissimilarities, there remain very striking links between the two. Both ascetic movements were felt by the hierarchy to be dangerously separatist. Both sought to bring seriousness and depth to the religion of nominal Christians. Both were accused of Monarchian tendencies in their doctrine of the Trinity, and of Manichee dualism in their ethic. Both had a lively interest in the demonic world. Both used apocryphal Gospels and Acts. Both movements enjoyed a strong following among women, and were alike accused of lapses into libertinism. The Messalians were at first accused of fasting too little, but later the accusation of fasting in Lent on Saturdays and Sundays is brought against the Messalians of Paphlagonia.[1] Both suffered complaint on ground of their voluntary poverty and vegetarianism.

At least it is worth raising the question, therefore, whether perhaps Egeria's expedition towards the Tigris was motivated by a desire to learn something at first hand of this evangelical movement spreading among the monks of that region. Conversely, when one considers the body of evidence for Syrians at this period finding their way into Gaul and Spain,[2] it is equally tempting to ask whether or not Priscillian himself may have been influenced by Messalian ascetics from Egypt and Syria.

The second Galician to be considered is Bachiarius. Gennadius of Marseille speaks of him as a man who left his home to become a wandering ascetic and who, to answer critics, found it necessary to address a profession of faith to the pope.[3]

---

[1] Anastasius Sinaita, *Quaest.* 64 (*PG* 89. 664). The evidence regarding the Messalians, apart from the homilies of pseudo-Macarius, is collected by M. Kmosko in the introduction to his edition of the Syriac *Liber graduum* (*Patrologia Syriaca* iii, 1926).

[2] Jerome (*In Ezech.* viii, on 27 : 16, *PL* 25. 267BC) comments on the energy and zeal of Syrian merchants penetrating every part of the Roman empire. Salvian (*De gubern. Dei* 4. 14) says the Syrians now control most of the trade in the Gallic cities, and are disliked and distrusted as cheats. Sidonius Apollinaris (*Ep.* 7. 17. 2) reports a monastery founded at Clermont by Abraham who was born by the Euphrates. The *Vitae SS. Patrum Emeretensium* (ed. J. N. Garvin, 1946) mention the presence in Emerita of a Greek physician and of Greek merchants coming regularly from the East (iv 1. 1; 3. 2). On the canon of Nîmes of 396 see above, p. 159; on Martin of Braga, below, p. 224.

[3] *Vir. inl.* 24.

The manuscript tradition has preserved two works under his name, the internal evidence of which suggests that he came from Galicia and wrote early in the fifth century, leaving Spain perhaps about the time of the Germanic invasion of 411. The profession of faith mentioned by Gennadius survives in two recensions.[1] Bachiarius complains in this work that merely to come from his province is to be suspected of heresy. He protests his correctness in both faith and morals. He rejects the libertinism of the Nicolaitans. On the Trinity he rejects both inequality and identity of the Persons. He holds the soul to be created, not (as some say) a part of God. He holds God to be indivisible. He holds that the devil was not born evil but is a fallen angel. He allows marriage, recommends married continence, and extols virginity. (Jerome himself could not have said it better.) He accepts both Old and New Testaments and admits no uncanonical books. He keeps fasts according to church discipline and humbly obeys bishops. He resents the distrust of those who doubt his integrity and suggest that he says one thing and means another.

This list of heresies disowned makes it obvious that Bachiarius must be a Galician *émigré* in Rome who needs to clear himself of Priscillianism. How unfair, he writes, that a whole province should be condemned merely because of one man.

The other work extant under his name is a less interesting and attractive piece. Entitled 'On the restoration of the lapsed', it is a harsh and even inhuman protest at the situation when an old friend and fellow ascetic (no doubt in Galicia) has lapsed into sin with a young woman, though in the past noted for his prayers and fasts. Expelled from his monastery by the superior (a deacon named Januarius) he has married the woman to avert scandal and the dangerous hostility of her offended parents. Bachiarius is appalled to think that the couple might now settle down to a

---

[1] For the text of Bachiarius see Dekkers's *Clavis* 568–70. *De fide* and *De lapso* are in *PL* 20. 1019–62, from Florio's edition. Of *De fide* J. Madoz printed a second recension in *Revista española de teología* 1 (1941), 463–74. Cf. A. Mundo in *Studia monastica* 7 (1965), 275–6. G. Morin ascribes to Bachiarius two ascetic letters (*Rev. Bénéd.* 40 (1928), 289–310, rp. in *PL Suppl.* i. 1035) recommending a three-week period of retirement for fasting and prayer, but presupposing the Christmas festival being observed on 25 Dec. (see above, p. 16). J. Duhr has a useful paper on *De fide* in *Rev. d'hist. eccl.* 24 (1928), 9 ff. But his study, *Le de Lapso de Bachiarius* (Louvain, 1934) is marred by fantasy, and impossibly dates Bachiarius *c.* 380. For a bibliographical note see F. X. Murphy in J. M. F. Marique (ed.), *Leaders of Iberean* [sic] *Christianity* (Boston, 1962), pp. 121–6.

respectable life together in the world. He calls on the former monk to renounce his marriage, to 'hate' the woman who is his partner in sin, and to re-enter his monastery cell where he is to torture himself with mortifications in expiation of his fault. Januarius is told to readmit him as a penitent, even though he was in deacon's orders. To Bachiarius it appears an intolerable defeat for the ascetic movement and for the Church itself if the couple are accepted in society.

The tract 'on the restoration of the lapsed' does nothing to illuminate the story of Priscillianism. The profession of faith, on the other hand, reflects the position of the first twenty years of the fifth century. It is important evidence for the extent to which Galicia has become virtually identified with the Priscillianist cause.

IV

THE HONOUR OF THE
MARTYR OF TRIER

The Council of Toledo

IN Spain the conciliatory work undertaken for the Gallic churches
by the council of Turin was paralleled by the synod held at Toletum
(Toledo) in the province of Carthaginensis in September 400.[1]
The object of this council was to put pressure upon the bishops
of Galicia to abandon their sympathy for Priscillianism, to discourage their clergy and people from venerating the martyrs of
Trier, and so to restore peace and harmony to the churches
throughout the Iberian provinces. Like the council of Turin, the
council of Toledo had before it as guidelines the letters of Ambrose
and of pope Siricius prescribing the conditions under which
recanting Priscillianists could be received back to communion.

According to the date prefixed to the Acts of Toledo in the
Hispana canonical tradition, the council met in the consulate of
Stilicho (i.e. either 400 or 405). The year varies in the manuscripts,
but the extant San Millán manuscript of A.D. 992–4 preserved
in the Escorial (d. I. 1) gives 400 (that is, Aera 438 by the Spanish
reckoning which followed the era of Augustus i.e. from 38 B.C.).
Internal evidence confirms 400. Both Ambrose (died 397) and
pope Siricius (died 20 November 399) are referred to as dead.
Simplicianus (died 15 August 400) is believed by the council to be
still living as bishop of Milan. The only surprise is that the bishops
at Toledo appear not to know the name of pope Anastasius who
succeeded Siricius on 27 November 399: the synod speaks of

---

[1] On the council of Toledo see Tillemont, *Mémoires* viii (2nd edn., 1713), 519–24,
794–7. There is a fine essay by Florez, *España sagrada* vi (Madrid, 1751), 49–129,
and a note by the Ballerini, commenting on Leo, *Ep.* 15, printed in *PL* 54. 1331–40.
Nothing written later on the subject as a whole is comparable in quality.

The Spanish tradition was aware of the relevance of the council of Turin to its
affairs. The Acts of Turin appear in the Hispana canon collection, and are cited at
the 12th council of Toledo, canon 4 (ed. Vives, p. 391 = *PL* 84. 474BC).

writing for confirmation of its decisions to the 'papa qui nunc est'. (Perhaps they had heard rumour of the aged Anastasius being ill and felt uncertain of his survival; he died in December 401.)[1]

The manuscript tradition of the Acts of Toledo 400 raises complex problems. The manuscripts of the Hispana canon-collection (Gonzalez's edition is reprinted in *PL* 84) transmit only certain parts of the Acts which were of interest at the time when the Hispana was compiled immediately after the fourth council of Toledo in 633;[2] and even of those parts that are thus transmitted one major piece seems to have no connection with the council of 400 at all. An annotated inventory of the material makes the situation clear.

(*a*) First, the Hispana gives a preface with the date and a list of nineteen bishops present. None of their sees is named except the last, Exuperantius of Celenis. This exception is probably to be explained from the fact that one of the decisions of the council was to reinstate at Celenis the bishop Ortygius who had been deposed and expelled by the Priscillianist bishops of Galicia. Since Exuperantius had prudently succeeded in dissociating himself from the Priscillianists and in taking his seat among the nineteen bishops in synod, the reinstatement of Ortygius will have created a considerable practical problem at Celenis, a diocese that might be much for one man but would certainly be too small for two.[3] Of the other bishops in the list, Patruinus or Petruinus is named first and evidently presided; from Innocent I's third letter it is clear that he was bishop of Emerita and so metropolitan of Lusitania. Hilarius is also mentioned in Innocent's letter as the

---

[1] Duchesne, *Liber pontificalis* i. 219.

[2] See canons 4 and 25 of the fourth council of Toledo (*PL* 84. 366–7, 374). On the Hispana, on which Spanish work is in progress, see F. Maassen, *Geschichte der Quellen und der Literatur des canonischen Rechtes* i (1870), 642–6, 667–716, and the survey by G. Martínez Díez, *La colección canónica Hispana* i (Madrid, 1966); thereon C. Munier in *Revue sc. relig.* 40 (1966), 400–10; K. Schäferdiek in *Zeits. f. Kirchengeschichte* 78 (1967), 144–48. The items of the first council of Toledo transmitted by the Hispana appear also in the ancient Spanish epitome (cod. Veron. LXI (59), s. vii), edited by Martínez Díez (Comillas, 1962) and in the St. Amand codex Paris lat. 3846, s. ix. The Hispana text in the eleventh-century Lugo codex lost in the Escorial fire of 1671 is enthusiastically reconstructed by C. García Goldáraz, *El códice Lucense de la colección canónica Hispana* (Rome: Spanish School of history and archaeology, 11, 1954) from the sixteenth-century notes of J. B. Pérez (below, pp. 179–80); the material hardly allows success, but the book is valuable.

[3] See above, p. 157, n. 3.

bringer of the report to Rome that led Innocent to write to Spain. Asterius or Asturius may be identified with probability from Ildefonsus of Toledo who mentions him as living about this time as bishop of Toledo.[1] One may speculate whether the Olympius present at the council is the distinguished Spanish preacher from whose sermons Augustine found a citation to throw at the Pelagian Julian of Eclanum, in which Olympus deplores the way in which original sin has caused faith to go astray upon the earth.[2] The other names in the list are men of whom there is otherwise no memorial: Aphrodisius, Severus, Serenus, Leporius, Aurelianus, Lampadius, Marcellus, Licinianus (Alacianus), Leonas, Jocundus, Lampadius or Lampius, Florus, Statius or Eustocius.

The preface notes that these same nineteen bishops appear 'in other Acts' as having given a verdict against the Priscillianists, but the compiler of the Hispana was not concerned to transcribe those other Acts containing this verdict. The remark betrays clearly that what the Hispana has preserved of the Acts of Toledo 400 is no plain transcript of the original conciliar record, but certain excerpts from it in which the editor has mingled his own comments with those pieces of the Acts that interested him. Whether this editor was the original mid seventh-century compiler of the Hispana is unclear. His date may be earlier than that. The Ballerini conjectured that he might be none other than Turibius of Astorga; but the nature of the material contained in the Hispana makes a rather later date, well after the time of the first council of Braga in 561, more likely.

(*b*) In the second place the Hispana preserves the opening sentence of Patruinus, the council's president:

Since in our churches each of us begins to do different things, and thence so many scandals arise that they produce schism, if it please you let us decree in common council the procedure to be followed by all

---

[1] *PL* 96. 199B. Ambrosio de Morales found in a codex Aemilianus (from San Millán de la Cogolla), written *c.* 930 and in his time in the Escorial, a list of the first nine bishops of Toledo: Pelagius, Patronus, Turibius, Quiricius, Vincentius, Paulatus, Natalis, Audentius, Asturius. See his *Los otros libros undecimo y duodecimo de la corónica general de España* (Alcala, 1577), fol. 8b. If the list concluded at Asturius, it is likely to have been drawn up early in the fifth century. On the probability that Audentius recorded as present at the council of Saragossa in 380 was bishop of Toledo, see above, p. 12.

[2] Augustine, *Contra Julianum* i. 8 (*PL* 44. 644–5); *Clavis* 558. Gennadius (*Vir. inl.* 23) shows Olympius' work to be an anti-Manichee tract arguing that evil comes from disobedience and is not inherent in creation.

bishops in ordaining clergy. I propose that the original rules of the Nicene council be perpetually kept, and that there be no departure from them. The bishops said: This has been agreed by all, so that if anyone, having knowledge of the Acts of the Nicene council, has presumed to do other than what is laid down and does not think that he must abide by that, then let him be held excommunicate, unless after correction by his brothers he emends his error.

Pope Innocent I noted with gratification this resolution of the Spanish bishops to adhere to the provisions of the Nicene canons in regard to ordinations.[1] At this period the importance of the canons of Nicaea was a leading theme in papal decretals. At the same time it is to be noted that the council of Toledo envisages the possibility that some bishops in Spain may not know the text of the canons. Their penalty of excommunication lies only upon a bishop who has ignored the canons of Nicaea after having read them, and who persists in maintaining his position when corrected by better-instructed brother bishops.

Patruinus' opening speech is an important step towards the introduction of a metropolitan system in the Spanish provinces, since the Nicene canons expressly give the metropolitan of the province the right to consecrate other bishops for the province and allow him an effective power of veto.

(*c*) Thirdly, the Hispana preserves twenty *capitula* or disciplinary canons. From these it appears that there had been some earlier provincial action in Lusitania. The first canon mentions a prior enactment by the Lusitanian bishops that deacons who lived with their wives without preserving strict continence should not be promoted to the presbyterate. The question had evidently been raised whether this ruling should have retrospective effect. What of 'vested interests'? No regard is to be paid to them: the council at Toledo provides that deacons who have begotten children before the Lusitanian ruling came into force should nevertheless be debarred from promotion to the presbyterate; it adds that on the same terms presbyters who became fathers might not be promoted to the episcopate. The date of the

---

[1] Innocent, *Ep.* 3. 5. 9 (*PL* 20. 492A). According to Innocent bishop Rufinus (whose name does not appear among the nineteen sitting in synod) apologized to the council for having consecrated bishops without metropolitan authority 'contrary to the Nicene canons' (3. 2. 5, 489B), which did not deter him from repeating his usurpations afterwards.

Lusitanian synod is unknown, but probably does not much precede the council of Turin of 398, to whose rulings its canon has so close a resemblance. Its cautious approach to the question of clerical celibacy is clear from the limitation of its restriction. The penalty of begetting a child is not to forfeit office, but only to lose prospects of promotion. At Toledo in 400 the bar to promotion is extended from deacons to presbyters; but again nothing is said to impose canonical penalties on presbyters in office whose wives embarrass them and their congregations by producing children. The motive for the strong encouragement given to clerical celibacy comes out in canon 5 which requires that all clergy shall attend the daily sacrifice. Communion requires abstinence.[1]

However, the canon makes it clear that the Priscillianist issue was the central problem. The canons of Toledo reaffirm the old ban of the council of Saragossa upon taking the eucharistic host away from mass (14), and upon the holding of devotional meetings ('collectiones') in women's houses. Other canons include provisions that no young consecrated virgin may be in an intimate situation with a 'confessor' (almost certainly meaning a celibate layman who would attend all daily offices and take part in the psalm-chanting),[2] or with any layman to whom she is not related; nor may she attend a dinner party except in the company of older women or widows (can. 6). No professed virgin or widow, unless the bishop or a presbyter is present, may sing antiphonal hymns in her house with a 'confessor' or even with her own servant. Vespers at the lighting of the evening lamp ('lucernarium') may not be read except in church or, if at home, in the presence of a bishop or presbyter or deacon (can. 11). A fierce canon prescribes that if the wives of clergy fall into sin, their husbands have a duty to lock them up in their houses with exceptionally severe fasting, though short of actually starving them to death; and they may not sit down to meals in their company (can. 7). The same rigorous note is struck by the excommunication of the widow of a bishop or presbyter or deacon if she remarries; not even a nun

---

[1] For the canons on celibacy see R. Gryson, Les Origines du célibat ecclésiastique (1970), pp. 179-81. The evidence of the councils of the Visigothic period shows that during the sixth and seventh centuries the requirement of clerical celibacy continued to cause much difficulty in Spain; see E. A. Thompson, The Goths in Spain (1969), p. 46.

[2] See B. Botte, 'Confessor', Archivum latinitatis medii aevi 16 (1941), 149-54.

may sit down to a meal with such a woman (can. 18). On the other hand, a note of liberal realism is heard in canon 17, laying down that so long as a man lives in an exclusive and 'monogamous' relation with a concubine to whom he is not legally married, the relation constitutes no bar to communion. The implication, that men ought not to regard themselves as entitled to sleep with their serving girls as well as their wives (as contemporary pagans generally did), is present but not spelled out.

The canons of Toledo endeavour to discourage clergy from combining their sacred office with duties in the civil service (can. 8), a practice which pope Innocent I (*Ep.* 3. 7) describes as endemic in the Spanish churches: the clergy (he complains) have continued practising as advocates or as servants of the government in carrying out their coercive instructions, and many who have been raised to the honour of the episcopate have previously provided spectacles and shows for the entertainment of the populace. Nevertheless, despite their own class, the bishops at Toledo are not entirely on the side of the authorities and of the rich. The eleventh canon mentions the need to protect clergy from violence at the hands of exploiting landlords, and threatens excommunication upon offending owners of estates. It must regretfully be noted that this penalty is laid down only for cases where the landowner has molested clergy and so affected the financial interests of the church. The canons of Toledo are less than a social programme for Spanish *latifundia*, and protect landowning rights, e.g. by the provision that none may be ordained unless his patron consents (can. 10).

The most difficult question facing the council was the right policy towards Priscillianism: should it be treated with gentleness or with severity? The 12th canon is revealing: it begins with the conventional rule that no cleric is free to forsake his bishop and join in communion with another bishop, but then adds a proviso that he may be received by the second bishop if that bishop is gladly welcoming back one who is abandoning the heretical schism and reverting to the catholic faith. On the other hand, any catholic Christian found communicating either openly or secretly with those who have been excommunicated in the past or who have been now censured at Toledo is to be reckoned among the Priscillianists. This canon envisages clergy with past Priscillianist associations, whose bishops are unwilling to be gentle and

generous with them. They must therefore find a home elsewhere
if they are to enjoy the catholic communion they now seek and to
be allowed to exercise their ministry. The council, in short, had to
provide for disagreement among the bishops about the right way
to deal with ex-Priscillianists.

(d) After the disciplinary canons the manuscripts of the Hispana
insert the note that this ends the council of Toledo: 'Explicit
constitutio concilii Toletani'. Nevertheless, the compiler goes on
to include a dogmatic statement or *regula fidei* with appended
anathemas. It has long been observed that this document survives
in two recensions. The long recension with eighteen anathemas
is preserved by the Hispana canonical tradition. But a few manuscripts of other canon collections, especially the Quesneliana,
preserve a short recension, which is ascribed to Augustine, and
the appended anathemas are twelve in number. The two editions
were edited together by A. de Aldama in 1934 in a critical dis-
sertation of great learning.[1] At the same time de Aldama sought
to make it plausible that both recensions should be associated
with councils at Toledo, the short recension (which shows every
sign of being prior to the long) belonging on this hypothesis to
the council of 400, the longer being an enlargement and adapta-
tion of it composed for submission to a council probably in or
soon after 447 (the time of Leo's correspondence with Turibius
of Astorga). There are difficulties, however, about this chain of
hypotheses.[2]

The differences between the two recensions are not minor
matters. The long recension asserts the 'Filioque' (5–6), declares
that in Christ two natures come together in one person (13),
condemns the beliefs that Christ is 'unbegettable' ('innascibilis')
and that his divine nature is subject to change (A. 6–7). Finally
it has a series of anathemas against dualism, astrology, the forbidding of lawful marriage, and the making of vegetarianism into
a general requirement (A. 13–18). So 'if anyone follows Priscillian's
sect in these errors and professes anything against the salvation

---

[1] A. de Aldama, *El simbolo toledano* i (Analecta Gregoriana 7, Rome, 1934).
The long recension is reprinted from Migne in an appendix to C. W. Barlow's
edition of Martin of Braga (American Academy in Rome, 1950), p. 288; also in
Lauchert, *Kanones*, pp. 177–81.

[2] The main difficulties are well stated by A. Barbero de Aguilera, 'El Priscilianismo:
¿ herejia o movimiento social?', *Cuadernos de historia de España* 37–8 (Buenos Aires,
1963), at pp. 33–5.

conferred by baptism, contrary to the see of St. Peter, let him be anathema' (A. 18).

The short recension, by contrast, is content to declare against Sabellian doctrines of the Trinity, against docetism, and against dualism. Where the long recension picks out for censure the doctrine of Christ as 'innascibilis', the short recension merely says 'If anyone has said and believed that the Son of God suffered as God, let him be anathema.'

As a declaration against Priscillianism (which is not mentioned), the short recension is soft in its impact. Other evidence, to be considered below, shows that the term *'innascibilis'* was the subject of hot controversy at the council of 400, which makes the silence of the short recension on this topic surprising. Prima facie, the long recension is much more directly concerned with the specifically Priscillianist questions as seen by their opponents. Nevertheless the long recension cannot belong to the council of 400 because of the presence of the 'Filioque' which is likely to betray the direct influence of Leo's letter of 447 to Turibius of Astorga (*Ep.* 15. 2). Moreover, the Acts of Toledo 400 lay before the Galician chronicler Hydatius, bishop of Aquae Flaviae 427–68. Hydatius knew that the council made a decree about the Priscillianists, drew up disciplinary canons, and reinstated Ortygius at Aquis Celenis. But he says nothing of a doctrinal statement such as a *regula fidei*.[1] Admittedly, arguments from Hydatius' silences need to be qualified by a note that the text of his chronicle has been transmitted in a corrupt condition, either enlarged and embroidered or excerpted and abbreviated; we cannot always be confident of having the text exactly as he wrote it. But it must remain more than doubtful whether this council of Toledo drew up any formal rule of faith. It is possible that both the short and the long recensions represent committee drafts of a later time, and that neither was produced by or at the council of 400.

The short recension's title indicates that it is not specifically drafted with Priscillianists in mind. It is simply a 'Rule of catholic faith against all heresies'. The long recension is not only against all heresies but specifically ('quam maxime') against the 'Priscilliani' (*sic*), and is stated to be a letter drawn up by the bishops of Tarraconensis, Carthaginensis, Lusitania, and Baetica and, at the

[1] Mommsen, *Chronica minora* ii. 16. See C. Courtois, 'Auteurs et scribes', *Byzantion* 21 (1951), 23–54, with corrections to Mommsen.

command of Leo, pope of the city, sent to Balconius, bishop of
Galicia. The bishops of the four provinces are then identified
with the council responsible for the twenty disciplinary canons of
Toledo. Accordingly, the long recension has a title indicating that
the *regula fidei* was the work of the council of Toledo of 400, even
if perhaps something of an afterthought. But this assertion is
irreconcilable with the further statement that it was sent to the
Galician bishop Balconius at the instruction of Leo the Great,
pope 440–61.

Balconius or Palconius turns up as bishop of Bracara in the
year 415. He is addressed in the extant letter by the presbyter
Avitus of Bracara written from Jerusalem, reporting the discovery in December 415 at Caphargamala near Jerusalem,
through special revelation, of the sacred relics of St. Stephen,
and promising to send 'some of the dust and, what is more
reliable and certain, solid bones' which have been secretly
obtained from the finder, the Greek priest Lucian, who had
succeeded in keeping for his own use, and no doubt profit, some
small part of his numinous treasure. Avitus intended that these
relics should be taken to Bracara by the hand of Orosius his com-
patriot. But in fact the relics ended by being divided between
Minorca, Ancona, and Uzalis in Africa, the Spanish provinces
at that time being wholly controlled by the Germanic tribes and
Orosius having no disposition to return to so dangerous a place.[1]
Avitus tells Balconius that his prayer is that the Lord will either
restore liberty to Spain or mollify those whom he has allowed to
prevail.[2]

The mention in the address of the long recension of Balconius,
if the bishop of Bracara is intended, is additional evidence that
this address is, or contains, fictional matter. It is certain that in

---

[1] The Vandals did not spare churches. In 429 they plundered the shrine of St.
Eulalia at Emerita (Hydatius, *Chron. min.* ii. 21). A Spanish inscription of this period
records the restoration of a shrine at Hispalis (Seville) 'despised and smashed by the
enemy': J. B. de Rossi, *Inscr. Christ. urbis Romae* ii. 296, no. 10. On healing at the
shrine at Ancona, see above, p. 3, n. 1.

[2] The two Latin versions of Avitus' letter 'domino papae Balconio' (*PL* 41.
807–18) are critically edited by S. Vanderlinden in *Études byzantines* 4 (1946), 178–
217. The career of Avitus is disentangled by B. Altaner in *Zeitschrift für Kirchengeschichte* 60 (1941), 456–68, reprinted in his *Kleine patristische Schriften* (TU 83, 1967),
pp. 450–66. He is probably identical with the Avitus who corresponded with Jerome
(*Ep.* 79. 106 and 124) when he was living near Constantinople. He is certainly not the
Origenist Avitus mentioned by Orosius as visiting Jerusalem before 414.

400 the bishop of Bracara was Paternus.[1] Moreover, while under the Roman imperial administration the metropolis of Galicia seems certainly to have been Asturica, Bracara became the administrative centre after the Germanic invasions of 409. The assumption, therefore, that in 400 the bishops of the four other provinces would have addressed themselves to the bishop of Bracara if they wanted to communicate with the principal bishop of Galicia is a tell-tale anachronism.

The most interesting fragments of the Acts of Toledo 400, however, are not those contained in the Hispana collection. For the mid seventh-century compiler the record of the Priscillianist debate was solely of antiquarian interest, and the three pieces concerned with this issue have been transmitted by a quite separate line of manuscript tradition. They have survived through a solitary manuscript which sadly perished in the seventeenth century but was fortunately studied in the seventies of the sixteenth century by two distinguished scholars of that golden age of Spanish humanist learning, Ambrosio de Morales (1513–91) and Juan Bautista Pérez (1537–97). At the time when they studied it the manuscript was in the Escorial. It was destroyed in the disastrous fire of 1671. Fortunately the excerpts from the Acts of Toledo were transcribed independently by both Morales and Pérez. The pieces from the Acts of Toledo were first printed by Morales in the eleventh book of the *General Chronicle of Spain*, published in 1577 at Alcala where he was then teaching.[2] Pérez's copy was included in a collection of conciliar documents which he put together in 1575 at the command of Gaspar de Quiroga, then bishop of Cuenca and inquisitor general, and sent to pope Gregory XIII. Pérez's manuscript survives in the Vatican Library (Vatic. lat. 4887). His material was available for the huge collection of councils of Spain and the New World compiled by Cardinal Sáenz de Aguirre, who made little use of it. Pérez's notes were consulted to better purpose by the Ballerini in the eighteenth century.[3] They have been printed in detail by

---

[1] This is attested in the council's verdict on the Priscillianist bishops (see below, p. 183).

[2] A. de Morales, *Los otros libros undecimo y duodecimo de la corónica general de España*, fol. 6b. On the Escorial collection see Gregorio de Andrés, *La Real Biblioteca de El Escorial* (Madrid, 1970); J. M. Sausterre, 'Les manuscrits de l'Escurial', *Scriptorium* 26 (1972), 326–33.

[3] For a general outline of the work of Morales and Pérez see G. Martínez Díez,

C. García Goldáraz in the third volume of his ambitious work on the lost Lugo codex of the Hispana,[1] also burnt in 1671. Collation of the printed texts of Morales and Pérez shows that Sáenz de Aguirre reprinted Morales's edition with minor improvements and a few errors.[2] Comparison of Morales and Pérez makes possible a more comprehensible and coherent text than either taken alone; but in general Pérez seems a more accurate witness to the readings of the lost manuscript. Morales and Pérez agree (against Sáenz de Aguirre) that the Escorial codex originated at the famous Castilian monastery of San Millán de la Cogolla, that is, the house of St. Aemilianus Cucullatus or St. Emilian of the Cloak, the ascetic saint who died in 574 and whose Life was written in the seventh century by Braulio of Saragossa.[3] As for its date, Morales gives a rough estimate that it seemed to him to be about five hundred years old. Pérez had evidently read the codex through with greater care, for he reports that the codex was precisely

---

La colección canónica Hispana i (1966), 31–40 and 43–52; since the three pieces on the Priscillianists are not included in the Hispana, he is naturally unconcerned with them. On Pérez see the Ballerini's notes in *PL* 54. 1334 and 56. 231–8. Sáenz de Aguirre's edition appeared in four volumes at Rome in 1693–4; second edition by J. Catalani (Rome, 1753–5) with additional notes; re-edited with the canons rearranged under subjects for canon lawyers by S. Pueyo at Madrid 1784–5 and 1850. Aguirre announced the plan of his work in his *Notitia conciliorum Hispaniae atque novi orbis . . quorum editio paratur Salmanticae* (Salamanca, 1686), where (p. 21) Pérez's labours are handsomely acknowledged; this rare book is at the Queen's College, Oxford, and the British Library. All editions of Aguirre's *Concilia*, except that of 1850, are in the University Library, Cambridge. (The British Library and the Bodleian have Catalani's edition only.) Pueyo's edition of the Priscillianist professions and conciliar verdict includes several conjectures for the improvement of Aguirre's text.

[1] *El códice Lucense de la colección canónica Hispana* (Rome, 1954), iii. 63–7.
[2] For the text of the three Priscillianist pieces J. Vives (*Concilios visigóticos . . . .*, 1963) reprinted Aguirre's edition without taking account of the material from Pérez printed in 1954 by García Goldáraz, on the basis of which Morales (= Aguirre) and Pérez can be improved upon. For a text resting on comparison of the two witnesses to the lost Aemilianus see below, p. 234.
[3] *PL* 80. 699–714; on this Life see A. Linage Conde in F. L. Cross (ed.), *Studia Patristica* 10 (*TU* 107, 1970), pp. 374–8. In his *Notitia conciliorum Hispaniae* (Salamanca, 1686), pp. 53–4, Sáenz de Aguirre asserts that the codex with the Priscillianist professions of faith is at Toledo. He says nothing of San Millán, nor of the date of the codex. Aguirre (born 1630) became a monk at San Millán (1645) before going on to professorships at Valladolid (1653) and Salamanca (1665). His reply to the Gallican declaration of 1682, *Auctoritas infallibilis et summa cathedrae S. Petri* (1683), won him his red hat in 1686. His heart went into the defence of the Ps.-Isidorian Decretals in the first volume of his *Collectio maxima conciliorum Hispaniae* of 1693. On his relations with Mabillon, to whom he sent a copy, see García M. Colombás, 'Aguirre, Mabillon y la Teología', *Revista española de Teología* 21 (1961), 153–66.

dated by the scribe in the year 962.[1] It was written in Visigothic script and was entitled 'Decreta canonum praesulum Romanorum' (so Morales).

The fact that this codex was written at San Millán de la Cogolla has been the cause of some confusion. The high authority of Friedrich Maassen has affirmed that the three pieces from the Acts of Toledo occur in the extant codex from San Millán which survived the fire of 1671 and remains today among the treasures of the Escorial, the codex d. I. 1 written in 994. This last codex Aemilianus has been the subject of detailed study, and while it contains the Hispana canon collection together with many papal decretals, it certainly does not have the three pieces from the Acts of Toledo concerning the Priscillianists.[2] Maassen, it is fair to add, had not seen the codex, and simply made mistaken deductions from the remarks of the Ballerini.

The three pieces consist of excerpts from the proceedings at Toledo concerned with the recantations of Symposius of Astorga, of Dictinius his son, and of a 'then presbyter' named Comasius who was also of the church of Astorga and no doubt succeeded Dictinius. Finally there is the formal verdict of the nineteen bishops about the terms of reinstatement for those disavowing Priscillianism and the decision to exclude the bishops who would not recant. Symposius and Dictinius did not want a separate church in Galicia. They wanted to be in communion with the catholic church. They solemnly abjured anything wrong that Priscillian had written, together with Priscillian personally. At a cross-examination on 6 September Dictinius seems to have been in the forefront of the battle: 'Hear me, most excellent priests;[3] correct everything, since to you is given the keys of the kingdom of heaven. But I beg of you that to us may be opened the keys of the kingdom, not the gates of hell. If you permit, I place all this before your eyes. For I reprehend in myself that I said that the nature of God and man is one.' The fragment continues with a series of excerpts from Dictinius' utterances before the council, all of which are designed to underline the unreserved and total

---

[1] Pérez's note is printed by García Goldáraz, iii. 31.

[2] F. Maassen, *Geschichte*, pp. 217 and 709. For a detailed analysis of the extant Aemilianus see G. Antolín, *Catálogo de los códices latinos de la Real Biblioteca del Escorial* i (1910), 320–68.

[3] 'Optimi sacerdotes.' Compare the address in the first Würzburg tractate: 'beatissimi sacerdotes' (p. 3, 6; p. 33, 7).

character of his submission. 'A little earlier I said, and now again I repeat: All that I wrote in my former understanding and in the beginnings of my conversion (*in principiis conversionis meae*) I reject with my whole heart . . . God's name excepted, I anathematize everything.'

Symposius followed: 'As for what has just been read in some parchment, in which the Son was said to be unbegettable (*innascibilis*), this doctrine, which proclaims two principles or that the Son is unbegettable, I condemn with the author. . . . Hand me the paper, I condemn with the very words used.' And when he had received the paper, he read from the text: 'All heretical books, and especially the doctrine of Priscillian according to what has been read today, where the Son is said to be unbegettable, I condemn with its author.' The presbyter Comasius then assures the council that he condemns whatever his bishop condemns; he regards God alone as a superior source of wisdom.

On the following day, 7 September,[1] the three from Astorga had to repeat the same assurances, and expressly recognized that it would be incompatible with the 'catholic and Nicene faith' to say that the Son is 'innascibilis'. They therefore condemned all books which Priscillian had written amiss, together with their author.

On the same day (7 September) the council of Toledo agreed upon the text of its final verdict. It is not easy to construe. The bishops explain: we have practised patience for a long time since the meeting of the council at Saragossa at which judgement was pronounced against certain individuals; but Symposius, who was present for only a single day, refused to accept the judgement. In view of all this, it was hard for us to listen to the persons mentioned.[2] However, Ambrose of blessed memory had sent a letter to us after that council (at Saragossa) to the effect that if they condemned what they had done wrongly and fulfilled the conditions which his letter contained, they might be received back to communion. In addition pope Siricius of blessed memory had written. They refused to attend the council called earlier to Toledo, to which we had invited them that we might hear why they had not fulfilled conditions which they themselves had

---

[1] Pérez gives 7 Sept. ('vii Iduum'), Morales 11 Sept. ('iii Iduum').

[2] 'arduum nobis esset audire iam dictos' (Morales); 'arduum nobis esse audire dicti' (Pérez); 'arduum nobis est audire dicta (*uel* Dictinium)', conj. Pérez.

proposed in the presence and hearing of Saint Ambrose. Symposius unambiguously replied that he had ceased to recite the names of those whom they have been calling martyrs. However, although since that time he has been deceived and led astray by many so that we discovered him to have been acting otherwise, yet he has been involved in no apocryphal writings nor with new sciences composed by Priscillian. Dictinius, who had almost[1] lapsed by some of his letters, condemns them all by his profession of faith, and has asked for correction and begged for pardon. He has acted as Symposius has done in condemning with their author everything that Priscillian wrote contrary to the catholic faith. It is established that Symposius was compelled by the multitude of the people to ordain Dictinius bishop, despite the decree of saint Ambrose that for the sake of peace he should retain the place of presbyter and should not receive increase of honour. They also confessed that they had ordained others for various churches which lacked bishops, having confidence that almost the entire laity of Galicia agreed with them. One of those so ordained is Paternus of Bracara.

At this point Paternus leapt to his feet and swore that, while he had once known the Priscillianist sect, after becoming a bishop he had been liberated from it by reading books of saint Ambrose.[2]

The council agreed that Paternus might remain in office in Bracara. Other bishops whom the council agreed to receive were Isonius who, though only recently baptized, had been consecrated bishop of an unnamed see by Symposius; Vegetinus who had

---

[1] *pene lapsum* was read in the manuscript by both Morales and Pérez. Florez (*España sagrada* vi, no. 159, pp. 109 f.) suggested the emendation *plene lapsum*, 'completely lapsed'. This correction is supported by Augusto Quintana Prieto, 'Primeros siglos de cristianismo en el convento jurídico asturicense', in *Legio VII Gemina* (León, 1970), 443–74 at 472, n. 161. But the council is concerned to justify its highly controversial decision to admit Dictinius to communion. Therefore *pene* is likely to be right.

[2] No special work by Ambrose on Priscillianism survives. However, it is irresistible to ask if Ambrose wrote for the Priscillianist situation the work, of which Caspari edited a fragment, on the origin of the soul, 'contra eos qui animam non confitentur esse facturam aut ex traduce esse dicunt'. It consists mainly of biblical quotations, so that authenticity is hard to judge, but the citations of IV Esdras are much in the Ambrosian manner. See the text in Caspari, *Kirchenhistorische Anecdota* (1883) i. 227–9 = *PL Suppl.* i. 611 (*Clavis* 170); G. Madec, *S. Ambroise et la philosophie* (Paris, 1974), pp. 260–7. There is irony in Ambrose's dependence on an apocryphon for an attack on Priscillianism. For Ambrose's large debt to this book see R. L. Bensly and M. R. James, *The Fourth Book of Ezra* (*Texts and Studies* iii. 2, 1895), pp. xxxii–xxxv.

been bishop somewhere since before the council of Saragossa; and Anterius, again of an unnamed see. The reception of Paternus and Vegetinus is declared to be absolute, without further quali- fication. The decision to receive Symposius and Dictinius and 'the rest who failed to come[1] to the council from the province of Galicia and who have always continued in communion with Symposius', on condition of their signature for the formula prescribed by the council, is made subject to the ultimate agree- ment of 'him who is now *papa* [evidently here meaning the bishop of Rome—the phrase is important testimony of the incipient tendency to call him 'papa' in a special degree] and of Simplicianus of Milan and of other bishops whose ratification is sought by letter. Meanwhile, Symposius, 'the devout old man', is to stay at home in his church and be very careful about those who will be given to him (apparently 'watchdogs' to see that he behaves properly under conditions approximating to house arrest); then he may hope for communion from those from whom he first received hope of peace in the future. A further decree is made regarding Dictinius and Anterius, that until such time as agree- ment is notified by letters from the pope or from Simplicianus of Milan, they are to ordain no bishops, presbyters, or deacons, so that they may know themselves to be only conditionally pardoned.

Four bishops remained recalcitrant. They refused the demand that they place Priscillian and his writings under anathema, for the simple and honest reason that if they were to do so they would lose the support of all their clergy and people. Of the four we know the names (Herenas or Herenias, Donatus, Acurius, Emilius),[2] not the sees. Not all their sees were necessarily in Galicia. One of Herenias' clergy cried out before the council, 'of his own accord, not under interrogation', that Priscillian was

---

[1] The text of the verdict is corrupt here. I read (after Pérez): 'Recepturi etiam in nostram communionem, cum sedes apostolica rescripserit. Reliqui [reliquos Pe] qui ex provincia Gallaecia ad concilium non venerunt [*cod.* convenerunt; *Morales* convenerant; non convenerant *conj.* Pueyo] et in Symphosii semper communione durarunt [*Morales* duraverant], acceptam formam a concilio missam [*Morales* accepta forma . . . missa] si subscripserint.'
If *convenerunt* is read, the reference is presumably to Isonius whose status is unclear under the verdict.

[2] Herenias (Pérez), Herenas (Morales). The name intended is perhaps Herennius, well attested in inscriptions. For Acurius Pérez gives 'ac Vrius'. From the epigraphic evidence one would expect either Acutius or Acilius; but Acurius is not impossible.

catholic and a holy martyr who had been orthodox to the end and
had suffered persecution at the hands of the bishops. Herenias
and the rest were promptly condemned for 'lying perjury', i.e.
for denying in the Manichee fashion that the Priscillianists really
believed the Manichee and Sabellian doctrines that they had been
authoritatively declared to hold.[1] The council concluded its
formal verdict by exhorting all bishops to beware that none of
those excommunicated by the council should hold private devotional meetings in women's houses and read 'apocrypha which
have been condemned'.[2] Anyone holding communion with them is
to be held an adherent of the sect. Indeed, those who accept them
are to be bound by an even graver sentence. Finally, Ortygius,
who had been expelled from Aquis Celenis, is declared to be reinstated. Nothing is said of the council's practical proposals for
dealing with the problem thereby created with Exuperantius.[3]

The council of Toledo had a mind almost as divided as that of
the council of Saragossa twenty years previously on the question
whether a hard or a soft policy should be adopted. To allay
critics likely to think them soft, the bishops' verdict expresses
itself in terms of strong censure of Symposius and Dictinius.
Moreover, the bold decision to accept them to communion on
condition of recantation is a responsibility that the council is
careful to try to share with churches outside Spain, especially the
great sees of Rome and Milan. Evidently the nineteen bishops
felt uncertain of their power to carry some of their colleagues with
them, and needed to look to Italy, perhaps also to Aquitaine and
Gaul, for reinforcement of their precarious authority. It was a
highly controversial decision to permit the ex-Priscillianist bishops
to remain in possession of their sees.

The death of pope Anastasius (probably on 19 December 401
after a long illness) and the succession of Innocent I on 22 December may have made Rome slow to react to the documents from
Toledo. Innocent's third letter is undated, but probably falls in
about 402 or 403.[4] The pope addresses the bishops assembled at

[1] See the formula for recanting Manichees cited, ch. I, p. 56, n. 1.
[2] 'Apocrypha quae damnata sunt': in view of Hydatius of Emerita's distinction
at the council of Saragossa between *damnanda* and *superflua* in relation to apocrypha
(above, ch. I, p. 23), the ambiguity of the wording here may be deliberate.
[3] Above, ch. III, p. 157, n. 3.
[4] *PL* 20. 485–93 reprints Coustant's text. Some time has elapsed since the council
of Toledo, which occurred 'dudum' (489B).

the synod of Toledo. He has had frequent reason to be anxious about the deteriorating dissension and schism among the Spanish churches. Bishop Hilary and the presbyter Elpidius have come to the apostolic see to report, at a formal meeting attended by the Roman presbyters, the deplorable state of discipline and disregard of the canons. The bishops of two provinces, Baetica and Carthaginensis, have so resented the milk-and-water peace terms with the Galicians that they have withdrawn from communion with all the others. It revives the old Luciferian spirit (of Gregory of Elvira in Baetica), Innocent shrewdly suggests, to feel animosity against the reception of those who have been converted by wiser counsel from the detestable sect of Priscillian. The treatment of Symposius and Dictinius has been displeasing to some, who seem to have felt that, if they were readmitted, they should not have continued in office as bishops but be treated as having lapsed and granted only lay status. But in the scriptures Peter's denial, Thomas' incredulity, even David's adultery, did not disqualify them for distinguished service to the Lord. Let all understand that the unity of the one body is the overriding necessity. The realization of this unity will be assisted by strict observance of the Nicene canons in regard to metropolitan authority. It is deplorable that two bishops, Rufinus and Minicius, the former of whom apologized to the council of Toledo for his usurpation, have been consecrating bishops in disregard of their metropolitan. Minicius' action in consecrating a bishop of Gerona is to be reviewed by the bishops of Tarraconensis, and the status of the bishops ordained by these two is meanwhile to be held in suspense. A bishop John, whose see is likewise not given, sent legates to the council of Toledo who there accepted in his name the reception of Symposius and Dictinius. He subsequently disavowed his legate's action. He must either submit to the council of Toledo's decision or resign his see.

Innocent contemplates with sadness the secularity of the Spanish bishops. Rufinus, already mentioned, and Gregory of Emerita have been promoted to the episcopate even though they compromised their baptismal promises by subsequently practising at the bar. Some bishops have continued working as government officials; others have been *curiales* and simply carried out the orders of the secular authorities. Some have become bishops who previously, as rich citizens, provided shows in the amphitheatre or the circus for the vulgar entertainment of the populace.[1] For the sake of peace Innocent accepts the situation, but on condition that such men are not ordained in future.

Innocent directs proper inquiry into a quarrel about Gregory, successor of Patruinus as bishop of Emerita, whose dignities and privileges appear to have been disregarded by someone (whether ecclesiastical or secular is unclear).

After repeating warnings against unsuitable ordinands Innocent concludes by ruling on the subject of clerical marriage. The requirement of 1 Tim. 3 : 2 that a candidate for the episcopate ought not to be twice married left it obscure whether a pre-baptismal wife counted. Many in Spain and elsewhere thought that baptism was a wholly new start in life so washing away the past that a previous marriage was among the stains obliterated; therefore it did not count as a marriage before God. In 397 Jerome had wholly refused to support the zeal of his lay correspondent Oceanus who asked for support in protest against a Spanish bishop Carterius (not at Toledo in 400 but perhaps the Carterius present at Saragossa in 380), who had married his first wife before baptism and after her death had married again. Jerome tells Oceanus that there are a vast number of bishops who are in an identical position and that he has no objection.[2] Innocent takes the opposite view, namely that marriage is an element in the order of divine creation and is in no sense part of the fallen world of sin from which baptism gives cleansing.

An echo of this controversy, with the probable implication that the influence of Priscillianist ideas north of the Pyrenees is not yet dead, can be heard in Innocent I's sixth letter of 20 February 405 addressed to Exuperius of Toulouse. Innocent reaffirms the policy of Siricius in regard to clerical celibacy; those clergy who have retained their wives are not to be promoted to higher grades. Exuperius had asked Innocent's judgement about baptized officials who had administered torture or even capital punishment; Innocent found no ruling among the precedents of the chancery, but did not think they should be excommunicated (above, p. 130, n. 6). Innocent's final words give Exuperius a

---

[1] Cf. Jerome, *Ep.* 69. 9, on the way in which yesterday's catechumen is today's bishop (no doubt Ambrose is in mind); yesterday in the amphitheatre, today in the church; in the evening at the circus, next morning at the altar; lately patron of actors, now consecrating virgins.

[2] *Ep.* 69.

list of the biblical canon (including fourteen Pauline letters), and warn him against apocrypha under the names of Matthias, James the less, of Acts of Peter or of John written by Leucius, or of Andrew by 'Xenocarides and Leonidas the philosophers', or of Thomas.[1]

From 407 onwards edicts outlawing Priscillianists begin to come from the imperial chancery. A law of that year imposes confiscation of property, ineligibility to accept any gift or legacy or to make contracts, and disqualification from making a valid will. Slaves are declared free to abandon Priscillianist masters. Any estate on which a Priscillianist meeting has been held with the knowledge of the landowner is forfeit to the Treasury. If the landowner was ignorant of it, he retains his land, but his steward or overseer is to be beaten with lashes tipped with lead and sent to the mines for life.[2] A further law of 410 forbids both the enlistment of Priscillianists in the imperial service and the granting to them of exemption from any curial duty.[3] By that time, however, the Priscillianist conventicles in Gallaecia had suddenly passed beyond the reach of government coercion.

The Germanic invasion

In 406 the Vandals, Alans, and Sueves poured across the Rhine in Gaul, and three years later, in the autumn of 409, penetrated the undefended passes of the Pyrenees. The Spanish provinces lay at the mercy of the invaders.[4] The chronicler bishop Hydatius paints a grim picture of the appalling sufferings of the population. Pillage and murder in the countryside was made worse by pestilence and famine, and hard-faced tax collectors in the cities. One woman, reduced to eating her own infants, was stoned by the mob. The four last plagues of the Apocalypse had come. The Romans, at first safe in the walled cities and forts, found the surrounding countryside so dominated by the barbarian enemy

---

[1] *PL* 20. 495–502. See Schäferdiek in Hennecke/Schneemelcher, *NT Apocrypha* ed. R. McL. Wilson, ii. 183. (German edn. ii. 121.)

[2] *Cod. Theod.* xvi. 5. 40 (Rome, 22 Feb. 407). A life sentence in Roman mines was not of long duration.

[3] *Cod. Theod.* xvi. 5. 48 (Constantinople, 21 Feb. 410) drafted with Montanists in mind; cf. xvi. 5. 59 (Constantinople, 9 Apr. 423).

[4] Jerome (*Ep.* 123. 16, to Geruchia) describing the ravages in Gaul and Aquitaine, adds that the invasion of Spain, long imminent, is fully expected.

that they had to submit.¹ Augustine mentions that while most of the Spanish bishops stayed to minister to their flocks some forsook their duties and joined the many refugees.² Salvian of Marseille saw in the invasion the anger of the Lord against that decadence from which Spain was no more exempt than Gaul.³

In time the invaders divided the Spanish provinces by lot between themselves: the Hasding Vandals and Sueves took Galicia, the Alans Lusitania and Carthaginensis, the Siling Vandals Baetica. Only Tarraconensis remained under precarious Roman tenure. Gradually, partly because they quarrelled among themselves, the barbarians came to uneasy terms with the Romans in Spain. The writ of the imperial tax-collector no longer ran,⁴ and not every Roman citizen was sorry to see the Vandals' arrival. Among those who had least reason to regret the domination of the Vandals and Sueves were the persecuted Priscillianists of Galicia. Under their new masters they were free to flourish without fear of the harsh edicts from Honorius' court at Ravenna which could not now be put into effect.⁵

Until 429 when under Sueve and Visigoth pressure the Vandals moved on to North Africa, they were engaged in almost continuous fighting in the Iberian peninsula,⁶ and the church can have had little outward peace. The imperial policy under Theodosius I and his sons was to assimilate the barbarians within Roman society and civilization. Not all Romans found this easy to accept in practice, and the external face of compromise often masked an inward sense of resentment and alienation from cruel invaders and malodorous immigrants, who greased their long hair, shaved their faces, and wore undignified garments such as trousers.⁷

---

¹ Sozomen, *HE* 9. 12; Hydatius, ed. Mommsen, *Chronica minora* ii. 17–18 is the main source; Olympiodorus of Thebes, *Frag.* 30 (Müller, *Fragm. Hist. Graec.* iv. 64, from Photius, *Bibl.* 80, p. 60*b* 35).

² Possidius, *Vita Augustini* 30. 5, citing Augustine's letter to Honoratus bishop of Thiabe (= *Ep.* 228. 5, *CSEL* 57. 488).

³ *De gubernatione Dei* 7. 12. 52.

⁴ Salvian, *De gub. Dei* 5. 5. 23; Orosius, *Hist. adv. paganos* 7. 41.

⁵ Leo, *Ep.* 15, praef. (*PL* 54. 680A).

⁶ On the Vandals in Spain it is hard to fill with flesh and blood the dry bones in Hydatius' chronicle. What can be said is well set out by C. Courtois, *Les Vandales et l'Afrique* (Paris, 1955; repr. Aalen, 1964), pp. 51–8; more briefly in H. J. Diesner, *Das Vandalenreich* (Stuttgart, 1966), pp. 27–30. For a broad survey see K. F. Stroheker, 'Spanien im spätrömischen Reich (284–475)', *Archivo español de arqueologia* 45–7 (1972–4), 587–605.

⁷ Hairgrease: Sidonius Apollinaris, *Carm.* 12. 6. Trousers were forbidden in Rome

Orosius

From western Spain one of those who found life intolerable under the barbarian occupation was Paulus Orosius, presbyter of the church at Bracara. Orosius left home in 414 and went to study under Augustine at Hippo, to be sent on by him to travel via Alexandria to Bethlehem where under Jerome's guidance he played a role in the Pelagian controversy. In 416 he was entrusted by his fellow presbyter Avitus of Bracara with the newly found relics of St. Stephen, to be taken from Palestine to the church at Bracara for enshrinement. But the dangers of travel in the Iberian peninsula made him stop at Minorca to deposit part of his precious treasure, and thence to return to Africa. There in 418, with some encouragement from Augustine (whose ideas about history and divine providence were certainly much above his head), he completed his historical work in reply to the pagans who thought that, while under the old gods of Rome all had gone well for the empire, the coming of Christianity had spelt political and social disaster.[1]

Both Orosius and Augustine affirm in strong terms that Orosius' motive in leaving Galicia for Africa was the disinterested love of learning.[2] It is easy to suspect that they are protesting too much, sensitive perhaps to unkind suggestions that Orosius had behaved as a hireling fleeing from his flock on the coming of the Vandal wolf. In his *History* Orosius frankly concedes that he left home because harassed by the barbarians.[3] Several passages in the *History* indicate that, while both Orosius' apologetic and imperial policy necessitated a friendly and favourable portrait of the barbarian invaders, his personal and private prejudices were unsympathetic to them.[4]

by edict in 397 and 399; long hair and garments of skin in 416 (*Cod. Theod.* xvi. 10. 2–4). Shaving: Jerome, *In Esaiam*, iii, p. 115 on 7: 21–2.

[1] For recent discussion of Orosius' *Historia* see T. E. Mommsen, *Mediaeval and Renaissance Studies*, ed. E. F. Rice (New York, 1959), pp. 325–48, rightly emphasizing the wide differences between Orosius and Augustine; B. Lacroix, *Orose et ses idées* (Montreal, 1965); F. Paschoud, *Roma Aeterna* (Rome, 1967), pp. 276–92; J. Straub, *Regeneratio imperii* (Darmstadt, 1972), pp. 299–303. Augustine's commendation of Orosius to Jerome is *Ep.* 166. 2.

[2] Augustine, *Ep.* 169. 13 to Evodius; Orosius, *Commonitorium* 1 (*CSEL* 18. 154).

[3] *Hist. adv. paganos* 3. 20.

[4] In places Orosius' *Historia* is for peaceful coexistence (1. 16. 2; 17. 3; 7. 38. 2). In 7. 41 the barbarian invasion is cheerfully interpreted as a mercy of God. Yet 5. 2. 2–3 and 6 reveal Orosius' very Roman heart. See above, p. 124, n. 1.

His first memorandum to Augustine asked for help in dealing with Priscillianism and Origenism. Two fellow Spaniards, both named Avitus, had (like Orosius) travelled abroad in search of the theological instruction that could not be had in Spain. One went to Jerusalem[1] and returned with a work by Origen, probably *On First Principles*. The other went to Rome and returned to Spain with writings of Victorinus (whether Marius Victorinus the Neoplatonist or Victorinus of Poetovio is unclear), which his namesake soon persuaded him to be inferior to Origen. Both Aviti rejected Priscillianism, but the situation was not improved by the theology they had acquired in exchange, viz. their propagation of Origenist speculations about the eternal creativity of God; the shared nature of 'soul' held in common by angels, men, and devils; the remedial, purging fire of divine judgement; the ultimate salvation of Satan; and the rationality of sun, moon, and stars.

A letter of Braulio, bishop of Saragossa 631–51, declares that Orosius was, like Dictinius, a convert from Priscillianism, who was put on the correct path by Augustine.[2] The report is late and unconfirmed. Moreover, it could be a false deduction from some words of Augustine in his letter to Jerome commending Orosius.[3] On the other hand, a Priscillianist past would not have been advertised by Orosius after his conversion, and the report must remain possible and doubtful.

It seems clear from Orosius' account that the only serious theology available in Galicia was under Priscillianist influence, so that those who wanted an alternative had to go elsewhere to find it.

The account of Priscillian in the memorandum to Augustine represents him as 'worse than the Manichees in that he accepted the authority of the Old Testament'. Priscillian is credited with speculating as follows: The soul is born of God and comes from a storehouse[4] giving a promise that it will fight before God and

---

[1] This Avitus cannot be the Avitus of Braga who obtained relics of St. Stephen and corresponded with Jerome (*Epp.* 79, and 106 and 124). See B. Altaner, *Kleine patristischen Schriften* (*TU* 83, 1967), pp. 450–66.

[2] *Ep.* 44 (PL 80. 693D); below, p. 230.

[3] Aug. *Ep.* 169. 13 (*CSEL* 44. 621) 'huic etiam ipsi Orosio ad quaedam interrogata, quae illum de Priscillianistarum haeresi et de Origenis quibusdam opinionibus, quas non recipit ecclesia, permovebant, uno libro non grandi quanta potui brevitate et perspicuitate respondi.'

[4] *promptuarium*, a favourite word in IV Esdras, cf. iv. 35, 41; vii. 32. The concept of a treasury containing souls is Jewish; cf. G. F. Moore, *Judaism* i (1927), 368;

be instructed by the adoration of the angels; it then descends
through certain spheres where it is captured by the powers of
evil. By the will of the conquering prince it is forced into various
bodies and is inscribed on a written bond as their property. On
this ground Priscillian affirmed the validity of astrology
('mathesis'), in the sense that he asserted that this is the bond
which Christ destroyed and affixed to the cross by his passion.

To support all this, Orosius proceeds to quote from a letter
written by Priscillian himself. As the Latin has caused commentators much difficulty, it must be transcribed:

Haec prima sapientia est in animarum typis divinarum virtutum in-
tellegere naturas et corporis dispositionem, in qua obligatum caelum
videtur et terra omnesque principatus saeculi videntur adstricti;
sanctorum vero [vero *om.* cod. B] dispositiones superare. nam primum
circulum et mittendarum in carne animarum divinum chirographum,
angelorum et dei et omnium animarum consensibus fabricatum patri-
archae tenent; qui contra formalis militiae opus possident, et reliqua.

The vocabulary of the piece abounds in words that occur in the
Würzburg tracts such as *obligatum, adstricti, dispositiones, chirographum, militia,* and no case could easily be made against Priscillian's
authorship on mere ground of style. But its content is problematic
and disturbing. The following rendering may be attempted:

The first wisdom consists in recognizing in the types of souls the
natures of divine powers and the disposition of the body, in which the
heaven and the earth are bound and all the powers of the world are
gripped; but the dispositions of the holy ones overcome. For the first
circle and the divine record of souls to be sent into the flesh are made
by the co-operation of the angels and of God and of all souls, and are
in the control of the patriarchs. Those on the opposite side who control the force of the zodiacal host . . . and the rest.

This at least appears to be the meaning of the text as edited by
Schepss. There is manuscript authority for omitting *vero* in the
fourth line, in which case Schepss's semicolon after *adstricti* must
also go, meaning 'and (to understand that) the disposition of the
body, in which etc., overcomes the dispositions of the holy ones'.[1]

The translation of the final phrase must be admitted to be a

J. Bonsirven, *Le Judaïsme palestinien au temps de Jésus-Christ* i (1934), 338–9. The
classic text is *b. Hagigah* 12b.

[1] Zodiacal powers control the body, divine powers the soul; the body is not
fully controllable by the good. Cf. above, p. 70.

venture that may be criticized as hazardous. On the face of it 'qui [*v.l.* quae] contra formalis militiae opus possident et reliqua' conveys no meaning at all. (This is partly because it is the beginning of a sentence that is torn away from what follows.) Babut throws in his hand: regarding the fragment as a forgery put under Priscillian's name, and cleverly using much of his vocabulary, he regards the unintelligibility of the last clause as somehow supporting his scepticism.[1] d'Alès translates the clause: 'En regard est la domaine de ceux qui possèdent l'œuvre de la milice formelle'[2] which is literal; but 'those who possess the work of the formal militia' cannot be called interpretative translation. He is surely correct, however, in treating *contra* as an adverb rather than a preposition. Vollmann has recently taken a knife to the Gordian knot and emends *contra formalis militiae* to *inferioris militiae*, that is, the order of demonic powers in the lower air.[3] The sense thereby gained is not implausible and Vollmann's emendation is no doubt a possibility. But it seems drastic and surgical. It is hard to be convinced that one is justified in tampering with the text which, at this point, has no significant variant in the manuscript tradition, until all possibilities have been explored.

The difficulty evidently centres upon the words *formalis militiae*, and the epithet is certainly surprising. *Formalis* in Latin usually corresponds closely to the English 'formal', that is, of anything having a set procedural form or conforming to a regular pattern. Nevertheless an adjective cognate with the substantive *forma* can obviously bear meanings that the noun can carry. It is easy to cite many familiar instances of *militia* being used of the host of heaven, whether angels or demons or sun, moon, and stars.[4] The significant fact here is that *forma* can occur in an astronomical

---

[1] Babut, *Priscillien*, p. 282, 'cette dernière phrase n'a d'ailleurs aucun sens'. The authenticity of the fragment is rejected by Paret, *Priscillianus*, p. 292; Schatz, *Studien*, p. 239, n. 4; accepted by J. Davids, *De Orosio*, p. 221.

[2] d'Alès, *Priscillien*, p. 18.

[3] *Studien*, p. 165, n. 50, rejecting as meaningless not only the transmitted *formalis militiae* but also Hilgenfeld's suggestion *contraformalis militiae*: *Z. wiss. Theol.* 32 (1889), 381.

[4] *Th. L.L.* viii. 965 cites (e.g.) Jerome, *Ep.* 121. 10. 13 'Militia caeli non tantum sol appellatur et luna et astra rutilantia sed et omnes angelica multitudo . . .' For Satan's *militia* cf. Hilary, *In Matt.* 12. 16. The sixth Würzburg tract (p. 77, 3) speaks of the 'militia principatum saeculi'. Priscillian's Old Latin Bible has 'militia caeli' at Hos. 13 : 4, cited in *Tract.* vi, p. 78, 27. Cf. i, p. 14, 17, of the planets.

or astrological context to mean a constellation or a sign of the zodiac. The *Thesaurus Linguae Latinae*[1] gives several instances, e.g. Ovid, *Metam.* ii. 78 'formas ferarum' (= signs of the zodiac) as a hazard to be passed on the way up to heaven; *Fasti* ii. 190 (of the Bear). Manilius (i. 60) and Firmicus Maternus (viii. 3. 5) offer instances of *forma* being used of celestial bodies and of the zodiac. Therefore there is no good reason to despair of the text transmitted at this point by all the manuscripts.

After the fragment quoted, Orosius continues with paraphrase and résumé: Priscillian (he says) taught that the names of the patriarchs correspond to parts of the soul—Reuben in the head, Judah in the breast, Levi in the heart, Benjamin in the thighs, and so on. In parallel to this the signs of the zodiac are assigned to parts of the body: the Ram (Aries) to the head, the Bull (Taurus) to the neck, the Twins (Gemini) to the arms, the Crab (Cancer) in the breast, and so on. Orosius concludes that Priscillian intends to imply that the powers of darkness are eternal, and that the prince of this world came from them; and Priscillian supports this doctrine from a book entitled 'The Memoir of the Apostles' (*Memoria apostolorum*; cf. above, p. 55).

In the *Memoria apostolorum* the Saviour is secretly questioned by the disciples, and interprets the parable of the Sower: the sower cannot have been good since he was negligent in wasting his seed by the wayside or in stony or uncultivated ground (Matt. 13: 3–5); accordingly the 'sower' is he who scatters the captured souls into various bodies as he wishes. 'In this book also many things are said about the prince of dampness and the prince of fire, intending to convey that all the good things in the world are done by art, not by the power of God. For it says that there is a certain Light-Virgin whom God, when he wants to grant rain to men, shows to the Prince of Darkness who, as he desires to grasp her, sweats with excitement and makes rain and, when he is deprived of her,[2] causes thunder by his groaning.'

Orosius' evidence, if correctly reported and interpreted, is highly damaging to Priscillian's reputation for sound doctrine. The *Memoria apostolorum* is evidently a gnostic gospel, perhaps

---

[1] *ThLL* vi. 1071; at vi. 1088 this passage of Priscillian is recorded but labelled 'sensu obscuro'.

[2] Read *ea* (for Schepss's *eo*) with the Ambrosian manuscript of the tenth century whose readings are recorded by G. Mercati, *Note di letteratura biblica e cristiana antica* (*Studi e testi* 5, 1901), p. 136.

a specifically Manichee creation; but it could be older than Mani.[1]

Though varying in detail, the main ideas here ascribed to Priscillian by Orosius are familiar from other sources for the mythology of the Manichees. The erotic myth explaining rain and thunder appears prominently in orthodox attacks on the Manichees such as the *Acta Archelai* of Hegemonius, Titus of Bostra, and Ephraem,[2] and is present in some pre-Manichee forms of gnosticism.[3] The first of the Priscillianist tractates attributes the same notion to the Manichees as a particularly disgusting thought: 'The Manichees, as sons of perdition and devils, may believe that they are given water by the devil's rain.' (p. 24, 14.) In the thought of the Manichees the Prince of Darkness is irrational brute desire,[4] so that the elemental crudity of the myth is expressive of a basic attitude.

The belief that thunderstorms are caused by demonic agencies invoked by human incantations is in no way distinctively Manichee. The classic testimony on this subject comes from Agobard of Lyon in the ninth century, who records with dismay that in his part of the world 'almost all men, noble and ignoble, city-dwellers and rustics, old and young' think hailstorms and thunder are caused by sorcery compelling storm-demons to act destructively (*De grandine et tonitruis*, PL 104. 147). This belief is treated by Porphyry (*De abstinentia* ii. 40) as a truth universally acknowledged.

A number of Manichee texts attest the importance in Mani's system of the twelve celestial powers who are 'members of the light of the eternal Father', 'twelve great gods, three in each of the four regions surrounding the first god', twelve elements

[1] R. A. Lipsius, *Die apokryphen Apostelgeschichten und Apostellegenden* i (1883), 75, thinks 'specifically Manichee'; this is not proved beyond doubt by the Light-Virgin, who appears in other forms of gnosis as well.
[2] *Acta Archelai* 9. 1–4; Titus of Bostra, *Contra Manichaeos* ii. 56, p. 60 ed. Lagarde (*graece*) = ii. 32, PG 18. 1196c. Ephraem, *Hymni contra haereses* 50. 5 f. Cf. H. C. Puech in Hennecke/Schneemelcher, *NT Apokryphen* i. 189 (E. T. p. 267). Augustine mocks the belief of Faustus the Manichee that thunder is caused by the *exactores* of light (*C. Faust.* 21. 12, CSEL 25. 584). On storm demons cf. above, pp. 53–4, and Ps. Justin (= Theodoret), *Qu. et Resp. ad Orthod.* 31.
[3] Puech (loc. cit.) instances Epiphanius, *Panar.* 25. 2. 4.
[4] See Puech's remarkable article 'Le Prince des Ténèbres dans son royaume' in *Satan = Études carmélitaines* (Paris, 1948), pp. 136–74, of which an English translation was published by Sheed and Ward, *Satan* (London, 1951), pp. 127–57.

who help in the creation of the primal Man.[1] As a mixture of
light and darkness and as a microcosm corresponding to the
macrocosm, Adam has a divine soul and a devilish body, or,
better, two souls, one being divine the other essentially
wicked.[2]

The identification of, or the association of a significant correspondence between, the signs of the zodiac and the twelve patriarchs is found also in rabbinic and cabbalistic speculation.[3] In
Valentinian gnosticism the twelve apostles are in control of re-
birth in parallel to the zodiac which controls physical birth;[4] and
as in the Clementine romance their number corresponds to the
twelve months.[5] There are early Christian sarcophagi on which are
figured the twelve apostles each with a star above his head.[6]

How necessary it was to make room within the Christian
scheme for the signs of the zodiac is shown not only by medieval
liturgical calendars, but by a fourth-century sermon of bishop
Zeno of Verona. Zeno offers his neophytes a Christian horoscope
contrasting animals allegorizing Christian virtues with the
threatening forms of the zodiac: you are under the Lamb, not the
Ram, the gentle calf instead of the Bull. Your Twins are the two
testaments warning you to flee idolatry, impurity, and avarice
which are incurable Cancer. Our Lion is that of Gen. 49: 9, our
Virgin is Mary teaching the Balance of equity and justice. You
tread down Scorpions and serpents. The more deadly Archer,
Satan, will give no cause for fear; nor will the deformed Capricorn
that he sends. All his arts are abolished by our Waterman, whom
the two Fishes in one sign follow—that is both Jew and Gentile

---

[1] See P. Alfaric, *L'Évolution intellectuelle de S. Augustin* (1918), p. 97, citing Aug.
Contra ep. Man. 16; *C. Faustum* 15. 5; the *Fihrist*, pp. 87 and 94, tr. Flügel.

[2] Alfaric, op. cit., p. 117, citing Aug. *Nat. boni* 46 (*CSEL* 25 (2). 886, 15); *Acta Archelai* 8; Aug. *De duabus animabus*, etc.

[3] Louis Ginzberg, *The Legends of the Jews* 5 (1925), 13, collects references. See also
E. R. Goodenough, *Jewish Symbols in the Greco-Roman Period* viii (1958), 167–218;
D. Feuchtwang, 'Der Tierkreis in der Tradition und in Synagogenritus', *Monat-
schrift für Geschichte und Wissenschaft des Judentums* 59 (1915), 241–67; some very
conjectural matter in E. Bischoff, *Babylonisch-Astrales im Weltbilde des Thalmud und
Midrasch* (1907).

[4] Clement of Alexandria, *Excerpta ex Theodoto* 25. 2.

[5] *Clem. hom.* ii. 23. Cf. J. Daniélou, 'Les douze apôtres et le zodiaque', *Vigiliae
Christianae* 13 (1959), 14–21.

[6] Instances from Arles and Manosque are cited by H. Leclercq, s.v. 'Astres',
DACL i. 3014. A major survey and inventory is given by Hans Gundel, art.
'Zodiakos' (1972), *PW* xa. 462–709.

Christians living by the water of baptism, sealed to become one people by the one sign of Christ.[1]

Zeno's sermon is in spirit and in a few details astonishingly close to a passage in the medieval rabbinic Midrash on Esther where the twelve signs are given a specifically Jewish meaning: Aries the passover lamb, Taurus = Joseph the ox (Deut. 33 : 17); Gemini the twin signs of Judah and Tamar; Leo = Daniel; and so on.[2] The material here could easily be older than the date of compilation of the Midrash; Zeno of Verona, like Ambrose of Milan, had personal contact with Jews, and exegetical influence is possible. The signs of the zodiac are not mentioned in the Talmud, but the Midrash on Numbers draws the parallel between the twelve tribes and the twelve months and the zodiac.[3] The twentieth discourse in *Pesikta Rabbati* (of about the fourth century A.D.) offers a moralistic interpretation of the zodiac.[4] Some ancient synagogues both in Palestine and in the Dispersion have mosaic decoration showing signs of the zodiac.[5] The Book of Creation, *Sefer Yezirah*, written perhaps between the third and sixth centuries, places in parallel in chapter 5 the twelve signs of the zodiac and the twelve parts of the human body.[6]

The tract *Shabbath* in the Babylonian Talmud contains a discussion of planetary influence at the day or hour of a man's birth, recording disagreements between different rabbis and concluding with the verdict of those who teach that no planet has any power over Israel.[7]

The allocation of different parts of the body to the control of the twelve signs of the zodiac is taught in the Manichaean *Kephalaia*, chapter 70, entitled 'On the body that it is constructed according to the form of the cosmos'. The same chapter of the

[1] Zeno Veron. *Tract.* i. 38 (ii. 43), pp. 105–6 Löfstedt, discussed by W. Hübner, 'Das Horoskop der Christen', *Vigiliae Christianae* 29 (1975), 120–37.

[2] *Esther Rabba* vii. 11.

[3] *Numbers Rabba* xiv. 18.

[4] *Pesikta Rabbati* 20; cf. 27–8. Rabbi W. G. Braude has translated these discourses in the Yale Judaica Series, vols. 18–19 (1968).

[5] e.g. the synagogues of Beth Alpha (E. L. Sukenik, *Ancient Synagogues in Palestine and Greece*, British Academy, 1934, pp. 33–5); Hammath by Tiberias (M. Dothan, *Israel Exploration Journal* 12 (1962), 153–4); Dura (C. H. Kraeling, *The Synagogue*, 1956, p. 42).

[6] See G. Scholem, *Major Trends in Jewish Mysticism* (London, 1955), pp. 77–8. There is a strange English version of this work by K. Stenning, *The Book of Formation* (London, 1923).

[7] *b. Shabbath* 156b.

Kephalaia refers to the Light-Virgin, who is an important figure in Manichee mythology,[1] and allocates the body's parts to the twelve signs in correspondence with the opinion that Orosius attributes to Priscillian:

Ram (Aries)—head
Bull (Taurus)—neck and shoulders
Twins (Gemini)—arms
Crab (Cancer)—breast
Lion (Leo)—stomach
Virgin (Virgo)—loins
Balance (Libra)—vertebrae (?)
Scorpion (Scorpio)—sexual organs[2]
Archer (Sagittarius)—loins
Horned goat (Capricorn)—knees
Waterman (Aquarius)—shinbones (or tibiae)
Pisces—soles of the feet.

The idea is not distinctively Manichee, but simply part of the regular stock-in-trade of ancient astrology. Almost identical lists appear in many other writers; e.g. Sextus Empiricus, Manilius, Vettius Valens, Porphyry, and Firmicus Maternus.[3] The allocation of limbs was given the technical term *melothesia*, and if each sign of the zodiac were subdivided into three divisions of ten degrees each, the body was then divided into thirty-six parts corresponding to thirty-six *decani* or Deans. The ancient texts differ on the question whether Deans are beneficial or maleficent beings.[4]

Orosius concludes his charges against Priscillian by declaring

---

[1] F. C. Baur, *Das manichäische Religionssystem* (Tübingen, 1831), pp. 219 ff; H. C. Puech, *Le Manichéisme* (Paris, 1949), p. 80 and n. 324. The chief sources are printed in Holl's edition of Epiphanius, iii. 60-1 (note on *Panar.* 66. 27. 1).

[2] The Coptic word may mean either bosom or genitals : see Crum, *Coptic Dictionary*, p. 111. Böhlig opts for the former; the parallel texts support the latter.

[3] Sextus Empiricus, *Adv. math.* 5. 21-2 (ed. R. G. Bury in Loeb Class. Libr., iv. 332-3); Manilius ii. 456-65; iv. 702-9; Vettius Valens ii. 36, pp. 109-11 Kroll; Porphyry, *Introductio in Tetrabiblum Ptolemaei* 44 (ed. Boer and Weinstock in *Catal. Cod. Astrol. Graec.* v. 4, 1940, p. 216); Firmicus Maternus, *Mathesis* ii. 24. In a third-century Rylands Papyrus (*P. Ryl.* 63) Plato learns a slightly different *melothesia* from an Egyptian prophet named Peteësis. An elaborate planetary *melothesia* survives in the Michigan papyrus 149 of the second century A.D. (ed. Winter, *The Michigan Papyri* iii).

[4] On *decani* I have collected the main references in my *Origen: contra Celsum*, p. 496 on *C. Cels.* viii. 58). A particularly interesting Hermetic tract on the subject is printed by J. B. Pitra, *Analecta sacra* v. 2, pp. 284-90.

that 'he spoke of a Trinity only in name: he asserted unity
(*unionem*) without any *exsistentia*¹ *aut proprietate*, and by omitting
"and" taught Father, Son, Holy Spirit, to be one, Christ.'
Augustine's reply to Orosius is, unfortunately perhaps for us,
more interested in Origenism than in Priscillianism, which he
quickly dismisses as a trivial variant of Manicheism, to the full
refutation of which he had already devoted several books.²
Nothing new is therefore to be learnt from Augustine's refutation
of the heresy as described by Orosius; and he had no access to any
document other than the memorandum which Orosius submitted.

That the stars and planets have a measure of control over human
destiny which is nevertheless conquered by the superior powers of
the redeemer is a doctrine that by the standards of the fourth
century cannot be fairly described as certainly and formally
heretical. The concluding verses of Rom. 8 make satisfactory
sense if they mean just this: 'height' and 'depth' are the points
when the heavenly bodies are in their strongest and weakest
positions to influence early things.³ The midrash on the Star of
the Magi in St. Matthew's gospel certainly signified to many
early Christians, perhaps to the author of the first Gospel, that
Christ's coming had conquered the power of the stars. Ignatius of
Antioch interprets the star in this sense,⁴ and for the Greek fathers
generally the argument is double-barrelled: on the one hand, they
make their own traditional sceptical arguments against horoscopes
and astral fate⁵ while on the other hand they affirm that from the
powers of evil and of destiny Christ has brought liberation.⁶

In the Latin West interest seems to have been less lively than in

¹ Orosius' rendering of *hypostasis* is of interest as an echo of the terminology of
Marius Victorinus (*Adv. Arium* i. 18. 45; 1. 230, Henry and Hadot; cf. iii. 8. 41,
p. 462).
² *Ad Orosium contra Priscillianistas et Origenistas* (PL 42. 669–78). I have been
able to consult a critical text of this work and of Augustine's *De haeresibus* in a Vienna
thesis by J. Leo Bazant Hegemark (Diss. Wien, Philosophische Fakultät, 1969).
³ This was pointed out by Lietzmann, ad loc. in *Handbuch zum Neuen Testament*
(4th edn., 1933). The new edition (1973) by Käsemann agrees. Cf. W. L. Knox,
St. Paul and the Church of the Gentiles (Cambridge, 1939), p. 107, n. 1 (to which many
texts could be added).
⁴ Ignatius, *Eph.* 19; *Protevangelium Iacobi* 21. 2; Clement of Alexandria, *Excerpta
ex Theodoto* 74–7.
⁵ See (e.g.) the sceptical tradition in Sextus Empiricus, *Adv. math.* 5; Cicero,
De divinatione ii. 42. 87 ff.; *De fato* 12–16.
⁶ See U. Riedinger, *Der heilige Schrift im Kampf der griechischen Kirche gegen die
Astrologie von Origenes bis Johannes von Damaskos* (Innsbruck, 1956).

the Greek East, perhaps in part because of the influential acids contained in Cicero's *De divinatione*, partly because there was simply no great quantity of Latin literature on the subject. In the time of Augustus and Tiberius, Manilius had written agreeable didactic hexameters expounding astrology, suffused with pantheistic emotion; but the *Astronomicon* gives an incomplete picture of its subject. In the fourth century in the West interest appears to have grown. About 335 the senator Firmicus Maternus, before his conversion to Christianity, wrote an encyclopedia of astrology (*Mathesis*); it is hard to know how widely this book was read, but the answer is probably not much. Both Manilius and Firmicus Maternus became popular in the Middle Ages, from the eleventh century, but cannot be seen to have been enthusiastically read before that time. Nevertheless it seems safe to presume that Firmicus Maternus wrote his encyclopedia because his contemporaries wanted such a book and, although Latin material on the subject is thin and jejune in comparison with the Greek texts, there is certainly a shift of interest towards astrology in the Latin texts of the last quarter of the fourth century. In Ambrosiaster's writings several passages attack astrologers, one of his 'Questions' being devoted to a long polemic.[1] Ausonius' grandfather Arborius was a considerable adept in astrology who left a horoscope of his grandson's life in a sealed tablet which Ausonius' mother brought to light.[2] As a young Manichee at Thagaste Augustine studied astrology, to which he was particularly attracted because it required of its practitioners no cultic acts or prayers. About 382 he was turned away from belief in it by Vindicianus, a well-known physician of Carthage, translator of Hippocrates and proconsul of Africa.[3]

As a generalization it may be ventured that the orthodox Latin West was more inclined to reject astrology as fraudulent than to

---

[1] *Quaest.* 115 is the main text. For other references see A. Souter, *A Study of Ambrosiaster* (*Texts and Studies* vii. 4, 1905), pp. 31–3. There is passing polemic in Ambrose (*Hexaem.* iv. 12–19) and Paulinus of Nola (*Ep.* 16. 4, to Jovius); but neither is concerned about it with the anxiety that Ambrosiaster shows.

[2] Ausonius, *Parentalia* iv. 17–22.

[3] *Conf.* iv. 3. 4–5; vii. 6. 8. On Vindicianus see *PLRE* i, s.v. Augustine's views on astrology, divination, and parapsychology are collected and discussed by E. Hendrikx in *Augustiniana* 4 (1954), 325–52. Particularly interesting is *Enarr. in Ps.* 61. 23 on a penitent Christian astrologer bringing his books to be burnt, where Augustine observes that pagan astrologers, on being converted to Christianity, often seek holy orders. On astrologer-clergy cf. Jerome, *In Sophon*, i, p. 680.

say that the valid power of the stars was overtrumped by the greater power of Christ. Accordingly, Priscillian's concession (if he made it) that the celestial bodies could be exercising some relative power over material things on earth would seem unusual and dangerous to pious ears in the West. Admittedly, however, there is an important exception to this generalization in Prudentius' *Apotheosis* 617 ff. where the Star of Bethlehem showed the Chaldean astrologers catastrophic consequences among the signs of the zodiac.

The allocation of the twelve parts of the body to the signs of the zodiac explains without more ado why Ithacius (and all sources dependent on him) discerned in Priscillian a dependence upon Mark the gnostic whose system was described by Irenaeus. Mark the gnostic seemed to present close parallels to Priscillian. He encouraged women both to utter prophecy and to perform liturgical, sacramental functions; he had a sensually magnetic effect on women; and he taught a cabbalistic magical mysticism based on the Greek alphabet, both as letters and as numbers. Above all, he believed that the signs of the zodiac were counterparts of a more transcendent Twelve, who were also symbolized by the twelve months and the twelve hours of the day. The physical body on earth mirrored the celestial form, the microcosm being a reflection of the macrocosm. Each of the twelve parts of the body was allocated two of the twenty-four letters of the Greek alphabet: the head—alpha and omega; the neck—beta and psi; shoulders and hands—gamma and chi; breast—delta and phi; diaphragm—epsilon and ypsilon; sexual parts—eta and sigma; thighs—theta and rho;—knees—iota and pi; tibiae—kappa and omicron; ankles—lambda and xi; feet—mu and nu.[1] Mark's alphabetical mysticism was a slight modification of the usual astrological doctrine which also allocated two letters to each sign, but in the order alpha-nu, beta-xi, gamma-omicron, etc.[2] Mark was also much addicted to apocrypha.[3]

Three related questions are raised by the *Commonitorium* of Orosius: From what source did he derive his information? Is his

[1] Irenaeus, *Adv. haereses* i. 13–21, especially 14. For elucidation see F. Dornseiff, *Das Alphabet in Mystik und Magie* (2nd edn., 1925), pp. 126–33; H. Leisegang, *Die Gnosis* (4th edn., 1955). Children learnt the alphabet in this order: Jerome, *In Hierem.* 5 p. 1019.
[2] F. Boll, *Sphaera* (1903), p. 471.　　　　[3] Irenaeus i. 20. 1.

fragment of Priscillian taken from an authentic letter? And is his picture of Priscillianist doctrine a true representation of the group's beliefs?

Writers like Babut who regard Priscillian as a maligned martyr of evangelical orthodoxy have wished to deny the authenticity of the fragment and of the opinions ascribed to Priscillian in the *Commonitorium*. But it is perfectly possible to affirm that Orosius is quoting a genuine piece of Priscillian without also going on to conclude that its author was a manifest heretic. We have no information about the context in which Priscillian said these things (if he did say them). The entire passage could have been Priscillian's exposition of an apocryphon, in which he was *warning* his readers against astrological or cabbalistic speculations. Orosius' method would then be analogous to that of Jerome in his letter to Avitus, where in a number of passages he ascribes to Origen opinions which Origen was only passing under review or even directly rejecting. The simplest method of polemic is to quote from a writer, as if his personal view, the opinions that he is stating but with which he is not actually identifying himself.

However, even if we may assume Orosius' good faith and if his fragment represents speculations towards which Priscillian was genuinely sympathetic, it is not clear that the division of the parts of the body among the signs of the zodiac, with the speculation that there may be a dozen parts of the soul under the yet higher authority of the patriarchs, is necessarily and formally heretical in both will and deed. That Priscillian really did stand close to this kind of speculation seems to be made probable by the defence (in the first Würzburg tractate) of the use of an amulet inscribed with the name of God in Hebrew, Latin, and Greek (above, pp. 54–5). Moreover, the first tractate quotes with warm gratitude the words of the Wisdom of Solomon:

God gave me true knowledge of all these things which exist, that I might know the disposition of the world and the power of the elements, the beginning and end and middle of months, the changes and divisions of the seasons, the course of the year and the position of stars, the natures of animals and the ragings of wild beasts, the power of the winds and the thoughts of men, the different kinds of trees and the powers of roots; all things that are hidden and manifest have I known.[1]

Above all, perhaps, there is the revealing sentence in the sixth

[1] *Tract.* i, p. 26 (amulet); p. 10 (citing Sap. Sal. 7: 17–21).

tractate (p. 73, 3–5) that 'although made by God, the nature of the body is called by the apostle *figura mundi et vetus homo*'.

To the first question, of Orosius' source, a reasonably confident answer can be given—namely, that Orosius drew upon the apologetic work of Ithacius (above, p. 145).

It has been recently pointed out (as a discovery made independently by both Puech and Vollmann)[1] that Orosius' anti-Priscillianist material has parallels in the *Indiculus de haeresibus* transmitted under the name of Jerome. As this work is cited by Augustine in 428, this work is to be dated early in the fifth century.[2] Three editions exist: the first, by Claude Ménard (Paris, 1617) is a rare book (inaccessible to me). The edition of Arévalo in the third volume of his great edition of Isidore of Seville (Rome 1793–1803) is reprinted by Migne (*PL* 81. 636–44). F. Oehler re-edited the work in the first volume of his *Corpus haeresiologicum* in 1856.

The manuscripts, which have been investigated by B. Hemmerdinger, are early: a ninth-century manuscript at Madrid (Academia de la Historia 80, in Visigothic script) represents one branch of the tradition. In the other, Italian, branch, it is transmitted with Isidore's *Etymologiae* and is found in three manuscripts of the eighth century, and two of the ninth century.[3]

The section on the Priscillianists may be translated as follows:

13. The heresy of the gnostics is a most impure body which has arisen from the above mentioned heresies, that is of Nicolas, Basilides, Marcion, as from certain deadly seeds of evil. Moreover, Mani, at a later time, is found to have walked in the same impurity. For the impurity of all those sects uses poisons that in Manicheism are united. . . . In addition it also has some points of its own.

14. These are the matters noted in Irenaeus' exposition: This heresy says that the soul does not sin; it holds it to be the substance of God,

---

[1] H. C. Puech in *Annuaire de l'école pratique des hautes études: Section des sciences religieuses*, 1960–1 (Paris, 1961), pp. 112–14. B. Vollmann in *PW* Suppl. xiv (1974), 532–4.

[2] Augustine, *De haeresibus* 81, cites *Indiculus* 38, on the Luciferians, as an anonymous tract. The *Indiculus* uses the original Greek of Irenaeus (e.g. for the account of Valentinus), not the Latin translation which Augustine is first to cite in the year 422 (below, p. 205). So a date nearer 400 than 420 seems likely.

[3] Wolfenbüttel: Weissenburg 64 (4148), s. viii med., from Bobbio (Lowe, *CLA* i. 40); Modena: Archivio Capitolare O. I. 17, written between 760 and 778 (*CLA* iii. 370); Cava: Archivio della Badia 2 (XXIII) written at Cassino 779–97 (*CLA* iii. 284); Vatic. Lat. 7803, s. ix; Vercelli, Bibl. Capitolare CXXVIII, ss. ix–x.

but from a contrary and alien substance to have assumed another soul of air, with an earthly body, which soul they call malign and devilish; and while it follows its own nature, the earthly body sins because of it; but the other soul[1] is of divine substance. By these doctrines it makes a place for its disgusting and accursed mysteries, in which by a magic prayer its angels are invoked, so that by their coming they may create bodies, which were once destined for Gehenna, and may burn them to the service of what seems to them a religious perdition.

15. For the rest it is shameful to say what execrable harm they do to themselves by their sacraments. Moreover, among those things that they think done by the power of another god, they fabricate the notion that claps of thunder are the voices of devils. They also say that the evil god, as souls pass as it were through ambushes planned by principalities, prepares traps for their perdition. As they go through each separate region of the heavens, the god offers them a present to compass their perdition. He also assigns to them commands which they are to fulfil; and thus the god's heaven, the cardinal points of the heavens, the Signs and the spheres of the Signs are contrary, and so it is as if for each substance there were an alien substance contrary to it.

16. For some of these (as Irenaeus, who was near in time to the apostles, reports) say that opposite the twelve signs of the zodiac stand the twelve patriarchs; and so other entities, which the wise of this world say to be either simple or twofold or threefold or fourfold or fivefold or sixfold or sevenfold, fight against equal and parallel forces of the holy ones. They also give the scriptures a corrupt interpretation affirming that the sons of promise are born not by a man having sexual intercourse but by the word of God, so that they do not say the Son is the only begotten of God. Desiring to get rid of the omnipotence of God, they maintain that God made all things not out of nothing but out of something, so that they may introduce the notion of two substances. These remarks are made as a partial account that the truth may be known. For it would be too long to enumerate all that we have known them affirm concerning the interpretation of the gospel miracles or concerning the pagan mysteries of Greek letters.

This account of the 'Manichees' has so many close parallels with the *Commonitorium* of Orosius that it seems certainly to be drawing upon the same source. The simplest hypothesis is to identify this source with Ithacius' *Apologia*. Already in 392–3 Jerome is aware that 'by some Priscillian is accused of the gnostic heresy,

---

[1] For *cetera* read *ceteram*.

that is of Basilides and Mark of whom Irenaeus wrote'.[1] The opinion that Priscillianism is dependent on Basilides and Mark reappears after 398 in Jerome's letter consoling Theodora, widow of the Baetican Lucinus. According to this letter Irenaeus is credited both with an account of the heretical doctrines of Basilides and Mark and with a statement, nowhere found in the Latin version of *Adversus haereses*, that Mark disseminated his heresy not only in the Rhône valley but also by the Garonne and in Spain.[2] This statement bears all the marks of direct Ithacian influence. Words to the same effect appear in Jerome's *Contra Vigilantium* of 406, and in his commentary on Isaiah (64: 4–5) written 408–10.[3]

On the other hand, in discussing deviant opinions on the soul in the letter to Marcellinus and Anapsychia, written 410–12, he refers to the question 'whether the soul has fallen from heaven, as Pythagoras the philosopher and all Platonists and Origen think; or whether it is an emanation of the substance of God, as the Stoics, Mani, and the Spanish heresy of Priscillian suppose; or whether souls, once created by God, are kept in a treasury, as some orthodox writers (*ecclesiastici*) stupidly assert'.[4]

The third view, not the second, is ascribed to Priscillian by Orosius. If the question of Priscillian's orthodoxy is to be at issue, then it is noteworthy that the doctrine of God creating souls then kept in a celestial repository is regarded by Jerome as a mistake rather than a formal heresy, and as a doctrine that has had substantial support in some orthodox writers.

In 1689 Henry Dodwell the elder cautiously suggested that the Priscillianist controversy provided the occasion for the making of the Latin translation of Irenaeus, whose existence is first attested in 422 by Augustine's quotations in his *Contra Julianum*.[5] The

---

[1] *Vir. inl.* 121. On the date see above, p. 7, n. 2.

[2] *Ep.* 75. 3. Irenaeus, *Adv. haer.* i. 13. 7, mentions only the Rhône valley.

[3] *C. Vigil.* 6 (PL 23. 345A+360B); *Comm. in Esaiam* xvii (PL 24. 622B–623A).

[4] *Ep.* 126. 1. I suspect the last sentence of being a reference to Ambrose.

[5] Aug. *C. Jul.* i. 3. 5; 7. 32. H. Dodwell, *Dissertationes in Irenaeum* (Oxford, 1689), pp. 390–410, denied that the Latin Irenaeus was already known to Tertullian, a denial for which he was mistakenly rebuked by J. E. Grabe in his preface to the Oxford edition of 1702. Dodwell's dating is strongly supported by F. J. A. Hort in Westcott and Hort's *The New Testament in the Original Greek* ii (1882), Introduction, p. 160; by H. Jordan, 'Das Alter und die Herkunft der lateinischen Übersetzung des Hauptwerkes des Irenaeus', *Theologische Studien Theodor Zahn dargebracht* (1908), pp. 133–92; and by A. Souter in W. Sanday and C. H. Turner, *Novum Testamentum S. Irenaei ep. Lugd.* (Oxford, 1923), pp. lxv–cxi. On grounds of vocabulary Souter

evidence for an origin in North Africa not long before 420 is persuasive, and the *Commonitorium* of Orosius, perhaps the *Apologia* of Ithacius, may well have given the necessary stimulus to the translator. If the evidence of Jerome and the *Indiculus* is rightly taken as an indication of the content of Ithacius' *Apologia*, the plausibility of Dodwell's conjecture is strongly reinforced.

Augustine's picture of Priscillian

Augustine's interest in Priscillianism first became conscious and lively as a result of Orosius' coming to Africa. He was in Italy in 386–7 at the time when feeling was running high about the Trier executions, and is therefore likely to have had some interest in 'Manichees' suffering the death penalty; but he expressly says that at that time he had no awareness of an independent sect of Priscillianists. In his 166th letter, addressed to Jerome in 415, he remarks that at the time when he was writing 'On the Freedom of the Will', between 388 and 395, he had never heard of the Priscillianists as a special group akin to the Manichees.[1] In his tract 'On the Nature of the Good' of 405 he writes with disgust of the alleged Manichee practice of mixing semen with the eucharistic elements. To dispel doubt whether or not the story was mere vile slander he adds that he had been assured by a catholic that under judicial examination Manichees had confessed to this obscene practice 'not only in Paphlagonia but also in Gaul', and had cited as their authority an erotic myth in the Manichean book called 'The Treasure' (*Thesaurus*).[2] Probably these confessions

judged the Latin Irenaeus to have been composed in North Africa between 370 and 420 by a Greek who did not know Latin well. Both Jordan and Souter thought plausible Dodwell's conjecture that Priscillianism provided a likely context. A late fourth-century date is also maintained by M. C. Díaz y Díaz, 'Tres observaciones sobre Ireneo de Lyon', *Rev. española de teología* 14 (1954), 393–9, who thinks the famous passage on Roman primacy (*Adv. haer.* iii. 3. 2) likely to reflect fourth-century concerns.

[1] Aug. *Ep.* 166. 3. 7.

[2] The myth is contained in excerpts from Mani's *Fundamental Epistle* and *Th saurus* cited by Augustine, *De natura boni* 44 and 47 (*CSEL* 25, 2. 881 ff.) See also *De haeres.* 46. Discussion in P. Alfaric, *L'Évolution intellectuelle de S. Augustin* i (1918), 306–7; id., *Les Écritures manichéens* ii (1918), 45–6, 63. The obscene eucharistic rite is pre-Manichee: see Epiphanius, *Panarion* 26, on which the silence of the commentators is broken by S. Benko in *Vigiliae Christianae* 21 (1967), 103–19. Epiphanius had met a sect of these licentious gnostics, whose women had attempted, no doubt unsuccessfully, to seduce him (26. 17. 1 ff.). For the Manichee myth of the seduction of the archons see Theodore bar Konai, tr. Pognon, p. 190.

extracted under torture in Gaul are to be identified with those of the Priscillianist trials at Trier. It is worth noting that Augustine's evidence for this practice actually occurring among the Manichees is very weak. It amounts to a hearsay report by a distant and prejudiced witness of confessions extracted by torture, given verisimilitude by a Manichee myth about super-human powers.

After the coming of Orosius to Africa Augustine's interest in the subject of Priscillian sharply increased. In his letter to Casul-anus concerning fasting on Saturdays, he goes out of his way to attack the scandal of fasting on Sundays, a practice demanded by the Manichees and defended (he adds) by the Priscillianists with texts from the canonical Acts (20: 7; 21: 11) which show Paul fasting at Troas on the first day of the week.[1]

In 419, in the third book 'On the nature and origin of the Soul', Augustine remarks in passing that in condemning the Priscil-lianists the catholic church has also condemned the belief that the soul once pre-existed the body and was then in a state of goodness.[2]

Augustine's principal account of Priscillianism was written in the year before he died, in the catalogue of heresies addressed to Quodvultdeus in 429. The seventieth chapter portrays the sect in language dependent partly on the *Indiculus*, partly on Orosius' *Commonitorium*, partly upon some of the hearsay reports about Priscillianist views on the acceptability of perjury mentioned in Augustine's letter to Ceretius (*Ep.* 237; see above, pp. 155-6). The chapter begins by following the *Indiculus* in observing that Priscillianism is a mixture of gnostic and Manichee doctrines, like a sewer into which several filthy drains run.[3] Then Augustine quotes his alleged Priscillianist justification of perjury: 'Swear, forswear, never betray a secret.' Finally Augustine enumerates a series of heretical articles mainly taken from Orosius: they believe the soul to be of the substance of God, but to have descended to struggle on earth, passing step by step through seven heavens and

---

[1] Aug. *Ep.* 36. 12. 28–9. That this letter should be dated after 414 is cogently argued by Vollmann, *Studien*, p. 58, n. 19.

[2] *De natura et origine animae* iii. 7. 9.

[3] Leo the Great was to borrow this phrase to apply both to Manichees and to Priscillianists: *Sermo* 16. 4 (A.D. 443) and *Ep.* 15 praef., *PL* 54. 679A (A.D. 447). It is echoed from Leo in Montanus of Toledo's letter to the church of Palentia (*PL* 84. 339D). It recalls Sallust, *Catil.* 37. 5.

encountering the evil prince who made this world and by whom souls are scattered into diverse bodies. They say men are under the power of the stars, and that our very body is put together from head to foot to correspond to the twelve signs of the zodiac. They avoid eating meats as unclean. They separate husbands and wives. They are worse than the Manichees in accepting all the canonical scriptures; and they give like authority to apocrypha. They allegorize everything in scripture that overthrows their error. They hold Sabellian views of Christ.

Apart from the conventional dualistic traits of vegetarianism and sexual abstinence and the resort to allegory, there is no point in Augustine's description of Priscillianism which is not derived from one of the three sources named above.

The seventieth chapter of the anonymous, so-called 'Praedestinatus', merely repeats Augustine's formulae.[1]

The influence of the portrait painted by Augustine and the *Indiculus* is clearly seen in the references to Priscillian in the *Commonitorium* of Vincent of Lérins, written in 434. In chapters 24–5 he refers to Priscillian as the most recent figure in a long line of gnostic teachers descended from Simon Magus, prone to disgusting enormity ('turpitudines'); his danger as a heretic is skilfully concealed by the huge number of quotations from scripture, both of the Old and of the New Testaments, with which his *opuscula* are full.

Turibius of Asturica

Augustine's adverse picture of Priscillianism did nothing to disturb the entrenched adherents of the sect in north-western Spain, a region which since 411 had been part of the Suevic kingdom beyond the reach of the Roman government. The Sueves had made Bracara their capital, so that administration and power had passed out of the hands of the Asturicans. If we could risk belief in the interpolated address of the long recension of the Acts of Toledo, the bishop of Bracara in the 440s would have been Balconius, not impossibly identical with the Balconius bishop of Bracara to whom Avitus the presbyter wrote about 416 (above, p. 178). Whatever his name, it looks very much as if from his position of leadership in the church of Suevic Galicia the bishop

[1] *PL* 53. 612.

of Bracara was giving no discouragement to a revival of Priscillianist allegiance in the churches. The Suevic king may have seen advantage in fostering a measure of religious dissent to mark off his domain from the other provinces. Accordingly, in a situation where rivalry between Asturica and Bracara would be only human, there is less surprise in finding the voice of protest against Priscillianism being raised at the very see which had once been its citadel in Galicia.

About 440–5 a new bishop was elected at Asturica, Turibius,[1] who had just returned to his native land after long years of absence in other provinces. His theological education had been outside Spain, and he adopted a very adverse view of the Priscillianists. Their love of apocrypha seemed to him especially full of danger to correct doctrine and sound morals. In Galicia he was disappointed and shocked to discover that the Priscillianist hold upon the churches had in no way decreased during his period of absence. Indeed, there were still several bishops who were understood to think well of Priscillian's cause. The feature which most distressed the newly elected bishop was the quiet mutual toleration that prevailed. Christians who were known to regard Priscillian as a martyr for truth received eucharistic communion side by side with those who did not, no man forbidding them. The barbarian domination of Spain made synods impossible, so that each bishop was left free to do as he pleased.

Turibius fears the use of apocrypha. Yet he protests that he does not doubt the miracles that the non-canonical Acts contain. Their narrative is no doubt true; the objection to them lies in the passages of doctrinal teaching composed and interpolated by heretics,[2] especially by Manichees who have particularly treated in this way the Acts of Thomas, Andrew, and John, and have produced a most blasphemous book, the *Memoria apostolorum*. From the Acts of Thomas the Manichees take their baptism in oil, not water. The Priscillianists interpret the apocrypha in an

---

[1] The spelling of his name varies in the manuscripts of Leo, *Ep.* 15, as can be seen from Vollmann's critical apparatus; e.g. Turbius, Torebius, Chorebius, Choribius, Toruvius, Thorybius, Thoribius, Torvulus, Torobius, Turibius. The Ballerini wrote Turribius. Hydatius has Thoribius.

[2] An exact parallel occurs at the beginning of the *Miracula beati Thomae apostoli*, where the author, perhaps Gregory of Tours, explains that, because some will not accept the Acts of Thomas as a whole, he has composed this book to record the miracles, which will please readers and strengthen the Church (M. Bonnet, *Acta Thomae*, 1883, pp. 96–7).

orthodox manner in public; and in such apocryphal codices as
Turibius has been able to find he concedes that he has discovered
no trace of the distinctive doctrines of the heresy; yet he knows
that they regard themselves as entitled to conceal their true
opinion, and suspects them of having either esoteric doctrines
not committed to writing or yet more secret books.

Turibius therefore made a digest of their opinions (evidently
from sources other than Priscillianist books), classifying their
doctrines under separate headings and also composed a reply to
them. He then looked about Galicia for sympathizers among the
bishops and found only two, Ceponius whose see is unknown,
and 'Idacius' whose see he does not mention but who is in all
probability identical with the chronicler Hydatius of Lemica,[1]
bishop of Aquae Flaviae.

Turibius' letter to Ceponius and Hydatius does not survive in
any now extant manuscript. It was found by Ambrosio de Morales
in the same San Millán codex of the tenth century, lost in the
Escorial fire of 1671, whence he first printed the Priscillianist
documents of the council of Toledo of 400 (above, p. 179). He
printed the letter in his history of Spain; and his transcript was
simply reproduced in the editions of Leo's letters by Quesnel and
the Ballerini.[2]

Turibius' letter is a cautious appeal for help in mobilizing
opinion. He concludes by submitting to the judgement of
Ceponius and Hydatius both his digest of Priscillianist propositions and his refutation of them, and by asking them to enlist the
aid of other bishops. As a very junior bishop, he lacked the
necessary personal standing to take a lead, and was evidently far
from certain that his move would be welcome even to those he has
decided to sound.

Hydatius of Aquae Flaviae responded to Turibius' appeal for
help by travelling to Asturica and sitting with Turibius at a
hearing of various 'Manichees' whom zealous inquiry had un-
earthed in the town. Hydatius records in his chronicle that he and
Turibius had sent a report of their proceedings at this examination

[1] Mommsen, *Chronica minora* ii. 3–4.
[2] Morales, *La corónica general de España* ii (1577), foll. 32b–33b. Aguirre mislead-
ingly asserted that Turibius' letter was preserved in manuscripts at Toledo: *Notitia
conciliorum Hispaniae* (Salamanca, 1686), p. 58. The Ballerini reprint is in PL 54.
693. Baluze's rash doubts about the letter's authenticity have found support only
from Künstle, *Antipriscilliana*, pp. 121–2; below, p. 215, n. 1.

to Antoninus, bishop of Emerita.[1] It can hardly be accident that their report was not sent to Bracara, but was addressed to the metropolitan of Lusitania. At this time Emerita was under Sueve domination. Hydatius records the city's capture by Rechila under the year 439, and it remained in Sueve hands for thirty years.[2] Nevertheless Bracara was the royal capital, and to report to Emerita seems a safe sign that in the capital Turibius' activities were not receiving keen backing.

Antoninus of Emerita was eager for the detection of Priscillianist or Manichee enormity. A Manichee named Pascentius from the city of Rome found that under bishop Turibius Asturica was an uncomfortable place, and took refuge in Emerita. There he was arrested and examined before Antoninus, who had him expelled from the province of Lusitania.[3]

Turibius did not limit his correspondence to bishops in Galicia and Lusitania. He also wrote a private letter (*epistola familiaris*) to pope Leo, accompanying copies of his memorandum (*commonitorium*) listing sixteen Priscillianist propositions and of his pamphlet (*libellus*) of refutation.[4] Much of the gist of these three documents can be discerned from Leo's reply, *Quam laudabiliter* (*Ep.* 15), dated 21 July 447, in which Leo cites the sixteen propositions and gives an authoritative condemnation of each of them as prompted by Turibius' *libellus*.

1. The Priscillianists deny the true doctrine of the Trinity and are Sabellian or Patripassian. (The charge occurs in Orosius' *Commonitorium*.)

2. They say (with the Arians)[5] that certain powers ('virtutes'),

---

[1] Hydatius, *Chron.* ad ann. 445 (*Chronica minora* ii. 24): 'In Asturicensi urbe Gallaeciae quidam ante aliquot annos latentes Manichaei gestis episcopalibus deteguntur, quae ab Hydatio et Thoribio episcopis, qui eos audierant, ad Antoninum Emeritensem episcopum directa.'

[2] Hydatius 119 'Rechila rex Suevorum Emeritam ingreditur' (sub ann. 439). cf. 245 (*c.* ann. 468): 'Legatorum Suevorum reditum aliquanta Gothorum manus insequens Emeritam petit.'

[3] Hydatius 138 (sub ann. 448): 'Pascentium quendam urbis Romae, qui de Asturica diffugerat, Manichaeum Antoninus episcopus Emerita comprehendit auditumque etiam de provincia Lusitania facit expelli.'

[4] See Leo, *Ep.* 15, praef. 2 and 15. 16. For *epistola familiaris* see 15. 17, and discussion by Vollmann, *Studien*, pp. 142–4. Leo makes it clear that *commonitorium* and *libellus* overlapped in text and subject matter. A critical text of *Ep.* 15 is given in Vollmann, *Studien*, pp. 122–38. The Hispana tradition has been edited by J. Campos in *Helmantica* 13 (1962), 269–308.

[5] Vollmann, *Studien*, p. 153, thinks it certain that the reference to Arianism is

which proceed from God, God did not at one time possess since his essence is prior to them. (This charge of teaching divine emanations does not occur elsewhere.)

3. They say that the Son of God is 'only-begotten' because he alone is virgin-born. (This charge occurs in the *Indiculus*, 16, and may be connected with the doctrine that Christ is unbegettable, 'innascibilis'; above, pp. 88, 182.)

4. They fast on Christ's Nativity and on the Lord's Day. (Cf. canon 4 of Saragossa, 380.)

5. They say the human soul is of divine substance (so Orosius' *Commonitorium*, and the disavowal of Dictinius at Toledo, 400).

6. They condemn marriage and procreation (cf. canon 1 of Saragossa; Filastrius, 84; Aug. *Haer.* 70.)

7. They say the devil was not a fallen angel, but emerged from chaos and darkness.

8. They say human bodies are formed by the devil (cf. Orosius).

9. They say the 'sons of promise' are born of women but are conceived of the Holy Spirit. (cf. *Indiculus*, 16; above, p. 204).

10. They say that souls here incarnate were previously incorporeal and sinned in heaven, thus lapsing and being imprisoned by aerial and sidereal powers in different kinds of bodies (cf. Orosius).

11. They believe in astral fate (cf. Orosius).

12. They allocate the parts of the soul to Patriarchs, the parts of the body to the zodiac (cf. Orosius).

13. The entire body of the scriptures is to be accepted under the names of the patriarchs, who symbolize the twelve virtues that work the reformation of the inner man. (This doctrine is not elsewhere attested.)

14. They put the parts of the body under the control of stars and signs of the zodiac (cf. no. 12, and Orosius).

15. They corrupt codices of the Bible and read apocrypha ascribed to apostles. (The charge of corrupting the biblical text first occurs here.)

16. They much admire the book by Dictinius, though it was condemned by its author (cf. the Acts of Toledo, 400. On the *Libra* see above, p. 154).

Leo's gloss on Turibius' statement. Turibius' charge was perhaps no more than that, like gnostics, the Priscillianists believe in aeons emanating from the supreme being.

Turibius' list of charges includes some information that may need to be taken seriously; because it is not obviously derived from the Apologia of Ithacius and is not therefore to be simply discounted as a stream from a polluted source. Turibius has made an attempt to acquaint himself directly with first-hand Priscillianist material. Admittedly his letter to Ceponius and Hydatius has to concede that he failed to find there the distinctive doctrines generally associated with the sect. He must therefore have turned to other sources for his list of offensive propositions. It is hard to believe that he is not directly dependent on the *Commonitorium* of Orosius, less certainly on Augustine.[1] Very probably he has used the records of the councils of Saragossa 380 and Toledo 400.

The transmission of the Acts of these two councils is, as we have seen, so incomplete that it is not really possible to say with confidence what the missing parts of the record did or did not contain.[2] The accusations of believing that the devil was not a being originally created by God[3] and that human bodies are of diabolical formation attribute to the Priscillianists what everyone (including the Priscillianists themselves—see *Tract.* v, p. 63, 21) knew to be true of Manicheism. The new, otherwise unattested propositions in Turibius' censure are numbers 13 and 15. The strong distinction in 9 between the sons of promise and sons born by natural birth is closely paralleled at the end of the sixth Würzburg tractate, which cites Luke 20: 34–6 (in a form also attested in Cyprian and some manuscripts)[4] contrasting the sons of this age who marry and beget children and the sons of God who neither marry nor procreate.

The same concluding passage of the sixth tractate includes a flight of numerological speculation which shows the Priscillianist

[1] Vollmann, *Studien*, p. 167, judges Turibius to offer good objective information derived from his personal contacts with Priscillianists, and denies direct dependence on Orosius or Augustine. I think dependence on Orosius probable, and that some discrimination needs to be exercised between the various propositions, some being conventional Manichee beliefs, others unusual and unparalleled in anti-Priscillianist charges, and therefore claiming greater attention and respect.

[2] Vollmann, *Studien*, p. 161, rightly remarks that in the extant documents of Toledo, 400, no demonology appears. The record is too fragmentary to allow the assertion that it was never mentioned.

[3] The origin of the charge that the Priscillianists denied Satan to be a fallen angel may perhaps lie in a phrase of *Tract.* v, p. 64, 19, of the devil 'cui[us] initium mendacii *natura* dedit'.

[4] Schepss, p. 81; see Wordsworth and White's Oxford Vulgate, i. 449.

interest in the symbolism of the twelve patriarchs, but is not
otherwise parallel to Turibius' thirteenth proposition that the
contents and limits of the entire canon of scripture are signified
by them. That for the Priscillianists the limits of the biblical canon
are a mystery explained by numerological principles exemplified
in the genealogies of Jesus is attested in the first and third of the
tractates (p. 32, 2; 55, 8; cf. above, p. 82). Turibius is our only
source to suggest that the sect also saw the same mysteries illumi-
nated by the patriarchs. Nevertheless the thought is so closely in
line with the number-mysticism of the Würzburg tractates and
their speculations about the concept of the canon that there is
sound reason to think Turibius has here preserved an authentic
Priscillianist notion. How the corpus of biblical writings was
actually divided into twelve parts we have no clue; but a twelve-
fold division would surely not be difficult to invent.[1]

If this reasoning is correct, then Turibius' continuation becomes
more important than may appear at first sight. He next reports
the Priscillianists as holding that the patriarchs also symbolize
'the twelve virtues that bring about the reformation of the inner
man'. This last doctrine is expounded in detail in one of the
principal surviving statements of Manichean systematic theology,
the tractate extant in an early medieval Chinese version of about
A.D. 900 edited and translated in 1911 by Chavannes and Pelliot.
There the twelve virtues which reform the inner man are 'forms
of the beneficent Light'.[2] Turibius (through Leo) is therefore the
earliest witness to this doctrine. The Pelliot tractate and other
Chinese Manichee documents do not use the title 'patriarchs',

---

[1] A passage near the end of the Priscillianist tract *De Trinitate fidei catholicae*
(above, p. 100) is sufficiently close to be noteworthy: 'Per hunc denique (filium)
omnes veteres prophetae fructum divinae promissionis, in cuius spem laboraverant,
consecuti, in unum perfectum virum, ad confirmationem corporis Christi, secundum
vocationis suae ordinem concorde membrorum societate concurrunt' (Morin,
Études, p. 204 = *PL Suppl.* ii. 1507). Cf. also Bachiarius, *De reparatione lapsi* 18
(*PL* 20. 1056B) where the reconstruction of the buildings of Jerusalem by men with
one hand on a sword, the other to build, symbolizes 'membra corporis angelicis
et patriarcharum virtutibus ut collapsa restruantur'.

[2] E. Chavannes and Paul Pelliot, 'Un traité manichéen retrouvé en Chine',
Journal asiatique, 10ᵉ série, 18 (1911), especially at pp. 568 ff. For other Manichee
texts on the same topic see E. Waldschmidt and W. Lentz, *Die Stellung Jesu im
Manichäismus*, Abhandlungen d. preuss. Akad. d. Wiss. 1925–6, no. 4, pp. 28–32;
and the same authors' edition of further Chinese documents, 'Manichäische Dog-
matik aus chinesischen und iranischen Texten', *Sitzungsberichte d. preuss. Akad. d.
Wiss.* (1933), xiii. 487, no. 137a: 'the twelve limbs of the new man, the twelve
radiant kings and the wisdom-light.' (Cf. p. 490, nos. 169–71.)

but otherwise there is no material difference in doctrine. Admittedly one cannot deduce with unreserved confidence that Turibius is faithfully reporting an actual Priscillianist doctrine, evidently derived from diffused Manichee ideas. It is also a possibility that the tradition he preserves came from one of his hostile anti-Priscillianist sources which was attributing to the sect a floating Manichee myth. Nevertheless, if one has to judge probabilities, it looks likely that Turibius' thirteenth proposition, just because it is mildly bizarre rather than manifestly and glaringly heretical, genuinely reports an idea current in Priscillianist circles which will have come in from the Manichee milieu. The Priscillianist insistence on the role and symbolism of the twelve patriarchs of the Old Testament (rather than of the apostles of the New) may raise the question whether perhaps the form of Manichee speculation which influenced Priscillian here may not have filtered through a Jewish, cabbalistic circle.

On 21 July 447 Leo replied to Turibius (the extant letter, *Ep.* 15),[1] congratulating him on his pastoral zeal for the true faith. Manicheism had lately touched Leo himself in the very citadel of Latin Christianity in the Roman church itself. In 443 he had held a grand inquisition at which on being examined before a mixed tribunal consisting partly of bishops, partly of distinguished lay judges, many seeming members of his church had confessed to being secret Manichees. Leo would blush to repeat to Turibius the disgusting practices that their confessions disclosed.[2] Leo's language strongly suggests that his special tribunal followed Roman judicial procedure and applied torture to the suspects. As he looked back on the Priscillianist trials of 385, he felt that the secular emperor's severity had been justified and had brought benefit to the Church, even though the only methods the Church itself could use were those of gentle persuasion.[3]

Leo echoes Turibius' horror that Priscillianism should continue to find among the episcopate either actual adherents or men who

---

[1] The arguments against the letter's authenticity advanced by Künstle, *Antipriscilliana* (1905), pp. 117–26, are universally rejected. His contention that the letter is a late sixth-century forgery, dependent on the Acts of the first council of Bracara, is liquidated by the fact that the letter is contained in cod. Paris. lat. 12097 dated 523 (Lowe, *CLA* v. 619). But Künstle saw correctly that the Acts of Bracara I betray no clear knowledge of Leo, *Ep.* 15.

[2] *Ep.* 15. 16. On the Manichee process in Rome see Caspar, *Geschichte des Papsttums* i. 432–5; Batiffol, *Le Siège apostolique* (1924), pp. 433–7.

[3] *Ep.* 15, praef. Leo's treatment of Roman Manichees was not gentle.

thought it pastorally inexpedient to pronounce anathema on the sect. He readily accedes to Turibius' suggestion that a general council of the Spanish bishops be held, through which pressure can be put upon deviating bishops. He therefore writes a (lost) letter to the bishops of the provinces Tarraconensis, Carthaginensis, Lusitania, and Galicia (the absence of Baetica is noteworthy), that they are to hold a general synod. But if such an assembly is for any reason impossible, there is to be a synod of Galicia, which Hydatius, Ceponius, and Turibius are to cooperate in convening. Leo says nothing of the practical problems which may arise if the bishop of Bracara is unsympathetic. He disapproves of the deep admiration for Dictinius' book *Libra*, but offers no advice to Turibius to help him meet the difficulty that in Asturica Dictinius was held to be a saint, to whom a principal church and monastery was to be dedicated.[1] His letter had provided Turibius with a strongly authoritative denunciation of Priscillianism as represented by its adversaries. He said nothing to help the Galicians towards reconciliation.

It is not certain that either the general council of Spanish provinces or even the local council of Galicia took place as directed by the Pope. Although Leo directs Turibius to coordinate his efforts with Ceponius and Hydatius, no express word of the existence of such a council occurs in Hydatius' chronicle of this period, in which events in north-western Spain naturally receive his special attention. Moreover Hydatius was, or at least became through Turibius' initiative, committed to the struggle against Priscillianism. A general council of bishops drawn from several provinces could hardly have been passed over. Admittedly the transmission of the chronicle is poor (above, p. 45). But that consideration does not greatly weigh here, since the transmitted text has a special entry to mention Leo's letter to Turibius, even giving the name of the Asturican deacon, Pervincus, who carried the letter from Rome to Spain. Hydatius significantly adds that 'by some Galicians a deceitful assent was given'.[2]

[1] Morales, *La corónica general de España*, book xi, ch. 5 (1577 edn., f. 10a) printed the epitaph of the thirteenth-century bishop Nonnus of Astorga, which threatens anyone moving the relics with anathema before Christ's judgement seat and before saint Dictinius. St. Dictinius' feast day, 2 June, is a double major at Astorga: cf. *Dict. Hist. Géogr. Eccl.* iv. 1219.

[2] Hydatius ad ann. 447 (*Chron. min.* ii. 24): '. . . inter quae [sc. scripta Leonis] ad episcopum Thoribium de observatione catholicae fidei et de haeresum blasphemiis disputatio plena dirigitur, quae ab aliquibus Gallaecis subdolo probatur arbitrio.'

Of an actual episcopal meeting either in Galicia or elsewhere he says nothing, but from the last phrase it is safe to conclude that either Leo's letter or a list of propositions closely based upon it was circulated for formal signature. Hydatius thought that the many Priscillianist sympathizers among the bishops had signed insincerely. Evidently they had readily condemned the offensive statements censured by Leo, but regarded themselves as free to honour Priscillian the martyr as much as before.

The question whether or not there was an actual council in Spain held in consequence of Leo's letters of July 447 hangs in part, however, on the evidence of the Acts of the first council of Bracara (561). According to the Acts the presiding bishop, Lucretius of Bracara, reminds his colleagues that Leo had written 'through Turibius notary of his see' to the 'synod of Galicia' against the Priscillianists. Here the title notary may seem surprising if the bishop of Asturica is intended. But the term need not mean a scribe or secretary, since at this date the Latin word can be used for an august representative figure.[1] We need not therefore hold (with the Ballerini) that Lucretius is referring to another lost letter of Leo, addressed about 448 to the synod of Galicia after he had learnt that a general council could not be held.[2]

Pastor and Syagrius

In his address to the synod of 561 Lucretius goes on to say that the bishops of Tarraconensis, Carthaginensis, Lusitania, and Baetica held council and composed a rule of faith against the Priscillianist heresy together with some 'chapters' (*capitula*) which they then sent to Balconius bishop of Bracara. From this sentence it is evident that Lucretius had before him the long recension of the Acts of Toledo (400) with its interpolated address. As we have seen, this long recension has been ascribed (especially since the monograph of Father de Aldama of 1934)[3] to a council

[1] See Blaise, *Dictionnaire latin–français des auteurs chrétiens* (1954, repr. 1975), s.v., for instances in Gregory the Great. The Acts of Bracara are in C. W. Barlow's edition of Martin of Braga (1950), pp. 105–15 = PL 84. 561–8.

[2] For the opposite opinion see the Ballerini's catalogue of Leo's lost letters in PL 54. 1222AB.

[3] A. de Aldama, *El simbolo toledano* i (1934). The same opinion (also held by Hefele in his history of the councils) is supported by K. Schäferdiek, *Die Kirche in den Reichen der Westgoten und Suewen bis zur Errichtung der westgotischen katholischen Staatskirche* (Berlin, 1967), pp. 82, 115.

hypothetically placed at Toledo in 447 resulting from Leo's letter of July 447. It has already been observed that the evidence for such a council is not strong, and that the name Balconius, while not impossible, looks like a forger's anachronism. He may have had before him some list of the bishops of Bracara and guessed that Balconius (who was certainly bishop in 416) was the recipient of the conciliar letter. A noteworthy suggestion, made independently by Morin in 1893 and Kattenbusch in 1894,[1] is that the long recension of the Toledo rule of faith is to be identified with the '*libellus* in the form of a creed' which was written by a bishop Pastor and was known to Gennadius of Massilia. Gennadius says that Pastor's document set forth almost all the orthodox faith, without mentioning names in its anathemas, except that he expressly condemned Priscillian. He gives no hint of Pastor's see or province, but the reference to Priscillian makes a Spanish see highly probable. Here Hydatius' chronicle may offer a further clue: against the year 433 the chronicle notes that 'in the region of Lugo Pastor and Syagrius were ordained bishops against the will of Agrestius bishop of Lugo'.[2] Hydatius likewise mentions no sees. If the Pastor of Hydatius' chronicle is rightly identified with the anti-Priscillianist bishop Pastor whose *libellus in modum symboli* was known to Gennadius writing about 470, then it does not seem extravagant to regard Agrestius bishop of Lugo as a hammer of the Priscillianists whose opposition to Pastor, if not Syagrius, may have either originated, or come to be associated, with the Priscillianist issue in Galicia. If, however, this identification is correct, the case for attributing the long recension of the Rule of Faith transmitted under the name of the council of Toledo of 400 to a hypothetical council of Toledo about 447 becomes weaker. The correspondence of Turibius and Leo includes no word about Pastor or Syagrius. It is safe to deduce that among the bishops in Galicia in 445–7 Turibius knew of no Pastor who might be expected to act in support of his initiative against the Priscillianists.

Gennadius devotes another chapter of his catalogue of Illustrious Men to a writer named Syagrius, and gives a summary of

---

[1] G. Morin, 'Pastor et Syagrius, deux écrivains perdus du cinquième siècle', *Rev. Bénéd.* 10 (1893), 385–94; F. Kattenbusch, *Das apostolische Symbol* i (1894), 158, 407.

[2] 'In conventu Lucensi contra voluntatem Agresti Lucensis episcopi Pastor et Syagrius episcopi ordinantur', *Chron. min.* ii. 22. That this Pastor is that of Gennadius, *Vir. inl.* 76, was held by Gams, *Kirchengeschichte von Spanien* ii. 1, p. 466.

his work on the Faith.[1] He says nothing to suggest that this Syagrius lived in Spain, nor that he disavowed Priscillianist prejudices which might make it plausible to identify him with the Galician bishop consecrated together with Pastor against the will of Agrestius of Lugo. Moreover, the content of the work as represented by Gennadius' summary is anti-Arian. According to Gennadius, Syagrius wrote to refute heretical argument that the names Father, Son, and Spirit should be replaced by more correct abstract terms, the Father being called unbegotten, uncreated, and solitary, so that whatever is external to him in respect of his *persona* is also external in respect of his nature; so (he adds) Syagrius showed that the Father can be called unbegotten even though scripture does not use the word, and that he begat of himself a Son 'in persona'—he did not make him—and of himself he put forth the Spirit 'in persona', the Spirit being neither begotten nor made. Gennadius adds that seven books on the Faith and on Rules of Faith are transmitted under Syagrius' name, but their variation in style precludes assigning all of them to the same author.

A tractate with a content closely corresponding to Gennadius' summary of Syagrius on the Faith was first printed in 1905 by Karl Künstle from six manuscripts, the earliest being written at Reichenau, 802–6, by the librarian Reginbert. There is a second ninth-century witness in a Fleury manuscript which passed from the Phillips library to Berlin in the nineteenth century. The work is ascribed by the manuscripts to Jerome and is entitled 'Regulae definitionum contra haereticos'.[2] The content makes it highly probable that this is the work summarized by Gennadius and that its author lived in the first half of the fifth century. Künstle freely conceded that the treatise is manifestly directed against Arianism and betrays none of the usual anti-Priscillianist features.

---

[1] *Vir. inl.* 65.

[2] Künstle, *Antipriscilliana*, pp. 142–59, edits the text; reprinted by A. Hamman in *PL Suppl.* iii. 132–40. The manuscript basis is: Karlsruhe, Aug. XVIII s. ix, Berol. 78 (Phillips 1671) s. ix, Remensis 295 s. xi, Oxon. Balliol. 147 s. xii, Paris. Mazar. 627 s. xiii, Oxon. Merton. 26 s. xv. The edition is the best part of Künstle's book. The important critical review of Künstle by Jülicher in *Theol. Lit.-Zeit.* 31 (1906), 656–9, does not question his view that Syagrius is anti-Priscillianist (and even accepts Künstle's absurd opinion that Leo's *Ep.* 15 is spurious). In general the hypothesis has been the most generally accepted speculation in Künstle's book, most of which is a maze of improbable conjecture. See E. Amann in *Dict. Th. Cath.* ixv. 2875–6.

Nevertheless he felt so confident of the author's identity with the Galician Syagrius mentioned in Hydatius' chronicle that he boldly made that identification the basis of a large-scale speculation about the character of Priscillianist developments of their doctrine of the Trinity. On the face of it, Künstle's argument puts the cart before the horse. If the tract were clearly anti-Priscillianist, his identification would be probable enough. But Syagrius was not an uncommon name at this period (apart from 'secular' instances, a bishop of this name was represented at the council of Nîmes in 396). The mere name is therefore a quite insufficient ground for taking the tract summarized by Gennadius to be the work of a Spanish bishop struggling against or disavowing Priscillianism.

It must, however, be conceded that Künstle's adventurous theory might conceivably be right, and that its basis can be widened by appealing to other obscure scraps of evidence whose anti-Priscillianist polemic is not questioned, however difficult they may be to interpret. It is worth scrutiny.

First there is Gennadius' notice of an explicitly Spanish bishop Audentius, probably the bishop of Toledo (above pp. 13 and 172) present at the council of Saragossa in 380. Audentius' book was written against Manichees, Sabellians, Arians, and Photinians. He argued that the Son is coeternal with the Father, and in particular that he did not begin to be divine at the time when he was conceived and born of the Virgin Mary.[1] Audentius' work may well have been the source whence Turibius took his third Priscillianist proposition, that the Son of God is called only-begotten because he alone is virgin-born (above, p. 212).

Secondly there is the fourteenth anathema in the long recension of the Rule of Faith ascribed to the council of Toledo: 'If anyone has said or believed that there is anything which can extend itself outside the divine Trinity, let him be anathema.'

Thirdly, there is the second anathema of the first council of Bracara (561), which condemns anyone who 'introduces some names of divinities outside the Holy Trinity, saying that in the very Deity there is a trinity of the Trinity,[2] as the gnostics and Priscillian say'.

---

[1] Gennadius, *Vir. inl.* 14.
[2] C. Tolet. anath. 14 (ed. de Aldama, p. 37) 'Si quis dixerit vel crediderit esse aliquid quod se extra divinam Trinitatem possit extendere, anathema sit.' C. Bracar.

To these pieces of evidence it is worth adding that in Leo's fifteenth letter Priscillianism and Arianism are linked in Leo's comment on the second of Turibius' propositions (above, p. 211). The evidence is unhappily too obscure to allow of any confident interpretation. One can do no more than speculate with diffidence. The tenacity with which the Priscillianist circle held to their master's modalist language is very clear from the Würzburg tracts, as is also their vulnerability to criticism on this point at a stage as early as the attacks of Ithacius. The evidence here surveyed would be compatible with the hypothesis that in an attempt to meet adverse criticism some Priscillianist theologian, perhaps Dictinius, set out to explain and defend the favoured language of the group regarding the Holy Trinity, and used some phraseology which suggested 'extension outside' the being of God who is Father, Son, and Spirit. But to propose such a hypothesis falls considerably short of accepting Künstle's proposal to identify Syagrius the author of the *Regulae definitionum* with a Galician bishop named Syagrius of a see in the *conventus* of Lugo. Despite the evidence that the Priscillianist doctrine of the Trinity occupied a rather larger place in the controversy than one would deduce from the great majority of the documents, the case for seeing the *Regulae definitionum* as an anti-Priscillianist tract, though not utterly impossible, is extremely weak.

One further conjecture is worth noting, namely the suggestion of A. C. Vega that Agrestius, bishop of Lugo, might be identified with the bishop Agrestius whose 'Verses on the Faith in the form of a Profession to Avitus the bishop' survive in a Paris manuscript of the eighth or ninth century. The verses include an insistence on orthodox Trinitarian doctrine, but otherwise have no special feature to link them with the Priscillianist movement. More probably this Agrestius was a Gallic bishop who addressed his verses about 500 to Avitus of Vienne.[1] Admittedly Agrestius

I, anath. 2 (ed. Barlow, p. 107) 'Si quis extra sanctam Trinitatem alia nescio quae divinitatis nomina introducit, dicens quod in ipsa divinitate sit trinitas trinitatis, sicut Gnostici et Priscillianus dixerunt, anathema sit.' The reference of the phrase 'trinitas trinitatis' is obscure unless perhaps it alludes to Manichee speculations about triads of entities derived from the Trinity, such as appear in the Coptic *Kephalaia*, ch. 7.

[1] The text of Agrestius' verses is printed in *PL Suppl.* v. 401 and the identification with the bishop of Lugo was argued by Vega in *Boletín de la Real Acad. de la Historia* 159 (1966), 167–209. Agrestius is re-edited with commentary by K. Smolak, 'Das Gedicht des Bischofs Agrestius', *Sitzungsberichte* of the Vienna Academy, 284/2 (1973).

of Lugo had Gallic connections; he attended the council held at Orange in 441,[1] and therefore can hardly have been generally understood to be a Priscillianist zealot, or his presence would not have been acceptable to his colleagues in the synod.

Priscillianism under the Sueves and Visigoths

The Arian Visigoths' dislike of the Manichees made it possible for Catholic bishops to harass Priscillianists within the Visigothic kingdom. About 530 two letters written by Montanus of Toledo,[2] metropolitan of the old province of Carthaginensis and bishop of a see now very conscious of what was due to it as the capital of the barbarian kingdom, disclose that at some churches in the territory, if not actually in the city, of Palentia (at the northern end of the province no great distance from Asturica), the custom has continued of commemorating Priscillian's name among the saints and martyrs. Montanus rebukes the Christians of the region for honouring the memory of an adulterer and sorcerer so rightly executed by the princes of this world, a heretic whose true teachings, together with a refutation, may be found set out in Turibius' letters to pope Leo. (Remarkably, though he knew it, Montanus never mentions Leo's reply.) In addition, the Palentians have caused Montanus further offence by inviting bishops from the Suevic kingdom in Galicia to attend the consecration of new basilicas, which has caused some alarm to the Visigoth king Amalaric (511–31), besides being contrary to church custom.[3] Moreover, certain presbyters have been disregarding episcopal rights by consecrating holy chrism.

Besides his letter to the faithful of Palentia, Montanus wrote on the same subjects to an otherwise unknown Turibius who, it appears, had previously held high rank in the world and in the

---

[1] See the list of bishops present, preserved only by the Cologne codex 212 (above, p. 158, n. 2), printed in C. Munier, *Concilia Galliae a. 314–a. 506* (1963), p. 87, no. 9, 'Ex provincia Gallecia civit. Lecentium Agrestius episcopus, Deudatus diaconus', rightly interpreted of Lugo rather than León by Schäferdiek, *Die Kirche in den Reichen der Westgoten und Suewen*, p. 114.

[2] The letters, preserved in the Hispana collection, are transmitted together with the Acts of the second council of Toledo of 531, and are printed in *PL* 84. 338–43 = *PL* 65. 51–8. They are not included in the critical text of the Acts of Toledo II by G. Martínez Díez in *Miscelánea Comillas* 41 (1964), 377–97.

[3] The fifth canon of the second council of Bracara (Barlow, p. 120), though disapproving, shows that for consecrating a new basilica a bishop was often able to charge a fee.

northern areas of Carthaginensis had attacked both pagan idolatry and Priscillianism, and had even converted some Visigoths to catholic orthodoxy. Since Montanus tells him to deal with any refractory clergy as a most severe priest ('sacerdos'), and refers at one point to 'your fellow bishop', it is certain that Turibius is a bishop, and that Montanus regards him as falling under the general metropolitan oversight of Toledo. Though Turibius' see is not mentioned, he is no doubt the bishop of Palentia. However, Montanus' letter to Turibius is evidently much more interested in asserting Toledo's primatial privileges in the kingdom than in stirring Turibius up to yet stronger action against Priscillianism. In fact the interest in primatial rights provided the reason for the preservation of the two letters by the subsequent tradition of Spanish canon law.

For the history of either catholicism or Priscillianism in Galicia in the period of Sueve domination, the sources are sadly silent with a single exception, pope Vigilius' letter to Profuturus of Bracara of 29 June 538.[1] This letter, written in answer to inquiries from bishop Profuturus, reveals the desire of the Galician bishops to keep the support of Rome in their struggle to survive in face of the Arianism of their Sueve rulers. Many were abandoning catholicism and conforming to the will of the barbarian king. Even so it is remarkable to note that Profuturus gave pride of place to questions arising out of persisting Priscillianist influences in north-western Spain. Is vegetarianism demanded of all truly dedicated Christians? May one omit the conjunction 'and' between the Son and the Spirit in reciting the *Gloria Patri*? Evidently the Priscillianist love of asyndeton (above, pp. 65, 199) has come to have large theological consequences.

The success of the Arian missionary Ajax in converting the Sueves to Arianism about 465–6[2] is likely to have resulted in a reaction among the bishops of Galicia. For it would have given them every motive for stressing their links with the catholic bishops in other provinces and therefore for playing down the Priscillianist hold upon their churches, even if that hold had been going no further than an episcopal willingness to countenance

---

[1] *PL* 69. 15–19; the date as in cod. Paris. lat. 1452, confirmed by ch. 5 which names 24 Apr. as the date of the following Easter, this being right for 539. See Schäferdiek, op. cit., p. 117.

[2] Hydatius, *Chron.* 232 (*Chronica minora* ii. 33 f.).

his commemoration as a martyr and to take no active steps to suppress the continued veneration of his tomb somewhere in the remote north-west.

The correspondence between Profuturus and Rome in 538 shows that at least by this date Priscillianism is no longer being protected from Bracara as may well have been the case a century earlier. The second conversion of the Sueves, from Arianism to Catholic orthodoxy about 555,[1] coincided with the advent from the East of the Pannonian monk Martin who founded a monastery at Dumium near Bracara and devoted himself to making Galicia safe for an organized monasticism that was free of any taint of Priscillianism. Abbot Martin was soon made bishop of Dumium, in which capacity he attended the first council of Bracara in 561. Later translated to be metropolitan, he presided at the second council in 572.[2]

Martin, the most interesting and original figure in sixth-century Spain, played a distinctive role as apostle of orthodoxy among the Sueves of Galicia.[3] The first council of Bracara, held on 1 May in the third year of the catholic king Ariamir and with his authority, marked a resolute attempt to reach a final solution of the Priscillianist problem. The council was attended by eight bishops under the presidency of Lucretius of Bracara. The Acts do not include any note of their sees, but from the record of the second council of 572 it is at least clear who represented Iria and Conimbriga.

Lucretius of Bracara began the proceedings with the observation that a long time has elapsed since synodical consultation and decision have been possible. But now, thanks to 'our son' the king, the bishops have been allowed to meet first to inquire into the precepts of orthodox faith, then to take note of the canons of the holy fathers, and finally to discuss clerical duty for the worship of God; so that errors due to ignorance or long neglect or disagreements and hesitations among the bishops can be dispelled.

The first item on the agenda is Priscillianism. In this most distant province ('in extremitate mundi et in ultimis huius provinciae regionibus') apocryphal texts find an easy entrance.

---

[1] Greg. Turon. *Virt. S. Martini* i. 11.
[2] Greg. Turon. *HF* 5. 37; Isid. Hispal., *Vir. inl.* 35 (PL 83. 1100).
[3] Venantius Fortunatus, *Carm.* 5. 2. 17–22; cf. Schäferdiek, op. cit., p. 123, n. 65.

Lucretius goes on to remind the synod of Leo's letter to the synod of Galicia sent by his notary Turibius, and of the rule of faith with appended chapters sent by the council of bishops of Tarraconensis, Carthaginensis, Lusitania, and Baetica, to Balconius, bishop of Bracara (see above, p. 178). Lucretius had the latter document read before the council, but the editor or scribe of the Acts could not be troubled to transcribe it, evidently feeling that for his generation it was unnecessary. Lucretius did not ask for the reading of Leo's letter to Turibius, and he may well have had no copy.[1] However, there follow seventeen 'chapters against the Priscillianist heresy', which are 'relecta', that is, a restatement of what has already been said. Most of them have a close relation to the propositions condemned in Leo's fifteenth letter, but are more probably excerpted from the *commonitorium* of Turibius than from Leo's extant reply to him.[2]

The list of censured propositions include familiar items: the Sabellian doctrine of the Trinity (1); the denial that the Lord was Son of God before his virgin birth (3); fasting on Sundays and on Christmas Day (4); belief that human souls or angels are of God's substance and pre-exist physical bodies (5–6); dualistic belief about the devil (7 and 13) who causes thunderstorms and droughts (8) and is maker of the human body (12); belief in astral fate (9)[3] and that the parts of the mind or body are ascribed to the signs of the zodiac (10); rejection of marriage (11) and of meat-eating (14). But some of the condemned propositions are new, or at least not found in Leo's letter to Turibius.

The second anathema has been discussed above (p. 220). The eighth, condemning belief that the devil causes storms, is not in Leo. Nor is the censure of vegetarianism in the fourteenth, which shows that the Priscillianists were thought to refuse even to taste oils in which meat had been cooked. Both Augustine and Profuturus (above, pp. 208, 223) mention the vegetarian question.

The fifteenth anathema condemns clergy or monks living with a woman other than mother or sister or aunt or next of kin by a bond of the closest consanguinity. They must not follow the

[1] Künstle, *Antipriscilliana*, p. 117, saw that Lucretius' words betray no certain knowledge of Leo, *Ep.* 15, a correct observation that led him into fantasies.
[2] Barlow, *Martini Bracarensis opera*, p. 81, thinks Braga still had a copy of 'the original letter compiled by Turibius and forwarded in the name of Pope Leo'.
[3] Belief in astral fate is picked out by Gregory the Great in 591 as distinctively Priscillianist: *Hom. in Evang.* i. 10. 4 (PL 76. 1111D–1112A).

Priscillianist practice of living in the same house as women who stand, so to speak, in an 'adopted' relation to them. This prohibition is new in this form; it seems to develop from the canon of Saragossa (380) and the sixth canon of Toledo (400), forbidding women to attend spiritual readings with men to whom they are unrelated.[1] It looks as if some Priscillianists had tried to protect themselves against criticism by going through some form of adoption of the spiritual partner.

The sixteenth anathema has quite fresh information. It condemns the Priscillianist customs of breaking the Holy Week fast at the third hour on Maundy Thursday by receiving communion at requiem masses and also of refusing to celebrate mass 'at the proper time after the ninth hour'.[2]

The seventeenth and last anathema echoes the fifteenth proposition in Turibius and Leo, condemning the altering of the text of scripture, all heretical tracts ascribed to patriarchs, prophets, or apostles, and the tractate which Dictinius wrote before his conversion.

The sixteenth anathema about Maundy Thursday is surprising and unclear. A possible source of light for interpreting it has been sought by Pierre David in a tract on Easter preserved in a number of manuscripts from the ninth century onwards, in some of which it stands with works of Martin of Bracara. A provisional text is available in C. W. Barlow's edition of Martin.[3] Whether it should really be ascribed to Martin is seriously doubtful. In some manuscripts there is no note of authorship, and elsewhere it is ascribed to Jerome. Pierre David conjectures that the tract may be Priscillianist and may illustrate the way in which the sect treated Maundy Thursday.[4]

The tract argues that Easter is rightly a movable feast and not, as until recently many Gallic bishops held, fixed on 25 March as the day of the resurrection. Easter may not occur earlier than 22 March because Christ redeemed the world on Thursday,

[1] This rule of Toledo is included by Martin of Bracara in his collection of canons from synods of the eastern fathers, no. 32, p. 133 Barlow.

[2] Barlow, p. 109.

[3] Barlow has translated it with Martin's other works in *Iberian Fathers* i (*The Fathers of the Church* 62, Catholic University of America, 1969). The Latin text is also in A. E. Burn, *Niceta of Remesiana* (Cambridge, 1905), pp. 92–110.

[4] P. David, *Un Traité priscillianiste de comput pascal* (Coimbra, 1951); thereon A. Cordoliani in *Revista de archivos, bibliotecas y museos* 62 (1956), 685–97.

22 March, which is also the date of the world's creation and also of the fall. The equinox is dated on 25 March; but one must subtract three to obtain the beginning of the world because three days of creation week passed before the sun was set on its course. The first 22 March was a Sunday, and the moon was created full. But the cycle of months and years prevents 22 March from being both Sunday and full moon in every year. So Easter may occur during a complete month, between 22 March and 21 April, on whatever day Sunday and full moon may coincide; and if Sunday and full moon do not coincide, then Easter Day is the Sunday after the full moon.

Reflection on the assumptions underlying this work shows that in the author's mind Maundy Thursday is the day of highest spiritual significance in Holy Week. Because of its relation to Easter, it commemorates both creation and fall which are said to have occurred on the same day.

Pierre David suggests that the tract's silence about Good Friday and the Passion would be explained if its author had docetic tendencies, as the Priscillianists were said by their opponents to have.

David's hypothesis is acutely argued and has attractions; but it is unnecessary and in the end rises to no more than an interesting conjecture. Much more light on the sixteenth anathema of Bracara is thrown by two African texts (to which David does not refer). The first is canon 28 in the Hippo Breviary: 'That the sacraments of the altar are to be celebrated only by fasting men, except on the day in the year when the Lord's supper is celebrated. But if after midday there is to be a commemoration of some dead persons, whether bishops or clergy or others, let it be only with prayers if those who make the commemoration are found to have dined already.'[1] The second text is in Augustine's fifty-fourth letter (to Januarius). Januarius has asked Augustine whether or not, as in some churches, the eucharist is to be celebrated both in the morning and in the evening on Maundy Thursday, and if, when it is celebrated only in the evening, one ought to remain fasting until

---

[1] C. Munier, *Concilia Africae a. 345–a. 525*, p. 41. The ancient western tradition disapproved, more than the eastern, of mass in the evening (except on Maundy Thursday). The newly printed Pauline commentary edited by H. J. Frede, ii (1974), 144, has the following comment on 1 Cor. 11 : 18–19: 'Usque hodie per rura Aegypti et Syriae die sabbati nocte post caenam ad ecclesias convenitur et est cernere saepe ebrios domini corpus accipere.' Cf. Socrates 5.22.43; Sozomen 7.19.8.

after mass. Augustine answers that one should follow local custom, though his own strongly expressed preference is for keeping
the rule of fasting, which is in fact the custom in Januarius'
church. Augustine does not forbid those who by custom break
the fast before the late mass on this day. He attempts to explain
the origin of the custom of having two masses on Maundy
Thursday by the hypothesis that, since in most churches it has
been usual to take a bath on this day, the morning mass was
provided for those unable to endure the strain of both fasting and
bathing and therefore needing food. The evening mass, then, was
kept for those who did not bathe and also kept their fast until
after the meal at the ninth hour.[1]

There is insufficient evidence to assess Augustine's theory to
explain the origin of the twofold mass. But that many churches
had two masses on Maundy Thursday is certain. Evidence survives for Capua in 546–7 when Victor drew up his Epistolary,
for Naples in the seventh century,[2] and for Rome. The Gelasian
Sacramentary provides both morning and evening masses for
the day, the morning, however, being pointedly distinguished in
the *Hanc igitur* as 'the *fast* of the Lord's supper' and an occasion of
penitential confession, the evening mass being the time for blessing holy oil.[3] None of the Italian texts, however, contains any
suggestion that either of the Maundy Thursday masses was
specially associated with prayer for the dead. Of this theme there
is an echo in a Mozarabic prayer for the feast of the Lord's supper
printed by Férotin (*Liber ordinum* 189). But that this day was not
in old Spain generally regarded as the occasion for commemorating all souls is shown by Isidore of Seville's observation that by
custom a special mass for the dead is said on Whit Monday.[4]
The only direct parallel, therefore, to the Priscillianist custom of
celebrating a requiem for the departed on the morning of Maundy
Thursday comes from North Africa. That parallel at least shows
that the custom was far from being distinctively Priscillianist.

Martin of Bracara felt strongly on this subject. He included in
his selection of canons from synods of the eastern fathers the
ruling attributed to the council of Laodicea that the Lenten fast

[1] Aug. *Ep.* 54. 7–8.
[2] G. Morin, *Anecdota Maredsolana* i (1893), 442 and 433.
[3] Ed. Wilson, xxxviii–xl, pp. 63–73 = Mohlberg, 349–94. A. Chavasse, *Le Sacramentaire gélasien* (1958), pp. 126–39, shows the antiquity of the formulas of the morning mass. [4] Isid. Hispal. *Regula monachorum* 24. 2 (PL 83. 894).

should not be broken on the fifth day of the last week of Lent (canon 50, p. 136 Barlow).

In Martin's anthology of eastern canon law several other canons are selected for their evident bearing on the Priscillianist problem. No individual bishop may refuse to attend a synod except on grounds of ill health (canon 19), or consecrate a bishop for a vacant see without a full council (canon 9) and without the metropolitan's consent (canon 3). Other canons forbid fasting on Sunday (57), vegetarianism on ground of principle rather than as a personal ascetic discipline (58), the reading of apocrypha in church (67), the use by clergy of magic and spells (59), and the resort by the faithful to the cult of moon or stars or the zodiac especially at the planting of crops or trees or at marriages (72). This last canon links up with Martin's endeavours, formulated in his tract *De correctione rusticorum*, to wean the peasants from folk magic and country superstitions.

Despite the title of his anthology of canons, Martin did not limit his collection of canon law to eastern synods. He inserted several enactments of the first council of Toledo of 400 (canons 23, 29–32, 43–4, 46, 51–2, and 63). He looked back to the anti-Priscillianist council as the principal source for Spanish ecclesiastical law.

By the time of the second council of Bracara in 572, thirteen years before the Sueve kingdom was suddenly conquered and absorbed by the Visigoths, Martin had been able to carry through a far-reaching reorganization of the church in the Suevic kingdom, with two provincial synods, the north having Lugo as its metropolis, the south Braga, the two together constituting the province of Galicia.[1] By this Martin helped the church to forget the frontiers and organizational forms of the old Roman province. Arianism is a thing of the past at the council of 572. The church of the Suevic kingdom is the church of the four ecumenical councils (the controversial fifth is ignored), and acknowledges the many local and regional councils. So it has itself authority to legislate as a local national synod for the churches in the kingdom. The main concern of the conciliar acts of 572 is to suppress simony, forbidding the bishops from accepting fees for ordinations or for providing holy chrism or for consecrating basilicas. Clergy are not to ask fees for baptisms under threat of violence,

---

[1] Cf. Schäferdiek, op. cit., p. 129.

or the poor will have no escape from perdition. It is forbidden for the Sueve landowners to build a proprietary basilica and then to divide with the clergy the offerings of the faithful. Evidently the construction of new churches has been funded in some cases by speculative finance in which the German landlords have had their capital costs met by being allocated half the recurrent takings. Each bishop must 'remember that he should not dedicate a church or a basilica before he has received the gift of the church and its endowment confirmed in writing; for it is highly imprudent if a church is consecrated as if it were a private house, without provision for the lighting costs and for the support of those who will serve it'. Otherwise the church (like a modern university) will be put into deficit if it accepts the capital benefaction without provision for running costs and overheads.

In the Acts of 572 only one echo of the Priscillianist affair can be heard. Some presbyters have been tenaciously continuing to celebrate masses for the dead after having broken their fast (presumably on Maundy Thursday). The tenth canon directs that this folly must cease on pain of deprivation.

In 585 the Sueve kingdom fell before Leovigild and his Visigoths.[1] The sudden reconversion to Arianism, followed in 589 by its equally sudden abjuration, must have created some temporary uncertainty. Of the fortunes of any surviving Priscillianists thereafter the sources give no information. That very occasionally such persons could still be met with as late as the middle of the seventh century is probable from the warning contained in a letter of Braulio bishop of Saragossa (631–51), to the Galician presbyter and monk Fructuosus who had written to ask advice.[2] Braulio treats Priscillianism with anxious respect: a heresy capable of misleading not only Dictinius but even Orosius, until he was corrected by Augustine, is insidious. Yet Fructuosus may remain proud of what Galicia has produced in the way of great ecclesiastical figures: Orosius, Turibius, Hydatius (the chronicler), and Carterius—of whom, unless he is the bishop present at Saragossa in 380 (above, pp. 13, 187), nothing is known.

Fructuosus was a zealous ascetic founding several monasteries in Galicia. His biographer makes no allusion to any confrontation

---

[1] Joh. Biclar. *Chronicon*, ad ann. XVII Leovegildi (*Chronica minora* ii. 217).
[2] Braulio, *Ep.* 44 (*PL* 80. 693D).

with Priscillianism.¹ The writings of Valerius of Bergidum (Vierzo) show life in Galicia in the latter part of the seventh century to have been exceedingly precarious, subject to civil disorder and incessant attacks by brigands, so that monasteries have to be built like fortresses.² In such circumstances the Galicians could hardly do more than try to survive.

The second half of the seventh century accordingly provides a probable niche for the *Consensoria monachorum*, a Galician work which in chapters 7–8 mentions an 'incursio repentina aut hostilitas'. Although the biblical citations are mainly Old Latin, it presupposes a coenobitic monasticism of which before Martin of Bracara there is no real evidence; the work is unlikely to be, as de Bruyne thought, Priscillianist.³

For the Spanish writers of the seventh century Priscillianism is not a living force which they must take measures to resist. The memory of the movement is strong enough to cause the compilers of the Hispana collection of canon law to preserve the canons of Saragossa, 380. It is tell-tale that of the first council of Toledo, 400, they preserve but the beginning of the Acts where the metropolitical rights of Toledo are referred to, the twenty canons, and then the interpolated, long recension of the rule of faith which cannot belong to this council. They are not interested in preserving the Priscillianist professions of faith and the council's ruling on the tenure of Symposius and Dictinius at Astorga (the reasons for the survival of which can only be a matter of conjecture in view of the loss of the San Millán codex containing them).

Neither Isidore of Seville nor Julian of Toledo had reason to be interested in Priscillian or in any who may have continued to treasure the martyr's honour. Naturally as an encyclopedist and antiquarian Isidore knows about them. In the *Etymologies* Isidore is content to record the date of Priscillian's emergence, and has a conventional note that 'the Priscillianists are called after Priscillian who put together in Spain a dogma combined from the error of the gnostics and the Manichees'.⁴ He includes Ithacius among the

---

¹ The *Vita S. Fructuosi* is well edited by F. C. Nock (Catholic University of America, 1946), and by M. C. Díaz y Díaz (Braga, 1974).
² *Vita S. Fructuosi* 7. Cf. E. A. Thompson, *The Goths in Spain*, pp. 318–19.
³ On the *Consensoria Monachorum* (PL 32. 1447 = 66. 993; *Clavis* 1872) see C. J. Bishko in *American Journal of Philology* 69 (1948), 377–95, rejecting de Bruyne's weak case for a Priscillianist origin, *Rev. Bénéd.* 25 (1908), pp. 83–8.
⁴ Isid. Hispal. *Etymol.* 5. 39. 37; 8. 5. 54. *Etymol.* 3. 27 distinguishes astronomy

illustrious figures of Iberian church history.[1] But during the first
half of the seventh century bishops of Seville had more serious
matters to occupy their minds. Isidore, it may be added, is well
aware that there continue to be clergy who consult astrologers
and fortune tellers. He presided at the fourth council of Toledo
in 633, the 29th canon of which threatens such clergy with in-
carceration in monasteries and austere penitential discipline.[2]
Moreover, the legislation of Visigothic kings of the seventh
century include edicts imposing harsh penalties on treasonable
consultation of fortune tellers and astrologers, nocturnal sacrifices, and sorcery practised to bring down storms on vineyards
and grain fields or to disturb the minds of men. The guilty are to
receive 200 lashes in public.[3] Neither Isidore nor the Visigothic
legislation associates Priscillianism with these enactments.

The leaders of the Spanish church in the seventh century no
longer write as men who fear to discover a Priscillianist under
their bed. This can be seen in the easy way that Julian of Toledo
feels able to make use of apocryphal texts without apprehension
that he may encourage para-Manichee speculations.[4] The dying
down of the controversy left the way open for iconography,
liturgy, and even theology to make freer use of apocryphal
legends about the Virgin or the apostles. So Isidore of Seville
attests, for the first time, the story that St. James came to Spain.[5]

The evidence points to the conclusion that by 600 or soon after
Priscillianism had become a spent force, hardly more than a bad
memory in the minds of men with time to be interested in the past,
in no serious sense affecting their judgement of the church's
contemporary tasks. In the seventh century there may still have
been country folk in the valleys of Galicia who remembered how
their fathers had sought strength and healing and had sworn
great oaths at Priscillian's tomb in the north-west. But they did
not create a problem for the Galician church, so far as can be

from the 'partly superstitious' astrology which assigns parts of the body to signs of
the zodiac, and casts horoscopes.

[1] *Vir. inl.* 15 (PL 83. 1092).
[2] PL 84. 575. See J. Fontaine, 'Isidore de Séville et l'astrologie', *Revue des études
latines* 31 (1953), 271–300, especially at p. 278.
[3] *MGH Leges* I. i, p. 257, 17; p. 259, 17 ff.
[4] Julian, *De sextae aetatis comprobatione* 2. 13 (PL 96. 568A) using Abdias (Fabricius,
Codex Apocryphus Nov. Test. p. 525); ibid. 2. 9 (565) speaks of Thomas in India,
Matthew in Macedonia, etc.
[5] PL 83. 151.

judged from the meagre sources for the period. Priscillian's permanent legacy came to be through his Pauline canons and no doubt also the gospel prologues, incorporated in manuscripts of the Vulgate and even penetrating the Latin liturgy. The Würzburg tractates remained without influence. What is now the solitary manuscript to preserve them was probably one of very few copies when it came into the hands of St. Bilihild in the eighth century.

There remains a speculative possibility that is worth recording by way of conclusion to this narrative. The shrine of St. James was first founded close to the north-west coast at Compostela in the diocese of Iria during the ninth century. The history of the site before that foundation is shrouded in mystery. Excavation beneath the great cathedral of Santiago nearly a century ago found an old Roman mausoleum with large granite blocks. Further digging during the years 1946–59 uncovered some baths of the third or fourth century and, under the nave, a large necropolis with graves of the fourth and fifth centuries, belonging to families of modest means. This necropolis has tombs facing east, and continued in use during the Sueve period. The orientation of these graves is out of alignment with the mausoleum and the supporting walls. No graffiti or inscriptions make any contribution to explain the site. The burials cease round about 600. The evidence would not be incompatible with the hypothesis that here were buried Christians who desired (as many in late antiquity) to be interred in proximity to some holy man. Without any document or inscription it is impossible to say who that holy man was.[1]

Was he Priscillian? The question cannot be answered on present evidence. But Compostela is in the right region for his shrine, and it would not be without analogy for a great orthodox centre of pilgrimage to be installed on an old site formerly associated with schism and heresy.

---

[1] There is a convenient summary of the results of the excavation in the excellent book by J. Fontaine, *L'Art préroman hispanique* (Zodiaque, 1973), p. 31, who asks: 'Près de quel corps saint a-t-on enterré *ad sanctos*, sous les futures et successives cathédrales de Santiago, du IVᵉ au VIIᵉ siècle?' A report on the dig, with plates, is given by M. Chamoso Lamas in *Compostellanum* 2 (1957), 225–74. Vollmann, *PW* Suppl. xiv, 517, refers to previous speculations on this subject.

APPENDIX

The Priscillianist Professions and the Judgement of the Council of Toledo

I t has been explained above (p. 179) that the principal anti-Priscillianist portions of the Acts of the Council of Toledo, 400, are not included in the normal Hispana collection, but have survived only through a codex from the monastery of St. Emilian which was brought to the Escorial under Philip II and perished in the fire of 1671. Fortunately the pieces concerning Priscillianism were twice transcribed, by Ambrosio de Morales, who printed them in his continuation of the chronicle of Spain, and by J. B. Pérez whose transcript is in the Vatican library (Vat. lat. 4887) and has been printed in the third volume of C. García Goldáraz, *El códice Lucense de la colección canónica Hispana* (1954). Morales's text was copied, with some modifications, in Aguirre's huge edition of the Spanish councils; and Aguirre's text has passed into all the standard conciliar collections such as Hardouin, Labbe, Mansi, and even the 1963 edition of J. Vives and others.

Since Pérez's notes and personal conjectures for the improvement of the text are of great interest, and suggest that his transcription of the manuscript may often have been more careful than that of Morales, the following edition of the Toledan pieces is intended to bring together what is known about this difficult text. In a few places I record conjectures by other editors using Aguirre, such as S. Pueyo's reorganized digest of Aguirre (Madrid, 1784).

In the apparatus M = Morales's text of 1577, P = Pérez's reading of the text of the manuscript, Pe = Pérez's personal conjectures:

Incipit exemplar professionum habitarum in concilio
Toletano contra sectam Priscilliani aera ccccxxxviii

Post habitum iam concilium Kalendis Septembribus tertio nonas
Septembres, post diversas cognitiones tunc habitas, sub die

1 Incipiunt exemplaria M   habitarum *om.* M   3 et tertio *conj.* Pe.   4 tunc
hab. *om.* P

octavo iduum Septembrium, domni Symphosii et domni Dictinii 5
sanctae memoriae episcoporum et domni sanctae memoriae
Comasii tunc praesbyteri excerptae sunt de plenariis gestis pro-
fessiones, quas inter reliquas habuerunt in concilio Toletano de
damnatione Priscilliani vel sectae eius:

Post aliquanta et inter aliquanta eodem tempore acta, Dictinius 10
episcopus dixit: Audite me, optimi sacerdotes, corrigite omnia,
quia vobis correctio data est. Scriptum est enim: *Vobis datae
sunt claves regni coelorum.* Sed peto a vobis ut claves nobis regni,
non portae aperiantur inferni. Haec, si dignamini, omnia ante
oculos pono. Hoc enim in me reprehendo, quod dixerim unam 15
dei et hominis esse naturam.

Item dixit: Ego non solum correctionem vestram rogo, sed et
omnem praesumptionem meam de scriptis meis arguo atque
condemno.

Item dixit: Sic sensi, testis est deus. Si erravi, corrigite. 20

Item dixit: Et paulo ante dixi et nunc iterum repeto, in priori
comprehensione mea et in principiis conversionis meae quaecumque conscripsi, omnia me toto corde respuere.

Item dixit: Excepto nomine dei, omnia anathemo.

Item dixit: Omnia quae inveniuntur contra fidem, cum ipso 25
auctore condemno.

Symphosius episcopus dixit: Iuxta quod paulo ante lectum est
in membrana nescio qua, in qua dicebatur filius innascibilis, hanc
ego doctrinam, quae aut duo principia dicit aut filium innascibilem,
cum ipso auctore damno qui scripsit. 30

Item dixit: Ego sectam quae recitata est, damno cum auctore.

Item dixit: Ego sectam malam quae recitata est, damno cum
auctore.

Item dixit: Date mihi chartulam; ipsis verbis condemno. Et cum
accepisset chartulam, de scripto recitavit: Omnes libros haereticos 35
et maxime Priscilliani doctrinam, iuxta quod hodie lectum est, ubi
innascibilem filium scripsisse dicitur, cum ipso auctore damno.

Comasius praesbyter dixit: Nemo dubitet me cum domno meo
episcopo sentire et omnia damnare quae damnat, et nihil eius
praeferre sapientiae nisi solum deum. Atque ideo nolo ne dubitetis 40

7–8 excerptae . . . professiones] *post* Septembrium M   7 sunt. *om.* P
8 reliquos M   9 eius+in hunc modum M   27 id quod M
32–3 item . . . auctore *om.* Aguirre   39 damnavit M et (*bis*) *om.* P   40 ne
om. P me M

aliud me esse facturum, aliud sensurum quam quod professus est
ac perinde quomódo dixit quem sequor episcopus meus. Quid-
quid ille damnavit, et ego damno.

AERA qua supra, sub die septimo iduum Septembrium, pro-
45 fessiones sanctae memoriae episcoporum domni Symphosii et
domni Dictinii et sanctae memoriae domni Comasii tunc praesbyteri:
Comasius praesbyter dixit: Non timeo frequenter dicere quod
semel dixisse me gaudeo. Sequor auctoritatem episcopi mei
50 Symphosii; sequor sapientiam senis. Teneo quod dixi; si iubetis,
ex chartula relegam. Omnes id sequantur qui voluerint vestro
haerere consortio. Et Comasius praesbyter ex chartula legit: Cum
catholicam et Nicaenam fidem sequamur omnes, et scriptura
recitata sit quam Donatus praesbyter, ut legitur, ingessit, ubi
55 Priscillianus innascibilem esse filium dixit, constat hoc contra
Nicaenam fidem esse dictum; atque ideo Priscillianum dicti huius
auctorem cum ipsius dicti perversitate et quos male condidit
libros cum ipso auctore condemno.
Symphosius episcopus dixit: Si quos male condidit libros, cum
60 ipso auctore condemno.
Dictinius episcopus dixit: Sequor sententiam domni mei et
patris mei et genitoris et doctoris. . . . . . . Quaecumque locutus
est, loquor. Nam scriptum legimus: *Si quis vobis aliter evangelizaverit*
praeterquam quod evangelizatum est vobis, anathema sit. Et idcirco
65 omnia quae Priscillianus aut male docuit aut male scripsit cum
ipso auctore condemno.
DIE qua supra:
Exemplar definitivae sententiae episcoporum translatae de
gestis. Episcopi dixerunt: Legatur scriptura sententiae. Et legit:
70 Etsi diu deliberantibus utrum post Caesaraugustanum concilium
in quo sententia in certos quosque dicta fuerat, sola tamen una
die praesente Symphosio, qui postmodum declinando sententiam
praesens audire contempserat, arduum nobis esset audire iam
dictos, tamen litteris sanctae memoriae Ambrosii, quas post illud

41 me *om.* M   facturum] futurum *conj.* Pe aliud esse P aliterve M   42 pro-
inde M dixit episc. meus qu. sequor M   44 vii P iii M   46 domni[2] *om.* M
49 dixissem et (ut M) gaudeam PM   50 teneo P sentio M   53 et[2] *om.* P
56 huius dicti M   62 *nomen erasum* M   65 male[1]] mali P   68 diffini-
tivae M   episcoporum *om.* M   69 scripta P   70 verum M utrum P
veritatem *conj.* Pueyo   71 sola *om.* P   73 esse P   73-4 iam dictos M
dicti P dicta *aut* Dictinium *conj.* Pe   74 ⟨lectis⟩ tamen?

concilium ad nos miserat, ut si condemnassent quae perperam 75
egerant et implessent conditiones quas praescriptas literae con-
tinebant, reverterentur ad pacem (adde quae sanctae memoriae
Siricius papa suasisset), magnam nos constat praestitisse patien-
tiam: et si prius indictum in Toletana urbe concilium declinarant
ad quod illos evocaramus, ut audiremus cur non implerent con- 80
ditiones, quas sibi ipsi, sancto Ambrosio praesente et audiente,
posuissent, patuit respondisse Symphosium se a recitatione eorum
quos dicebant martyres recessisse, ac dehinc deceptum tentumque
per plurimos secus aliqua gessisse reperimus, nullis libris apocryphis aut novis scientiis quas Priscillianus composuerat in- 85
volutum; Dictinium epistolis aliquantis pene lapsum, quas omnes
sua professione condemnans, correctionem petens, veniam postu-
larat: quem constat, ut Symphosius fecit, quaecumque contra
fidem catholicam Priscillianus scripserat, cum ipso auctore da-
mnasse. Ceterum extortum sibi de multitudine plebis probaret esse 90
Symphosius ut ordinaret Dictinium episcopum, quem sanctus
Ambrosius decrevisset bono pacis locum tenere praesbyterii, non
accipere honoris augmentum. Confiterentur etiam illud quod
alios per diversas ecclesias ordinassent, quibus deerant sacerdotes,
habentes hanc fiduciam quod cum illis propemodum totius 95
Galliciae sentiret plebium multitudo; ex quibus ordinatus Paternus Bracarensis ecclesiae episcopus in hanc vocem confessionis
primus erupit ut sectam Priscilliani se scisse, sed factum episcopum liberatum se ab ea, librorum lectione sancti Ambrosii,
esse iuraret.   100

   Item Isonius nuper baptizatum se a Symphosio et episcopum
factum, hoc se tenere quod in praesenti concilio Symphosius
professus est, esse respondit.

   Vegetinus vero olim ante Caesaraugustanum concilium episcopus factus, similiter libros Priscilliani cum auctore damnaverat; 105
ut de caeteris acta testantur, de quibus qui consuluntur episcopi
judicabunt.

   Herenias clericos suos sequi maluerit, qui sponte nec interrogati

---

75–77 condemnasset . . . egerat . . . implesset . . . reverteretur P   papa adaeque
s. mem. Siricius suasisset P   80 et audissemus M   implessent M   83 quod
P quae M   tentumque PM praeventumque *conj.* Pueyo   84 nonnullis *conj.* Pe
85 aut M vel P   86 plene Florez   87 suam professionem P sua professione
Pe   postularet MP   91 Symphosium MP   92 bonae M   93 confitentur M   96 ordinatus est M   98 et sectam M   99 lectione librorum M
103 esse *om.* M   105 damnaverit P   108 Herenas M   maluerit P maluerat M

Priscillianum catholicum sanctumque martyrem clamassent,
110 atque ipse usque ad finem catholicum hunc esse dixisset per-
secutionem ab episcopis passum. Quo dicto omnes sanctos iam
plurimos quiescentes, aliquos in hac luce durantes, suo iudicio
deduxerit in reatum. Hunc cum his omnibus, tam suis clericis
quam diversis episcopis, hoc est, Donato, Acurio, Emilio, qui
115 ab eorum professionibus recedentes, maluissent sequi consortium
perditorum, decernimus ab sacerdotio submovendum: quem
constaret etiam de reliquis verbis suis convictum per tres episcopos, multos quoque praesbyteros sive diacones, cum periurio
esse mentitum.
120 Vegetinum autem, in quem nulla specialiter dicta fuerat ante
sententia, data professione quam synodus accepit, statuimus
communioni nostrae esse reddendum. Paternum, scilicet pro
catholica fidei veritate et publicato haeresis errore, libenter
amplexi, ecclesiam in qua episcopus fuerat constitutus tenere
125 permisimus, recepturi etiam in nostram communionem cum
sedes apostolica rescripserit. Reliqui qui ex provincia Gallaecia ad
concilium non venerunt, et in Symphosii semper communione
durarunt, acceptam formam a concilio missam si subscripserint,
etiam ipsi in caelestis interim pacis contemplatione consistant,
130 expectantes pari exemplo quid papa qui nunc est, quid sanctus
Simplicianus episcopus Mediolanensis reliquique ecclesiarum
rescribant sacerdotes. Si autem subscriptionem formae quam
misimus non dederint, ecclesias quas detinent non retineant;
neque iis communicent qui reversi de synodo datis professionibus
135 ad suas ecclesias reverterunt.
Sane Vegetinum solum cum Paterno communicare decrevimus.
Symphosius autem senex religiosus, qui quae egerit supra scri-
psimus, in ecclesia sua consistat, circumspectior circa eos quos ei
reddemus futurus: inde expectabit communionem unde prius
140 spem futurae pacis acceperat.
Quod observandum etiam Dictinio et Anterio esse decrevimus.
Constituimus autem ut priusquam illis per papam vel per sanctum

110 dixisse P dixisset *conj.* Pe   114 diversorum episcoporum P   ac Urio P
115 professione recentes M   118 diaconos P   122 scilicet *conj.* Pe licet
PM   123 publicato *conj.* Pe publicatae PM   126 reliquos *conj.* Pe reliqui
PM   127 non venerunt *conj.* Pe convenerunt P convenerant M non convenerant Pueyo   communionem P duraverant M   128 accepta forma . . . missa M
129 interim *om.* M   133 retentent P   134 iis P his M   137 qui quae
M quaeque P   scribimus M   138 consistet P   142 ut *om.* M

Simplicianum communio redditur, non episcopos ab illis, non praesbyteros, non diacones ordinandos; ut sciamus si vel nunc sciunt, sub hac conditione remissi, tandem synodicae sententiae 145 praestare reverentiam.

Meminerint autem fratres et coepiscopi nostri enixe excubandum ne quis communione depulsus collectiones faciat per mulierum domos, et apocrypha quae damnata sunt legant, ne communicantes his pari societate teneantur. Quoniam quicumque hos 150 susceperint, certum est eos etiam graviori sententia retinendos esse.

Fratri autem nostro Ortygio ecclesias de quibus pulsus fuerat pronunciavimus esse reddendas.

144 presbyteres P   145 sciant M   146 praestare debere *conj.* Pueyo
150 has M   154 pronunciamus M

INDEX

Abelard 4, 160
Abgar 166
Abortion 37
Abraham, abbot 167
Acci (Guadix) 4
Acholius of Thessalonica 153
Acts, apocryphal 77 ff., 87, 156
Acurius, Galician bishop 184, 238
Adamites 140
Advent 14
Aemilianus, St. 180
Agape 20, 37
Agobard of Lyon 129, 195
Agrestius of Lugo 218, 221
Agroecius 147
Aguirre, Sáenz de 180, 210, 234
Ajax, Arian missionary 223
Aland, K. 102
Alans 42, 188–9
Albertus Magnus 99
Alcoholism 149
Aldama, A. de 176, 217
Aldazábel, J. 7
Alfaric, P. 196, 206
Alföldi, A. 118, 134
Alms 70, 72
Altaner, B. 178, 191
Altar of Victory 114–16, 136
Alvaraz, M. E. 157
Amalarius of Metz 15
Amann, E. 219
Amantia 62–3
Amantius of Jovia 118
Ambrose 3, 6, 18–19, 26, 28, 32, 35, 40, 43, 70, 72, 93, 97, 111 ff., 133–8, 148, 151–4, 158, 161, 164, 170, 182–3, 187, 197, 200, 197, 205, 236–7
Ambrosiaster 16, 18, 25, 31, 56, 74, 76, 82, 85, 88, 105, 200
Ammianus Marcellinus 52–3, 75, 142–3
Ampelius 128
Amulets 54–5, 202
Anastasius I, Pope 153, 170–1, 185
Anastasius Sinaita 140, 167
Anastasius, emperor 143
Anatolius, hermit 10
Ancona 3, 178

Andrés, G. de 179
Anemius of Sirmium 117
Animals, divine symbols 91 ff.
Anterius, Spanish bishop 184, 238
Antichrist 9, 62
Antiphons, Great 15; antiphonal hymns 174
Antolín, G. 181
Antoninus of Mérida 211
Anysius of Thessalonica 153
Apocrypha 23–4, 38, 56, 63–4, 77 ff., 93, 98, 119–20, 151, 166, 185, 188, 208 ff., 212, 214, 232, 237, 239
Apollodorus 52
Apostles as zodiac 196; legends 232
Apuleius 51
Aquitaine 11
Arborius 200
Arévalo, F. 60, 203
Arianism 5–6, 30, 76–7, 117–18; link with Priscillianism 220–1; Visigoths 222
Ariminum, council 6–7, 13, 117, 131
Aristotle 51
Arles 11–12, 161 ff.
Armenius 144
Arnobius 52
Artemius, Gallic bishop 129
Asarbius (Asarivus) 47, 144
Ascension Day 4
Astrology 75, 176, 191–204, 225, 232
Asturius of Toledo 172
Athanasius 26, 44, 52
Audentius of Toledo 12, 172, 220
Augustine: curses 3; St. Antony 9; Consentius 11, 154; bare feet 17; ritual habit 19; Manichees 23, 37, 143, 195–6; amulets 54; Easter 75; Filastrius 91; Baalsamen 96; Acts of John 105, 156; Gratian 114; Ambrose 117, 165; picture of Priscillianism 122–4; 206–8; fault in ordination intransmissible 147; oaths 150; lying 150; Vandals 189; Irenaeus 205
Augustus, superstitious 75
Aurelianus 144
Ausonius 36–7, 44, 144, 200

Auxentius, Arian 90, 127
Auxentius of Toledo 12
Avitus of Braga 178, 190
Avitus of Vienne 221
Babut, E. C. 8, 13, 25, 33, 37, 40–1, 48,
  50, 103, 133, 162–4, 193, 202
Bachiarius 16, 59–60, 167–9, 214
Balconius of Braga 178–9, 208, 218
Ballerini, P. & G. 170, 180, 210, 217
Balsamus 96
Baptism 19
Barb, A. A. 53
Barbelo 96
Barbero de Aguilera, A. 176
Bare feet 17–19
Barlow, C. W. 217, 225 ff.
Barnes, T. D. 7
Baronius, C. 151
Barrow, R. H. 116
Baruch Apocalypse 75
Batiffol, P. 4, 28, 39, 215
Baumstark, A. 106
Baur, F. C. 198
Bauto 43, 112, 123
Bélin, J. A. 99
Berger, S. 59, 102
Bernays, J. 44
Bilihild 63, 233
Binionites 56, 77
Binns, J. W. 40
Bischoff, E. 196
Bishko, C. J. 231
Bishop, W. C. 15
Blockley, R. C. 143
Boethius 15
Boll, F. 201
Bonner, C. 19, 70
Bonnet, M. 79
Bordeaux, council 43–8
Botte, B. 15, 17, 174
Bowers, W. P. 2
Box, G. H. 82
Braude, W. G. 197
Braulio of Saragossa 13, 180, 191, 230
Bribery at court 40–2
Brice of Tours 162
Brisson, J. P. 15
Britto of Trier 42–3, 126, 133–4, 145
Broomsticks 21
Brou, L. 15
Brown, P. 141–2, 150
Brox, N. 54

Bruyne, D. de 58–9, 103, 109–10, 231
Bulhart, V. 6
Burkitt, F. C. 79, 103
Burn, A. E. 226
Buddha 97–8
Cabaniss, J. A. 15
Cabié, A. 4
Caesaraugusta, *see* Saragossa
Caesarius of Arles 84
Caesarius, Claudius 45
Calendar 74, 99
Callimachus 52
Callinicon 125
Cameron, A. 114
Campenhausen, H. von 60, 135
Campos, J. 211
Canon of scripture 81–4, 214; *see*
  Apocrypha
Canons, Pauline 58–62
Capital punishment 130 ff., 187
Carterius 13, 187, 230
Caspar, E. 28–9, 215
Caspari, C. P. 131, 183
Cassian, John 17, 124, 155, 162
Catalani, J. 152, 180
Catiline 20, 206
Cavallera, F. 38
Celibacy 24–5, 29–31, 35, 60, 68, 70 ff.,
  105, 147, 168, 173–4, 187
Celsus 141
Ceponius 210, 213, 216
Chamoso Lamas, M. 233
Chapman, H. J. 49, 59, 102–9
Charisms 21, 60, 79–80
Chastagnol, A. 45, 114, 163
Chavannes, E. 214
Chavasse, A. 228
Cheese magic 53
Christ 85–91
Christmas 16–17, 212
Chronopius 45
Chrysostom, John 9, 18–19, 54, 118
Church, mother 74
Cicero 52, 151, 199–200
Cirot, G. 27
Clarke, G. W. 1
Clement of Alexandria 18, 196, 199
Clement of Rome, 1; Clementine
  homilies 196
Clercq, V. de 5, 22
Colombás, G. M. 146, 180
Comasius of Astorga 181

Compostela 233
Concubinage 175
Confessor 174
Consensoria monachorum 231
Consentius 11, 154–5
Consistory 138
Constantine the Great 4, 53, 127
Constantine, usurper 115, 162–3
Constantinople, *see* Councils
Constantius of Orange 126
Constantius II 6, 26, 115, 128, 142
Consultationes Zacchaei et Apollonii 9, 100, 146
Cordoliani, A. 226
Corssen, P. 102
Coster, C. H. 40
Councils: Antioch (*328*) 46, 153; Aquileia (*381*) 117–18, 127, 130; Ariminum 13, 117, 131; Bordeaux (*384*) 43–8; Braga I (*561*) 172, 217; Braga II (*572*) 224–30; Carthage (*254*) 1; Constantinople (*381*) 131; (*536*) 19; Elvira 1–3, 30, 54, 130, 140; Francfort (*794*) 163; 'Laodicea' 228; Mainz (*813*) 19; Milan (*390*) 143; Nicaea (*325*) 33, 127, 173, 182; (*787*) 132; Nîmes (*396*) 158–9, 167, 220; Rome (*378*) 128–9, (*382*) 42; Serdica (*342*) 5, 22, 34; Toledo I (*400*) 27–9, 56, 69, 152, 170 ff., 234 ff.; XII (*681*) 170; XVII (*694*) 3; Trier (*386*) 145; Turin (*398*) 132, 160–5, 170; Valence (*374*) 13–4, 42.
Courcelle, P. 146
Courtois, C. 45, 177
Crocodiles 21
Crops, fertility 2, 53
Crum, W. E. 198
Curses 3, 52
Cyprian 1, 90
Cyril of Jerusalem 19, 148

Dale, A. W. W. 1
d'Alès, A. 8, 38, 136, 193
Damasus, Pope, 17, 23, 26, 33–5, 38–45, 49–51
Daniélou, J. 196
David, P. 226
Davids, J. A. 8, 193
Deaconesses 159–60
Deane, H. A. 130
Decans 198
Decret, F. 143, 156

Delehaye, H. 84
Delphidius 36–7
Delphinus of Bordeaux 12, 36, 43–4
Demons, *see* Satan, Storm-demons
Devos, P. 38, 166
Dexter, Nummius Aemilianus 5
Díaz y Díaz, M. C. 206, 231
Dictinius 69, 153 ff., 181 ff., 212, 216, 230, 234–9
Dierich, J. 48
Diesner, H. J. 135, 189
Dihle, A. 116
Diocletian 141
Dionysius Areopagita 19, 132
Dobschütz, E. von 102
Docetism 35, 55
Dodwell, H. 205
Dölger, F. J. 19
Domninus of Grenoble 126
Donatism 16, 131, 147
Donatus, Galician bishop 184, 238
Donatus presbyter 236
Dornseiff, F. 201
Dothan, M. 197
Dubois, J. 7
Duchesne, L. 12, 26, 28–9, 42, 133, 162–5
Dudden, F. H. 130, 135–6, 151
Duhr, J. 168

Eadie, J. W. 142
Easter 226–7
Eclipses 51–2
Edessa 79, 166
Egeria 5, 15, 86, 142, 166–7
Egger, R. 118
Elias Apocalypse 81
Elpidius, Priscillianist layman 20, 27, 37
Elpidius, Spanish presbyter 186
Elvira 1–3, 30, 54, 130, 140
Emilius, Galician bishop 184, 238
Encratites 143
Endelechius 54
Enoch 80
Ensslin, W. 29, 42, 135–7
Epiphanius 140, 149, 195, 206
Epiphany 4, 9, 16–17
Ephraem Syrus 98, 195
Esdras IV, 74, 183
Étienne, R. 43
Eucharist 14, 23, 99
Euchrotia 36–46, 61–3, 144
Eugenius 124
Eulalia, St. 178

Eulogius, charismatic monk 129
Eunomius 88
Eunuchs at court 112
Euodius 122, 139, 143
Eusebius of Caesarea 46, 96
Eusebius of Emesa 52–3
Eutropius, presbyter 146
Exuperantius of Aquis Celenis 157, 171, 185
Exuperius of Toulouse 187–8
Ezra 74, 183

Fabre, P. 132
Fasting 14, 16, 18, 166, 207, 227–9
Faustinus 6–7, 90
Faustus of Mileu 78, 98–9, 195
Feder, A. 5, 15
Fees for sacraments 222, 229
Felicissimus 144
Felix IV, Pope 153
Felix of Trier 126, 133, 145–6, 157–65
Férotin, M. 2, 7, 16–17, 30
Feuchtwang, D. 196
Filastrius of Brescia 4, 9, 17, 24, 78–81, 86, 91, 119
Filioque 176–7
Finkel, A. 82
Firmicus Maternus 198, 200
Fischer, B. 59, 84
Flacilla 7
Florez, E. 8, 152, 170, 183
Fontaine, J. 9, 20, 45, 83, 136, 232–3
formalis 192–4
Fortunatian of Aquileia 58
Frede, H. J. 81–2, 90
Frend, W. H. C. 40
Fritzsche, O. F. 60
Fronto 154
Fructuosus of Braga 13, 230–1
Fructuosus of Tarraco 1
Funke, H. 142

Gaiffier, B. de 7, 84
Galla, Priscillianist 37–8
Galla, empress 123
Gams, P. B. 28
García Conde, A. 27
García Goldáraz, C. 171, 179–81, 234
Gaudentius of Brescia 18, 177, 165
Gelasius, Pope 31; Decree 84, 93, 110
Gennadius 12, 60, 146, 167–8, 218–20.
Gförer, A. F. 82
Ginzberg, L. 196

Giraldus 3
God 72, 89; *see* Monarchianism
Goffinet, E. 74
Gonzalez, F. A. 1
Goodenough, E. R. 196
Gothofredus, J. 36, 113
Gottlieb, G. 114, 119
Grabe, J. E. 205
Gratian 26, 35, 39, 41–2, 61, 111 ff., 129
Gregory the Great 82, 128–9, 139; on Priscillianism 225
Gregory of Elvira 6–7, 13, 30, 90, 101, 186
Gregory of Mérida 186
Gregory of Tours 45, 78, 112, 133, 150, 224
Griffe, E. 31, 163
Grumel, V. 135, 137
Gryson, R. 31, 159
Guadix 4
Gundel, H. 196
Gundlach, W. 163–4

Hairgrease 189
Hamman, A. 16, 100
Harnack, A. 4, 90, 103
Hartberger, M. 48
Hebrews, epistle 58, 61
Heckenbach, J. 18
Hefele, K. J. 164, 217
Hegemark, J. L. B. 199
Hegemonius 91, 195
Hell 62, 151
Helpidius, *see* Elpidius
Hemmerdinger, B. 203
Hendrikx, A. 200
Heracles 52
Heraclian of Sirmium 131
Herenias 184–5, 237
Hermes Trismegistus 98, 198
Heros of Arles 162
Hilarion 140
Hilarius, Spanish bishop 171–2, 186
Hilary of Poitiers 5, 11, 15, 65, 68, 70–4, 76, 95–6, 88–9, 193
Hilgenfeld, A. 48, 102, 193
Hill, D. E. 53
Himerius of Tarraco 13, 16–17, 29, 31
Hippolytus 18, 95, 130
Holl, K. 198
Honigmann, E. 142
Honorius 115, 163, 189
Hort, F. J. A. 205

Huemer, J. 4
Huns 142
Hydatius, chronicler 45, 157, 166, 177, 188 ff., 210–11, 213, 216, 218, 230
Hydatius of Mérida 12, 20 ff., 31 ff., 50–1, 61, 125, 146, 148, 156–8
Hyginus of Cordoba 6, 12–13, 20, 25, 31, 36, 38, 125, 134, 145–6

Ialdabaoth 94–5
Iamblichus 18, 141
Iconoclastic controversy 131
Idacius, *see* Hydatius
Ignatius 199
Ihm, M. 151
Ildefonsus of Toledo 12, 172
Illuminism 10
innascibilis 88–9, 176–7, 182
Innocent I, Pope 72, 130–1, 153, 163, 173, 175, 185–8
Innocent IV, Pope 139
Innocents, Holy 17
Instantius 20, 25, 27, 31–40, 44, 64, 145; as author of tractates 48–9
Ioel 96
Irenaeus 1, 9, 22, 201, 203–6
Isidore of Seville 7, 17, 21, 82–3, 145, 224, 228, 231–2
Isonius 237
Ithacius of Ossonuba 20–2, 40–3, 46–7, 61, 203; charges 51–6, 126 ff., 145; exile and character 148–9; end 157–8

Jacoby, F. 19
James, St., in Spain 232–3
James, M. R. 74–5, 183
Januarius, correspondent of Augustine 19, 75, 227
Jerome 4–9, 13, 16, 20–2, 37–8, 58, 69, 75, 105, 118, 121, 140, 142, 144, 152, 155–6, 167, 187–8, 190, 193, 200–2, 205–6
'Jerome', *Indiculus* 87, 203–4
Jews in Spain 2; sabbath 75; Callinicum 125; nudity 140
John of Antioch 124, 140
John of Lycopolis 124
John, St.: Acts 78, 87, 105, 156; Apocryphon 91–2; *Comma* 90
John Baptist, St. 19
John the Deacon 19
John, *see* Chrysostom
John of Nikiu 142

John, Spanish bishop 186
Jones, A. H. M. 138
Jordan, H. 205
Jordanes 118
Joseph (*Hypomnesticon*) 24
Jülicher, A. 4, 90, 219
Julian 9, 115, 140–2
Julian of Aeclanum 172
Julian of Toledo 2, 232
Justin II 131
Justina 43, 111 ff.
Justinian 143
Justus of Lyon 126
Juvenal 52
Juvencus 4

Käsemann, E. 199
Kattenbusch, F. 218
Kauffmann, F. 118, 127
Kelly, J. N. D. 7
Keys, power of 127, 181
Kidd, B. J. 28, 149
Klauser, T. 96
Klein, R. 116
Kmosko, M. 167
Knots 18
Knox, W. L. 199
Koch, H. 75
Kraeling, C. H. 197
Künstle, K. 90, 210, 215, 219–20
Kunkel, W. 138

Lacroix, B. 190
Lactantius 130
Laeuchli, S. 1
Lafontaine, P. H. 159
Langgärtner, G. 164
Laodiceans, epistle 24, 58, 81–2
Latronianus, 144, 151
Lauchert, F. 46
Laurence, St. 3
Lazarus of Aix 32, 162–3
Leclercq, H. 196
Leisegang, H. 201
Lentz, W. 214
Leo I, Pope 16, 23, 83, 131, 154, 189, 207, 211 ff., 225; sacramentary 165.
Leosibora 94
Leovigild 230
Leucadius 111
Lezius, A. 154
Libanius 116
Liberius, Pope 30

Lietzmann, H. 48, 199
Linage Conde, A. 180
Lindos, Heracles-cult 52
Lippold, A. 124
Lipsius, R. A. 195
Litigation 38, 44, 127
Liutprand of Cremona 7
Lof, L. J. van der 142
Lowe, E. A. 62–3
Lucan 3, 52
Lucernarium 174
Lucian 52; on sorcerer's apprentice 21
Lucifer of Calaris 6, 26, 203
Luciosus 6, 13
Lucius 6, 13
Lucretius of Braga 217, 224–5
Lugo 157
Lydus 51

Maassen, F. 158, 171, 181
Mabillon, J. 180
Macarius *notarius* 131
'Macarius', homilist 140, 167
MacCarthy, B. 59
Macedonius, *mag. off.* 40–4
Madec, G. 183
Madoz, J. 168
Magic 2, 51–6, 139–40
Magnentius 124
Magnus 139
Maier, J. 95
Mainz, council 19; Ambrose at 126; Bilihild at 63.
Malalas 142
Mani and Manicheism 21–4, 34–5, 37, 39, 46–50, 78, 94 ff., 141 ff., 156, 185, 194–8, 156, 185. 'Manichee' as term of abuse 146
Manilius 194, 198, 200
Mansilla, D. 4
Marcellina, Ambrose's sister 117, 137
Marcellinus, Luciferian 6
Marcellinus, Maximus' brother 112–13
Marinianus 41
Mark of Memphis 20–1, 145, 152, 201
Marrou, H. I. 162
Martial 52
Martialis, Spanish bishop 1
Martin of Braga 153, 224–30
Martin of Tours 7, 9, 20, 44–5, 54, 111, 124, 133, 146 ff., 158, 161
Martin, J. 48
Martínez Díez, G. 171, 179–80, 222

Martín Patino, J. M. 15
Martyrs, Acts of 84
Mary, Virgin 16, 86, 196
Matthews, J. F. 40–2, 54, 113, 116, 136
Maundy Thursday 226–9
Maximian, emperor 134
Maximin, vicarius of Rome 128
Maximus, Magnus 42–3, 46, 111 ff.; executes Priscillian 144
Maximus of Ephesus 141
Maximus of Turin 160
Médard of Noyon 159
Melothesia 198
Memoria Apostolorum 55, 194–5, 209
Memphis 21
Mercati, G. 15, 73, 100–1, 194
Meslin, M. 119
Messalianism 93, 140, 167
Metrodorus of Scepsis 19
Michael, E. 64
Midrash 82, 197
Minicius, Spanish bishop 186
Minucius Felix 52
Misgeld, W. R. 116
Mocsy, A. 119
Mommsen, T. 45
Mommsen, T. E. 190
Monarchianism 56, 86 ff., 199, 223; prologues 102–9
Montanus of Toledo 165, 207, 222–3
Moon 51–3, 75
Morales, A. de 172, 179 ff., 210, 216, 234
Moreira, A. M. 5
Moricca, U. 48
Morin, G. 16, 48–9, 64, 100–2, 168, 218
Moschus 3, 19
Mundo, A. 168
Munier, C. 14, 171
Murphy, F. X. 168
Mursa 118
Musurillo, H. A. 1
Mutzenbecher, A. 160

Nagel, P. 78
Narses 111
Nat, P. G. van der 4
Nautin, P. 7, 119
Nebroel 95
Nectarius 34
Nicolaitans 55, 168, 203
Nisibis 142
Nock, F. C. 231
Noize, M. 99

Noonan, J. T. 37
Notarius 217
Novatianists 1, 72: on capital punishment 130
Nudity 18–19, 139–40

Oaths 20, 52; not binding in evil cause 125; at Priscillian's shrine 150
Obscenity 52, 55, 139–40
Occult 18, 21, 51 ff., 99–100; *see* Astrology
Oil 51–2
Olympiodorus of Thebes 189
Olympius, Spanish bishop 172
Oost, S. I. 123
Ophites 92
Oppenheim, P. 18
Optatus 90, 131, 150
Orbe, A. 100
Origen 71, 77, 191, 198, 202
Orosius 42, 55, 57, 112, 121–2, 124, 145, 154, 189 ff.
Orpheus 98
Ortygius of Aquis Celenis 157, 171, 177, 185, 239
Ossius of Cordoba 1, 4–5, 7, 52
Ovid 18, 52, 194

Pacatus 111, 113, 122, 124, 144, 150–1
Pacianus of Barcelona 1, 4
Palanque, J. R. 42, 114, 122, 135–6, 163–4
Palladius of Helenopolis 19, 22, 124
Palladius, Illyrian bishop 127
Palladius, on agriculture 52
Pannonia 117–19, 122
Paredi, A. 136
Paret, F. 193
Pascentius, Manichee 211
Pastor 217–18
Paternus of Braga 179, 183–4, 238
Patriarchs, twelve 212–15
Patricius, *fisci patronus* 144
Patripassianism 47, 50, 90; *see* Monarchianism
Patroclus of Arles 161–5
Patruinus of Mérida 157, 171–2
Paul, St. 1, 45, 127; Priscillian's canons 58–62; *Visio Pauli* 84
Paulinus of Adana 52
Paulinus, Life of Ambrose 136, 139, 151
Paulinus of Nola 12, 40–1, 43, 54, 132, 150, 200

Pausanias 52
Pearce, J. W. E. 117, 123
Pelagius 37, 39
Pelliot, P. 214
Pentecost 4
Peregrinus 49, 57–62, 159
Pérez, J. B. 171, 234
Pérez de Urbel, J. 100
Perler, O. 122
Persia 141–2
Peter the Deacon 15
Peterson, Erik 93
Petrus de Natalibus 151
Philo of Libya 6
Philostratus 19, 150
Phoebadius of Agen 12–13
Physiologus 92–3
Piganiol, A. 136
Pitra, J. B. 51, 198
Pizzolato, L. F. 113
Plato 198
Pliny the Elder 18–19, 51–2, 75, 141, 157
Plutarch 19, 52
Polybius 12
Poncelet, A. 151
Ponticianus 9
Pontifex maximus 114, 165
Porphyry on storm-demons 195; on toleration 116, on zodiac 198
Postumianus 9
Potamius of Lisbon 5
Praedestinatus 208
Préaux, C. 51
Presbytery 31
Priscillian: emergence 8, 11, 21; ascetic practices 14; influences on, 22; supported by Instantius and Salvianus 20, 25 ff.; accused at Saragossa 26–7; appeal to Symposius and Hyginus 31; bishop of Avila 33; validity of election denied 34; exiled by Gratian 35; visit to Euchrotia 36–8; petition to Damasus 27, 34, 38–9; reinstated by Gratian 40; appeal from synod of Bordeaux to Maximus 43, 125 ff.; disavows Manicheism, heresy, lechery, and sorcery 47–56; teaching 57–110; date of trial at Trier 132–8; trial and execution 128 ff.; venerated as martyr 150–1, 238; Galician shrine 150, 233
Proclus 51
Procula 36–7, 44, 46, 62, 143

Proculus of Marseille 29, 126, 160–3
Proculus Gregorius 40–1
Profuturus of Braga 223–4
Prosper of Aquitaine 44, 124, 132, 148, 150
Protevangelium Jacobi 199
Prudentius 4, 13, 201
Puech, A. 8
Puech, H. C. 195, 203, 205
Pueyo, S. 180, 184, 234
Punishment, capital, 130 ff. 187
Pythagoreanism 18

Quaestor sacri palatii 40
Quintana Prieto, A. 150, 183
Quispel, G. 79

Ramos y Loscertales, J. M. 8, 48, 50
Rauschen, G. 135
Recemundus of Elvira 7
Regul, J. 103
Regula Magistri 84
Reichenau 219
Reitzenstein, R. 96
Remigius of Reims 159
Requiem masses 2–3, 228, 230
Revenge 2–3
Riedinger, R. (U.) 92, 199
Rogation processions 19
Roman primacy 4, 26, 38–9, 184, 206
Rossi, G. B. de 178
Rudolph, K. 95
Rufinus, Spanish bishop 173, 186
Rufinus of Aquileia 77, 93, 127
Rufus, Spanish bishop 10, 139

Sabellianism 7, 87; *see* Monarchianism
Sabinus of Placentia 40
Saclas 94–5
Sáenz de Aguirre, *see* Aguirre
Sallust, historian 20, 206
Sallustius, neoplatonist theologian 141
Salvian of Marseille 163, 189
Salvianus, Priscillianist bishop 20, 25, 27, 31, 33–8, 40, 49
Samaritans 131–2
Santiago 233
Santos Otero, A. de 109–10
Saragossa, council (*380*) 12–15, 19–20, 23–30, 39, 46, 48; alleged second council (*ca. 395*) 28–9
Satan 95, 193, 195, 212–13
Sausterre, J. M. 179

Savio, F. 160, 164
Schäferdiek, K. 78, 171, 217, 222–3
Schatz, W. 9, 99, 193
Schepss, G. 47–8, 192
Schlumberger, J. 52
Schmid, W. 54
Schneemelcher, W. 78, 109–10
Schenke, H. M. 95
Scholem, G. 95
Schwab, M. 96
Schwank, B. 149
Scilly Isles 144–5
Secundianus, Arian bishop 127
Sedulius 108
Seeck, O. 111, 113, 122
Serdica, council (*342*) 5, 22, 34
Servius 18
Severus Acilius 4
Severus, Sulpicius 5, 9–10, 13, 20 ff., 111–13, 117, 121, 132 ff.; 149–50, 158, 161, 165
Sextus Empiricus 198–9
Sibyl 98
Sidonius Apollinaris 167, 189
Sigonius, C. 30
Simonetti, M. 5–7, 90, 93
Simony 229
Simplicianus of Milan 184, 238–9
Simplicius of Vienne 163
Siricius, Pope 16–17, 29–30, 40, 115, 121, 147–8, 164, 170, 182, 237
Sirmium 117
Sittl, K. 64
Smelik, K. A. D. 79
Smolak, K. 221
Socrates, historian 117, 122, 227
Sophronius of Tella 53
Sorcery 2, 51–6, 139–40
Souter, A. 200, 205
Sozomen 117, 127, 189, 227
Spanodromos 22
Speyer, W. 18
Stein, E. 163
Stephen, St., relics 3, 178, 190
Stimming, M. 63
Storm-demons 53–4, 195, 225, 232
Straub, J. 190
Stroheker, K. F. 4, 42, 189
Sturhahn, C. L. 78
Suda 120
Suevi 188 ff., 208–9, 211, 223–4
Suetonius 75
Sukenik, E. L. 197

Index

Sulpicius Alexander 112
Sulpicius, *see* Severus
Syagrius 218–19
Symeon Stylites Junior 131
Symmachus 41, 43, 114–16
Symposius of Astorga 13, 27–9, 31, 69, 145, 152 ff., 181 ff., 234–9
Sympronianus 1
Syrians in West 167

Taeschner, F. 102
Talmud 197
Tardieu, M. 92, 95
Tertullian 1, 93, 89
Thecla 24
Themistius 113
Theocritus 52
Theodora 205
Theodore of Studios 14, 132
Theodore bar Konai 92, 94, 206
Theodoret 42, 96, 108, 195
Theodosius I 6–7, 26, 28, 42–3, 112 ff., 120 ff.
Theognitus, Gallic bishop 138, 148
Theophilus of Alexandria 124
Theophilus of Ephesus 132
Theophrastus 52
Thomas, St. 78–80; Apocalypse 110; Acts 188, 209
Thompson, E. A. 29, 140, 231
Thunder, *see* Storm-demons
Tiberianus 47, 144–5
Tibullus 19, 52
Tillemont, L. S. Le Nain de, 133, 135, 164, 170
Time 76
Titus, Letter of 109
Titus of Bostra 37, 195
Toledo, primacy 223; episcopal list 172; *see* Councils
Toleration 116–17, 127–32
Torture 53, 129, 139, 151, 187
Tovar, A. 21
Tranoy, A. 45
Transmigration 91
Treu, U. 92
Trinity, treatise on 100–2; *see* Monarchianism
Trousers 189
Tuentius 165
Turibius of Astorga 16, 25, 78–9, 83, 154, 172, 208–18, 230
Turibius of Palentia 222–3

Turner, C. H. 14, 79, 100

Unguent 51–2
Unnik, W. C. van 19
Urbica 44
Ursacius of Singidunum 5
Ursinus, antipope 45, 128
Usuard, 7
Uzalis 178

Vagaggini, C. 159
Valence 13–14, 42
Valens, emperor, 114, 142
Valens of Mursa 5, 118
Valentinian I 42, 120, 127–8, 140, 142
Valentinian II 43, 111 ff., 133 ff,
Valentinus, gnostic 196, 203
Valerius of Bergidum 75, 166, 231
Valerius of Saragossa 13
Valio 111
Vandals 178, 188 ff.
Vanderlinden, S. 178
Varady, L. 119
Varro 51
Vega, A. C. 2, 221
Vegetarianism 60, 79, 119, 176, 223, 225
Vegetinus 28, 183, 237–8
Venantius Fortunatus 224
Vergil 4, 75
Vettius Valens, astrologer 198
Victor, Aurelius 112
Victor of Capua 228
Victorinus Marius 191, 199
Victorinus of Poetovio 191
Vigilantius 12, 74, 139
Vigilius, Pope 223
Vincent of Beauvais 99
Vincent of Lérins 60, 69, 208
Vincentius, presbyter 6
Vindicianus 200
Virgins 14, 174
Visigoth conquest of Galicia 230
Visio Pauli 84
Vives, J. 2, 15–16, 180, 234
Vollers, K. 102
Vollmann, B. 8, 16, 28, 48, 64, 66, 100, 133, 136, 193, 203, 207, 211, 233
Volventius 40

Waldschmidt, E. 214
Waldstein, W. 31
Wilmart, A. 15
Wine 23

Index

Wytzes, J. 116

Zahn, T. 80–1, 100, 106
Zelzer, K. 79
Zeno the Isaurian 42
Zeno of Verona 19, 24, 64, 72; on zodiac 196
Ziegler, J. 42

Zodiac 51, 154, 192–204, 208, 212, 225, 232
Zonaras 120
Zoroaster 97–8
Zosimus, Pope 29, 32, 39, 161–5
Zosimus, historian 42, 112, 114, 116, 122–3, 140
Zwierlein, O. 116